POP CULTURE AND POWER

POP CULTURE AND POWER

TEACHING MEDIA LITERACY FOR SOCIAL JUSTICE

DAWN H. CURRIE AND DEIRDRE M. KELLY

UNIVERSITY OF TORONTO PRESS
Toronto Buffalo London

© University of Toronto Press 2022
Toronto Buffalo London
utorontopress.com
Printed in the U.S.A.

ISBN 978-1-4875-0759-6 (cloth) ISBN 978-1-4875-3656-5 (EPUB)
ISBN 978-1-4875-3655-8 (PDF)

Library and Archives Canada Cataloguing in Publication

Title: Pop culture and power : teaching media literacy for social justice / Dawn H. Currie and Deirdre M. Kelly.
Names: Currie, Dawn, 1948– author. | Kelly, Deirdre M., author.
Identifiers: Canadiana (print) 20210395834 | Canadiana (ebook) 20210395907 | ISBN 9781487507596 (hardcover) | ISBN 9781487536565 (EPUB) | ISBN 9781487536558 (PDF)
Subjects: LCSH: Social justice – Study and teaching. | LCSH: Popular culture – Study and teaching. | LCSH: Media literacy – Study and teaching. | LCSH: Popular culture – Social aspects. | LCSH: Social justice and education. | LCSH: Popular culture in education. | LCSH: Teaching – Social aspects.
Classification: LCC LC192.2.C87 2022 | DDC 370.11/5 – dc23

We wish to acknowledge the land on which the University of Toronto Press operates. This land is the traditional territory of the Wendat, the Anishnaabeg, the Haudenosaunee, the Métis, and the Mississaugas of the Credit First Nation.

University of Toronto Press acknowledges the financial support of the Government of Canada, the Canada Council for the Arts, and the Ontario Arts Council, an agency of the Government of Ontario, for its publishing activities.

To teachers who, like our study participants, include media literacy in their teaching for social justice

Contents

List of Illustrations   xi

List of Tables   xiii

Acknowledgments   xv

1 Teaching for Social Justice: Pop Culture in the Classroom   3
   Multiliteracies and Redesign of the Future   4
   Accounting for Pop Culture and Power   9
   Moving Forward   17
   Pop Culture and Power   18

2 Agency and Power as Media Engagement   22
   Agency as Key to Redesign   23
   Power of Media Engagement   25
   Fostering Political Agency   38

3 *Pop Culture and Power*: Teaching as Research   41
   Shape Shifting: Designing a Multiple Case Study   42
   Research Setting and Recruitment of Participants   44
   Phase 1: A Seminar on Pop Culture in the Classroom   46
   Phase 2: Researching Pop Culture in the Classroom   59
   Conclusion   61

4 The Monopoly Project: Meaning Making through Board Game Production   63
   DAWN H. CURRIE, DEIRDRE M. KELLY, AND PAULINA SEMENEC
   Research Setting   65
   The Monopoly Project   65
   Student Redesigns   72
   Promoting Critical Media Literacy through Games   77
   Conclusion   85

5 *The Hunger Games*: Using Popular Film to Learn about Power 87
  DAWN H. CURRIE, DEIRDRE M. KELLY, AND LJ SLOVIN
    Research Setting 89
    The Hunger Games Project 90
    Promoting Critical Media Literacy through Role Play 102
    Conclusion 112

6 Celebrity Marketing: Gender Performances in Popular Music 113
  DAWN H. CURRIE, DEIRDRE M. KELLY, AND ZAVI SWAIN
    Research Setting 114
    Project Planning 115
    The Celebrity Marketing Project 117
    Promoting Critical Media Literacy through Gendered Pop Music 132
    Conclusion 141

7 Are You Being Hailed? Advertising as a Venue for Critical Media Literacy 143
  DAWN H. CURRIE, DEIRDRE M. KELLY, AND AMY CLAUSEN
    Participants 144
    Lesson Planning and Preparation 146
    Research Setting 149
    Identifying Identities: Are You Being Hailed? 150
    How Is the Meaning That Hails Us Constructed? 155
    Reconfiguring Commercial Texts: What Do You Have to Say? 162
    Promoting Critical Media Literacy through Magazine Advertising 165
    Conclusion 170

8 Agency Revisited: Pop Culture in a Participatory Classroom 172
    Unpredictable Affect: Coping with Unforeseen Moments 173
    Agency Informed by Affect 177
    Student Identities Matter: They Shape Agency 179
    The Audience Is Everything 181
    Texts as Context: Intertexuality in Meaning Making 184
    Affect Reclaimed as Agency: The Pleasure of Redesign 186
    The Teacher as the Learner 193
    Multidimensional Reflexivity in Lesson Planning 195

9 Power Revisited: Harnessing Media Engagement to Social Change 201
    Teaching Media Literacy as Social Change 202
    A Social Ontology of Media 203
    Into the Classroom: Promoting CSL through Fairy Tales 207

Digital Capitalism Poses New Challenges, Deepens Older Ones 212
CSL as Informed Judgment through Reflexive Interrogation 218
Promoting Student Reflexivity 223
"What Kind of World Do You Want to Live In?" 227

Appendix A: Course Syllabus for CSL Seminar 233

Appendix B: Writing and Other Homework Activities – CSL Seminar 2012 245

Appendix C: Ethics and Example of Parent/Guardian Informed Consent Letter 248

Appendix D: Details from the Hunger Games Project Lesson Plan 253

Notes 257

References 273

Index 301

Illustrations

2.1 Concept map of power (inspired by Allen, 1999/2018) 26
4.1 The "Food Group" modifies their game board using yellow sticky notes 69
4.2 The *Hamunopoly* board 72
5.1 Working on hideouts 96
5.2 "We have a winner!" 100
6.1 Student drawing to describe a male versus female human 119
6.2 Student drawing to describe a male versus female human 120
6.3 Student drawing to describe a male versus female human 121
6.4 Student drawing to describe a male versus female human 122
7.1 "Empowerment discourse" in a Nair ad identified by Isla 157
7.2 Isla's mapping of themes identified for Triumph undergarment ad 159
7.3 Diana's Hollister ad culture-jamming project in progress 164
9.1 Concept map of critical social literacy and related terms 228
9.2 The relation of CSL to reflexive interrogation and informed judgment 229

Tables

3.1　Interrogating media texts and media engagement　58
8.1　Teacher reflexivity when using popular culture in the classroom　199
9.1　A social ontology of media texts　206
9.2　Student reflexivity during media engagement　226
A.1　Hunger Games Project resource cards　254
A.2　Assessment of learning in the Hunger Games Project　255

Acknowledgments

The motivation for *Pop Culture and Power* grew out of our dismay as witnesses to the appropriation and resignification of feminist discourse by the very corporate actors it criticizes. Working from cultural studies, we questioned how critical media literacy, employing pop culture, can challenge the corporate takeover of social life, including those processes intending to promote social change. It is difficult, if not impossible, to individually identify the wide range of colleagues and friends who, over the years, encouraged and joined us in the struggle to teach for social justice in times of educational retrenchment.

We do individually acknowledge and thank our Graduate Research Assistants who undertook field work: Amy Clausen, Paulina Semenec, LJ Slovin, and Zavi Swain. We acknowledge and thank other assistants who worked on our project: Rachel Goossen, Kerria Gray, Bert Lobb, Katherine Lyon-Tanner, Sheila Martineau, Michele Murphy, Megan Ryland, and Kerry Watts. Our study was also made possible by educators who volunteered their time: Dan Blake, Yvette Cassidy, Natalie Chu, Amy Clausen, Yue Lu, Mary, Olivia, Liz Schulz, and Jane Spencer. Of course, our research could not have been undertaken without K-12 student participants, along with their parents and guardians who supported their participation in the study.

As our ideas and analyses took shape, we owe a special thanks to David Beers for patiently reading an early draft of the entire manuscript and offering his editorial advice, as well as to Al at the White Spot where, over a course of years, we met regularly to plan and debrief the research and writing. Al often ushered us to a cozy booth with a window, ignored the overflow of papers, books, and devices as we settled in to work, and sometimes regaled us with stories of his early years working at the restaurant chain.

We thank Nora Kelly and Quinn Kelly. They patiently, and with good humour, indulged the curiosity of two aging feminists about youth culture, and Nora generated ideas for the cover for *Pop Culture and Power*.

We also acknowledge and thank Meg Patterson, our Acquisition Editor, for supporting our project, and her colleagues at the University of Toronto Press, as well as unknown reviewers. Thanks, also, to Judy Williams for her careful attention to our manuscript during the copy editing process.

We acknowledge the Social Sciences and Humanities Research Council of Canada for financially supporting the research on which this book is based, and the UBC Scholarly Publication Fund for financially supporting publication of *Pop Culture and Power*.

Finally, we thank our partners, Brian and Dave, for their support, patience, and love.

POP CULTURE AND POWER

1 Teaching for Social Justice: Pop Culture in the Classroom

> What I see from kids is a "fish in water" phenomenon where they've never known anything outside constant media and advertising bombardment ... Just imagine! They've never known a world where their lives aren't constantly mediated.[1]
> – Liz, director of a media education program in Vancouver, talking with one of the authors

This book explores media as "the water" in which we all live but which we often fail to question. So normalized are the commercial media of everyday life that they have been dubbed "popular culture."[2] But why should we care about what Liz refers to as "constant media bombardment," which she worried is displacing face-to-face interaction, even when between friends? How do youth engage with media texts? How do we, as researchers (and thus as "experts"), understand "media" as the object of our investigation? As teachers as well as researchers, we ask: How can media literacy prepare media users – adults as well as youth – for participation in the twenty-first century?

We are not alone in raising these kinds of questions. The context of our research (carried out in 2013) includes the saturation of our lives with new media technologies. Today, most Canadian households own game consoles, laptop and desktop computers, cell phones, MP3 players, and so on; the proliferation of technology since 2000 gives youth (in theory, more than reality)[3] almost unlimited access to media. For example, in Canada, 99 per cent of students in Grades 4–11 can access the internet outside of school (Steeves, 2014, p. 1), increasingly via cell or smartphone, with, for example, 85 per cent of eleventh graders having their own cell phone (Steeves, 2014, pp. 1, 10).[4] Accompanying the rise and ubiquity of digital media is the need for a robust and critical media education for youth, who are commonly yet erroneously portrayed as uniformly prepared for the digital era (see boyd, 2014, chap. 7) – a generation for whom print-based literacy is no longer sufficient. As Luke et al. (2017) point out:

> How we can enlist and harness these [digital] media to learn to live together in diversity, mutual respect, and difference, addressing complex social, economic, and environmental problems, while building convivial and welcoming, just and life-sustaining communities and societies is the key educational problem facing this generation of young people and their teachers. (p. 252)

The complexity of teaching includes the vast diversity of media that children and youth encounter every day, from flashy billboards to multimodal messaging online. At the same time, the interactive nature of Information and Communication Technologies presents new opportunities for media production. Young people will not be adequately prepared to navigate this landscape if literacy is based on simply *reading* and *writing*, no matter how adequate these may have been for previous generations.

Within a growing body of work promoting literacy for the twenty-first century (e.g., Jenkins et al., 2006; Lankshear & Knobel, 2007; Hobbs, 2010; Alvermann & Hinchman, 2012; Hoechsmann & Poyntz, 2012), the New London Group (NLG)[5] has been perhaps the most influential voice.[6] Their international collaboration produced what they called a pedagogy of "multiliteracies" designed to address "the multiplicity of communication channels and media, and the increasing salience of cultural and linguistic diversity" (1996, p. 63). Their pedagogy reflects changes in the uses, proliferation, and functions of systems of communication. Following current conventions, we refer to new social media, emphasizing the two-sided nature of media engagement; youth are both consumers and producers of media. As argued below, multiliteracies helped displace the view of youth as passive media consumers through an emphasis on media engagement as participation in shaping the future.

Multiliteracies and Redesign of the Future

According to Kress (2000), a member of the NLG, individuals can no longer be seen as "mere users" of cultural resources, including those made available through new technology; rather, they also need to be seen as innovators and drivers of change:

> It is a need on the part of individual makers of texts/messages which leads them to stretch, change, adapt, and modify all of the elements used, all the

time, and thereby change the whole set of representational resources with its internal relations.

An adequate theory of semiosis will be founded on a recognition of the "interested action" of socially located, culturally and historically formed individuals, as the remakers, the transformers, and the re-shapers of the representational resources available to them. (p. 151)

The NLG described conventional literacy education as outdated and authoritarian. Multiliteracies, by contrast:

focuses on modes of representation much broader than language alone ... Multiliteracies also creates a different kind of pedagogy, one in which language and other modes of meaning are dynamic representational resources, constantly being remade by their users as they work to achieve their various cultural purposes. (NLG, 1996, p. 64)[7]

Their approach to teaching multiliteracies is structured around the concept of "Design" as forms of meaning. *Design* can refer to either "the organizational structure (or morphology) of products, or the process of designing" (pp. 73–4). They maintain that any semiotic activity, including using language to produce or consume texts, involves three elements: Available Designs, Designing, and the Redesigned (pp. 73–4). Every moment of literacy as meaning making involves the transformation of available resources. Kress (2000) claims that this approach displaces media literacy as "critique" – a static process that limits creativity – with Design, as "deliberate deployment of representational resources in the designer's interest" (p. 156). In other words, as media producers, youth are redesigning the social world:

Configurations of subjects, social relations, and knowledges are worked upon and transformed (becoming The Redesigned) in the process of Designing ... Transformation is always a new use of old materials, a re-articulation and recombination of the given resources of Available Designs. (NLG, 2000, p. 22)

The emphasis the NLG gives to *redesign* interests us because they connect media engagement to social change: "Designing will more or less normatively reproduce, or more or less radically transform, given knowledges, social relations, and identities, depending upon the social conditions under which the Designing occurs" (NLG, 2000, p. 22).

The twentieth-century view of literacy education for youth as "inoculation" against media's harmful influences has been displaced by the task of preparing youth to redesign their world. While multiliteracies has been adapted, revised, and elaborated (and criticized) by a number of literacy researchers and educators (for example, see Jenkins et al., 2006; Lankshear & Knobel, 2007; Alvermann & Hinchman, 2012; Albers, 2018; Penuel & O'Conner, 2018), emphasis on media users as *remakers* of the semiotic landscape remains a central premise of "critical literacy" based on media engagement as an opportunity for youth to "design social futures."[8] To become "critical" is widely accepted as an overarching educational goal as well as a goal for media literacy. In general, *critical thinking* refers to analysis and evaluation of knowledge claims in order to make reasoned judgments about their veracity. Emphasis is given to logic and evidence applied in an objective manner (see Hitchcock, 2018). In contrast, when teaching media literacy, we invoke *criticality* to attend to power relations, embodied by media texts, that enable specific claims to be made. Identification of these relations empowers media users to assess whether knowledge claims work to reconstitute – or to challenge – existing social inequities (see Kellner & Share, 2009; also see chapter 9). As we elaborate in upcoming chapters, our notion of *critical* media literacy implies a necessary connection between critical judgment and practices that work towards a more equitable future.

In principle, we share the goals of the NLG authors. As noted by Janks (2010), however, the challenge is that "Some redesigns are conservative in that they seek to maintain dominant interests whereas others strive to transform social relations in order to achieve greater equity" (p. 184). Like Penuel and O'Connor (2018), we ask how literacy can promote redesign that challenges the exclusions and inequalities that characterize the contemporary social order.

Evidence is mounting that youth are connected through new media in ways that encourage them to challenge their experiences of oppression. For example, Szucs (2013) documents how a network of young women redefined "virginity." Through open dialogue made possible by social media, they shared their experiences of, and feelings about, heterosexuality. Relying on "biological ambivalence of the cultural myth of the broken hymen," for instance, they questioned what it means to be "a virgin." Rejecting definitions that are often invoked (by adults) to limit girls' sexual experimentation, these girls reworked seemingly fixed, biological notions of sexuality. Through online exchanges of opinions and experiences, they redefined virginity as "whatever you make of it" (p. 128). While we do not endorse a view that "anything goes," Szucs's research illustrates how embodied experience can call established meanings into question and invite alternative meaning making. It also highlights the contested nature of meaning making. At a perhaps more visible level, social media hashtags such as #MeToo and #Black Lives Matter are examples of the potential for using new media to promote widespread social change.

Despite these encouraging examples, a number of teachers who have enthusiastically embraced media production in their classroom have experienced mixed results. Gainer (2010), for example, found that while the racialized minority students in his middle-school extracurricular program identified racist stereotypes in the movie *Dangerous Minds*, their own video production perpetuated sensationalistic storylines rather than offered a counternarrative by depicting their daily lives at school. Facing a similar outcome, Rogers (2017) analyses a series of films created by his students during a class addressing social justice issues. His program, *What's Up Doc?*, was motivated by commitment to a participatory pedagogy that made room for critical social commentary by his students. In contrast to his intentions, student designs often perpetuated, rather than fully resisted, marginalizing discourses and demeaning visual representations that authorized sexist and heteronormative assumptions. This outcome demonstrates the power operating on, in, and through media texts that does not cease to operate simply because critical or participatory pedagogies have been employed (also see Ellsworth, 1989; Luke & Gore, 1992; Rogers, 2016; Wheeler, 2012). Rogers recommends that teachers include opportunities for critical self-reflection on the part of student filmmakers.

Stack (2010) draws attention to the complications of such self-reflection. When students produced videos in her media education class, some White boys traded on hegemonic masculinity and whiteness to legitimate their subjectivity vis-à-vis the Other. They took inspiration from satirical news shows like *The Daily Show with Jon Stewart* and *The Colbert Report* – a genre where creators ironically play with stereotypes to challenge them but, however unwittingly, can end up reinforcing prejudice. During the same activity, the girls and racialized minority students "repeatedly told heartfelt stories of marginalization and the effects this has on them" (p. 211); one such video focused on a girl's experience of racism and membership in an Aboriginal drumming group. White boys in the class distanced themselves from a consideration of institutional racism through raising questions about "political correctness" and minorities "taking things too seriously" (p. 208). Stack emphasizes that educators need to challenge hierarchies among peers that determine who is "given" a voice and who has influence during classroom media projects (also see Stack, 2008, 2009). Media production raises questions about "Who gets to say what and how do they get to say it?" (Stack, 2010, p. 204).

What we find missing in the expanding field of literacy education is guidance on how the redesign encouraged by student media production can equip youth to "radically transform given knowledges, social relations, and identities" (NLG, 1996, p. 75) in ways that do not simply reconstitute dominant culture. We ask how pop culture can be used in the classroom to support the redesign of more just futures. We chose the venue of "pop culture" based on our previous research exploring how girls engage with "girl power" culture (Currie, Kelly, & Pomerantz, 2009). Moreover, the inclusion of pop culture can render formal curriculum more responsive to the experiences and values of youth (Giroux & Simon, 1989; Hill, 2009).

In this era of Big Data, where people's online media engagement is increasingly commodified, inquiries like ours into how youth navigate the contemporary media landscape have taken on new urgency. To navigate games on the internet or use corporate-owned social networking sites, people of all ages must endure a constant barrage of pop-up ads and submit to data-mining techniques. Furthermore, as old boundaries between various media (for example, the telephone and the television) are becoming blurred so that the forms and functions of these technologies converge, a context has been created where "the power of the media producer and the power of the media consumer interact in unpredictable ways" (Jenkins, 2006, p. 2). This unpredictability has fostered widespread worry among parents, teachers, and media commentators that new technologies are having a negative impact on youth (see Twenge, 2017; but also see Denworth, 2019).

These worries were magnified during the Trump era; much of the 2016 election, and debate since, concerned the trustworthiness of media information.[9] In this context, Hyslop (2017) argues: "telling the difference between real and 'fake' news can be tricky for even the savviest media critic. But it's about to get much harder, thanks to new technologies." This challenge is not only relevant to adults; research indicates that youth – despite being dubbed "digital natives" (Prensky, 2001) – in both the USA and Canada have difficulty "telling fake [online] accounts from real ones, activist groups from neutral sources and ads from articles" (Domonoske, 2016, p. 2; see also Wineburg et al,, 2016). Disconcerting to some (including us), at time of writing Google – whose revenues mostly derive from internet advertising – presented itself as a solution through its online safety and empowerment program for kids, "Be Internet Awesome."[10] As evidenced by these concerns, the cultural texts mediating young people's everyday knowledge are a powerful influence and, as such, the site of political struggle.

Along with others, we are interested in engaging youth themselves in this struggle, through literacy that enables them to question and to challenge the media in their lives: a *critical* literacy can – and in our view *should* – foster healthy scepticism towards media content, no matter who its author. This scepticism encourages interrogation of the everyday texts and associated practices that mediatize our understanding of ourselves, of our social world, and of our place in that world. What values are embedded in media messages? Whose purpose do they serve? Who might they devalue or exclude? What kind of reality is being constructed? What kind of future becomes unimaginable as a result? And so on. This kind of interrogation can promote critical judgment about media engagement, as readers but also as creators of media texts. As Jenkins et al. (2006) note, we become political actors when we understand our decisions in political terms (p. 10); one goal of *Pop Culture and Power* is to explore how such understanding can be fostered through media literacy as a vehicle to promote social justice (see also Gee, 2018). Such literacy must, in our view, connect "changing media images, political statements, news reports, internet websites, [and] the language of laws ... [to] material effects upon" peoples' lives (Luke, 2013, p. 138). Theoretically speaking, how can we understand the power of media to shape the social world and our understanding of it? *Pop Culture and Power* explores our answer, as materialist feminists, to such a question.

Accounting for *Pop Culture and Power*

Our feminism originates in our participation in women's liberation as a political movement promoting equality. This participation is based on our identities as "women," employing an intersectional[11] understanding of "identity." While our visibly gendered identities, at times, have been interpreted as a signifier of incompetence or devaluation, being White, cis-gendered, and able-bodied women grants us privileges not afforded all women. As materialists, our commitment is to change in the material world, and not simply cultural change. Changes in the material conditions of everyday life are needed if we are to achieve equality for everyone (see, e.g., Couldry & Mejias, 2019; de Roock, 2021). Like Fraser (1989), our research as well as our teaching keeps an eye to the aims and activities of oppositional groups working for social justice.

By calling ourselves *materialist* we signal belief in a reality that has been forged, over time, through coordinated social activities, reminding us that language-in-use always takes place in specific contexts. Following Gee (2004), those contexts include "the material setting, the people present (and what they know and believe), the language that comes before and after a given utterance, the social relationships of the people involved, and their ethnic, gendered, and sexual identities, as well as cultural, historical, and institutional factors" (pp. 28–9). The meanings we ascribe in such contexts are important because they guide our embodied interactions.

These interactions are with others, but include engagement with established knowledge as cultural sediment that predates our entry into the social world; much of that cultural engagement takes place through "schooling" that excludes or marginalizes experiential learning. What we make of, and what we do with, experiential knowledge is, in part, open to individual negotiation. By specifying *embodiment*, we signal that individuals are located by birth in a social order that differentially structures their experience according to their class, gender, race, physical ability, and so on. Processes that structure this order are part of what we include as "material" conditions of media engagement operating below the level of ordinary consciousness. Critical social literacy (CSL) is about bringing these processes into analysis through interrogation of the power of media to orchestrate meaning making (hence social action) across geographically and culturally disparate populations. In the words of Mirra et al. (2018): "Teachers and students must analyze not only the text itself, but also the roles of the creator, the audience, and the stakeholders" (p. 14) who benefit from media production and dissemination. Based on this feminist materialism, our research interests over the past two decades share the vision of a more equitable and inclusive world, made possible, in part, through teaching for social justice. But what does it mean to teach for social justice?

As argued by Kelly (2012), teaching for social justice implies a vision that will always be contested and provisional. It is important to see both teaching and the struggle for social justice as ongoing, always changing processes. "It would be self-defeating for educators to employ unjust or harmful practices in service of teaching their vision of a better, more just and humane society" (Kelly, 2012, pp. 137–8). For this reason, we embrace the ambiguity of the phrase "teaching for social justice." In this project we supported the use of curriculum that draws student attention to injustice, raising questions about social change, and pedagogy that promotes a participatory and inclusive classroom. As we describe in chapter 8, in the reality of the classroom these idealized intentions bring challenges for teaching with pop culture.

Setting the contested nature of teaching for social justice aside for the moment, we share the vision of Fujino et al. (2018). Drawing on Freire (1972), they view education as "a practice of freedom [that] ... demands critique of, and intervention in, social problems and structures of oppression. We seek to create a society where people learn not merely to be governed but to govern, with mutual respect" (p. 69). Our practices as educators are based on anti-oppressive pedagogies and engagement in struggles to democratize public institutions, including schooling. By *democracy*, we mean participation extending beyond electoral politics, to grassroots activism, "engagement in associations or civic organizations, egalitarianism, and dialogue across differences to solve collective problems" (Kelly, 2014, p. 389), what Fujino et al. (2018) call "active social citizenship" (p. 69).[12] Children and youth need opportunities in school and other settings to experience participatory citizenship by practising it; at other moments, they need to be recognized as "full-fledged political actors" in their own right (Kelly, 2014, pp. 391–2). The question is, how can literacy education promote such experience?

Answers to this kind of question are open to multiple interpretations and are not self-evident until the broad value statements they imply are put into practice within "the messy political realities of schools" (Kelly, 2012, p. 137). We recognize, too, that promoting participation in the classroom does not take place under conditions of individual teachers' making. Those conditions are material, but also include cultural resources through which students make sense of themselves as everyday agents and formulate their vision of what kind of world is imaginable. Historically, institutional practices – including Eurocentric curricula, a "transmission" model of teaching, standardized testing, ability grouping, streaming, and zero-tolerance discipline policies – have selectively discouraged (if not prevented) young people from exercising their political vision making in school and beyond. As argued by Giroux (2004), corporate media, with their neoliberal[13] emphasis on the individual and privatized responsibility, place limits on what youth might imagine. One goal of our professional work as teachers is to broaden what young people can imagine as possible.

Our participation in the feminist movement has shown us that the future is never already written. As late-career researchers, we have witnessed (and participated in) the emergence of Women's Studies and, subsequently, Girls' Studies. We also have witnessed, however, the ways that women's liberation – as resistance to what feminists named *patriarchal capitalism* – can be appropriated by the same interests it emerged to protest (also see Fraser, 2009).[14] Within popular culture, commercial interests lay claim to what it means to be "a girl," notably promoting "emphasized femininity" – an appearance-based femininity fostering girls' preoccupation with gaining boys' approval and sexual interest (Connell, 1987; see Currie, 1999; Currie, Kelly, & Pomerantz, 2009). To challenge the workings of such institutional forms of oppression requires joining forces with others in pursuit of common interests. Thus, we are interested in understanding processes that work to foster – or inhibit – collective action for social change.

Mainstream media are implicated in these processes, in part by coordinating meaning making in ways that support the status quo. As we explored how girls take up – or resist – this coordination through their engagement in commercialized pop culture, we became interested in critical literacy for youth. Themes that we carried into the current project include media consumers as agents of meaning making; the power of commercial media over youth, exercised through the ability of corporate interests to shape everyday meaning making (hence behaviour); and the power of youth to reject, resist, and rewrite their future as shaped by these interests. Underlying these themes are interrelated issues of "agency" and "power" – two topics we find underdeveloped in much of the literature on critical literacy. *Agency*, as the capacity for youth to take action, is key to "redesign"; it thus informs the classroom activities described in *Pop Culture and Power*. In order for student agency to be directed towards the design of more equitable futures, as elaborated in upcoming chapters, we explore media as a venue for the operation of power. Given how our thinking on agency and power informs our current project, they are discussed at length in the following chapter. In the remainder of this chapter, we locate our project within the actualities of teaching media literacy in Vancouver, British Columbia, where our research was conducted; we initiated our project through exploratory interviews with three local media educators.

Getting Started: Moving from Cultural Studies into Literacy Research

Historically, the critical study of media texts has meant uncovering the "false consciousness" embedded in popular culture (see Luke, 1997). As a result, media education often became "an exercise in students' endurance of the teacher's proselytizing approach of warning students of the media's harmful effects" (Alvermann, Moon, & Hagood, 1999, p. 24). Such an approach not only fails to address the pleasure of media engagement but also replays the binary thinking – of "authentic" versus "false" representation – that we reject (see Kellner, 1990 on this point). In contrast, Janks et al. (2014) claim: "What makes critical literacy *critical* is its concern with the politics of meaning: the ways in which dominant meanings are maintained or challenged and changed" (p. 6). Along these lines, our initial thinking was inspired by the claim that a *critical* approach requires:

> … analysis of the production and political economy of media and the emergence of new forms of digital and consumer culture [combined] with textual and contextual analysis of a wide range of artifacts – from TV and film to Barbie dolls and YouTube – as well as discussion of audience reception and the social effects of media. (Hammer & Kellner, 2009, pp. ix–x)

Our research goal was to explore how such a comprehensive approach to media literacy might be facilitated using popular culture in the classroom. We became particularly interested in entertainment culture, which, in this era of corporate social media platforms, has become increasingly intertwined with advertising across its various forms (games, movies, music, etc.). We asked ourselves whether, and how, this culture can be harnessed to teaching critical media literacy that promotes greater inclusion and equality. We already had some ideas from our earlier work in cultural studies. To assess their practical utility, we interviewed local media educators working with youth. We intended for these interviews to inform the design of our project, to ensure that it would be relevant to the actual, ongoing work of media educators. What might they tell us about the kinds of media, but also pedagogy, that would be most relevant for using popular culture in the classroom? Three key informants shared their experiences with us: Dan, a retired high school teacher who taught media studies during his teaching career and, at the time of our interview, worked with educators; Mary, a master's student at the University of British Columbia (UBC) who recounted her experiences of teaching media literacy as a recently graduated elementary school teacher; and Liz, the educational director of a large nonprofit organization promoting media literacy. For brevity's sake, below we highlight interview themes that shaped our thinking about how to proceed; as we will see, these themes foreshadowed challenges we encountered once in the classroom.

START WITH MATERIAL RELEVANT TO YOUTH

Liz, who works with both teachers and youth, emphasized the importance of teaching from where students "are at":

> I can tell you right now that what's going on is not getting talked about openly by anyone, for the most part. Kids are having those conversations [about popular culture] behind closed doors ... They're accessing all kinds of stuff, let alone the constant messaging around gender roles and all of those kinds of social messages that are completely unexamined ... They're getting this stream of information about social responsibility at the elementary school level – that "Care Bear" style talk – and then the real world is happening.

To enable youth to navigate this contradictory environment, Liz experimented using different media that "bombard" young people – ads, music, online videos, film. She soon discovered that starting where youth are at means dealing with student investment in pop culture:

> We cannot touch Lady Gaga with a 10-foot pole. We cannot have critical discussions about Lady Gaga. She is like a deity, and you can't do that! You've immediately alienated your audience. Don't even *try* to talk about Lady Gaga. We've tried on numerous occasions, different approaches, different educational strategies. No. Sorry ... Welcome to adolescence!

14   Pop Culture and Power

In short, whether acknowledged or not, popular culture already operates in the classroom, in ways that educators may not anticipate. Giroux (2004) coined the term *public pedagogy* to describe the political, but also educational, force of dominant media culture. Despite the challenges this raises, relevance is necessary to give lessons situated meaning as opposed to abstract, textbook meaning. Starting with media already familiar to students also helps to validate them as "knowers."

MEDIA IDENTITIES CAN BE PERSONAL INVESTMENTS FOR YOUTH

As a feminist filmmaker and activist, Liz is comfortable with controversial topics. She admitted, however, that there are topics where she is in "over her head." She emphasized: "I'm not a gender expert. I'm not a sexuality expert. I'm not a sex ed expert, even." In a context where youth are "all accessing hard-core porn," Liz cites gender as "probably our most challenging thing that we do, *ever. Period.*" But Liz is not alone. After Liz viewed *Sexy Inc.* (a National Film Board of Canada documentary on hypersexualization in commercial culture and its influence on young people) with teachers,

> The conversation kept coming up about [the teachers] just feeling kind of helpless around what their young girls were saying and what their young boys were saying. The ingraining of those kind of social gender roles and how that was playing out in the classroom – what they were getting asked [by youth] and what was happening [to them]. And at the same time, parents' complete active resistance to having any open conversations about this outside of very highly prescribed and scripted sex ed conversations.

Liz described discussions concerning gender as "more than an uphill battle." Popular sentiments surrounding feminism contribute to the challenge:[15]

> I get adolescence – you don't want to put yourself out there. And especially now that the "F" word is no longer "fuck," it's feminism. So, we end up with these situations where young people are afraid to even voice if they have a problem [with sexism in media] because feminism's the dirty word. And so, when we integrate all those things, we try not to make it about feminism, but it is about feminism, *absolutely.*

THE INSTITUTIONAL CONTEXT OF TEACHING MATTERS

As a new teacher, Mary saw how important popular culture was to her Grade 4/5 students. Noticing her young students' engagement with the song "Runaway" by the rapper Ludacris, she decided that they needed guidance in what they were listening to:

> It was subtle, but there were allusions that this young girl had prostituted herself. It wasn't explicit, but she was on the street, working on the street. And they [the children] were singing along to the lyrics. And there were also allusions to drugs and sex, as well. It was just a rap, hip-hop song ... They were just singing along, and I didn't know if they even understood what they were singing.

When her students asked whether they could bring the song into class for one of their music appreciation sessions (a practice Mary encouraged), she consulted with her vice principal. Despite her VP's approval of using the music, a torrent of parent complaints put Mary's teaching under intense scrutiny for the remainder of the year. Uncertain whether she would "go that route again," Mary revisited her reasoning at the time:

> I thought, "If you're listening to it already, and you've memorized all the lyrics, then I want to help you understand it. And I want to be able to process it with you." The response that I got [from parents] is that it would've been preferable to just gloss over it. Like for the parents, it was okay that they [their children] were listening to it [only] because they didn't understand it ... [the idea was that] "We don't need to talk to them about it because they're too young to get it."

In the end, Mary was left on her own to wonder, "What do I name, and what am I allowed to name?"[16]

PARENTS, AS WELL AS TEACHERS, HAVE A STAKE IN LITERACY
Mary's experience confirmed what we already believed: using popular culture in the classroom would implicate us in the everyday, small p politics of teaching youth – through "minute-by-minute choices and decisions" (Janks, 2010, p. 188).[17] Dan as well as Mary recounted struggling with expectations on the part of not only colleagues but also parents about what constitutes education. Dan explained that many people conflate education with a narrow view of schooling in basic "skills" (the 3 "Rs"). When Mary replaced cursive writing with media activities, one mother of a Grade 5 student challenged her: "She was like, 'How is he going to learn to write a cheque?' ... And the spelling tests – people are so attached to those. Wow! Like, they were up on the fridge." Despite the negative outcome for Mary that followed parental complaints, she nevertheless maintained that educators must be prepared to accept the

affective investments that parents and guardians hold towards "appropriate" schooling: "people are attached to their ideas of what it [education] is. Their fears are that you're spending all day with their kids, and that you are influencing them. *How* are you influencing them?"

ALTHOUGH RISKY, MEDIA PRODUCTION CAN ENHANCE LEARNING

Consistent with her commitment to "guide" inquiry rather than "preach" about media, Liz found that having students make their own media could help them explore topics she felt she had to avoid addressing head on:

> We've seen some really profound moments with students who have not only engaged with a [sensitive] topic but found ways to articulate that for themselves and been really excited about that. And nervous at the same time, but [they] played with ideas [for example, about gender stereotypes] in the films they've produced. That comes up fairly frequently when students have carte blanche to do whatever they want with their video projects.

At the same time, Liz acknowledged that giving students free rein was also risky; they do not always produce what teachers might hope for. In some cases, teachers who were apprehensive but initially willing to "take the leap" into student video production could lose their nerve as a result:

> It can run the whole gamut, from teachers who are totally unintimidated and just diving in there, even when they don't know what they're doing, all the way through to teachers who genuinely feel helpless. And don't always undertake the projects again because in many cases the videos that are produced are problematic when it comes to social values, especially the school's values.

As voiced by Liz, and echoed by other media educators (see Buckingham, 1998b; Stack, 2010), student media may not only surprise but also disappoint teachers. We took this advice as a warning against the temptation to fantasize youthful media production as evidence of their "empowerment" – a theme that we frequently encountered in literature that celebrates youthful media agency.

ALTHOUGH INTERESTED, TEACHERS ARE OFTEN UNPREPARED

When the exploratory interviews were carried out in 2011, very little formal curriculum on media education existed for teachers in British Columbia (BC). We were aware that the cohort of teachers currently practising in BC would likely be inadequately prepared in media studies, given that it was not mandated as a distinct subject area at the time of our project.[18] Since the inception and implementation of our project, a number of literacy educators have begun to call for teacher education in media analysis (see, for example, A. Butler, 2020; Kellner & Share, 2019; Buckingham, 2019). As recounted by Dan:

> I am a bit sceptical about what is being offered as a media literacy course [in schools]. I tutor students now. I did see a course outline for one student of mine last year that had "media" as a component of the course outline. I kept asking him, "So when are you doing the media?" [laughter] … "Well, we're going to watch a film for the last two weeks." So that was it. I have a nasty suspicion that for some teachers that constitutes their "media course."

Dan's experience illustrates what can happen when interested teachers lack media education. Compounding lack of education, there is very little prepared material to guide teachers into new terrain. Resources that were available in the past had been developed by educators independently; when they retired, their initiatives retired as well.[19] Based on his experience of working with teachers through the BCTF (the provincial Teachers' Federation), Dan further noted:

> When you start talking about something that doesn't immediately appear to belong [in the curriculum], then they just kind of say, "I don't know. I don't really have time for that. I'd love to do it. It sounds great, but I don't have time to do it. How am I going to fit it in? What am I going to take out?"

Moving Forward

Given that Liz had worked with "hundreds and thousands of kids" by the time of her interview, we were eager to benefit from her experience. Deirdre asked her how she chooses media for her workshops. Liz shared her guiding principles:

> First one would probably be obviously something that is engaging and controversial enough to provoke debate and discussion while, at the same time, not being so sensationalized that it's being ridiculous. [For example, "the kids can't get past the boobs"] … The second piece is trying to choose something that is very, very relevant … The third one is, of course, walking the lines of – depending on the age group, depending on what's appropriate and what we can get away with … How much can we get away with while, at the same time, not lose our audience? … And of course, you want, at the same time, to respect the boundaries of students who may have either religious viewpoints, conservative viewpoints, or just may not be exposed to

these things. Like many [young people] have caps on what they're allowed to watch by parents. You have to balance those pieces. So, then the other one we're looking for is really something that's immediately thought- and conversation-provoking ... You're dealing with an audience that's so media saturated, it had better be *good* stuff.

In sum, themes from our interviews with local educators echo much of what we found in published sources, including what Dehli (2009) reports after talking with media educators in the Canadian province of Ontario (also see Hoechsmann & Poyntz, 2012; Buckingham, 2003a; Buckingham et al., 2005; Alvermann, Moon, & Hagood, 1999).

We took into consideration that the cohort of teachers currently practising in British Columbia would likely lack education in media analysis (in retrospect, this was the case). On that basis we decided that a professional development seminar in media analysis for teachers interested in joining a project to pilot media activities in their classrooms would be a promising way to proceed. This strategy would result in a number of benefits. It would leave major decisions about what kind of media, for what kind of subject matter and grade level, to practising teachers. It would help attract participants for our project while supporting their interest to continue media activities after our project. From a researcher's point of view, a preparatory seminar would also encourage the design of classroom activities that reflect how we are thinking about media literacy. Finally, as we discuss in chapter 3, it would enable us to pilot curriculum that could support teacher education at our university. In this way, *Pop Culture and Power* emerged as a teaching as well as research project.

Pop Culture and Power

Chapter 2 elaborates our approach as influenced by cultural studies, specifically through our interest in agency and power. In the context of our materialist feminism, we follow Buckingham and Burn (2007), who maintain that "literacy should not be seen as a set of disembodied cognitive skills, but as a set of social practices ... embedded in social contexts and social relations." These practices "involve forms of social action that have social purposes and consequences" (p. 328). Reflecting our interest in the social nature of literacy, we treat media as the operation of power working through symbolic communication, taking forms that do not require face-to-face interaction. Like Jenkins (2006), we distinguish between the media technology that enables communication (that is, determines the *form* of communication) and the messages embedded in that communication (that is, the *content* embedded in that form of communication) in order to think about literacy as engagement with both the form and content of media (pp. 13–14). For now, we set aside questions about the relationship between form and content.[20] Because our focus for the seminar concerns symbolic communication – as opposed to communication technologies – when we refer to *media*, unless otherwise specified, we are directing attention to *media texts*. When we refer to *media literacy*, we are directing attention to *meaning making* through media engagement. Further, because media practices are activated in a context of social relations (see Burwell, 2010; Gee, 2008, p. 198; Christensen & Morley, 2014), technological competence will not determine whether media engagement will subvert rather than perpetuate inequality (see, e.g., Rogers, 2017; Stack, 2010).

The term *popular culture* entered the cultural studies lexicon during the 1970s, at Bowling Green State University (BGSU) in the USA and at the Birmingham Centre for Cultural Studies in the UK. Its emergence challenged academic focus on culture as the "highbrow" work of talented artists. At BGSU, Ray Browne studied Mickey Mouse and Madonna, for example – topics generally viewed as not worthy of scholarly attention. Rival definitions for *popular culture* (viz., *pop culture*) emerged. Storey (1993) identifies multiple definitions,[21] each positing a competing understanding of how pop culture is produced. Given our interest in redesign as social change, we have been influenced by approaches that recognize media consumers as simultaneously media producers (see, for example, McRobbie, 1991). Youth do not passively internalize the meanings and values of established culture, as implied by many media critics (for discussion, see Moje & van Helden, 2005). Rather, they redeploy them as resources at hand for their own cultural production, together with other available resources, such as tacit knowledge of the world gained from practical experience.

As will become apparent in the following chapters, given our view of media as a vehicle for the operation of power – rather than as power itself – we are interested in the relations and practices through which media are produced and disseminated. In our theoretical work, we therefore distinguish between culture produced by corporate interests, for purposes of its exchange value as a commodity (such as print, film, online magazines), and culture produced by everyday people for its practical use (its use value).[22] The latter includes cultural production on Facebook, Twitter, TikTok, and YouTube (see, e.g., Kellner & Gooyong, 2010; Pomerantz & Field, 2021).[23] While we do not, like Fiske (1989), see cultural production by everyday people as, necessarily, resistance to corporate media interests, the distinction between commercial culture and culture produced by everyday people is analytically significant. It reminds us that while commercial culture works to sustain the status quo, we, as everyday cultural producers, have the power to challenge or reject dominant meaning and to create alternative culture. At the same time, we recognize that the boundary between "commercial" and "everyday" culture is not always empirically distinct; commercial culture remains relevant to audiences because it incorporates everyday experience and desires, while also being a cultural resource for media consumers (see Schäfer, 2011). Clearly, in light of the notion of designing as the appropriation of available meaning, the distinction between commercial and popular culture is not readily apparent without taking analysis deeper, to include its production.

One complication is the common practice of designating what we would call *commercial media* – such as film with box office appeal and much youth music – as "popular culture" or "pop culture." To be consistent with the existing literature, we use the term *pop culture* as a descriptive category that embraces both commercial culture as a source of available meaning and culture produced by media users that expresses their everyday meaning making. The significance of our theoretical distinction between the everyday and the commercial production of media will become more evident in chapter 2, where we distinguish between the agency of media production and the societal conditions through which media production takes place. Such a distinction enables us to analyse media as a venue for the operation of power.

Chapter 3 describes the design of our study, which unfolded in two distinct phases. Here, the reader will see how *Pop Culture and Power* is both a teaching and a research project. As design research (see Mehan, 2008), we initiated our project with a professional development seminar in media analysis for practising teachers, informed by our theorization of media as a venue for the operation of power. During the seminar, participants designed classroom activities, four of which were piloted in the second phase of our study as case studies (presented in chapters 4, 5, 6, and 7). These activities address social justice issues through the use of board games (for Grade 4/5), film (for Grade 6/7), music videos (for a Grade 11/12 Marketing class), and advertisements (with teenage girls in an out-of-school setting). These cases enable us to draw general observations about the challenges, but also opportunities, of using popular culture in the classroom to promote social justice. They enable us to revisit how agency and power operate in a space where media messaging shapes precisely what critical media literacy hopes to challenge. Based on our cases, we introduce a distinctly *social* approach to media literacy, what we call "critical social literacy." By treating youth as agents of social change, critical social literacy attends to media engagement as an embodied activity, through which youth have the opportunity to exercise their power to redesign a more equitable and sustainable future. Doing so entails critical interrogation of both available design and media production that offers alternatives. Our hope is that by the end of *Pop Culture and Power*, readers will not only understand what we mean by such literacy but will adapt and extend it through their own work as teachers and researchers; by sharing our project, our intent is to inspire deeper investigation into how media engagement can be harnessed to better futures.

2 Agency and Power as Media Engagement

By encouraging students to make texts about things in the world that matter to them; by focusing on what they produce rather than on what they consume; by harnessing their creativity and by helping them share what they make with audiences of their own choosing, we will help them to understand what literacy is for. In doing so we give them the *power* to name their world.
— Hilary Janks (2013a, p. 238, emphasis in original)

In a review of mass media studies, Dahlgren (2015) credits cultural studies for raising questions about the operation of power. Giroux (2004) identifies tenets of cultural studies relevant to research in media literacy, including its embrace of theory, its emphasis on context, its transdisciplinarity and reflexivity, and its attention to the wide range of everyday cultural forms. In thinking about the redesign promoted by critical media literacy, our previous work in feminist cultural studies gave us a place to start (see Currie, 1999; Currie, Kelly, & Pomerantz, 2009). It made us attentive to issues surrounding agency and power – two themes that are implicit in considering media production as a vehicle of social change, but underdeveloped in much writing on how critical media literacy plays out in the classroom.[1] The concept of redesigning social futures too often assumes, rather than problematizes, *agency* as the capacity for intentional action. Without a framework for understanding the operation of power, we can mistake the agency expressed by redesign for social change itself.

Perhaps ironically, this conflation of agency and power has a long history in cultural studies. In the UK, Hebdige (1979) and Willis (1990), for example, drew on Lévi-Strauss's (1966) notion of bricolage to characterize youth as recombining semiotic resources to subvert intended meaning. The sign values associated with clothing, as well as other cultural objects, were combined in ways that parodied "proper" adult sensibility, encouraging subcultural theorists to celebrate the agency of these "redesigns" as resistance. By contrast, McRobbie (1991) found nothing to celebrate in schoolgirls' semiotic resistance to the official policy of their all-girls' school. By coding "femininity" in their self-presentation – for example, by wearing make-up along with their required school uniform – their resistance, in effect, propelled them along the path of traditional womanhood, unwittingly reproducing female subordination. McRobbie thus drew attention to the conflation of agency with resistance, hence agency with power.

We find a similar conflation in literacy research that celebrates student media production as heralding a more equitable future.[2] We have already seen in chapter 1 that media production by youth does not necessarily challenge the social exclusions and inequalities characteristic of dominant culture. For this reason, "agency" and "power" could not be ignored in our current project. For us, *agency* refers to the human capacity for self-directed action, exercised individually and collectively, within historically given conditions that enable and constrain possible lines of action. The meaning making exercised during media engagement is an example of agency. *Power* refers to the capacity to shape meaning making in specific ways, while recognizing the intentionality of self-directed action: as agents, human actors have the capacity to shape, challenge, and resist what happens. As a quality of hierarchical relations given by the social order, power often operates through processes below the ordinary level of everyday consciousness. One goal of critical media literacy is to bring processes that shape meaning making into consideration. In this chapter we draw together what we have learned from our previous research, along with the research of others, to explore how agency and power inform media engagement, hence influence teaching literacy. In the concluding chapters, we revisit the agency of media engagement and power of media production in ways that benefit from the case studies that comprise the bulk of *Pop Culture and Power*.

Agency as Key to Redesign

Agency is a characteristic of people (and not "things," such as technology), exercised either individually or collectively. In our work we differentiate *agency*, as expressed in the everyday practices of youth, from *power*, as those social processes that shape their agency in specific ways. We emphasize "shape" – in contrast to "determine" – in recognition of the intentionality of action in pursuit of a conscious goal. At the same time, we acknowledge that much of what shapes human action operates through processes below the ordinary level of everyday consciousness that cannot be directly observed. Included in those processes is the power of media messaging. Today youth negotiate both their goals and actions within a context of increasingly commercialized (and complex) pop culture. Some commentators maintain that the inclusion of this culture in the formal curriculum "allows for a more democratic space because it validates the personal histories, experiences, and values of students" (Hill, 2009, p. 250). While we share this belief, we also acknowledge that bringing media engagement into the classroom subjects it to adult surveillance – a point that is not lost on youth themselves. It is not that this engagement otherwise remains outside the school; on the contrary, it can enter the classroom in unexpected ways (see chapter 8 for an extended example).

One obvious, but often overlooked, expression of agency as cultural production in the classroom is negotiation of identity, commonly believed to be the hidden "mandate" of "adolescence." Our previous interest in girls' agency thus focused on their identity performances, both within and beyond school. "*Girl Power*" (Currie, Kelly, & Pomerantz, 2009) explored how practices of "girlhood" are coordinated by public discourses that shape the subject as an agent, enabling this subject to reshape her own girlhood. As Gonick (2003) argues, such a process entails a "double movement between a subject speaking/writing her way into existence" by reworking available cultural resources and, "in the moment of doing so, also subjecting herself to the constitutive force and regulative norms" informing this movement (p. 10).[3]

At the same time as recognizing "girlhood" as a social and not simply personal identity, we acknowledged that as self-determining individuals, not all girls share the goal of achieving idealized girlhood, based on what Connell (1987) calls "emphasized femininity," nor do they equally have access to such an identity, given its valorization of a specific physicality displayed through visible consumption of "the right" cultural resources (see Currie, Kelly, & Pomerantz, 2009, chap. 4). Both the formulation of goals and the opportunities to achieve them are influenced by an individual's location in the social order. As materialists, we remain mindful of the relationship between identity as the sense of "being a certain kind of person" and identity as shaped by the given socio-cultural order. The approach in *Pop Culture and Power* echoes Moje and Luke's (2009) metaphor of identity as "position": "Identity as position takes into account discourse and narrative ... but also acknowledges the power of activities and interactions ... artifacts ... space and time ... and embodied difference" (pp. 430–1). Our social position grants us access to specific discourses of "being in the world" and forms of articulating that being, as well as the material and other cultural resources that consolidate identity as an expression of "authentic" selfhood.

Among the processes that operate in this way, everyday media produce consumers with both a need and a desire to perform their identity as autonomous, through practices valorizing "difference" from others. One result is naturalization of what feminist cultural critics trouble as *socially constructed* – identities that cohere around taken-for-granted signifiers of gender, "race," (hetero)sexuality, adolescence, and so on. In *Pop Culture and Power*, we attend to the dilemma this naturalization brings for teaching critical media literacy. As producers of the future, youth are simultaneously the product of the already given social order and the producers of the future order; their identities – hence sense of self – are implicated in processes that critical media literacy encourages them to scrutinize. Recognizing this dilemma is necessary if, as teachers, we want to foster student redesigns that challenge available design. One goal of *Pop Culture and Power* is thus to explore how this dilemma plays out in the classroom through an understanding of how power informs the agency of media engagement by young people.

Power of Media Engagement

Power is conflated with agency in everyday talk when we refer to "powerful people" because their agency has far-reaching effects on others. Following from our discussion above, this agency is afforded by their location in the social order, one that bestows the individual in question a status or authority that sets them apart from others. In other words, power is a characteristic of the functioning of the social order and not a "personal" quality: it is a characteristic of a historically specific configuration of social relations and the practices those relations afford. (Some) people exercise power over others through the agency made possible by the specific relations of their social positioning.

We agree with Lukes (2018): "How we think about power affects, indeed consists in, or constitutes, what we think is possible for others and for ourselves and what is not" (p. 48). It is therefore important to explore power in relation to media engagement, in particular to redesign. In the absence of such a discussion, within media studies "power" is often used as a synonym for *domination*.[4] To deepen our understanding of how media engagement is an exercise of power, we draw on the work of philosopher Amy Allen (1999/2018). Accepting a broad definition of *power* "as the ability or capacity of an actor or set of actors to act" (p. 128), she complicates this definition through her interrelated concepts of "power-over," "power-to," and "power-with," describing how they help us differentiate between the exercise of power as domination, resistance, and solidarity.

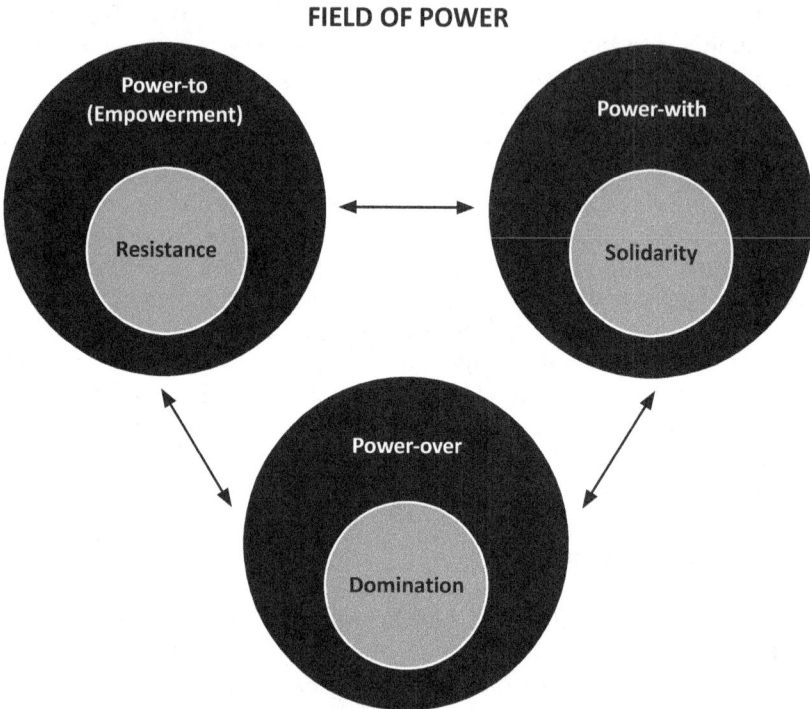

Figure 2.1. Concept map of power (inspired by Allen, 1999/2018)

It is important to note that Allen resists referring to these subordinate concepts as "distinct *types* or *forms* of power" (p. 129). This is because while the analyst may focus on, say, power-over, power-to and power-with may also operate in a given situation. Her concepts are tools to aid comprehension of complex power relations present within any specific interaction or set of interactions; just as for agency, the exercise of power is situation-specific and relational (see figure 2.1). Allen thus opens the door to a materialist approach by noting the importance of accounting for the "background social conditions" that enable "these particular power relations" to operate (p. 130). Identification of these conditions of possibility helps us, both as teachers and as researchers, to identify what kinds of media activities can foster students' exercise of power through redesign. Allen's feminist conception of power supports the goal of teaching media literacy for social justice. It illuminates the "complex and interrelated array of systems of domination" (p. 122) – racism, sexism, heterosexism, class inequality, ableism, and colonialism, to name only some – thereby helping social-justice-minded educators and their students understand, critique, and challenge unjust power relations.

Power-Over

One expression of power is the exercise of *power-over*, which generally takes place in the context of an unequal relation between two or more actors. *Domination* is a subset of power-over; it "entails the ability of an actor or set of actors to constrain the choices of another actor or set of actors in a nontrivial way and in a way that works to the others' disadvantage" (Allen, 1999/2018, p. 125). Critical media literacy emerged from an assumption that media (at the time, referred to as "mass media") operate as a form of power-over, as "tools for the reproduction of the status quo" (Sholle, 1994, p. 22). Within this perspective, Peter McLaren described critical media literacy in terms of "decoding the ideological dimensions of texts, institutions, social practices, and cultural forms such as television and film, in order to reveal their selective interests" (quoted in Sholle, 1994, p. 19). This approach promoted media education as "ideology critique"[5] based on an ability to identify how mass media distort our perceptions of reality. By trafficking in a "false" versus "real" dichotomy, ideology critique encourages identification of misrepresentation, especially evident in advertising (see for example, *Killing Us Softly 4* [Kilbourne, 2010] and earlier films in this series). While intending to protect youth from media's harmful effects, this approach can foster "media cynicism" rather than media literacy informed by an analysis of how the power of media works. Moreover, it can encourage students simply to mimic criticisms raised by their teacher (see, e.g., Alvermann, Moon, & Hagood, 1999).

Against this common view that media derive power from their content, Dorothy Smith (1990a) argues that ideology does not rest in the *content* of commercial media – the categories that give it meaning – but rather in the *practices of meaning making* it encourages. These practices hinder critical interrogation if available categories of meaning are readily accepted as "common sense" – something that does not require investigation (see also Hall, 1992, 2000). By "detach[ing] meaning from the lived processes of its making," media texts provide material conditions for cultural reification (Smith, 1990b, p. 168);[6] freed from the necessity for personal interaction, text-based messaging confronts its reader as a "thing" – as a fait accompli. The goal of critical literacy is not simply to critique media content, but to interrupt the process of meaning making that the text invites. In the final analysis, ideology critique fails to enhance the agency of students as meaning makers. It is not simply that this approach characterizes media texts as more or less perfect reflections of the social order, but that it characterizes youth as passive consumers of media content; in this way, it does not support the view of youth as redesigners of their social future.

At the same time, we do not dismiss the importance of media critique. We have in mind Chung's (2005) report of an activity where youth were instructed to identify "false or questionable realities" in cigarette advertising. As educator, Chung concluded:

> The students seemed to have no trouble articulating the intended and implicit messages of a cigarette ad [making people feel that through the use of cigarettes they fit in, that they are cool, that they are happy] ... it is likely that they might fail to scrutinize the negative aspects of smoking if not guided to analyze the ad critically. (p. 21)

In this way, while an emphasis on "techniques of visual [and textual] manipulation" (Chung, 2005, p. 21) may not meet our view of a fully "critical" literacy,[7] it has the potential to increase students' level of consciousness about the values and motivations embodied by media texts. In this context, media critique identifies media culture as a site of political struggle: it can offer a first step towards deeper interrogation of media in general.

Despite our criticisms of literacy as "inoculation" of youth from the harmful influence of media domination, we do not deny the power that media exercise over everyday life. Once normalized, their power-over can play out in ways that, conditioned by habitualized social practices, fade from consciousness. Like Smith, our goal is to make power and its operation visible, in our case to show how power works through media. Smith does so by tracing the operation of power through what she calls "textually mediated discourses" – of psychiatry, news making, the fashion and beauty industry, and her own discipline of sociology (Smith, 1990b). Power operates through text-based procedures of describing, naming, and classifying the social world in ways that normalize a specialized form of social organization, working through everyday practices while appearing to be independent of the meaning-making activities of subjects.

Smith illustrates this process by describing how women's magazines promote the self-regulation of a culturally and historically specific "femininity." They do so through the mechanisms, techniques, and procedures of knowledge making embedded in the text (for elaboration, see Currie, 1997, 2001). Self-regulation as a social and not simply individual process comes through the ability of magazines to replicate and disseminate a text-based discourse of femininity that provides "a standpoint for the [reader] from which her own conduct or the conduct of others can be examined. This consciousness of self is the lived moment bringing local settings under the jurisdiction of public textual discourse" (Smith, 1990b, p. 168). Hidden are the social relations that benefit from practices fostered by these magazines. Meaning making from this text is ideological, not so much as a result of the meaning of womanhood embodied by the text, but as a result of accepting this socially constituted meaning as "the way that things are." The womanhood promoted by commercial interests has been normalized, while the nature of the gendered relations objectified in the text – and the activities they orchestrate – disappear from consciousness.

As corrective to this practice, Smith (1990a) shifts attention from text-based knowledge as already constituted to *knowing* as an embodied activity of meaning making, a shift that restores "the subject in the object":

> Knowing, of course, is always a "subjective" activity, that is, an activity of a particular subject. But *knowing* in this sense cannot be equated with perception or cognition; it always involves a social dimension, the coordination of activities among knowers vis-à-vis an object that is known in common ... Knowing is still an act; knowledge discards the presence of the knowing subject. We are to look therefore for the actual socially organized practices and relations expressed in that concept of knowledge. (p. 66)

In other words, while text-based "knowledge" (read: available design) presents itself as an already constituted object for consumption, knowing (read: meaning making) is an activity of embodied subjects, materially as well as discursively located in the world as an effect of social organization. As such, the power of media originates in what Smith calls *relations of ruling* working *through* textually mediated discourse. Keying off her work, we saw teaching literacy as less about recognizing the authenticity of any specific communication (although messages, of course, matter) and more about understanding how media exercise power by coordinating individual meaning making as a social process.

Within this context, we asked: How can educators foster the agency of critical meaning making by helping youth "analyze media as a space where power is created as well as contested" (Marshall & Sensoy, 2013, p. 32)? One answer is to bring into analytical focus representational practices that naturalize socially constructed meaning (see, e.g., Iyer & Luke, 2011). Stereotyping has been a common, and useful, tool in realizing this goal. "*Stereotypes* get hold of the few 'simple, vivid, memorable, easily grasped and widely recognized' characteristics about a person, *reduce* everything about the person to those traits, *exaggerate* and *simplify* them, and *fix* them without change or development to eternity" (Hall, 2000, p. 104). As such, and especially in contexts of unequal power, stereotypes discursively position certain groups outside the norm and operate to socially exclude them, based on difference that has been devalued or vilified. As a shorthand representation, stereotyping offers an economical way to avoid dealing with the complexity of group membership and variation among individual members of social groupings. Because stereotypes employ visible markers of social identities (e.g., gender) that make us immediately knowable to others, they are common in advertising and animated media, two popular venues for teaching literacy because their texts are short, visual, and accessible across age groups. In these venues, stereotypes normalize specific identities and affirm their social status through the assignment of cultural values to various social groups. Critical media literacy takes students beyond simple recognition of misrepresentation when their understanding of stereotypes, and of other analytical tools, enables them to explore how the text "works" – how power operating through media reconstitutes the social order while normalizing its operation. Elsewhere (Kelly & Currie, 2020) we explore the challenges of using stereotyping to teach critical media literacy.

An example of using stereotypes to teach for social justice comes from Linda Christensen's media unit on cartoons (2017; see also Bullock & Zhou, 2017 for analysis of Disney's *Aladdin*). Posing questions that help her high school students identify stereotypes embedded in cartoons, Christensen (2017) described her strategy as

> a way of getting students to understand critical lenses we bring to literature and life: the way we look at men and women in society, the way we look at class issues, the way we look at race issues, the way we look at language issues. Those are critical lenses that I want students to develop so that they stop reading just to find the storyline, or who the characters are, or how the characters change, and instead *read as a way to investigate society*. (Para. 13, emphasis added)

Christensen (2017) "want[s] to enlist them in imagining a better world, characterized by relationships of respect and equality" (p. 23). Evidence that her goal is being accomplished, at least in part, comes when her students connect cartoon themes to "elections, ads, video games, and contemporary movies" (p. 27). We characterize Christensen's cartoon unit as engaging her students in what Janks (2018) calls small p politics – activities at the local level that begin to question the "power-over" that media exercise. We do not celebrate this kind of agency as "empowerment," but we do see it as a potential bridge to broader, more collective action, discussed below.

While many people mistakenly equate power-over solely with domination, subtler accounts point out that some power-over relationships can be authoritative and legitimate, assuming they do not involve abuse (see Lukes, 2005). The relationship between teachers and their students is one of power-over; if teachers conflate their power-over students with domination, teachable moments can be lost. Josephine Young (2000) provides such an example. As a feminist mother and teacher homeschooling four boys, two of whom were her sons, with hindsight Young recognized how uncomfortable she felt prompting the boys to question and challenge their "common-sense" beliefs about gender. "There were many times," she acknowledges, "when I failed to exercise power over the boys by initiating a critique or calling attention to a gendered inequity" (Young, 2000, p. 332). By realizing that not every instance of power-over is domination, teachers (and parents) may feel more authorized to engage in overt instruction or otherwise create awareness of alternative viewpoints – in Young's case, about gendered identities and inequities. In our work, teaching literacy is an exercise of power; whether recognized or not, teachers shape the meaning-making practices of their students. In chapter 8 we discuss how teachers can reflect on how they exercise that power through practices that support teaching for social justice. These practices enable teachers like Young to transform self-critique of past action into what Schön (1995) calls reflection-in-action – reflexivity that enables educators to respond to unexpected (and perhaps uncomfortable) moments as they unfold. We analyse how unbridled student agency "disrupted" intended learning during one of our case studies, suggesting how such a disruption might be transformed into a teachable moment through meaningful teacher interventions.

The power that teachers hold over their students' learning is evident in lesson planning. As we shall see in our case studies, teachers could join our project only because they had the authority to design classroom activities using pop culture to promote teaching for social justice. Mary's interview reminds us (see chapter 1), however, that authority is circumscribed – by mandated curriculum, regulation through school policy, the supervision of teaching practices, and the parents and guardians of young people. As for agency, the opportunity for teachers to exercise their power in the classroom is itself shaped by the institutional context of learning as schooling. We remain mindful of this context when exploring issues addressed in *Pop Culture and Power*.

Power-To

Some theorists consider *power-to* as the "primary understanding" of power – "as the ability to effect outcomes, not the ability to affect others" (Morriss, 2006, p. 126). In Allen's (1999/2018) approach, power-to is "the ability of an individual actor to attain an end or series of ends"

(p. 126). Because power-to expresses agency, Allen argues that *empowerment* is "roughly equivalent" to her definition of power-to, whereas *resistance* is a subset of power-to: "We can define resistance as the ability of an individual actor to attain an end or series of ends that serve to challenge and/or subvert domination" (p. 126, i.e., resistance as politicized agency).

For our purposes, student redesign is the exercise of Allen's power-to. Citing a Pew study, Jenkins et al. (2006) claim that more than half of American teens have produced media, in that they have "created a blog or webpage, posted original artwork, photography, stories or videos online or remixed online content into their own new creations" (p. 6). In the classroom, critical media literacy affords opportunities for students to experience power-to, through meaning making as the production as well as consumption of media. As Hoechsmann and Poyntz (2012) contend:

> the boundaries between the analytic work of media education and the creative work of media production are porous. One supports the other and, in many ways, thinking of media literacy outside of the way young people articulate their ideas and experiences through creative work makes little sense. (p. 101)

Because remix and mashup are now facilitated by digital technologies, youth are often seen as "experts" in these practices. As classrooms become more "wired," students can create computer-assisted redesign exhibiting the technical polish previously seen only in professionally created media designs.[8] At the same time, teachers need not be limited by access to technologies. Cut and paste is a longstanding, hands-on technique of collage, for example, that can be used to juxtapose counterimages (see Kenway & Bullen, 2006, p. 535 for examples).

Common activities with youth as an exercise of power-to include redesign of media texts through culture jamming that enables students to "talk back" to cultural producers. As "an interruption, a sabotage, hoax, prank, banditry, or blockage of what are seen as the monolithic power structures governing cultural life ... culture jammers seek to introduce noise into the signal that might otherwise obliterate alternatives to it" (Harold, 2004, p. 192). Teachers can inspire students through examples where culture jamming has fostered protest movements. Such an example is the "subvertisement," created by Greenpeace, of Unilever's TV ad "Dove Onslaught" (Ogilvy & Mather, 2007; see Kelly, 2010, pp. 283–4).

Unilever's original ad presents rapid-fire images that remind the viewer of the unrealistic images perpetuated by the beauty industry and related problems such as disordered eating and cosmetic surgery, all set to a catchy song that starts with the lyrics "Here we go." The ad ends with this message: "Talk to your daughter before the beauty industry does." Greenpeace International (2008) created a parody of this ad, called "Dove Onslaught(er)," for use in a successful environmental campaign. Its video uses the same barrage of images, only this time what is depicted is the deforestation of Indonesia by the palm oil industry, the human and environmental costs, and the use of palm oil to make Dove soap – all to the song lyrics of "There they go." The parody ends with this message: "Talk to Dove before it's too late." According to Greenpeace's website (2009), the "viral video" resulted in tens of thousands of protest emails to Unilever, which then met with Greenpeace and agreed to an immediate moratorium on deforestation for palm oil in Southeast Asia, among other things. This example illustrates how redesign of media can foster social change.

Culture jamming in the classroom offers an opportunity for youth to make their own media by using the same tools and techniques that give commercial media power-over them (see Kenway & Bullen, 2006). Classroom activities can take the form of "hacking" ads and "tweaking" messages that an audience expects to see to produce something else, something both playful and political, enacting what Harold (2004) calls "pranking" (see Kenway & Bullen, 2001) or others call "subvertising" (see Chung & Kirby, 2009; Gordon et al., 2018 on what they call "counter-advertising"). By sharing their productions with classmates, culture jamming can encourage students to reflect on their own media responses while developing a language to "talk back" to media creators.

Remix similarly appropriates and changes cultural materials to create something new, but most commonly it refers to audio mixing in music and song recording, while mashup was originally used to describe songs that fused two different styles of music.[9] Laughter (2015) maintains: "a remix is a new version of an existing text, while a mashup takes pieces of existing texts to create something new" (p. 268). Within multiliteracies, Knobel and Lankshear (2008) attend to "a more specific sense of remix, one associated particularly with fan practices and undertaken using the capacities of computers to remix music, digital images, texts, sounds, and animation" (p. 23). Jenkins et al. (2006) call the appropriation that characterizes this kind of remix a "core" skill or competency for our "emerging participatory culture" (p. 56). Specifically,

> digital remixing of media content [music, film clips, images, etc.] makes visible the degree to which all cultural expression builds on what has come before. Appropriation is understood here as a process by which students learn by taking culture apart and putting it back together ... Appropriation may be understood as a process that involves both analysis and commentary. (pp. 32, 33)

Given their popularity among youth, Burwell (2013) describes remixes as "surprisingly potent forms of public pedagogy, not only revealing subtexts but also acting as a springboard for analysis ... Not only do remix videos uncover media culture's dominant ideologies and commercial roots, but they also suggest ways that media texts might be reimagined" (p. 207).

This optimism about student redesign, however, has been challenged by Luckin et al. (2009). Presenting data from the UK, they show that (somewhat contra Jenkins et al., 2006) the more sophisticated use of Web 2.0 tools is not as prevalent among youth as might be thought, given their relative accessibility. Those few youths who are involved as producers and publishers do not demonstrate the use of "higher order thinking skills" (p. 100). Equally important, they found that "it is teachers who have inspired the use of Web 2.0 tools in a more complex or sophisticated manner." Overall, their data reveal "little evidence of critical enquiry or analytical awareness, few examples of collaborative knowledge construction, and little production or publishing outside social networking sites" (p. 100; see also Lu, Hao, & Jing, 2016). In short, while media production made available by new digital technology is a promising exercise of political agency (see, e.g., Jenkins et al., 2016; Andersen, 2017), the ability to use technology will not necessarily, in itself, challenge the power that media hold over youth (Schäfer, 2011; Buckingham, 2019; de Roock, 2021). Burwell (2013) reminds us: "it remains crucial for young people to *discuss, describe,* and *critically reflect* on digital media" (p. 206, emphasis in original). The classroom is one such place where this kind of critical engagement can accompany student media production.

Gainer and Lapp (2010) point out that appropriation can include meanings that students bring into the classroom: "literacy as remix positions readers as active meaning-makers who blend understandings based in prior knowledge and experience with new information as they construct new understandings from textual transactions" (p. 58). These meanings may not correspond to the formal curriculum. An important example of enhancing power-to arises when critical media literacy enables students from non-dominant backgrounds not only to identify how they are being misrepresented (as through stereotyping) but also to articulate experiences that may not be included in official curriculum.[10] Their alternative interpretations of the social world, however, may put them into conflict with their classmates: in chapter 1, we saw how White boys in Stack's (2010) media lesson dismissed the girls' experiences of racism, complaining about "political correctness" and that minorities can "take things too far." Stack's experience echoes Liz's caution that encouraging independent meaning making can put students at risk of peer censure. Teachers often have to make decisions in the moment about whether and how to respond to student ideas, especially to "offensive" remarks (e.g., racism, sexism):

> There are times when, honestly, kids have said stuff that is very racist or very offensive and absolutely sexist all the time. They don't even, half the time, acknowledge that they're being sexist in their own comments. And then you have to have a response, you have to manage your own response [laughs] as a facilitator ... How much are you going to call it out? How do you, at the same time, not offend that individual who did take a risk in speaking, even though they have misspoken? (Liz, the media educator interviewed early in our study)

Clearly, validating the agency of independent meaning making by students complicates what we described above as teachers' power-over students' learning. How this contradiction will be resolved is situation-specific; in our view, resolution requires commitment on the part of the teacher to honour rather than stifle student agency as meaning making.

By honouring student agency, teachers must negotiate precisely what many educators attempt to hold at bay – pre-cognitive, erotic, embodied affect that can disrupt well-planned lessons about the sexism or racism embedded in media culture. We have seen, for example, that despite extensive experience in media education, Liz "could not touch Lady Gaga with a 10-foot pole." Liz's response was one of "avoidance"; while we attribute her response to the context of her situation,[11] such avoidance can prematurely foreclose an opportunity for critical reflection. Resolution engages teachers in what has been called "the politics of pleasure" (see Luke, 1994; Alvermann, Moon, & Hagood, 1999). Given our interest in pop culture as public pedagogy, a secondary research question emerged: How can the pleasure of pop culture be harnessed to critical media literacy?

Power-With

Allen (1999/2018) defines power-with as "the ability of a collectivity to act together for the attainment of an agreed-upon end or series of ends" (p. 127). In our project we view it as the collective exercise of power-to, already implicit in much of what we discussed above. In Allen's framework, *solidarity* is a subset of power-with: "the ability of a collectivity to act together for the agreed-upon end of challenging, subverting, and, ultimately, overturning a system of domination" (p. 127). She equates it with *collective empowerment.* In our work, this experience of solidarity is a necessary, but not sufficient, condition for transforming small p into capital P politics. While small p politics is about "the micro-politics of everyday life" and "the minute-by-minute choices and decisions that make us who we are" (Janks, 2013b, p. 33), by contrast:

> Politics with a capital *P* is about government and world trade agreements and the United Nations' peace-keeping forces; it is about ethnic or religious genocide and world tribunals; it is about apartheid and global capitalism, money laundering and linguistic imperialism. It is about the inequities between the political North and the political South. (p. 33)

Janks's notion of politics thus echoes our materialism, by connecting social issues taking place in local settings to extra-local conditions that perpetuate global inequities. By promoting social justice in this way, we view capital P politics as the desired – but not inevitable – outcome of critical literacy.

Strategies to promote experiences of power-with characterize teaching for social justice. Consensus exists that critical media literacy, likewise, cannot be achieved through traditional, top-down pedagogy, what Dehli (2009) calls the "transmission" model of teaching (p. 68). As argued by Kellner and Share (2005):

> A major challenge in developing critical media literacy ... results from the fact that it is not a pedagogy in the traditional sense, with firmly established principles, a canon of texts, and tried-and-true teaching procedures. It requires a democratic pedagogy which involves teachers sharing power with students. (p. 373)

Both our preliminary interviews with media educators and existing literature emphasized the need for participatory pedagogy that includes activities such as class discussion, group media projects, and peer-based learning by giving and receiving feedback from classmates. This kind of *collaborative learning* is characterized as promoting "collective intelligence" that mimics much out-of-classroom learning through activities such as crowdsourcing or the collectible card game Pokémon, where fans, "who each know some crucial detail about the various species [aka categories], constitute a collective intelligence whose knowledge is extended each time two youth on the playground share something about the franchise" (Jenkins et al., 2006, p. 40). This kind of intelligence promises what the NLG (1996) calls "productive diversity" that can result when "the multiplicity of cultures, experiences, ways of making meaning, and ways of thinking" are harnessed (p. 67). Relatedly, rather than see intelligence as a *possession*, the concept of *distributed cognition* (expanding one's mental capacity by using tools such as databases and Wikipedia) emphasizes *accomplishment*. It corresponds to the differentiation Smith (1990a) maintains between "knowledge" as an already constituted thing and "knowing" as an ongoing activity.

A relevant example of power-with emerged during completion of our manuscript, appearing in a newsletter from the school that Deirdre's daughter attended before university. As a school-based activity, it begins with an existing parody of the first few Harry Potter books and then invites students to participate in what NLG calls redesign:

A VERY POTTER MUSICAL
The High School theatre class is going to adapt *A Very Potter Musical* for the stage at WH. **This show is a "Fan tribute" and is not licensed. We are calling a one day intensive "adaptation" of the script.** Anyone who would like to be in this show is asked to come to the intensive adaptation of the script day. Currently the show is 3 hrs long and we want to do it in less than 2 hrs. This is a deep dive into the script with a reading and adapting of scenes. We will be looking at the show with a critical lens. The musical is definitely for teens. Not a hard fast line but in that direction. **The whole show is on YouTube. There are scenes that we are not using for a variety of reasons.** We are using the show as an opportunity to learn and think about theatre.

This example illustrates the characteristics of a participatory culture that "shifts the focus of literacy from one of individual expression to community involvement": low barriers to artistic expression and civic engagement, strong support for sharing, informal mentorship, belief by participants that their contributions matter, and some degree of social connection among participants (Jenkins et al., 2006, p. 7). In *Pop Culture and Power*, we explore the challenges of using pop culture to foster this kind of participatory ethos in the classroom (see chapter 8). One dilemma is that, in many ways, education as schooling is itself "parallel to mass media, as an industrial-era institution with one-directional learning and teaching" (Kupiainen, 2013, p. x). Within this context, fostering a participatory learning environment requires a degree of flexibility not typical of an authoritarian, transmission pedagogy: a participatory classroom culture requires teachers who are comfortable in relinquishing, when appropriate, their institutionalized power-over student learning.

As indicated by Liz during her interview, media production by students can be one such instance when teachers need to "let go" of complete control. Despite the discomfort that this might invoke, for her it resulted in "some really profound moments" as students not only engaged with a (sensitive) topic, but also "found ways to articulate that [topic] for themselves and [become] really excited about that." She emphasized that such a result "comes up fairly frequently when students have carte blanche to do whatever they want with their video projects." While we would not characterize students exercising either power-to or power-over in the classroom as engaging in capital P politics, we view this exercise as an important experience in how to speak to power.

Fostering Political Agency

In summary, our goal for teaching critical media literacy is to harness the agency of media engagement to embodied experiences of political agency, when possible beyond the classroom. New social media have been identified as an opportunity for youth to exercise their political "power-with." Relying on online networks rather than hierarchical organizations, activist movements can be adaptable and flexible, while the speed and scale at which they can operate has been greatly enhanced by communication technologies (Gonzalez-Bailon, 2015; for an overview of internet activism, see Kahn & Kellner, 2004, 2006; Jenkins et al., 2016). We thus share optimism about the potential for new social media to support the work of social activists, while remaining well aware of challenges that can arise.[12] As Gonzalez-Bailon (2015) points out, "technologies never determine the outcomes of what are essentially human dynamics" (p. 513):

> Protest movements are not caused by social media activity; social media offer just a vehicle (one of the many) to help a protest movement rise from the shadows; the crucial explanatory factors are still social and economic, if not historical. (p. 515; also see Fuchs, 2014)

In short, commentators identify new communication technology as support for political action. In our work, media offer a venue for the exercise of power; media engagement can thus support social justice. As will become apparent in the remainder of *Pop Culture and Power*, our goal is to explore how critical media education can help youth mobilize this support, drawing on Allen's concepts of "power-to" and "power-with."

The teaching context obviously makes a difference about what *can* be done (see, e.g., Friedman, 2011; Pelo & Pelojoaquin, 2006–7). We do not claim – or expect – that becoming politically aware is an inevitable result of even the best-planned media activities. As noted by Liz:

> Social justice is certainly not something that every student cares about at all! I know it's naïve to say this: I kind of thought they would care a bit about equity, especially if they're from a west-side [economically privileged] school. You can count on it that they *don't*. You can count on it that they've never experienced

enough difficulty in their lives based on social inequality to have any context of what that looks like, or why that matters at all ... They're living in a generation where they're the target audience for millions of advertisers. Car ads are aimed at children who are eight and nine. That's their target audience. If you were raised like that, wouldn't you think that that's all that mattered?

When thinking about our project, we further recognized that not all teachers (or schools) are committed to learning that promotes social justice.[13] As Mary noted during her interview, when describing her experience of teacher education:

There was a lot of resistance to the half course on equity by people who didn't feel like they needed to teach about homophobia [and racism], for example ... like, "I don't have to do that." They felt like they should just be able to teach a "normal" class, whatever that was ... I encountered a lot of that.

In considering our interviews with local educators, we decided to recruit teachers not simply on the basis of their interest in using popular culture but also their commitment to teaching for social justice.

Like cultural studies, our notion of critical media literacy is "motivated by a desire to maintain some ground for optimism in the face of the overwhelming and quite reasonable pessimism that confronts anyone looking at the contemporary world" (Grossberg, 2009, p. 41). Literacy education offers what Giroux (1987) calls a pedagogical and political mechanism through which to promote social practices necessary to support social movements fighting for the imperatives of a participatory democracy. Based on a collaborative pedagogy, critical media education encourages students to ask "who gets to say what and why" (Stack, 2010, p. 212). Because this type of critical reflection is not inherent in student engagement with media, Janks (2013a) asks: How can our teaching

contribute to a world in which our students at all levels of education become agents for change? How can we produce students who can contribute to greater equity, who can respect difference and live in harmony with others, and who can play a part in protecting our environment? (p. 227)

While Janks points out that different disciplines will have different answers, she places hope in literacy education. We consider critical media literacy as a "place to start." As noted by Liz,

in defining critical thinking, for me it's about uncovering layers. That's absolutely what it is. And that means there's no right answer, right? It can keep going down and down and down, depending on how far you read into it. But for someone who might be new to it, or for whom their tendency is really not to look at things that way, even one layer down can be interesting and can be revelatory for them to say, "Oh, that also could mean that to someone else? Huh. I never thought about it that way." ... It's a pretty cool moment.

It was within the context of such optimism that we designed our current study. Using pop culture to teach for social justice must take student agency beyond the activities of simply redesign. To support the changes Janks (2013a) describes, teaching for social justice requires an understanding of media as a venue for the operation of power: redesign, in itself, does not result in social change. What does teaching critical media literacy look like when student agency, expressed as redesign, is an exercise of power? *Pop Culture and Power* answers this question in a two-phase study, described in the following chapter as both a teaching and a research project.

3 *Pop Culture and Power*: Teaching as Research

... any meaningful pedagogic theory has to be able to take account of the experience of classroom practice; and that practice is a site on which new theoretical insights and challenges can be generated.

– David Buckingham, 1998a, p. 11

This chapter explores how *Pop Culture and Power* takes account of classroom practice to generate theoretical insight into media as a vehicle for the operation of power that can be harnessed to teaching for social justice. Our study took place in two phases: the first phase entailed the design and facilitation of a professional development seminar in media analysis for teachers, the second assessed our theoretical framing of the seminar by piloting media activities in participants' classrooms. Taking the form of design research, our project "concentrates explicitly on improving practice and simultaneously building theory that advances fundamental understanding" (Mehan, 2008, p. 82).

When we initiated our study, Dan (a retired teacher working to promote media studies in public school, interviewed for our study) indicated that few, if any, teaching resources for using pop culture were readily available in our region (in fact, in the province of British Columbia). Commentators since have begun to direct attention to the need for teacher education in media analysis. Given the ubiquity of television, smart phones, popular music, film, video games, digital platforms, and advertising, Kellner and Share (2019, p. 5) argue it is irresponsible to ignore media as public pedagogy. A reconstruction of education should provide critical media literacy (CML) to teachers, as well as to students and citizens (also see Buckingham, 2019; A. Butler, 2020). Because media education was not a required part of the teacher education program at our university at the time, we asked how our study might contribute to teacher education by developing curriculum for practising teachers wanting to upgrade their capacity to teach media literacy.

Dan's claim about the lack of resources was subsequently confirmed by our teacher participants, who were attracted to our project because of their interest in using pop culture, despite lacking a background in media studies.[1] This context influenced the framing of *Pop Culture and Power* as both a teaching and a research project. This chapter elaborates on our project design, followed by a description of demographics in the province of British Columbia where our study took place. We then overview the two phases, both organized to address the themes introduced in chapter 2 – agency and power. By understanding how the power of popular culture shapes student agency as meaning making, we can better understand how teachers might use media literacy to support social justice.

Shape Shifting: Designing a Multiple Case Study

As academic researchers but also teachers, like Buckingham (1998a) we are committed to *praxis* – building theory that explicitly aims to improve practice. While motivated by theoretical interests, we wanted our project to address practical concerns of teachers: How to use pop culture in ways that meet the requirements of mandated curriculum in their subject area, while stimulating student interest in issues of social injustice. We were determined also to support the ongoing interests of potential teacher participants in continuing to teach media literacy. In the end, these practical commitments shaped the design of our project. Prioritizing the practical nature of our undertaking, we moved away from the idea that, as researchers, we would preselect the medium to be researched in a classroom setting. Instead, we saw teachers as best equipped to choose media that would support their ongoing teaching. Our project would necessarily be exploratory, informed – but not driven – by the theoretical commitments outlined in the previous chapters.

Exploratory research seldom unfolds as smoothly as retrospective accounts imply; ours was no exception. The innovative nature of qualitative researching means that a research design requires ongoing "critical and creative thinking" rather than being treated as a "fixed product" (Mason, 2002, p. 46). Our innovations resulted in a project where we ourselves engaged in teaching media education (to teacher participants), and subsequently researched the outcomes of our teaching practice. This design had some obvious benefits – it ensured that the classroom activities for our project would fit into teacher participants' regular workload, with minimal intrusion on their busy schedules. From a research perspective, teacher designs would ensure a good fit between student participants and selected media, with their designs incorporating our theoretical interests: our project does not assess the practices of teacher participants, but rather the potential efficacy of using the various media strategies that inform the cases in our study. As a multiple rather than singular case study, it also enables us to say a lot more about the complexity of student engagement with media. The complications of our design, however, became increasingly apparent as our project unfolded. For example, the activities designed by teachers for each case study required an extended series of classroom sessions (at least five), generating much more data than anticipated, especially video data. While case study chapters have been written with coherence in mind, these data captured the "messiness" that can accompany the "unscripted" learning that critical media education requires. We discuss the implications for lesson planning in chapter 8.

What caught us by surprise was the protracted delay in gaining institutional approval from our university. Reviewers' concerns did not rest with the possible exploitation of youth as research participants or the desire to ensure that participating schools would benefit from our work. Rather, reviewers questioned our dual role as "teacher researchers."[2] They expressed concern as to whether teachers we recruited were *required* to attend the seminar, and, if so, they asked: "Is it possible that [teacher] students will feel undue influence to consent to the research project or complete the research assignments, if it [whether or not they gave consent] is known to the instructors of the course who will be assigning the grades?" In addressing their queries, we explained the intertwined and simultaneous processes of design research:

> In the first [process], researchers "intervene in the activity by participating in its design" (Mehan, 2008, p. 82); in the case of this proposal, the intervention is our design of the critical media education course. In the second set of intertwined processes, researchers develop methods to study the activities they have designed; in the case of this proposal, our primary tool will be the reflexive journalling done by course participants (the students and ourselves) ...
>
> We hope to create a new course (or series of workshops or both) based on our experience of piloting this course. We want to give participants the option of taking the course for credit and for a mark. This has the added advantage of making this a more authentic experience for us as instructors piloting the course and for students who are participating in a formal learning experience. Given this situation, the distinction between what is research and what is the course is not as clear-cut as implied in the comments from the Ethics Reviewers.

44 Pop Culture and Power

As the reviewers were members of an institution of higher education – dedicated to teaching and not just research – we were disappointed that they did not seem fully informed about research practices common in the field of education. There is a growing literature that attests to the challenges faced by researchers who are also teachers wanting, in some sense, to study their own practice (see Metro, 2014; Hemmings, 2006). We attribute these challenges to the institutional regulation of knowledge production (see also Appendix C for more details on our ethical protocol). In the end, only one adult – a parent – raised questions about the activities that young students were being asked to participate in. In response to a letter of informed consent sent home with Grade 4/5 students, this parent asked:

1. Media Literacy – Can you please elaborate on exactly what is meant by this term, as it is very general? What types of media? Why is it being promoted and for what purpose? What are some examples of the advantages/disadvantages of childhood media literacy?
2. Development of Learning Activities – can you explain what type of learning activities will be developed? What will be the purpose of them?
3. Will the media literacy be associated with any marketing?

Together, Deirdre and the teacher (Yvette) who designed the learning project (discussed in the following chapter) addressed these concerns to the satisfaction of the parent(s) involved. We remain curious about why more adults did not question the role of youth as "research subjects."

Research Setting and Recruitment of Participants

Much of what we were able to learn about teaching critical media literacy through a literature review did not take place in Canadian classrooms (but see Dehli, 2009; Hoechsmann & Poyntz, 2012; Stack, 2009, 2010). While there are many points of similarity between Canada and Australia as past colonies of Britain, as well as between Canada and the USA, both media education and research on media literacy are situated practices. Below we describe a prominent feature of the local site where our project would take place: the multicultural nature of Vancouver, British Columbia.

More than one-fifth of the population of Canada belong to what Statistics Canada calls "visible minority"[3] groups, the three largest such groups being "South Asians, Chinese and Blacks" (Statistics Canada, 2017, *Growth of the visible minority population*, para. 7). That figure is significantly higher in major cities like Vancouver; in 2011, over half of the population in the largest cities within the Vancouver CMA (Census Metropolitan Area) belonged to a "visible minority" group, predominantly South Asian and

Chinese (Statistics Canada, 2013). Today, Vancouver (alongside Toronto and Montreal) is where half of all immigrants and recent immigrants to Canada reside (Statistics Canada, 2017); in 2016, immigrants represented 40.8 per cent of Vancouver's population (Statistics Canada, 2017, table 1). Despite its current ethno-racial diversity, the province's name, British Columbia, highlights its White, European, English-speaking settler roots. Most Canadian students have to negotiate both Eurocentric curriculum and Eurocentric culture, where "whiteness" is the unmarked norm. Within this context, we recognized that while teacher participants recruited into our study would likely have limited backgrounds in media studies, they would necessarily be the experts on teaching within this complex context.

One element that remained constant, and informed our ongoing decision making, was the commitment to media literacy as teaching for social justice. As noted previously, this commitment is based on the belief that media engagement can be harnessed for social change. Recognizing that not all teachers share such a commitment, we emphasized "teaching for social justice" during recruitment. Deirdre advertised the project by word of mouth and by distributing a brochure through her professional network of teachers. This brochure described our project as a "professional development research project" that would be carried out from a social justice perspective. Because we were piloting curriculum that we hoped to offer regularly at UBC, the seminar schedule mirrored our university's fall term with sessions to be held weekly over a three-month period (September through December, 2012). We indicated that our goal was to identify "What models of media education will best prepare students to be informed consumers of commercial culture and thoughtful, engaged members of our democratic society." We identified the kinds of questions that would frame the seminar component of the project:

- What are some key concepts that help us to analyse media?
- How do people's social investments and identities influence their interpretations of media messages?
- What difference might age, gender, sexuality, culture, class, religion, and immigrant status make in terms of how young people negotiate meanings of media "texts"?
- What are the challenges and barriers to bringing popular culture into the classroom?
- How can teachers honour students' pleasure in popular culture while fostering the "learned pleasure of analysis"? (Recruitment Brochure)[4]

Recruitment of teachers proved to be more challenging than anticipated, for a number of reasons.[5] Four graduate research assistants hired on the project were also enrolled in the seminar. We introduce teachers participating in Phase 2 and research assistants completing the field work in following chapters.

Recruiting teachers was, *de facto*, recruiting their students as participants in Phase 2. We are sensitive to the role that adults play in regulating the lives of youth. Vadeboncoeur (2005) points out:

> The teachers supervise the students, and are themselves supervised by the administration. The students, internalizing the teacher's gaze, begin to regulate their own behaviour in school, and supervise their siblings (and parents) at home. Hierarchical surveillance is self-reproducing and perhaps one of the most powerful lessons of schooling. (p. 10)

We are aware that researchers as well as teachers can participate in the hierarchical surveillance of youth.[6] We continue to ask whether critical literacy can actively work *against* what Vadeboncoeur describes as processes that limit, rather than enhance, young people's horizons. How? This questioning is at the heart of teaching critical media literacy as a political undertaking.

From the outset, we did not treat students as a captive audience for our project; given that we grant young people agency in making meaning from their classroom experiences, we viewed them as agents able to make decisions about their participation in research activities. As well as securing approval from the school boards and principals of the schools where teachers were employed, letters of informed consent were distributed to all parents or guardians,[7] and assent was sought from student participants. The two school boards and three school principals we contacted were very supportive of our project. School settings as research sites for our project, as well as the specific student demographics, are described in each case study chapter.

Phase 1: A Seminar on Pop Culture in the Classroom

The goal of our seminar was to translate our theoretical understanding of media as a venue for the operation of power into "a pedagogy that guides teachers and students to think critically about the world around them; [that] empowers them to act as responsible citizens, with the skills and social consciousness to challenge injustice" (Kellner & Share, 2019, p. 14). To enhance participants' ability to use pop culture in their classrooms, not only during the study but afterwards, we keyed off Kellner's (1998) notion of a media-literate person as "skillful in analyzing media codes and conventions, criticizing media stereotypes, values, and ideologies, and thus reading media critically." Such literacy empowers people to "to discriminate and evaluate media content, to dissect media forms critically, and to investigate media effects and uses" (p. 108).

In keeping with this notion of "a media-literate person," our seminar was designed to engage participants in critical media analysis. The challenge was to use our theoretical understanding of media as a venue for the operation of power to explore what might remain invisible: how the meaning making encouraged by media texts operates as coordinator of social practice. This coordination operates through media engagement and can be uncovered when the analyst decodes the conventions, frames, and ideologies of media texts; identifies the relations and practices of media production; and explores how and why audiences make diverse meanings of any given media offering (see, e.g., Buckingham, 2003a; Kellner & Share, 2005). These analytical tasks became seminar themes, described below. Each theme explores the power of media to "make things happen," promoting learning that could help teachers harness this power to their students' redesign of a more inclusive and equitable future. To enhance this learning, we organized the seminar around a series of conceptual tools. We selected tools that can be employed across varying subject areas and grade levels. Because our intent was to support their teaching beyond our project, these tools were drawn from the existing literature on media analysis, enabling participants to follow up on themes that interested them.

Below we elaborate seminar content, organized around the themes outlined above. This content is the context within which the case studies were produced as a situated practice of using pop culture to promote CML (the now outdated syllabus is included as Appendix A; prompts for writing and other homework activities appear in Appendix B). The discussion below, therefore, helps account for what was accomplished in participants' classrooms; in keeping with design research, our analysis of each case study is an assessment of our own thinking about how to promote critical media literacy, and not of teacher participants' teaching. Our overview of seminar content also provides the basis for our retrospective discussion of how teaching for social justice might be deepened through our distinctly social approach to media literacy.

Theme 1: The Power of Media Operating as Available Design

As we elaborate below, Smith's notion of "textually mediated discourse" enables us to treat media not simply as a cultural artifact, but as the material product of human activities. In *Pop Culture and Power*, "discourse" takes the form of, but goes beyond, written/spoken/visual texts to include ways to think and talk about – hence act in – the world. In other words, the practice of literacy as meaning making informs action in the social world. It does so, however, within the social context described in chapter 1, which includes "the material setting, the people present (and what they know and believe), the language that comes before and after a given utterance, the social relationships of the people involved, and their ethnic, gendered, and sexual identities, as well as cultural, historical, and institutional factors" (Gee, 2004, pp. 28–9). The challenge is to understand *how* everyday media texts (such as those of pop culture) work to "make things happen." While a full answer to such a question lies far beyond our seminar, we chose strategies that could support the ability for teachers to foster students' power-to analyse available design, both individually and through collaboration.

As argued in chapter 1, social regulation of meaning making happens when the established discourses of everyday life become taken for granted; they disappear from our consciousness even as they inform our actions. Critical media literacy aims, therefore, to bring this regulation into consciousness, opening the opportunity for resistance and discursive renegotiation (Rogers, 2017, p. 206). In our seminar, how power operates through practices of meaning making was rendered visible through conceptual tools that facilitate critical interrogation. We drew from critical discourse analysis, for example, to interrogate how the text, as a concrete manifestation of a rule-bound system of signification, constructs meaning that is offered to readers as a (more or less) accurate reflection of social life, orchestrating how we experience "reality" by giving us categories for its appropriation. In our project, critical media literacy identifies how taken-for-granted meanings are discursively constructed through culturally and historically specific practices of symbolic signification, raising further questions about motivations embedded in available design.

A useful tool comes from James Gee's (2011a, b) concept of "figured world." This concept supports recognition of how the social world is brought into consciousness through the ability for the discourses embedded in media texts to "build things" (Gee, 2011b, p. 171). Drawing on Holland et al. (1998), we used "figured world" to refer to

> a socially and culturally constructed realm of interpretation in which particular characters and actors are recognized, significance is assigned to certain acts, and particular outcomes are valued over others. Each is a simplified world populated by a set of agents (in the world of romance: attractive women, boyfriends, lovers, fiancés) who engage in a limited range of meaningful acts or changes of state (flirting with, falling in love with, dumping, having sex with) as moved by a specific set of forces (attractiveness, love, lust) ... These collective "as if" worlds are socio-historic, contrived

interpretations or imaginations that mediate behavior and so, from the perspective of heuristic development, inform participants' outlooks. (pp. 52–3; also see Bartlett & Holland, 2002)

This example illustrates how concepts from critical discourse analysis enable us to explore the text as more than an inert object standing "outside" the world of the reader; they reveal the power of "textually mediated discourse" to authorize specific visions of the world.

Given our interest in understanding how media texts enable action through the (potential) construction of subjects as well as their social world, over a series of seminar sessions we introduced questions that interrogate what textually mediated discourse "builds":

- What is being accomplished?
- What "figured world" is constructed?
- What social identity is being constructed (by the speaker, by the text)?
- What social relationships are being sustained or re/negotiated?
- What practice is being facilitated or accomplished?
- What value system is being communicated?

We also posed questions that reveal what remains hidden:

- What discourses are being referenced without being acknowledged?
- What is not being said but is necessary for the text to make sense? (adapted for our seminar from Gee, 2011b)

In summary, critical interrogation of the values, predispositions, and desires constructed by the text reveals how social practice is embedded in the text. To explore how a text might support specific actions, we keyed off Althusser's notion that ideology "recruits" readers, "transforming" them into subjects. His notion of *interpellation*

> can be imagined along the lines of the most commonplace everyday police (or other) hailing: "Hey, you there!" ... Assuming that the theoretical scene I have imagined takes place on the street, the hailed individual will turn around ... he [sic] becomes a *subject*. Why? Because he had recognized that the hail was "really" addressed to him, and that it was *really him* who was hailed [and not someone else]. (Althusser, 2004, p. 321)[8]

While we did not characterize media as "ideology" (because such an interpretation encourages a search for "authentic" representation), we found it useful to introduce the idea that textual processes invite us into their figured world by "hailing" us. If we are successfully hailed, we take up the subject position offered by the text. From this position we look at the world from inside textual categories in the way Dorothy Smith describes (see chapter 2); what we see, how we feel about what we see, and how we respond to what we see come to seem obvious or natural. From this perspective, Althusser argued that when successfully hailed, we "misrecognize" both ourselves and the social world; we occupy an imagined *but lived* relation to reality.[9]

Also interested in the relationship between a text and its reader, Ellsworth (1997)[10] draws on film theory to explore how this imagined relation can be resisted. Filmmakers make assumptions and have wishes, consciously or not, about to *whom* their film is addressed:

> a film is composed, then, not only of a system of images and unfolding story. It is composed of a structure of address to an imagined audience ... Given the commercial interest of filmmakers, it [mode of address] is about the desire to control, as much as possible, how and from where the viewer reads the film. It's about enticing a viewer into a particular position of knowledge towards the text, a position of coherence from which the text works, makes sense, gives pleasure, satisfies dramatically and aesthetically, sells itself and its spin-off products. (pp. 24, 28)

Successful interpellation supports a "preferred reading" (Hall, 2004) of the text, where readers adopt the categories of meaning embedded therein. Interested in social change, Ellsworth attends to how audiences can refuse or subvert the subject position and associated pleasures offered by any social text. Refusal begins through awareness of how we are addressed by the text:

> Once you figure out the relationship between a film's text and a spectator's experience, for example, you might be able to change or influence, control even, a spectator's response by designing a film in a particular way. Or, you may be able to teach viewers how to resist or subvert who a film thinks they are, or wants them to be. (Ellsworth, 1997, p. 22)

Recognizing the ability of the text to invite us into its figured world brings the constructed nature of selfhood into the interrogation. "People's identities mediate and are mediated by the texts they read, write, and talk about ... In other words, texts and the literate practices that accompany them not only reflect but may produce the self" (Moje & Luke, 2009, p. 416; also see Weedon, 1987; Davies, 1989; Buckingham &

Sefton-Green, 1994). This construction of our sense of selfhood testifies to the ultimate power of media.

For the seminar, we devised an activity that enabled participants to experience how the text invites readers into its figured world, using a travel ad from a popular print magazine.[11] The image was, simply, an empty chair, sitting among palm trees on a deserted beach. Given that this activity was held during the bleak rainy weather typical of Vancouver winters, it hailed virtually all participants, generating rich discussion. There was general consensus that this figured world was designed to appeal to hard-working, winter-weary Canadians, by evoking a desire for sunshine and the peace and quiet associated with vacationing. In effect, the empty chair is offering "me," the reader, a subject position in the ad's figured world. But we recognized that not all readers are able to occupy that subject position and participate in the pleasure of sitting on this sunny beach; only readers able to purchase tickets to the tropical South and freely travel away from domestic responsibilities can experience it. This recognition led us to consider whom the text does not address: Canadians without sufficient wealth or without paid vacation. It also ignores, but requires, local hotel workers who clean up after wealthy guests, and who are likely to be living without the luxury of taking a vacation. In the final analysis, we decided that the text hails readers who desire to vacation in the South, where a Canadian dollar can buy luxuries not experienced at home. This interrogation thus led us to ask whose desires are being addressed by this text, and how its preferred reading naturalizes the global inequalities upon which its figured world depends. Interrogation reminds us that media are the product of intentional human action, directing our attention to the social relations of media production and the social practices those relations (attempt to) coordinate.

Theme 2: Power Exercised as Media Production

Animated film for children, especially, reminds us that the already-given meanings of everyday culture are the product of human activity (see Christensen, 2017). Political economy can direct attention to those activities by giving visibility to the ownership of media corporations producing entertainment for youth and the politics of media regulation. It thus locates popular culture in the social world of organized human activities motivated by historically specific relations of ruling. These activities include the routine work of studio artists, filmmakers, reporters, editors, photographers, and so on (see Burwell, 2010; for newsmaking, see Smith, 1990b, chap. 4), working with specific intention. The power of pop culture is thus traced to the vested interests and practices that sustain current meanings ascribed to relations of age, gender, family, and class (for example) as relations of social inequality that now extend to the global level.

Discussed in our seminar, Kenway and Bullen (2006) describe a classroom activity that can bring the vested interests and practices of media production into view. Treating consumer-media culture as a "pedagogical machine," they promoted critical media literacy by appropriating and repurposing the corporate practice of "cool hunting": mining youth subcultures to poach marketable signifiers of what is "cool" among young consumers. Their teaching strategy engages young learners in a "cultural and social biographical analysis of the objects of cool in their own consumer culture" (p. 526). This analysis asks

> simple questions of who made the object and where it originated ... When does an object lose its coolness and why? What is its exchange value in terms of the identity, solidarity or pleasure the consumer derives and how does this equate with the functional uses of the product? (p. 526)

By making the social origin and life of cultural objects (e.g., an i-Phone) visible, Kenway and Bullen's pedagogy offers students "ways of understanding how they use consumer culture as a resource in identity building and how, at the same time, *they* [students] are used by consumer-media culture" (p. 524). Kenway and Bullen suggest that students make "the backstage reality the object of investigation" (e.g., how music videos are produced), to demystify or unmask the "marketing intent" of "consumer-media culture" (p. 527). We would take this activity one step further through an exploration of the labour conditions under which information and communication technologies are produced. A Samsung production site in China has been reported to employ 14- and 15-year-olds (which is below the legal working age in China; see Barboza, 2014), while Samsung produces its Galaxy S9 and S9+ smartphones under conditions that expose young female workers in Vietnam – most in their twenties – to reproductive hazards (Minh Hang & DiGangi, 2018). Online searches for these backstage stories would, by all accounts, lead students to articles by UN Human Rights experts, for example, introducing students to capital P politics by connecting local media consumption to globalized processes of media production.

Although receiving much less attention for teaching media literacy, classroom discussion of the regulation of media through various government agencies and consumer organizations can also connect media literacy to issues of social justice. The topics of internet safety and "cyberbullying" are especially relevant for today's youth, and offer many examples of potential government action that students could research and debate. Regulation of cyberbullying that goes beyond existing hate speech laws, for example, raises questions of how to balance freedom of expression with the safety of persons (Kelly & Arnold, 2016, pp. 539–41). A fruitful area for investigation and class discussion is proposed legal remedies, ostensibly aimed to safeguard youth from cyberbullies, but all too often at the cost of infringing on privacy rights by ceding surveillance powers to telecommunications companies and police (pp. 541–2).

Theme 3: Power at Play – Student Media Production

While commercial media offer teachers an accessible way to introduce how power originates in the relations and practices of corporate cultural production, interrogation can shift – and, in our view, *should* shift – to media produced by young people. Media production offers youth an opportunity to challenge corporate meaning making. Included in the contemporary access and control of media production is the emergence of new technologies (e.g., video-sharing sites, image-editing software) that facilitate the creation of technically accomplished texts by everyday people. These technologies thus have the potential to give meaning making by youth the reach and polished appeal that was once reserved for corporations: texts produced by "private" individuals become, almost instantly, "social" communication through Twitter, for example.[12] In this context, Kellner and Share (2007) advise:

> While not everyone has the tools to create sophisticated media productions, we strongly recommend a pedagogy of teaching critical media literacy through project-based media production (even if it is as simple as rewriting a text or drawing pictures) for making analyses more meaningful and empowering as students gain tools for responding and taking action on the social conditions and texts they are critiquing. (p. 9)

To give seminar participants a hands-on feel for how media production can be an exercise of power by their students, we created an in-class activity involving rescripting scenes from a Hollywood comedy. We showed clips from the Arnold Schwarzenegger film *Kindergarten Cop* (Reitman, 1990), selected to feature gender and sexual stereotyping through conflation of sex, gender, and sexuality. After participants used various discourse analysis tools to interrogate the film, we divided them into two groups and assigned each the task of rewriting and role playing a key scene from the movie that might suggest an alternative ending. We instructed the groups to "try to challenge the gender or other stereotypes (figured worlds or traditional storylines) that your group discerns." Debriefing questions included: "How, if at all, were stereotypes or traditional storylines challenged? By reversals? Other ways? Were the rewritten scenes funny? Why or why not? Which rewritten scene did you feel was most successful at challenging the stereotypes? Why?"

One challenge in moving from "teacher agency" – how teachers engage media texts when preparing lessons – to student agency is the unpredictability of student responses. Existing research shows that youth draw on available resources for meaning making that include media texts, but also on what they already know, often resulting in new meaning or meaning making in ways that subvert the primacy of commercial culture (see Guzzetti, Elliott, & Welsch, 2010). Smith (1987) points out that while meaning making draws on cultural resources readily at hand, we also draw on a "practical consciousness" that comes through everyday activities, and that enables us to competently engage with others in the social world. Because practical consciousness can be at odds with the meaning conventional knowledge provides, it can become a force for social change. Readily available, established knowledge, however, may "dominate and penetrate the social consciousness of the society in general, and thus may effectively control the social process of consciousness in ways that deny expression to the actual experience people have in their working relations of everyday life" (p. 55). A *disjuncture* can arise between "the world as it is, known directly in experience and as it is shared with others, and the ideas fabricated externally to that everyday world and provided as a means to think and imagine with" (p. 55). This disjuncture, which is more likely to be felt[13] by those marginalized from the benefits of mainstream society, can open the possibility for alternative meaning making through redesign. As in feminist struggles, it can become a force for social change.

As Burwell (2010) reminds us, young people's responses to media culture are never either entirely compliant or creatively resistant; their actual responses are likely to be context specific and thus, at times, contradictory (p. 395). Without an appreciation of the complexities of media engagement, student responses to media in the classroom can catch teachers by surprise (see, e.g., Gainer, 2010). Liz (a media educator we interviewed early in our research), for example, recounted how heterosexualized media could shut down the kind of disciplined critique hoped for by adults, illustrating how deeply social identities are implicated in young people's engagement with media, including media they produce. The challenge for teachers moving from an analysis of texts as "specimens" to media engagement as an embodied event is to understand how identity is implicated in student meaning making (hence, literacy). Recognizing the complexity and range of ways that identity is theorized in literacy studies (see Moje & Luke, 2009; Buckingham & Sefton-Green, 1994), during the seminar we emphasized the intersectional nature of identities to discuss how not only age but also gender, class, sexuality, family background, and racialized identities are implicated in youth's meaning-making practices. Intersectionality reminds us that youth are members of multiple, overlapping communities, both within and beyond the classroom. These communities are not based on simply age, gender, race, class, and so on, but also on personal interests and peer group affiliations that may not be readily apparent. Intersectionality thus highlights how a constellation of identity processes can have complex social effects in terms of the operation of power among students and not simply between the teacher and her students (see Jorba & Rodó-Zárate, 2019). Teaching critical literacy needs to recognize as well as respond to these complexities.

Also contributing to the unpredictability of student media responses is the way that pleasure can obscure the operation of power through media texts, especially if pleasure is derived from dominant discursive frames. We do not read simply with our "intellect" (as knowledgeable decoders of texts) but also with our bodies when the text elicits palpable "feelings" (Barthes, 1975). Ideology has done its work when dominant meanings "feel right," discouraging us from recognizing – let alone challenging – their constructed nature (see Hall, 1986; Jenkins, 2007, p. 3). Affective responses have been amplified by the multimodality of pop culture that engages more of our senses in immersive ways: for example, music videos are visual as well as aural, while video games can influence senses of sight, sound, touch, and perception of bodily movement. As argued by Kellner and Share (2005), to competently use the internet, young users must be able to convey not simply their thoughts but also their feelings (pp. 370, 381): for both theoretical and practical reasons, CML must interrogate how affect shapes our engagement with media texts. The challenge is to acknowledge embodied responses in our understanding of how media work as a venue for the operation of power. Because these responses can only be experienced through media consumption, during in-class activities seminar participants explored their own pleasures in various images and written texts. As described earlier, given that our seminar was held during Vancouver's bleak rainy season, responses to exotic travel advertisements generated good class discussion.

Engaging seminar participants as embodied readers of media texts (as opposed to students of media studies) drew attention to the way that any text can, often unexpectedly, give rise to a range of readings. After exploring their own affective responses to a series of media texts, seminar participants used what they learned through self-study to explore texts written by fans on FanFiction.net – the largest website of its kind in the world. As homework, we instructed participants to "choose a topic that interests you" and "explore the kinds of texts produced by fans on this topic." We asked them to analyse these texts to identify "the kinds of skills being demonstrated" and the "kind of learning taking place" on the part of fans. Each participant had also been given, by lottery, one of the critical discourse analysis tools introduced during previous sessions, with instructions to discuss how that tool helped them analyse their chosen text. As homework was discussed during the seminar, participants were alerted to what they might encounter in their own students' work by identifying "what surprised them" about FanFiction.net audience responses and analysing why. The point is that because the reception of media messages is shaped by the identity, life experiences, and affective investments of individual readers, as well as the reading context, teachers cannot predict how young students will respond to pop culture introduced as "educational" material. The challenge in lesson preparation is that the embodied response to any text depends not only upon its "preferred reading" – which can be uncovered through textual analysis – but also its reception as a situated encounter – something that cannot be read off the text.

While analysing media content necessarily focuses on the text, *teaching* critical media literacy draws attention to media engagement as a social activity that brings the text and reader together. The text is no longer treated as an inert "thing" to be interrogated: it becomes a site of active meaning making by embodied actors. The text does not construct only a figured world – as suggested already, it engages readers in the construction of their subjecthood. Unlike choosing textual specimens for semiotic analysis, embodied responses to media messaging cannot be "planned." We heightened awareness of the complexity of media reception among seminar participants through written assignments. For example, participants reflected on what they enjoyed about media consumption as youth. With seminar tools in mind, they subsequently analysed their childhood enjoyment. Beyond describing what they enjoyed, participants were prompted to reflect on their enjoyment. They were asked: "How did you interact with this cultural artifact? What context were you in? How did you feel at the time? How do you feel about your pleasure now, as an adult? Why? What was so striking about the experience you describe that it lingers in your memory so long?" Written assignments were supplemented with readings by teachers who described their experience of youth engagement with pop culture.

Designing tools that teachers could use in their classroom teaching was shaped by a number of practical issues that limited what we could address – the timeframe for the seminar, the busy schedule of practising teachers, background preparation of seminar participants, the demographic profile of students who would be involved later, and so on. Table 3.1 summarizes the tools we used to design the seminar, indicating the kinds of interrogation these tools support. This table offers elements for a comprehensive, distinctly *social* literacy that uncovers what Liz, cited in chapter 2, called "layers" of media analysis. As she noted, "even one layer down can be interesting and can be revelatory," generating what she called "a pretty cool moment" in her teaching.

While we introduced relevant concepts and analytical tools through "overt instruction" (NLG, 1996), we attempted to model the independent meaning making required when teaching critical media literacy. The concepts and tools we introduced above were used by participants, either individually or in groups, to analyse media texts during the seminar. As well as encouraging individual reflection on personal media engagement – through written assignments and journalling – group discussion invited peer-to-peer learning. It was not our intention to provide a model or a prescriptive way of working with media. Rather, we wanted teachers to be able to take their grade level and subject area, as well as their mandated teaching goals, into consideration when using pop culture in their classrooms. Because we base our approach on literacy as the production of knowledge about the social world rather than simply a critique of media as representation, it can be incorporated into multiple subject areas (see Moje, 2007, p. 3). In fact, none of the teachers in our project taught "media" as a distinct subject area; participants joined our project because they were interested in learning how critical media literacy could help them teach for social justice while using popular culture. Like Luke and Freebody (1999), we see the tools in table 3.1 as a "family of practices," combined and used as appropriate to specific teaching goals and contexts. The culminating assignment for teachers in our seminar was to design a unit aimed at promoting critical media literacy through the use of pop culture. Teacher participants each identified relevant tools for media activities in their classrooms, based on considerations such as grade level, mandated teaching, student demographics, school policy and culture, and so on. Each participant identified one or two themes (such as "Who does this text want me to be?" to explore issues of identity in magazine texts) and worked with one or two appropriate tools (such as "interpellation" and "mode of address").

In summary, our seminar was designed to offer teachers a metalanguage for thinking, talking about, and using pop culture in their

Table 3.1. Interrogating media texts and media engagement

Guiding question	Teaching tools or resources
How does the text work to construct a "preferred reading"?	*For functional literacy:* Semantics; discourse analysis tools; visual functions of form, colour, placement, page layout, etc.; digital functions of screen format; functions of audio *Interrogation through class discussion of both commercial and student media:* • What does the text say? • How is its message conveyed? • What difference does the image, colour, music, etc. make? • And more …
Where does that meaning come from?	*For analysing power:* Political economy of media production and circulation; institutional regulation of media production; practices of everyday media production (technical and social) *Interrogation through class discussion of both commercial and student media:* • Who produced this text? For what purposes? • What kinds of practices produced this text? What motivates these practices? • What social relations sustain the production of this text? How do these relations relate to the values embedded in the text? • Who has been historically excluded from media production and circulation? How does this influence what we see? • What is needed to change current practices of media production? • And more …
How do actual readers make meaning from the text?	*For critical media literacy:* Identity, intersectionality; mode of address; figured world; media audience research and theory; embodied affect *Interrogation through class discussion, individual journalling, or both:* • What kind of reader is constructed by the text? • How is this reader invited into the world constructed by the text? Who is excluded? • How does this text address me, as reader? • What values are promoted by the text? What values are discounted? • How do I respond to the text? Why? How might others respond? • Could an alternative meaning be constructed? By whom? Why? How? • What kinds of practices are promoted by this text? • And more …

classrooms. This metalanguage shares some of the "taxing criteria" described by the NLG (1996):

> It must be capable of supporting sophisticated critical analysis of language and other semiotic systems, yet at the same time not make unrealistic demands on teacher and learner knowledge ... It should be seen as a toolkit for working on semiotic activities ... Teachers and learners should be able to choose from the tools offered. They should feel free to fashion their own tools ... Furthermore, the primary purpose of the metalanguage should be to identify and explain differences between texts, and relate these to contexts of culture and situation in which they seem to work. (p. 77)

We began to refer to our interpretation of critical media literacy as "critical *social* literacy," a term that Davies (1997) coined some time ago and that we elaborate in chapter 9 (see, e.g., figure 9.1 for a concept map that locates *critical social literacy* in relation to its allied terms: *literacy, critical literacy,* and *critical media literacy*). While literacy teaching necessarily focuses on a text, our approach emphasizes the social rather than textual nature of literacy as meaning making. As Smith (1999) notes, meaning that sustains the social world is not a property of language (discourse) but of *social interaction* (p. 110). The social world is not accomplished by texts on their own; to imply so would misattribute agency to meaning embedded in the text rather than assign it to social practices of the embodied readers of the text. In support of teaching for social justice, the goal of critical social literacy is to understand how power works *through*, not *as*, media text.

Phase 2: Researching Pop Culture in the Classroom

As outlined above, our project took the form of a multiple case study. The media for the cases included board games (in a Grade 4–5 classroom); film (specifically, *The Hunger Games* in a Grade 6–7 classroom); music videos (for a Grade 10–11 marketing class); and magazines (with girls aged 16–18 as an extracurricular project). Each case uses media to promote its teaching for social justice. Individual cases are each described in the following four chapters. Data for each case consist of teacher work during our seminar (for example, homework, including written drafts of classroom activities, also presented in our final seminar session); field notes by our research assistants during implementation of the activities; interviews by various members of the research team, conducted throughout the project; video recordings of classroom activities in progress; case study reports written by our research assistants; focus group discussions, most facilitated by Dawn and Deirdre, held with students upon completion of classroom activities; and, for some of the activities, student output (written work, drawings, etc.). To maximize the consistency of data generation for Phase 2, our research assistants not only enrolled in the media education seminar but also completed a three-month media research course for graduate credit, designed specifically for this project, taught by Dawn and Deirdre during Phase 2.

At the beginning of Phase 2 (February 2013), we added research questions that reflect our interest in the "politics of pleasure" (Alvermann, Moon, & Hagood, 1999; also see Luke, 1994):

1. How does pleasure work through media engagement?
2. How can pleasure be harnessed through popular culture when teaching critical media literacy to youth? (That is, what tools promote the "pleasure of analysis"?)
3. How does the affect evoked by media texts work to normalize (or, alternatively, to destabilize) meaning making, contributing to (or challenging) the ideological effectiveness of dominant media messages? (meeting notes)

In other words, how can media come to "feel" like an accurate representation of "the way things are meant to be," and how can this feeling be disrupted through critical media literacy? These questions reflect our interest in student redesign as a vehicle supporting social change. As our project unfolded, it became increasingly apparent to us that there are no definitive answers to the question of "how" to use popular culture in the classroom. Paraphrasing Allan Luke (2018), we decided that while there is no single "right way," "there are more productive ways" (p. 2) to use pop culture in the classroom.

FROM THE DRAWING BOARD TO THE CLASSROOM

The following chapters describe and analyse four projects designed by teachers and piloted in their classrooms during Phase 2. While each case study draws upon the seminar in unique ways, all reflect participants' commitment to teaching for social justice (albeit variously defined). Each project, in a different way, uses tools from the seminar to foster student experiences of the operation of power, not only of power-over through media critique, but also of power-to and power-with through redesign. To enhance the utility of the case studies for practising teachers, we describe the teaching philosophies of teacher participants and identify their intended learning outcomes, formulated during the seminar, before we move into their classrooms to describe "what actually happened." In this context we identify the successes of each case, while documenting unexpected challenges that emerged and analysing how such challenges might be dealt with. While each case study might be read individually, the advantage of a multiple case study design is that it can offer in-depth understanding of common features across all the cases in relation to complex contextual conditions (Yin, 2009, p. 18). As Stake (2006) maintains:

> a single case is only meaningful in the context of other similar cases. The single case is of interest because it belongs to a particular collection of cases that share a common characteristic or condition. To understand this characteristic or condition better, we study its single cases or manifestations. Some cases may provide particular information and not much else, while some cases may provide insight into relationships not yet recognized, illuminating a complexity common to the group. The point is that it is not necessary to analyze each case in a standardized manner; moreover, while data come primarily from the cases studied, other relevant data may also be analytically useful. (p. 4)

In effect, a multiple case study enables us to assess the utility of our seminar tools across a range of pop culture. Following Stake (2006), each classroom project is analysed as a unique case, identifying what it tells us about using the featured media. Drawing on our emerging notion of critical social literacy, we discuss how teaching for social justice could be deepened. Two chapters following the case studies then analyse our data as a whole by exploring "common features across all the cases in relation to complex contextual conditions" (Yin, 2009, p. 18). In chapter 8 we revisit agency – exercised by students but also by teachers – in the context of participatory pedagogy inviting independent meaning making. Chapter 8 thus deepens our understanding of how pop culture can be used in the classroom. As design research, in chapter 9 we revisit our initial teaching about media as a venue for the operation of power, in order to explore how critical social literacy can harness the small p politics of media redesign in the classroom – as demonstrated in all four case studies – to what Janks (2018) calls capital P politics taking place beyond the classroom. In doing so we elaborate how critical *social* literacy promotes media engagement as an exercise by youth of their power-to – and power-with – to redesign a more just future.

Conclusion

To recap, in this chapter we have described *Pop Culture and Power: Teaching Media Literacy for Social Justice* as design research. As a contribution to teacher education, *Pop Culture and Power* explores teaching in two contexts: the first concerns the authors' teaching CML to teachers, the second teaching in public schools and an extracurricular setting. As research, *Pop Culture and Power* takes the reader through two simultaneous but distinct analyses. While data generated in the first context enabled us, as university educators, to deepen our understanding of teaching CML to teachers, data generated in the second teaching context enable us to explore how using CML to teach for social justice played out in actual classroom settings (in contrast to a "contrived" research setting).

This chapter tells the story of Phase 1, anticipating Phase 2 of our project. The professional development seminar in Phase 1 outlines our provisional answer to the question: How can critical media literacy support teaching for social justice when using pop culture? In tandem with our research assistants, we worked with classroom teachers as they translated seminar tools into learning activities that made sense for their particular students and pedagogical aims. Tools from the seminar guided inquiry into media texts and media engagement, encouraging students to question and disrupt media that might otherwise remain taken for granted as natural and therefore unchangeable. The following chapters thus enable us to elaborate how pop culture was used in actual classrooms, informing our approach to critical social literacy as a tool for teacher education.

4 The Monopoly Project: Meaning Making through Board Game Production

DAWN H. CURRIE, DEIRDRE M. KELLY, AND PAULINA SEMENEC

The media literacy component of [redesigning *Monopoly*] is to build awareness of [students'] broader world by ... recreating objects that they see or games that they see, and, in the process of recreating them, [increase students'] understanding [of] how much is deliberately placed as opposed to haphazardly present.
– Yvette, post-project reflection

Yvette had an interest in media literacy for her Grade 4/5 class for some time before our seminar. For her, media literacy is "a gentle way of getting them [children] to discover the end of their childhood [chuckles]. Trying to find a gentle way and being a guide rather than a stick, and leaving them enabled and not victimized or traumatized." She includes media literacy in her "guidance" because "There's very little out there that's not without a message, without an agenda of some sort. Even Shakespeare had an agenda." Yvette identified board games as an example of an "everyday text" with a message. Previously, Yvette had used *Monopoly* in the classroom "as a way to develop social skills and to practise basic math skills and the concept of taking turns." In contrast, and inspired by Buckingham and Burn (2007) during our seminar, her Monopoly Project was designed to "move [students] beyond the passive player identity, get more into the innovative player identity" (for more on the value of game play, see Gee, 2008, 2018). This intention reflects her view of students as "producers" rather than simply consumers of media and our view of youth as meaning makers.

There was little research with younger children for Yvette to draw on (see Buckingham et al., 2005, p. 43). She was attracted to Buckingham and Burn's (2007) argument that games function through "the indicative mood (that is, showing us the world) but also in the imperative mood (that is, urging us to take action upon that world)" (p. 327). In their discussion of "game literacy," Buckingham and Burn focus on two key elements of game construction: rules (that structure game behaviour, hence outcomes) and economies (the quantified resources determined by the game designer, for strategic use by players) (p. 334; cf. Beavis, 2014). Yvette structured these two elements into her project. Her plan was for students to create board games based on their own rules. She reasoned that, "in general, classroom teachers would like students to play by rules and work through the ideal society – not necessarily deal with the messiness of real life. Games can start that way because they're very structured and isolated [from reality]. They can be a good place to start." But Yvette saw more in *Monopoly* than a good place to start: she saw how the unequal distribution of resources that results from the rules of *Monopoly* parallels our economic system.

Yvette based her project on the popular *Monopoly*, not only because it is widely accessible, but also because it originated as a teaching activity that illustrates the negative consequences of a capitalist economy that concentrates resources in private monopolies. While there have been many innovations since its debut in 1903, the principles of play remain faithful to designer Elizabeth Magie Phillips's[1] intentions: players move around the board buying or trading properties, developing their properties with houses and hotels, and collecting rent from opponents with the goal to drive other players into bankruptcy. What Yvette planned was for teams to merge, from about six to eventually one, to play the game until the "natural end": "If they really push it to the very end, how can they really win when no one else has money? ... In reality, we're all in one world and [if] one person has all the money, then what?" In other words, Yvette was hoping that, once familiar with the outcome of playing by the rules of *Monopoly* (unequal distribution of game resources), her young students would question – if not reject – the basic premise of capitalism. Her underlying logic was to start with something that reflects the structure of their world, but then to raise fundamental questions about that world for her young learners. At the same time, she acknowledged that rather than plan lessons with the "idealized" student identity in mind, students must be able to start with what they know and with who they are. As their guide, Yvette designed activities to prompt critical reflection as students moved through the Monopoly Project.

Paulina joined Yvette as our research assistant. She shared Yvette's premise that "students become engaged learners when they start with what they *already* know ... Through media production, students become 'researchers' of their own world." Moreover, Paulina noted the importance of encouraging students "to notice that these things are socially constructed with particular ideologies and audiences in mind." Given that Yvette wanted to launch her project through *Monopoly* as a critique of monopoly capitalism, their shared interests in promoting social justice provided a platform for their work together.[2]

Research Setting

Yvette's school, Centennial Elementary, is located in Vancouver's Lower Mainland, in a culturally diverse neighbourhood. The school, which enrols about 400 students in Kindergarten to Grade 7, prides itself on sustaining a positive learning environment in which every student will succeed. This means that teaching staff members work collaboratively to ensure that each student's literacy needs are supported. As a result, Centennial is designated as an "Early Intervention" school: Kindergarten and Grade 1 students receive small group and one-on-one support for reading and writing.

Yvette had 29 students in a Grade 4/5 split. She described her class: "mixed ethnicities, socio-economic groups, and ability groups. I have a number of students who have written output issues, and I have a student who is on the autism spectrum ... I've got two Aboriginal students." While all 29 of Yvette's students (11 girls and 18 boys) participated in the Monopoly Project, 23 also participated in our research (we received parental consent and assent to film 19 students and to interview 20 students, while six students did not submit consent forms). Paulina attended almost all the class sessions to observe and record activities, while LJ, another of our research assistants, filmed during one of the game creation sessions, enabling Paulina to interview teams.

On her first visit to Centennial, Paulina expressed surprise at "how nice (and big!)" the school was. Judging from photos of employees adorning the hallway, she noted: "most of the teachers at the school are female, and White." Her field notes give a sense of the school culture. Paulina described some of the posters on the walls:

> I notice one that says: "Homophobia is just as wrong as racism – think before you speak." In the centre of the poster is an image of a stop sign with the phrase, "That's so gay!" crossed out ... As I wait, I notice two posters right outside of Yvette's classroom – one is a poster for the UN Convention on the Rights of the Child – in child-friendly language. (Paulina's field notes)

The Monopoly Project

While preparing her project during the seminar, Yvette reasoned that a class activity around creating a game would be exciting for students, while offering opportunities for the kind of reflection that promotes critical literacy. She proceeded from the assumption that learning comes when, after carefully deconstructing texts to develop awareness of what "makes them work," students could alter or produce a new text as a means to understanding the complexity of such a creation. This learning objective reflects Yvette's belief that "teachers are charged with preparing students to become critically aware members of society. That is the nature of civic responsibility." Her goal was to balance pleasure with critique. Yvette saw redesign as offering

> a balance between analysis and production with a move away from binaries [high- and lowbrow culture] and a promotion of self-reflexivity along the way. This approach includes acknowledging that students come with expertise; that the pleasure popular culture produces is valuable and worth retaining; and that students may produce multiple readings and derive multiple perspectives from popular culture texts.

At the outset, Yvette acknowledged that not all of her young students might have access to the internet at home; she sought a medium that did not require "high tech" or "expensive" equipment (see Flores-Koulish & Smith-D'Arezzo, 2016 on this point). Yvette based the design of her project on dimensions of literacy identified by Green (1988): *operational* literacy (following established structure/rules); *transformational* literacy (awareness of systems of rules but going beyond to create new rules); and *distributed* literacy (learning through many sources at different times on an ad hoc basis, as happens during collaboration and cooperation). The Monopoly Project moved students through these three dimensions, engaging them in redesign of *Monopoly*'s figured world. Her project was to be initiated through students playing *Monopoly* to ensure a common understanding of the structure and rules of standard board games (operational literacy). Once a shared understanding of game play was in place, Yvette would encourage students to criticize and revise the design and rules of conventional play in preparation for collaborative creation of something "new" (transformational literacy). Journalling, class discussion, and peer feedback (distributed literacy) would be incorporated into each stage, as part of the learning process that took place over several class sessions.

Yvette would assess student learning through classroom observation and periodic journal writing. Upon completion of their new games, teams would make a formal presentation to their classmates as a graded assignment. A Grade 6 class was also invited to play the new games, giving Yvette's students an opportunity to consider how their game might address diverse audiences.

Stage 1: Learning to Play

The purpose of Stage 1 was to familiarize students with the figured world of *Monopoly* and the practices required to participate in that world through basic rules of game playing: taking turns and handling money, understanding how a "win" is constituted. During the seminar Yvette reflected on her lesson plan:

> After the first few games students will analyse various components of the game layout and playing structure. It can be developed as the students start to understand the "rules" and the goals of the game. Over the course of several games, some more "critical" observations may start to emerge – perhaps through strategies, or feelings, or values of the various players' experiences. Areas of class discussion could include changing the goals of the game; examining who is present or absent and why that might be; the structure of the board and whether there is value or meaning in what the playing pieces represent; and the notion of winning. What ideas and assumptions are present in the game framework and what things are absent? Another area of focus is the notion of pleasure – what kinds of "fun" are derived from playing? Does it apply to all players? Could it?

Prompts to facilitate student reflection in their journals included: Should all players play by the same set of rules? What makes the game "fair"? Why is that? Fair for whom? Because the goal of Stage 1 was to open the door for innovation, Yvette was hoping that this reflection would prepare students for "moving beyond the game" as it already had been designed.

By the second session, Yvette was encouraging students to think of their own rules. She retrospectively described this stage of the activity:

> And then the second time we played would be another hour and a half, just to build some fluency ... The third time was to troubleshoot things that didn't work out. A big part of that for them was making sure that the banker was also a player because they had tended to put the banker out. And then, by about the fifth hour, we had started moving into what I call the "international realm," where they could borrow money or trade money from one another. So, there was an option there for some international, in quotations, monetary movement, and so the game speed was beginning to pick up.

As basic as this first stage may sound, Yvette informed Paulina that many students had never played a board game before, so this introduction was essential. It gave students the necessary common understanding of game play before collaborating on the design of their own, potentially alternative, games.

Stage 2: Moving beyond the Game

The goal of Stage 2 was to encourage students to think about how the game itself, and the rules for game play, might be changed. Yvette urged students to modify whatever they wanted about the game, keeping the principle of fairness while having fun in mind. Prompts to facilitate reflection included: Did anything change? How did you feel this time playing the game? Do you want to continue? Why? Or why not? What makes this changed version more, or less, fun? Did your or anyone's behaviour change?

Once small groups formed teams, they were to decide, through *agreement*, on the rules for their game. A "Food Group" immediately began to work together to decide on rules for play. They were soon busy putting sticky notes on their *Monopoly* game board and making alternative "chance" cards). Paulina noticed that this group was the most involved in changing the rules of the game. As she paused to watch them, they told her that *Monopoly* did not have any food, so they decided to organize their game around popular food chains like Burger King and Tim Horton's. As their play progressed, they added bathrooms as well as a hotel stop. Yvette later told Paulina that the Food Group was playing the game in the way she had imagined, and that she hoped some of the other groups would catch on to all the possibilities of modifying the game.

At this stage, class members were all beginning to alter the layout of their boards (see figure 4.1). Yvette asked students to take out their journals and to think about three things:

> The first is to think about the game as a participant. The second is to think about the game from a designer point of view – the "designing head." She asks them to think about what they want to include or not include in a game. And finally, she asks them to write about what makes the game enjoyable (or not) to play. It takes a long time for the students to get settled into writing, and Yvette has to pause often in order to get their attention and then to keep them focused on writing. (Paulina's field notes)

This journal writing exercise was consistent with Yvette's lesson plan, where she outlined that students would be "[making] predictions in their journals about how they envision the game play [and recording] their feelings and past experience playing *Monopoly* thus far. When did they enjoy the game the most/least? Why?" At this point, most students were getting better in their counting abilities as well as redesigning their board games. At the same time, this was also a stage where students not experiencing "success" were getting frustrated; conflict could emerge:

The Monopoly Project: Board Game Production   69

Figure 4.1. The "Food Group" modifies their game board using yellow sticky notes

> The room is somewhat chaotic at this point ... I learn that the girls got upset because someone in another group was throwing something, and also that the group couldn't agree on the rules of the game. (Paulina's field notes)

A few minutes later, however, the group was back together playing their game. There were two groups, though, that appeared uninterested in their games, while one student abandoned his group completely.

As chaotic as the classroom appeared at first glance, Paulina observed a lot of collaboration and negotiation among various groups. This part of the activity seemed to fulfil two specific Language Arts learning outcomes that Yvette had stipulated in her project plan: "Listen purposefully to understand and analyse ideas and information" and "Select useful strategies when interacting with others." Additionally, Paulina saw this stage of the project as meeting other objectives in Yvette's project plan. Yvette had noted that students would be "[developing] an understanding of the main and multiple strategies of play and an understanding there may be more than one end-goal in the game." As Paulina observed the students play, she noted that many of them were demonstrating these understandings.

As Stage 2 ended, Yvette announced the next activity – students would create their own games:

> For homework, she asks them to write about the strategies they tried in their game and about what worked and what did not. She asks them, "Does it mean that we didn't learn anything if it didn't work?" A few of the students say "No." She asks them to think about what would make a game fun to play if they were to design their own, and to consider how long it will be. (Paulina's field notes)

Stage 3: Creating New Games

During this final stage students again worked in small groups. Yvette recounted:

> The kids were allowed to sort of self-select ... I tried to open it up so if they were working in groups, there were jobs and interests available to them. And, certainly, with the creation of the game, I did not insist that they work in large groups, to accommodate different interest levels and different skill levels.

Most of the groups were same-sexed, which Yvette claimed was not surprising for this age.[3] Teams were reminded that another class (Grade 6) would be coming later in the term to try out their games. They were instructed to consider how they would modify the game for different age groups and different abilities. Group work reflects Yvette's philosophy that "learning comes through discussion and not just the ones that occur around the teacher but that much learning among children is constructed through their conversations – even ones that adults do not acknowledge as worthwhile." Because she wants *each* of her students to succeed, she was prepared to give them "creative freedom" in all aspects of game redesign.

To stimulate her students' imaginations, Yvette's original lesson plan included an activity using Sara Perry's picture book, *If*. Its two-page spreads present artful watercolours paired with such strange possibilities as "If zebras had stars and stripes ... ," "If the moon were square ... ," and "If worms had wheels ... ." Although some of the ideas and pictures are whimsical to the point of being downright creepy ("If caterpillars were toothpaste ... ," "If toes were teeth ..."), the hypotheticals are designed to inspire flights of fancy. One illustration, for example, features a large, hairy warthog with a sparkling crown and the text, "If ugly were beautiful ... ." Yvette's goal was to have students describe what they see in *If*, and practise imagining the possibilities to "what if" questions. Keying off this activity, Yvette created prompts for her students' new games: What *must* a game have to make it fun? What if everyone could win? How would that work? What adaptations or modifications could be made to reflect "the rest of the (world's/country's) population or reality as Canadians in the game? Or current timeline? Or environment? Or ...?"

Upon hearing Yvette's explanation of creating a game, the room buzzed with anticipation:

> Some students ask questions about the design of their board game (use of materials, pizza boxes, etc.) and they seem excited when Yvette tells them "*You* are the designer" ... One of the students asks Yvette: "Can we just use the *Monopoly* game?" Once again, Yvette tells them they can design any kind of game they want, but that they should think about the strategy and goal of their game. Yvette tells them to think about the "experience" they had while playing *Monopoly*, and asks them to think about what made playing the game enjoyable for them. (Paulina's field notes)

During the following two sessions, students created games and prepared their class presentations. Paulina observed each team as they finalized their projects:

> One group is still busy making game pieces out of playdough, while others are putting the final touches on their rules sheets. A few of the students have actually prepared a script that will help them with their presentation, and many students have printed the rules for their games. Taylor, who made a game called Resources, put all his game pieces in mini zip-lock bags, and created a game board that can be folded into the box ... The *Hamunopoly* team is busy playing their game when I come around. Their board game is very colourful, and there are many little toys on it (including Hamun [Hamtaro] erasers and Nicole's Winnie the Pooh toy) [see figure 4.2]. The Shopping Game is also coming along nicely ... They tell me they are ready to present, and so I try and track down some other students in the hallway. I see Amelia and Ariana working near the stairs, so I ask them what they're doing. They are acting out their presentation, and have memorized what they want to say about their game ... I notice that the Dice Wars group is hanging around the stairwell, but I'm not sure what they're doing. They seem to just be chatting, and goofing around, and I guess from their behaviour that they are also ready to present! (Paulina's field notes)

In later viewing the videos, we noted that not all the students were so productively engaged. Lego-opoly, a game created by two boys, caught our

72 Pop Culture and Power

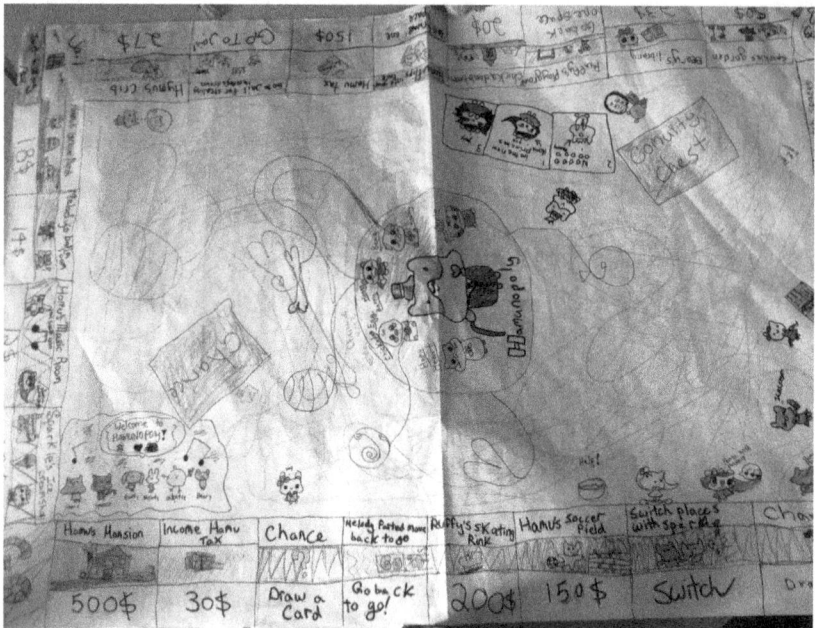

Figure 4.2. The *Hamunopoly* board

attention. These boys had constructed various figurines and machines from Lego pieces and were playing what appeared to be a military-style game. Neither boy could explain the rules to Paulina. When one stated that he likes "mass destruction," which he illustrated by smashing his playing pieces on the board, the other chimed in that it was "part of their game."

Class presentations took place over several sessions and were filmed for our research. Each team set up their game in the centre of the classroom, with desks arranged as a gallery. The result of this project was a variety of games that ranged in complexity. Most games followed the *Monopoly* template, while some new games closely resembled those from Stage 2; whether or not games keyed off *Monopoly*, all looked familiar.

Student Redesigns

The format for each presentation followed Yvette's instructions: presenters opened by indicating the name of their game and held up their board for classmates to see the final product; teams described how to play their game and explained the rules, often reading from a neatly typed Instructions sheet, also held up for inspection; each team indicated the intended audience for their game, but also how the game could be adapted to accommodate different abilities (by making the game "easier" or "harder"); and each team concluded by listing the materials needed to make their game.

Even though students often looked inattentive during their classmates' presentations, there were many eager volunteers for class discussion. Yvette called on students by name, after reminding them that "positives come first." Class discussion thus opened with comments such as "It looks like you worked really hard," "It looks really original," and "Your game looks like fun." The level of detail in classmates' questions signals not only engagement in the activity, but also how students were thinking through their own experience of game creation. Some questions concerned the construction of the game. For example, classmates asked: "How did you make the shopping bags?"; "Where did you get the idea for the pieces?"; "How long did it take you to make all the pieces?" Other questions concerned the mechanics of play: "How much do you pay if you land on …?"; "But what if there's like an attack and somebody puts it like right there and your road's right there? Can they do that?"

In these kinds of questions, we see excited pleasure in the problem solving that Yvette's participatory pedagogy promoted. As Jenkins et al. (2006) note, questions posed to peers in this way are "productive explorations": they have "no right or wrong answers; they emphasize creative thinking rather than memorization; they allow diverse levels of engagement; they allow students to feel less intimidated by adult expertise" (p. 24). For example, when Ariana and Amelia indicated that they did not know how to adapt their game for different players, a classmate offered suggestions. These types of exchanges imply that most of the students were engaged in the kind of "deconstructive process" that Yvette had in mind: using "traits" and "objects" that they observe in the world "to recreate objects, and" – to reiterate the opening quote by Yvette – "in the process of recreating them, understand how much is deliberately placed as opposed to haphazardly present." To illustrate how the Monopoly Project encouraged these kinds of outcome, below we briefly describe three games.[4]

Shopping Cart

Hannah and Isabel designed their new game, *Shopping Cart*, after *Monopoly*, which they described as "the normal game." Their game board has the same layout as *Monopoly*, but the girls turned the properties into familiar stores (for example, Old Navy, Home Sense, Apple, etc.) and restaurants (for example, White Spot). Hannah explained to Paulina:

"*Monopoly*'s fun. And, I guess, it's kind of easier not to make up your own rules. Trying to just go with the old rules and change it around a bit." For their presentation the two girls set up their pink board game in the centre of the room. Both seemed at ease as they described their game to classmates, displaying items, such as "shopping bag" tokens, to their audience. How closely their game resembled *Monopoly* is apparent in their presentation to classmates:

> You start where it says "go shopping." And your playing pieces are little shopping bags. And then there are stores that you can buy. And on every five of these you get checks. Over here is mall security, and you have to pay $100, or you have a chance card … This one says, "Lose $90." And then over here you have the free parking place where you can get the free parking money. Then these are the pieces you're supposed to put on the place you've bought, so you know that you've bought them. In the same colour as your shopping bag. But you can only put ten down, and don't squish them. (Isabel)

After an extended description of how to play, Isabel explained how to win: "To win the game, all the other players must have no money. Also, you can't mortgage your properties. You can also win the game by having the most money at the end of the game." She added: "This game lasts up to three hours at most. If your mom or dad calls you and tells you to stop playing, you may delay the game or the person with the most money wins." While Isabel claimed that this game would be fun for "ages three and up," when she was asked who might want to play, the gendered nature of the game came into their discussion: "I think like probably girls, Grades 2 to 6, would like this. I don't think boys would like this one too much." Hannah went on to claim that while boys might like to go shopping, they would most likely "Go to the game store and like the video game store or something. But like – girls are more like clothes shoppers." As a further reason, she pointed out that "the board's all flashy and pink."

For this team, the most fun was designing the board. During one of the game creation sessions, the girls were excited to show Paulina how they had replaced the logo for *Monopoly* – a male figure in a top hat – with a female figure carrying two shopping bags, which Hannah explained were full of purchases from Best Buy. The most challenging part for them was "Probably just figuring out what to do for a board game. Which like we couldn't really figure out a theme. Like we couldn't decide if we should do – I don't know. We wanted to do different stuff, but we finally decided that we should do shopping because we both like shopping" (Hannah). Their pleasure in making this game was evident in videos. These two girls worked together well; at one point, Hannah placed her arm around Isabel's shoulder for the camera.

Pencil Hockey League (PHL)

PHL is an NHL-themed game created by three boys: Nate, Isaac, and Matt. The boys made a "rink" in the middle of their game board, so when you land on a certain spot in the board, you get to go to the "playoffs" (a quick game of pencil hockey in the rink). During game creation one of the boys told Paulina that they chose hockey "Because there's a *real* hockey *Monopoly*, but it – it costs *$50!* [looks upset], so we thought we will do this one." As Isaac explained: "We thought baseball would be hard to do on this kind of place. Like how are you going to hit it? And if it goes out, like it can go really far."

When Paulina videoed this group on a game creation day, one boy was busy writing out the names of hockey stars that players could buy. He told Paulina that Wayne Gretzky, for example, was an "expensive" player: he would cost "more than 2,900 [dollars]." The three bantered a bit over the cost of various hockey stars, deciding that each game player will need to start with a million dollars. At this point Matt blurted: "We will need *two* packs of *Monopoly* money!"

In a focus group after completion of their game, Matt recounted that they had played their game while it was being created as a strategy to decide on rules: "We already had about half the rules, so it was good enough to play." One challenge was to decide on a winner. Nate eventually came up with a solution: "You had to play a hockey game with your pencils for the winner. Also, like you had to buy players, which were the properties. You had to buy three properties and win five games." This team made final changes after the Grade 6 class tested their game. Isaac explained: "They said it was just sort of a fun game. And then they said you could improve it by making more chance cards because we only had like five." Importantly, some of these older "test" players cheated. This was a bit surprising and resulted in the addition of a referee.

Making the actual board was also a challenge for the *PHL* team. Isaac explained: "Like we made hockey nets to shoot at. We had challenges, how to fold them down and fold them back out without getting them crushed. Which was hard." He told Paulina that the fragile nature of their construction alerted the boys to the need for special rules:

> We shoot on the nets with these little ... beans. And we made a rule. It's that you're responsible for the beans if they break. So, if you break a bean, you have to pay 50 bucks into the bank ... Because they can't just break them for

76 Pop Culture and Power

fun, and they can't just stab them with their pencils until they break. 'Cause we would get in trouble for them doing that. So, they have to pay 50 bucks. And if they broke them on purpose, they would have to pay 300 of their *Monopoly* money to the bank. Sometimes they might think it's fun to break it. So, we wrote that rule down.

When Yvette asked them how they "solve disputes," Nate replied: "Rock, paper, scissors," suggesting that this method would avoid further conflict.

Truth or Dare

The *Truth or Dare* game, designed by Ariana and Amelia, interests us because Yvette admitted that she found it "a little unsettling." The premise of the game is that each player will roll a die and land on either a "truth" or a "dare" spot on the board. The designers decided that the game will be for four players, and that there will be several levels of dares and truths (from easy to more difficult). They also included a money component to their game; if someone lands on a dare but does not want to do it, they have to pay a "fee." When Paulina asked the girls how they got the idea for their game, Ariana claimed that although *Truth or Dare* is popular among young people, "they don't have a board game yet because they can't figure out how to have a winner." Asking how they solved this problem, Amelia explained: "People lose money. Just like regular *Monopoly*. Until we can find something better, we'll go with that."

The girls maintained that the most fun was making *Truth or Dare* cards:

AMELIA: Yeah. But sometimes we got really stuck.
ARIANA: We want people to be – like embarrassed, but we want like –
AMELIA: We want them to be embarrassed, but, yeah –
ARIANA: One of them is like, "Have you ever pooped your bed?"

Given that winning was based on the amount of money a player held, they attached different amounts of money, to be gained or lost, according to the level of the truth or dare: for level one, $10; level two, $30; and level three, $50. They had different kinds of *Truth or Dare* cards: "extreme, smell, bugging dares, and writing dares." They described a "bugging dare":

ARIANA: So, like, one dare card says, "Pull the hair of a person of your choice lightly."
PAULINA: [Gasps].
ARIANA: Person must be opposite gender.

PAULINA: Why do they have to be opposite gender?
AMELIA: It just seems more fun ...

The girls decided that *Truth or Dare* would be fun for kids "Grade 4 and older," "maybe high schoolers," but "it wouldn't be fun to people like 100 years old."

On Presentation Day, the girls introduced themselves and their game in chorus and then took turns explaining how their game worked, often finishing each other's sentences or interrupting to make clarifications. In conclusion to their class presentation, they thanked classmates by name for both inspiring their game idea and testing early versions. Their presentation ended with a loud "Have fun!" – again in chorus and this time with a bow. It was obvious that these two girls worked well together and that both were having fun. Perhaps keying off the girls' enthusiasm, their audience broke protocol by jumping straight into the question-and-answer activity, as if the "positives" of their game were self-evident.

Promoting Critical Media Literacy through Games

As illustrated above, beyond introducing youth to basic skills for exercising power-with – turn taking, counting, conflict resolution, and so on – games (such as *Monopoly*) construct a figured world for players who become participants in this world. Players experience this figured world as they take up subject positions structured by the game and interact with other players according to the rules of the game. Games thus engage players through a mode of address that offers children an opportunity to try out new (or impossible) situations in a safe environment; in game play, mistakes are not as costly as in "real" life. In this way games of all sorts, non-digital and digital (e.g., video, console, phone), are pedagogical. Kellner and Share (2005) thus define literacy in ways that would include game play. This is because

> "Literacy," in our conception, comprises gaining competencies involved in effectively learning and using socially constructed forms of communication and representation. Cultivating literacies involves attaining competencies in practices in contexts that are governed by rules and conventions. (p. 369)

Along these lines, Jenkins et al. (2006) argue that computer games foster procedural literacy as a capacity to reconfigure knowledge in order to look at problems from multiple vantage points. Through game play, learners can develop a greater understanding of the rules and procedures that shape everyday experiences (p. 27). Sharing this premise,

Yvette had hoped that experiencing the "problem" of rules that result in the unequal distribution of resources would encourage her young students to resist, or even challenge, the everyday world of capitalism. While their experience of "power-to" would be limited to the realm of game play, Alvermann and Hagood (2000) maintain that the act of deconstructing and reinscribing discourse – such as that promoted by *Monopoly* – demonstrates to learners the possibility of actual systematic change. The challenge is to harness change to the promotion of social justice. What have we learned from the Monopoly Project that would help us meet such a goal? Below we identify learning that was accomplished in the Monopoly Project, exploring how children's games more generally can promote critical media literacy. We also suggest how games like *Monopoly* might afford opportunities to deepen learning about social justice issues, recognizing that grade level determines what is actually feasible. At the same time, we acknowledge that making alternative games would not be an easy task for Yvette's young learners, given that it requires a player to take a step back from their immediate experience to "engage in some hard, systematic analysis" (Buckingham, 2016, p. 8).

In our view, *Monopoly* has three distinct characteristics that make it an ideal venue to promote critical media literacy: (a) *Monopoly* is an instructional text structured by rules that govern the behaviour of players; (b) it constructs the figured world of monopoly capitalism with embodied players taking up roles of property owners and consumers; and (c) it invites an exploration of how the commercialization of *The Landlord's Game* by Parker Brothers has transformed *Monopoly* into a game that can normalize, rather than challenge, the existing order. From this perspective, *Monopoly* has the potential to be a venue for exploring pop culture as the operation of power; the operative word here is *potential*. Below we explore what might maximize this potential, drawing attention to the kind of learning that this project fostered, while recognizing the challenges Yvette faced. We draw on a post-project interview with Yvette and five focus group discussions that LJ and Dawn held with 18 student participants after final class presentations. While the interview data captures Yvette's reflections on her project, the focus groups were an attempt to capture the experience of project activities from the standpoint of participants.

In choosing *Monopoly* to introduce game playing, Yvette considered how this game originated as a critique of monopoly capitalism, intended as an educational tool. As a social justice advocate, she hoped young players would experience and, thus, also recognize how the competitive rules of capitalism structure unfair outcomes. Through this experience, players could "build awareness of their broader world" as the basis for designing new games. Yvette anticipated that this move would come through recognition that "Once you have all the money, then what? ... If you have all the power, then what?" As we have seen, however, most of the students employed the *Monopoly* template in their redesign rather than question or go beyond it. As a result, Yvette initially voiced disappointment with student creations: "What I had hoped for was a natural movement beyond the established rules. That maybe happened in one, possibly two games, but for the most part students worked within the established rules." This outcome made Yvette uncertain about reaching her "ultimate" goal:

> I don't think I achieved the learning objectives as I envisioned them because, ultimately, I wanted to bring this back to a larger reflection of how our society works, and the pluses and minuses of a capitalist society ... So, in some respects, I don't feel I met my objectives.

Upon further reflection, however, she concluded: "On the other hand, I realize *now* that like any kind of literacy building, you have to put in the background work." These kinds of self-negotiations meant that, in the final analysis, Yvette was satisfied with the outcome of the Monopoly Project:

> But, even if they weren't able to attach it to the social studies component of understanding constructed social rules, I do think that they had a lot of practice time negotiating rules and understanding how a game is constructed and that rules and conflict resolution are a necessary part of having a game. So, in some respects, I'm quite satisfied that a lot of thinking went into it.

The Monopoly Project illustrates Jenkins et al.'s (2006) claim that it is easier for students to see how rules operate in a game than to recognize how rules structure everyday life (p. 15). Yvette implied that her disappointment reflected, in part, her unwillingness to "interfere" in the creative process that might emerge through teamwork. As teachers, we understand her disappointment. Against Yvette's self-criticism, below we identify challenges that, while observed in her activity, originate outside her classroom. These challenges draw attention to children's games as venues for the operation of power. While power operates through the rules of play – as Yvette contended – it also operates through game elements that are taken for granted; in *Monopoly* these elements include winning through competition. These taken-for-granted elements, as much as the more obvious elements such as rules, shaped the agency of student design.

Buckingham (2003a) reminds us that educators engaging students in creative activities are often disillusioned when learners reconstitute readily available design. In the context of media production, he claims that this response is rooted in the fear of "imitation" as a practice of reproducing dominant culture. He argues that this fear derives from "a wider suspicion of the deceptive pleasures of popular culture" (p. 124): teachers often see imitation as an inherently unthinking process through which young people simply internalize and reproduce dominant messages. One way teachers attempt to avoid this problem is to render media production a "safer" activity by requiring the demonstration of critical thinking, a requirement that can stifle creativity (p. 125). Within this context, we view Yvette's willingness to give her students relatively free rein as a courageous experiment that fostered significant learning. The reinscription demonstrated during this project can be used to encourage students to interrogate the mediated totality of their lives, by identifying and exploring connections between ideas they encounter – such as those underpinning *Monopoly* – and their everyday experience. As Kellner (1990) notes, and as we later suggest, as well as connections students can identify *contradictions* (p. 24) or what we call, following Smith (1987), *disjunctures*.

In this activity, although students did not challenge the capitalist logic embodied by *Monopoly*, they recognized that their lived experience is mediated by market mechanisms. We have in mind the *Shopping Cart* and *Pencil Hockey League* games. For Hannah and Isabel, we surmise that shopping (for clothes) is a significant (and pleasurable) event in their experience of being "girls." We found it interesting that Nate, Isaac, and Matt transformed hockey as a favoured Canadian sport into a commodity – a facet of their game that, in fact, accurately reflects "reality." In both projects, students recognized, but could not "name," economic processes of capitalism, even though these processes motivated their choices. These youthful innovations remind us that as early as Grade 4/5, children have not escaped messages of competitive capitalism, even with limited actual experience of the economic world.[5] Without an alternative "text" – for example, one explaining how the current economic system contributes to unequal social outcomes – we would not likely see the kind of critique of capitalism that Yvette anticipated. Instead, students drew on what they knew. What they knew, we point out, was mediated not only by market relations but also by their gendered identities. It seemed self-evident to Hannah, for example, that boys would not want to play on their "flashy" pink board featuring clothing stores. Her reasoning illustrates how the experiential knowledge Yvette's students brought to the Monopoly Project normalized the kind of social processes that critical media literacy attempts to challenge.

One way to challenge such normalization is to broaden students' experiences through game play offering alternatives to what "normally" exists – to what is taken for granted in game play. This approach is counterintuitive to Yvette's logic of starting with what they already know. For many students, *Monopoly* entered into game construction as Yvette's young students tried to figure out how to end their game: "We just had trouble to find out like who's the winner. 'Cause it's really hard to find out who's the winner in *Truth or Dare*. So, instead, we just did like normal *Monopoly* – like whoever wins, [is] whoever has the most money. Because there's money in our game" (Amelia). It is instructive (and ironic, given Yvette's hope that students might come to question the rules of capitalism) that this team was following what they thought were Yvette's instructions:

> DAWN: Do you think you could've designed a game maybe where there wasn't a winner? Since that was the hardest part [for your group].
> AMELIA: Well, yeah. But that's what the teacher asked [laughs] ... She asked, "How are you going to win?"

For appropriate grade levels, an alternative design that might foster new thinking could be *Class Struggle*, a board game based on a Marxist challenge to capitalist logic. Although not a board game, "World without Oil" – an online game designed for high school students – offers an "alternative reality" where players engage in "a collaborative imagining of the first 32 weeks of a global oil crisis" (Eklund, 2020, homepage; also see Cheung, 2020 on doma.play, a multiplayer online "game to beat the housing market"). Lesson plans included in this teaching resource promote "collaborative grassroots simulation to engage students with questions about energy use, sustainability, the role energy plays in our economy, culture, worldview and history, and many others" (*Lesson plans*, para. 1).

A further strategy for the Monopoly Project might be to trace the transformation of Lizzie Magie's original game – *The Landlord's Game* – over the past 100 plus years since its emergence.[6] Such a history documents not only the commodification of everyday entertainment, but also legal battles accompanying culture as "intellectual property." For example, a number of unauthorized "parodies" of *Monopoly* have emerged over the years, resulting in trademark wars that illustrate the complex relation between market processes and the commodification of entertainment. In Yvette's project, how this commodification becomes normalized is visible in the *Pencil Hockey League* game; the designers of this game questioned how much various hockey players would cost, but they did not question why hockey stars like Wayne Gretzky could be "bought and sold." An instructive example on how entertainment can normalize social relations is *Ghettopoly*. This game keys off *Monopoly* but replaces its properties with racist icons (such as a massage parlour, a peep show, and a pawn shop) and players with characters representing racial stereotypes (such as "thugs," "drug dealers," "hos," and the like). Wikipedia reports that *Ghettopoly* generated US$8,790,000 in profits for its creator, David Chang. Through online research, students could follow litigation surrounding this board game – not arising from its embedded racism, but rather from issues surrounding intellectual property rights when Hasbro, maker of *Monopoly*, sued Chang.

In summary, while some adult observers might describe the innovations in the games produced during the Monopoly Project as "limited," we take the view that they reflect the restricted range of experiences that these young students brought to the classroom. What students knew included *Monopoly* – something their teacher had introduced – which they combined with everyday experiences: school, shopping, hockey, and so on. In retrospect, we are not surprised (or disappointed) with student redesigns. We point out that Yvette's students did not simply reiterate identical *Monopoly* texts – they brought experiential knowledge, however limited, into their creations to render the figured world of *Monopoly* more familiar. By giving young learners free rein, she legitimated the value of their experiential knowledge. The Monopoly Project thus generated pleasure for students by enabling them to give expression to their own ideas and lived experiences in ways that could be shared with classmates. This pleasure speaks to the fact that we confront a cultural world that, for the most part, is not of our making. Children's redesigns are an attempt to reconcile their subjective experience and desires with the objectified interests (in profitability) and ideas (of what we will want, hence buy) of corporate production. Pleasure in doing so can be seen in the pride expressed by Isabel, working in the group that "foodified" *Monopoly*: "We created it, and it's *our* game [gestures to her chest] ... Nobody else can say, 'We made it.' Only us can say 'We made it ... we *made* it!'" As Hannah, co-designer of *Shopping Cart*, exclaimed: "It's kind of like an artist; if you make a mistake, you can make it into something." We see the pleasure generated by redesign as a "teachable moment," one where the "inadequacy" of available design can be questioned and subsequently challenged. This project fostered the pleasure of creative agency as an experience of both "power-to" and "power-with." Yvette was able to promote this outcome without requiring artistic ability or specialized material (also see Alvermann, 2018 on her similar experience). Yvette's young students were productive working with everyday resources, such as pizza boxes, stickies, glue, crayons, favourite toys, and so on. We cannot help but think that Yvette's own creativity in designing the Monopoly Project helped to "level the playing field" for her learners.

In conclusion, given the age of Yvette's young students, we should not be surprised that their creative redesigns highlight, but are circumscribed by, their limited experience, resulting in student productions with a familiarity that could be mistaken for imitation. Overall, her students' redesigns help illustrate how power operates through the commodification of children's everyday culture. As a commodity, *Monopoly* embodies the social context of its production – a point we elaborate in chapter 9. The challenge is to give students the freedom to draw on what they know, to begin where they are at, without naturalizing the given world. We point out that schooling is a rule-bound institution – younger students typically have little say in rule making. They are rewarded for compliance to classroom codes of practice. Much of the pleasure expressed during the Monopoly Project can be attributed to following classroom rules. Clearer or more stringent instructions from Yvette would not have necessarily led to "better" learning because students might have simply imitated her instructional text.

Paradoxically, rules may also offer comfort to Yvette herself: the game she found "unsettling" – *Truth or Dare* – consciously challenged unspoken rules of classroom "civility" (through dares such as embarrassing classmates, having them pull another's hair, or unexpectedly "hug the teacher"). The audience response to this game, in particular, was notably expressed as "fun." Although disruptive, we are tempted to see violation of classroom rules as a potential for inviting deeper learning about the unspoken regulation of everyday social life. As we see in upcoming chapters, unexpected student responses can offer a "teachable moment"; being able to take them up is one of the challenges of using pop culture when teaching critical media literacy. In chapter 8 we explore how teacher reflexivity can help meet these challenges.

In addition to learning through the design of games and the creation of rules required for fair play, Yvette chose board games because she saw them as a way to promote the experience of exercising "power-with." The pleasure generated by working with others was apparent when Neil claimed, "It's fun to win and all, but it doesn't matter that much," and classmates in the same focus group agreed. Elizabeth emphasized, "I don't think it's necessarily more fun [to win]. I think it's just if you're – if you're more competitive, you think you *have* to win, but if you just want to enjoy the game, you don't really care about winning." In fact, the camaraderie of game play meant that the Monopoly Project did not seem like a lesson at all for many students:

> NEIL: Normally in class time, you don't get much time to, like, make new friends and play with your new friend – with your friends.
> AUDREY: We have so much free time!
> ELIZABETH: [Laughs].
> NEIL: Like in math or something like that ... this was kind of like a period where you could work together with your friends, and like in math you can't really work together with your friends.

These expressions of pleasure resonate with the social elements of online game play identified by Delwiche (2010): engagement, identification, and interaction (p. 180). *Engagement* refers to the intensity of focus that can emerge as players become involved in game activities; at times, players can become so engrossed as to "lose themselves" in game play. Engagement encourages players to identify with their game character and with the broader narrative that delineates the character's choices, hence interactions with other players (p. 184). As for online game play, in *Monopoly* this interaction is shaped by the rules of play, but also by individual players' responses to other gamers. Paulina observed in her field notes how the "fun" resulting from group work drew out some of the quieter students. Because players are rewarded for certain behaviours, the positive feelings that are evoked by following rules could help explain why it might have been difficult for Yvette's students to move out of the competitive logic fostered by the rules of *Monopoly*. This "reward" for compliant media engagement tells us a lot about the power of popular culture as public pedagogy; the challenge is to capture and repurpose this pedagogical potential. Yvette's teaching philosophy – to act as a "guide" when necessary, rather than "teacher" – helped her build on this potential.

Yvette instructed her students to consider their intended audience, with classmates providing feedback on how their ideas were received by their peers as well as by their teacher. Such a process can be used to prompt reflexive (re)consideration of the values, motivations, and purposes guiding media production (something we return to in chapter 9). This is a small but first step in rewriting the cultural landscape through what Levy (2010) calls "collective intelligence": "the capacity of human collectives to engage in intellectual cooperation in order to create, innovate and invent" (p. 71). He argues that this capacity can operate at any scale, from work teams to huge networks or even to our entire species. Collective intelligence is characteristic of a knowledge-based or "information economy," such as that supported by recent developments in communication technology. We thus see the collaboration exercised by Yvette's young students as preparation for the more complex and networked world of online media production, of which games are one example. Many commentators see collaborative media production as a goal of critical media literacy, and many equate it with the "empowerment" of youth (Kellner & Share, 2005; for criticisms, see David Morley in dialogue with Miyase Christensen [Christensen & Morley, 2014]; Buckingham, 2008). Like Berliner (2018), we prefer to view media production by children and youth as participation in an ongoing struggle, rather than as "evidence" of their empowerment.

Conclusion

In the end, we attribute the success of Yvette's project to both the nature of board games – characterized by structured rules – and a pedagogy based on Yvette's trust in her students' creative capacities. Like us, Yvette conceded that no matter how limited their innovations, they testify to learning that social texts are not "fixed truths," but rather constructions. This learning can lay the ground for challenging, and perhaps reconstructing, the "truths" embedded in social texts in ways that validate the experiential knowledge of youth as a legitimate understanding of the social world.

While we could not find any statistics on the amount of time Canadian youth spend in board game play, in a national survey, 59 per cent of students in Grades 4–11 report playing games as their top online activity – 71 per cent of boys and 47 per cent of girls. Relevant in the case of Yvette's Grade 4–5 class, online game activity peaks among students in Grade 5, with 77 per cent of students listing it as their top activity (something done daily or weekly) (Steeves, 2014, pp. 17–18).[7] Within this context, the relevance of games (of all types) makes them attractive media for teaching media literacy.

Yvette chose games because she wanted to introduce media literacy by starting with something her students already knew. Her logic was that by taking *Monopoly* apart to learn what makes it work, students could produce new games as a means not simply to understand the complexity of game creation but also to raise questions about the economic structure of their world: Yvette's project was designed for her students to become researchers of their own world. With hindsight, Yvette realized she had underestimated how difficult it would be for her young learners to recognize the figured world of *Monopoly* as following the rules of monopoly capitalism that operate in their lived world and that lead to unfair social outcomes. The challenge she unexpectedly faced was not that students lacked experiential knowledge of that world – indeed, "commodification" characterizes more than one student redesign – but that they had no readily available "counter text" to draw upon. Rather than reject capitalism, her students normalized its available design. Upon reflection, we think such redesigns would have been challenging for many in most age groups. This is because the assumptions underpinning the neoliberal capitalist worldview are, at present, solidly entrenched; no clear rival to this reigning commonsense has yet to emerge (for further discussion, see Fraser, 2015).

For the moment, it is worth noting that Yvette, as herself a learner, planned to build on the results of her Monopoly Project in the following year: "I have a split [class] again next year, and I have some students returning. I'm going to look at revisiting this, now that I know some students have this as background ..." Like Yvette, as researchers we are also learners; our learning concerns critical media literacy as a tool when teaching for social justice. We present our learning about classroom practice in chapter 8, along with practical advice for teachers wanting to use pop culture, and in chapter 9, where we revisit our initial thinking about critical media literacy as support when teaching for social justice.

5 *The Hunger Games*: Using Popular Film to Learn about Power

DAWN H. CURRIE, DEIRDRE M. KELLY, AND LJ SLOVIN

We had some good [class] discussions about power and where it comes from and that it's not exactly clear-cut. It ... might depend on weapons, it might depend on influence, it might depend on alliances.

– Jane, post-project interview

As a teacher, Jane sees pop culture as a "jumping off point for the development of literacy skills, social awareness, and critical thinking." She reasons: "If we tap into the 'flow' of media swirling around students all the time, we create little 'eddies' of social interaction where meaningful conversations can occur." Jane believes that media literacy can start at "any" age because it allows youth

> to engage with and participate in the world around them ... young people today are exposed to more depictions of reality and alternative realities than ever before. Through television shows, news, games, movies, and social media, they hear and see things that resonate with them and that they have questions about. The classroom can provide a safe and supportive place for ideas and impressions to be verbalized and either strengthened or reshaped.

The use of popular film to promote critical media literacy among her Grade 6 and 7 students appeals to her because "We need to use whatever media students are exposed to in their home lives to inform and develop skills which will ensure students are developing awareness of their own value system in relation to what they see" (for more along these lines, see Souto-Manning & Price-Dennis, 2012).

Jane had an idea before enrolling in our media seminar of using *The Hunger Games* in teaching about government:

> We had done *The Giver*[1] and had lots of talk about rules and laws and things like that, and dystopias. And then I was thinking about *The Hunger Games*. It's another dystopia. I just wanted to use it as a lead-in to government ... The main thing is just to have a fun activity to start government with ... I don't think it's earth-shatteringly deep or anything like that [laughs]. But it's about trying to create circles that we come back [to], right?

Like Jane, LJ (our research assistant who teamed up with Jane) does not believe that it is good to "protect" youth from media. When young, LJ

> was instructed through public outcries and pointed censorship that the media is entertaining but potentially dangerous and I should be aware of being duped ... When media was presented in my classrooms, it was usually prior to school breaks as intentionally laidback time or it was superficially discussed. There was *media* and then there was *education*.

Reflecting on their media engagement as a youth, LJ admitted feeling "somewhat betrayed":

> I think of the Disney movies I watched growing up and the experience of revisiting these movies as an adult. I was shocked at the intense level of sexism, homophobia, and racism in these movies. Moreover, I was shocked that I was allowed to watch these movies as a kid without any follow-up discussion of the oppressive imagery, characters, plotlines, and language ... I was consuming them and making sense of them in my own mind.

LJ believes that "with early instruction in critical literacy, I would have been able to engage with the racist, classist, ablest, heterosexist, and sexist messages that are rampant in all of those movies while also understanding the enjoyment I received from watching them."

Besides shared interests in media education for youth, Jane and LJ brought complementary knowledge to their collaboration; while Jane knew her students very well and their capacity to deal with the explicitly violent material in *The Hunger Games*, LJ's background in theatre fitted well with Jane's commitment to an activity that would entail role play. Together, they designed and implemented a project inspired by the wildly popular *Hunger Games*.

The Hunger Games by Suzanne Collins is the first in a trilogy of novels developed into four films. The first of the series, used for this case study, concerns a dystopia set in a country (Panem) consisting of a wealthy Capitol and 12 Districts living in various states of poverty. This country is presented as post-apocalyptic North America. Every year one boy and one girl are chosen by lottery from each district to participate in a compulsory televised death match, called the "Hunger Games." These Games serve as punishment for past rebellion against the Capitol. The story's narrator, Katniss, lives in the poorest district, where people die of starvation on a regular basis. The 24 participants in the Games are called Tributes. The winning Tribute and their home district are rewarded with food, supplies, and riches. The purpose of the Games is to entertain the Capitol while reminding the Districts of the power of the Capitol.

The Hunger Games has been interpreted as a "powerful critique of economic injustice and capitalist ideals" (Marshall & Rosati, 2014, p. 20), making it a useful venue for teaching for social justice. In an interview, Collins claims that her novel gives readers the freedom to explore issues "like the vast discrepancy of wealth, the power of television and how it's used to influence our lives, the possibility that the government could use hunger as a weapon and then, first and foremost to me, the issue of war" (quoted in Marshall & Rosati, 2014, p. 20). Jane chose *The Hunger Games* as a bridge between a literary unit – where the students read about dystopias – and lessons on government. In presenting her lesson plan during the seminar, Jane maintained:

> The kids will be constructing the world through playing out the game. They will construct identities and relationships, and these will be ripe for discussions of power. This will lead into a discussion of Canadian government. I want to emphasize how power comes from a lot of places. A concern for social justice will emphasize the way that power is something they can take and exercise.

Research Setting

West Glen Elementary School (WGES) is a dual-track (English and French) Kindergarten to Grade 7 school located in a middle-class, predominantly single-family neighbourhood in greater Vancouver. The red-brick architecture reveals the school's age: WGES was established in 1908, with several additions and renovations up until 2006. Enrolment during recent years has held steady at around 600 students a year, making WGES one of the bigger schools in the district. Approximately 18 per cent of families accessing WGES report speaking a language other than English at home, and about 13 per cent of the students are designated as speaking ESL (English as a Second Language). The School Plan (2015–16) indicates that WGES values diversity and honours Aboriginal culture specifically. Social justice is supported through the study of governance and restorative justice and through the exploration of ancient civilizations.

The goals for WGES centre on "literacy, written expression, math and social responsibility." WGES is also known for its focus on music, fine arts, and drama. Important to the case study described in this chapter, the School Plan embraces a goal of "communication including written expression with a focus on clear, well organized presentations with attention to audience and purpose." The school's vision is to "allow each student to demonstrate growth relative to his or her individual potential." WGES prides itself on a "strong spirit of giving to others and demonstrating positive global citizenship." The school motto reads: "Is it Safe – Is it Kind – Is it Fair?" (School Plan, 2015–16). Also important to the project in this chapter is the large play area surrounding the school, which Jane described as "an amazing playground – we have one of the biggest playgrounds, I think, probably in the school district." In addition to the usual playground equipment and soccer field, the school property contains an area of large conifer trees housing picnic benches and tables. The school webpage emphasizes that WGES ensures "a positive playground environment" so that students feel "safe and secure." The importance given to outdoor play is reflected in WGES school protocols: "all students need to be outside unless determined to be a rain day which will only be called when there is torrential rainfall." Parents and guardians are instructed that students need to come to school with proper footwear and clothing.

Jane's class consisted of 10 Grade 6 students and 19 Grade 7 students. Jane maintains this split can have advantages: "I kind of like it at this time of year because the Grade 7s aren't quite as wild when they're tempered a bit with the Grade 6s." The bigger challenge comes from kids with "identified [learning] issues" and "then quite a few ADHD [Attention Deficit Hyperactivity Disorder], too ... I have one with autism and three that have IEPs [Individualized Education Plans] for ADHD and learning disabilities. And one student who doesn't speak English. And one ESL." There were 20 boys, whom Jane described as "very thoughtful," and nine girls. According to Jane, "Most of them are pretty normal kids." She then clarified: "middle class and, you know, they're very involved. They have a lot of after-school activities."

The Hunger Games Project

In designing an activity, Jane and LJ drew on elements from across Jane's curriculum: physical education, social studies, drama, and language arts. From the seminar they worked with mode of address, relationship building, identity building, Gee's (2011b) notion of "figured worlds," and typologies of power. Jane wanted a lesson based on experiential learning that could be shared by all her students:

> It's pretty hard to come up with ways to teach government that are a little more active. I think it's good to have a point of reference. You always have that common experience you can go back to and say, "Well, remember when this happened." You don't know what the kids' experiences are with any kind of government or any kind of law making. So, it's good to have those common experiences that they can draw on as we go along.

LJ's co-facilitation was fuelled by interest in how students would engage with their character and experience of the game, especially around "power":

> I view the activity as a starting point for broaching the topic of power. Through role play, the students will be in situations that lead them to experience powerfulness and powerlessness. By critically debriefing with an emphasis on this element, we can challenge the students to question power and open up a space for them to take up empowerment work in their own lives.

LJ saw this potential learning outcome as a goal of promoting social justice.

In the final analysis, the Hunger Games Project combines tools from our seminar to promote learning outcomes that support social justice: modelling fair play; applying critical thinking skills to a range of problems and issues; describing the purposes of rules, laws, and government; developing personal responses and supporting them with opinions and judgments; forming opinions and modifying viewpoints to gain further understanding of self; explaining how works of communication relate to the broader context of world issues; and addressing an audience through persuasion. These goals were included in BC's provincial "prescribed learning outcomes" at the time. Ideally, students would also gain a nuanced understanding of power and of empowerment through experiences structured by role play. Assessment of learning was to be primarily through observation, although students' written work, consisting of reflection essays assigned as the project unfolded, was also used for that purpose.

To enhance role play, Jane and LJ prepared character cards describing background information that illuminated each character's motivations, as well as fears that could influence their participation in the Game. Their descriptions included the skills and weaknesses that each character brings to the playing field (see Appendix D for details). To prevent the temptation for students to key off the original screenplay, Jane and LJ decided that the characters described on these cards should not resemble ones from the book or movie. One important consideration in designing the project was the necessity for students to become immersed in the activity: experiencing "power" requires that student actors step outside themselves into their assigned role. This immersion would be facilitated through costume creation, giving students an opportunity to design and display their imagined character. Jane and LJ also expected that costume creation would enhance the pleasure of role play. Because the game includes an "Audience," Ms. Knight's Grade 6/7 class attended the first two sessions and – in their role as Audience – the presentations held during the third session as well as the re-enactment of *The Hunger Games*. Besides Jane and LJ, two other adults were present throughout the project: Phil, a teacher's aide who worked with the student with autism, and our research assistant, Katherine Lyon, who videoed most of the sessions.

Watching The Hunger Games *Film*

Students were prepared by watching *The Hunger Games* film in class (Jacobson, Kilik, & Ross, 2012). Jane emphasized to her students that the goal of the project is "experience," specifically "feeling" how power operates:

> The purpose is to discover who has power within the movie. So, when we do the re-enactment, we want to experience that. So, we're looking for the emotion that you feel. If you felt things were not fair, or if you felt that you didn't have any choices on how things were done.

In this way, Jane drew her students' attention to their affective responses to the film.

Role Play

The second session opened with class discussion of role play, essential to the experiential learning Jane desired. Jane reviewed the guidelines: (a) stay in character, (b) stay within the bounds of the arena, (c) follow what the cards indicate, (d) be respectful of the Capitol's decisions and the Audience, and (e) no physical contact except with a card – the cards represent food, water, weapons, abilities, and obstacles. She felt that students should be given an opportunity to volunteer to play members of the Capitol because these roles entail decision making that could be uncomfortable for some students. The rest of the students were assigned to Tribute roles. Jane and LJ had created 24 different characters for Tributes – 12 males and 12 females, split into Districts. They opted for four Game Masters instead of splitting the Capitol into Game Masters and a President, limiting the number of different levels of characters in the Game.

As Jane walked around the room with a stack of character cards, fanned out but turned face down, students randomly drew their Tribute role:

> The room is full of chatter as the students get their characters, and I can hear them turning to each other to discuss strategy. Many have ideas already about what the "strong" cards are, even though we didn't make any cards that are more likely to win than others. I can hear a lot of kids talking to each other about their cards, highlighting the "best" parts. One boy, who's wearing a neon orange sweatshirt and toque, is flaunting his card. Another student is reading his card, impressed. Then he says: "Doesn't say you're going to win though." (LJ, field notes)

Jane emphasized that the character cards were not based on the book or the movie, which meant that everyone could influence their chance to win. She explained the rules of the activity: "When the Game begins, you must play in role. You can only use the skills and resources on your [character] card." To illustrate the importance of resource cards, Jane indicated that if a player had a starvation card, for example, they would have to run around and look for a food card that might be hidden around the play area. As well, someone in the Audience could supply them with such a card. Jane emphasized: "This is a game built on trust. Like any game, if you don't play by the rules, it's not fun for anyone."

Owing to the deluge of questions by eager participants, explaining the project took longer than budgeted in the original plan. The questions were very specific: "Can you only pick one box [from the cornucopia]? Can we steal? What if two people have the same weapon?" The students were very concerned about how fairness factored into the game. They described potential scenarios that could unfold during play, asking how Jane or LJ would handle them: "What if I have a slingshot card, and I'm going to steal someone else's card, but they have a bow and arrow – can they kill me?" Students also seemed very concerned about the rules that protected their right to win the game. Jane had difficulty subduing the class. Despite a few mixed responses to their assigned characters, Jane and LJ were encouraged by how excited the students generally seemed about the activity.

Jane announced that the Tributes would make presentations on the following day. Their goal was to gain Sponsors from the Audience or Game Masters, who could assist players by providing resource cards. This element of the project thus drew on "mode of address," although Jane did not name it as such for her young learners. The session closed as Jane assigned the first written essay, an "In-Role Reflection" on identity building and self-presentation. Students were instructed to describe their character and how this character felt about the upcoming Game. Prompts included: How does it feel to be in that role, to act as that person? Who are you doing your presentation for? Who are you doing your costume for? How are you acting? For whom? The goal of this assignment was to enhance commitment to assigned characters for the upcoming Game.

Despite some initial groaning as students read their character cards, written work suggests that students, overall, took up the role play enthusiastically. Most essays keyed off their character card, reciting the "biography" and "skill set" from their card in the first person. Students embraced new identities with comfort, including a cross-gender identity:

> I am Ashley, the female Tribute from District 10 ... Since I was little I have never been really devoted to sports, usually quitting in the first few weeks, so as a result I am not very fit. So, I will have to rely on my intelligence to overcome any obstacles I may face and to give me the best advantage in making me successful in the games. I have been committed to school, so I am very adapted to using my brain to solve problems. To give me an advantage even before the games start, I am currently formulating complex strategies. (Kyle)

Kyle was one of the few students who considered fighting against the Capitol: "During these games I will devote myself to rebelling against the Capitol to convince all the Districts that there is a better world than the one we live in."

Engagement in role play was also evidenced when students took ownership of their character's affect:

> My name is Spahgett Pashtadringus. I am from District 10 ... I was selected to join the Hunger Games, which makes me worry about my family. I would think about losing the Hunger Games and not about winning it. People started to encourage me to win. I started to feel brave after all the encouragement, and I felt like I would win. (Theo)

> Today I feel upset and overwhelmed because I just got picked as a Tribute from District 2, where we specialize in weaponry for the Hunger Games. I am shy, and I am afraid I will not get along with the other Tributes. (Madison)

Overall, reflection essays signalled a high degree of commitment to role play. In the words of Robert: "It's an experience. You want to get the most out of it."

Tributes were given time for group discussion about their role in the activity, the strategies they wanted to employ, and their concerns for the Game. Jane's goal was to promote learning through the experience of being a group member, met through relationship building within the group and negotiating how the group wants to understand their role in relation to others. Students identified collective goals and assigned leadership as a group. They also discussed whether they wanted to be united as a District by forming alliances. This session closed with a barrage of "What if" questions, most pertaining to the use of weapons. As a general answer, Jane and LJ both emphasized how weapons (indicated on resource cards) must be used according to the character being played. With few exceptions, everyone was on the edge of their seat, raising their hands, physically reacting to answers, and laughing and smiling a lot.

Setting the Stage

The third session was designed to encourage students to further immerse themselves in their role play through hideout construction, costume design, and preparation for class presentations. The purpose of presentations by Tributes (to be done during the fourth session) was to gain Sponsors, who could assist them during key moments of the Game. Because each Tribute had only one minute for their presentation, Jane warned them to be very clear on the most important information or impression that they wanted to relay. This session thus fostered learning about presentation of self, which Jane defined as "the idea of selling yourself by the way that you dress or the way that you talk." In this context, she gave her students instructions about costumes:

> The costume can be as simple or as elaborate as you want ... For your costume, you have to ask yourself, "How am I going to endear myself to the Audience? How am I going to get their attention so that they remember me and send me stuff [resource cards] when I need it?"

LJ noticed that one girl had a behind-the-scenes book on makeup and outfits from *The Hunger Games*, while one of the boys had brought a blue wig.

Although faithfully following their character cards, students were learning about media production. With Jane acting as director, students participated in staging a performance by casting characters, designing costumes and scenery, anticipating their audience, and taking up acting roles. This learning was enhanced through student construction of props for their enactment (see figure 5.1). When this activity was announced,

Figure 5.1. Working on hideouts

there was a flurry of questions: "Can the Game Masters choose where to put them? Can we put leaves on them?" When Jane asked for volunteers, almost the entire class raised their hands. She remarked to LJ that the excitement level always mounts whenever her students get to do something outside and whenever a lesson "doesn't involve pencils."

Stepping into Character

When LJ arrived on the following day, they could see students getting ready for the costume parade and character presentations:

> Some of the kids look fantastic in the costumes. A few of the districts planned matching costumes. The boy from District 3 (electronics) has a very elaborate costume with a headset and wires draped around his body. The boy from District 1, who I am standing and waiting next to, is wearing a faux fur coat. He is a bit nervous about presenting and asks me what he should say. The two girls we are waiting on run in and get into their spots. One is the girl from District 1. She is wearing a polka dot black and white dress, pearls, and a feather scarf/shawl. The other is the girl from District 2. She is wearing an entirely golden outfit. She made a headdress with wings on it and a shield that says District 2 on the back. (LJ, field notes)

Ms. Knight set up a microphone, and each District came up in a pair to give a little speech:

> The presentations are fairly hectic. I announce the District, the students walk in while one of Ms. Knight's students, a boy with bright red hair, points

to the front of the class ... Some of the students take the microphone with confidence and seem to already know exactly what they want to say; the boys typically present with more confidence. The Audience seems to enjoy the presentations. There's a lot of laughter and lot of smiles. (LJ, field notes)

The stage presentations went rather quickly. Each group followed the same pattern: keying off their character cards, participants introduced themselves ("I am ...") and informed the Audience, "I am going to win because ..." Most of the groups did not use anywhere near the one minute allowed. Many Audience members made notes while the Tributes presented. The last students to enter were the four Game Masters, who also made presentations. Three of them were dressed very sharply – suit jackets for the boys and a brimmed hat, glasses, and dress blazer for the girl. They each recited one part of a small speech they had prepared, closing with the most famous lines from the movie: "Happy Hunger Games and may the odds be ever in your favour!"

In class discussion that closed this session, Jane challenged students to examine what worked and didn't work well during their presentations. They brainstormed around the importance of rehearsing their lines, the success of wacky costumes, and how to "really get into character." Jane gave tips: she advised students to project self-confidence by looking up and maintaining eye contact with their audience. Discussion then transitioned to the upcoming performance of the Game, now just a few days away. As class discussion focused on the particulars of the game, LJ noted:

It seems like a few kids have taken the time to memorize different cards because when they ask questions about the rules, they cite the details of the cards, nearly verbatim. For instance, one kid asks a question about the backpack card and, in asking the question, illustrates that he knows exactly what the backpack card says on it. All of the students, except one, seem very engaged. Everyone is looking at Jane, often smiling, sometimes turning to the student next to them to share a laugh or smile in reaction to an answer or question. (LJ, field notes)

Questions again centred on "what if" scenarios, giving Jane the opportunity to bring something up that she heard about. Apparently, Tributes had been trying to bargain with the Game Masters, using candy as a bribe. All four of the Game Masters admitted that multiple students had approached them. This behind-the-scenes strategizing provided a poignant contrast to the students' prior obsession with fairness. Jane reminded participants that they were all working "on the honour system."

Re-enacting The Hunger Games

The weather had been very pleasant during the two weeks prior to the Game. On the day of the actual role play, it was cold, pouring rain, and windy. None of the kids, however, seemed to mind. Jane asked who might head out and set up the hideouts; she had no trouble finding volunteers. LJ noted:

> I can hear the kids chatting about the game and strategy. I see that one kid has the second *Hunger Games* book out on his desk. There are a bunch of kids asking questions about the game, talking animatedly, and discussing strategy with each other and Jane. Kyle comes in from helping set up and is covered in mud but doesn't seem fussed about being dirty. (LJ, field notes)

Hideouts dotted the soccer field, now covered in puddles, and the forested play area. A large umbrella with a plastic tarp served as the cornucopia, set in the centre of the soccer field. For the re-enactment, as in *The Hunger Games*, most of the resource cards were stashed around the cornucopia with a few hidden in the play area. Students were lined up at the door with district numbers pinned on their back. Jane had a megaphone and busily organized the Tributes in a line. The Game Masters all wore brightly coloured pinnies. Ms. Knight rallied the Audience; many of her students were also in costume. They chatted and huddled together. Some stood atop playground equipment to gain the best view. Phil, the teacher's aide, was dressed in a yellow slicker and armed with a megaphone. He was to act as President by announcing who was officially "out." Jane was a bit anxious, uncertain that everything was well organized. Despite her concern, the role play unfolded quickly, albeit rather hectically:

> Jane announces the start of the first official West Glen Hunger Games and "May the odds be ever in your favour!" She then makes a starting noise with the megaphone. It's really exciting! The beginning is very fast paced. Many students rush off to the cornucopia, grab supplies, and then rush off, shoving the supplies into their pockets as they search for safety. Other students head straight for the forest and look for cover. (LJ, field notes)

Alliances were immediately apparent to Jane, who pointed them out to LJ as they both watched the Tributes run around. Students were travelling in packs, from two up to four or five. It was difficult to be sure what was going on. The weather added an element of chaos. The district numbers worn by each Tribute tore off in the rain, and it wasn't long before everyone was covered in mud. All the resource cards were constructed from paper and thus falling apart. While Jane was restocking the cornucopia, the Game Masters set fire to the southwest quadrant. LJ announced the fire over the megaphone, adding that anyone in that sector was "out." Jane and LJ both ended up restocking supplies throughout the Game, not having anticipated how far-flung all the cards would get and the necessity of ensuring a constant flow of resources. All these unexpected issues had to be dealt with as Jane and LJ ran around in the rain. They had to keep track of the progress of the Game and the whereabouts of all the students while revising the activity. It felt a bit out of control to LJ, who commented: "It's difficult to be sure what is going on." After 10 minutes, Jane limited the playing field to the forested area to consolidate the game.

The Game itself lasted only 20 minutes. By the end, all the kids were muddy and exhibiting a lively energy. The last three Tributes were boys:

> They make a triangle in the forest and size each other up. One of the boys gets a card from the Game Masters and wants to appeal to the Audience for a Sponsor but in the process, he gets killed by one of the other surviving Tributes. Very soon after, Sam triumphs. It's 11:20. Jane declares him the winner as he throws his remaining supplies in the air, exuberantly, and does a little leap. Everybody claps [see figure 5.2]. Ms. Knight takes her class to head inside. She tells me they are going right in to discuss everything and that she thought it was "brilliant." (LJ, field notes)

As everyone headed inside, students mobbed Jane, asking when they could play again. Jane let the class know that they would and directed students to sit on the carpet, so they could talk about their experience. To stimulate reflection before the students did their second writing assignment, Jane debriefed students on the goals of the project. Because the key aim was to introduce the themes of power and rules, Jane encouraged the students to think about how these themes were experienced during the activity. Discussion was animated; Jane systematically called on students by name, but there were far more volunteers eager to answer her questions than could be accommodated. Jane referred to their earlier work on characterization, urging the students to consider how their experience of power related to their staged character throughout the Game.

When she asked how many started out in an alliance, an overwhelming majority raised their hands.

> Jane asked what broke them down. One boy said that selfishness tended to break down the alliances. Another said traitors and betrayal. One said secret alliances ... Kyle said that you formed alliances because you really wanted to win ... Jane asked why alliances were so successful. The kids brainstormed

100 Pop Culture and Power

Figure 5.2. "We have a winner!"

that with an alliance, you could gain trust, pool resources, and kill other Tributes. You were stronger together. (LJ, field notes)

Later, Jane told LJ she thought the alliances would be a productive way to talk about party politics in the upcoming unit on government.

Jane encouraged the class to talk about who they thought had the most power, and ways that power was misused during the activity. They had many different ideas for who had the most power: "kids who were in alliances, kids who broke alliances, the Game Masters, or the President":

> Another kid said Phil [the President] did because he could decide if a person was dead or not. Chloe said that people who had the bow and arrow had the most power because it was the best weapon. Another kid said that the main alliance of boys had the most power. Jane asked if it was because of how many they were. The student responded that yes, they were able to share resources, but in the long run their numbers were bad because they ended up having to kill each other. The next student responded that the Game Masters had the most power. Then a student chimed in saying that he believed that people who broke alliances had the most power because of their unexpected betrayal. Mia said that people in alliances had the most power, not when they broke them, but when they worked in a group. A person on their own was easier to kill than a person who was part of a bigger group. (LJ, field notes)

When students brought up examples of the misuse of power, they spoke about unfairness. For instance, "Mia argued that it was unfair when [the Game Masters] sent the fire into the SW quadrant. That was how she was 'killed.' She just happened to be in that area. There was nothing she could do, and it was unfair" (LJ, field notes).

Since affect was emphasized in our seminar, Jane also questioned students about how they felt while playing. They talked about feeling annoyed, frustrated, and defenceless. The context of these feelings was an intense focus on fairness. Jane opened space for the students to talk about the pleasure of the activity by asking what they liked about the game. Again, hands shot up. Many students said they really liked the beginning because it was fast-paced and intense, just like the book and movie. A few students recounted specific moments that had been highlights for them.

Following lively discussion, students wrote an Out-of-Role Reflection. Using Gee's (2011b) "figured world" concept, Jane and LJ prompted students to think about what world is being created through the role play, what is "normal" in this world, and how they know what is normalized. They also reviewed types of power, drawing on Jane's overall lesson planning: the power of the Capitol, the power of individuals, the power of influence, and the power of the group. Students were asked to compare *The Giver* (used for the prior learning unit on ancient Egypt) and *The Hunger Games*. Essays indicated that Jane's goal to introduce notions of *power* as structured by various roles was effective. Student work identified how power worked through a hierarchy, but most students recognized that Tributes were not necessarily completely "powerless":

> The person with the most power was the President. The President decided if a Tribute was alive or dead ... The Audience has power too. They are the ones to choose who to sponsor. The Tributes have lots of power at the presentation because if they make people like them then they get Sponsors ... An alliance has power ... Most people have more strength working with someone. (Mia)

> In the games I think the Game Masters had the most power because they can change the rules any time that they want and kill anybody they want. Then the Sponsors come next because they can choose who they want to win by giving them parachutes to survive like water, food, and medicine. Next comes the Tributes. I think that only some of the Tributes have power. Some of the Tributes who had power are the ones who were travelling with others and the ones with good weapons like bows and arrows, ropes. (Madison)

As well as introducing a typology of power (corresponding to power-over exercised by governments, power-to exercised by individuals, and power-with by the collective), Jane had intended for participants to "experience" its operation through the hierarchy of roles. Success in meeting this goal was evident when students described power stemming from the structure of the Game, and not just from their character role (as in the earlier assignment):

> At the beginning, I thought I had a lot of power because I was notified that I have a large number of Sponsors. But there was a lack of assistance, limited by Panem's very own President, PHIL. Phil denied the sponsors of mine to send in food. (Nicholas)

As Jane had intended, one student, Andrew, related his experience to government. His essay concluded:

> My game experience can relate to the present political structure in Canada in the sense that you join a political party to be surrounded by people with influential power and a similar goal in mind ... like politics, I became estranged from my political party [and was] left to rot away on the streets or in this case "die."

Promoting Critical Media Literacy through Role Play

Jane's initial idea was to design a "fun" activity that would enhance her teaching on government, an otherwise "dry" topic for children. The intended learning objectives for this case study are complex, cutting across several subjects: from *drama*, developing characters and using persuasion; from *social studies*, understanding rules, laws, and government; from *health and career*, modelling fair play, developing personal responses and supporting them with opinions and judgments, modifying viewpoints to gain further understanding; and from *language arts*, learning how works of communication relate to the broader context of world issues. What unites these objectives is an understanding of the operation of power, as both a personal and collective capacity. In this sense, the Hunger Games Project supported Jane's teaching for social justice by exploring how power works through individual behaviour as well as rules governing the collective behaviour that reconstitutes social inequality. Role play further promoted media literacy: the students' re-enactment of *The Hunger Games* engaged them in activities associated with movie production. They scripted characters; acted in ways to "hail" an audience; created and organized visual props (costumes and hideouts); and so on. Below we analyse how Jane's goals were met, while also suggesting how learning could be deepened. Our reflections are informed by three group discussions that LJ and Dawn held with 12 student participants (four girls and eight boys) after completion of all project activities.

Student Experiences of Role Play

The novelty of Jane's project is that it structured learning about the operation of power through the simulated experience of feeling powerful/powerless. As in the movie, the re-enactment worked to the general disadvantage of the Tributes, although there was an opportunity for Tributes to influence the outcome. Overall, participants could variously experience different ways that power can operate: through class structure, by the elite (power-over, exercised by the Capitol); through individual skill and personal influence (power-to, exercised by Tributes); and through the group (power-with, exercised through alliances). Jane aimed for her students to reflect on their experience of power in terms of the class structure of Panem and the rules of the Game. She wanted the students to ultimately be able to contrast a dictatorship, the figured world re-enacted during the Game, to a democratic government as an upcoming lesson topic.

Virtually all participants arrived at the conclusion that the rules governing the Game (namely, a dictatorship) were "unfair," given that not every player had an equal opportunity to "survive." Both the distribution and effectiveness of the weapons that influenced a Tribute's chances of winning were deemed to be unfair. Although individual Tributes might acquire weapons as the Game opened (by running to the cornucopia and grabbing a box of resources), distribution of weapons was ultimately controlled by the Capitol: the President, the Game Masters, and the Audience. Moreover, while some of the boxes could disadvantage players because they were devoid of weapons or contained "starvation" cards, the boxes could result in ambiguity:

> ROBERT: When people picked up some boxes, they were freaking out because inside their boxes – like Nicholas had a box, and it had both thirst and hunger inside. He had to find food right away. And he had no weapons inside. So, it was kinda weird ... I think someone should *give* it to them –
> KYLE: Yeah. Like the Game Masters – "You're thirsty." 'Cause at the beginning of the Game, you're more looking for supplies. You're not –
> ROBERT: You're expecting something good and – Oh. If you had a thirst card, no one would know after five minutes that you're dead. So, thirst didn't do anything to you. Because no one would know if you had it.

At this point, Eva jumped in: "The boxes weren't really fair. I got a small box and there was a ton of cards. And David got a really big box [gestures], and there was only one card [Dawn and LJ chuckle]."

In this context, individual Tributes had limited opportunities to influence their chances for "survival." They could break the rules by cheating (e.g., by attempting to bribe Game Masters, as happened before the actual role play); they could attempt to secure sponsorship through self-presentation before the Game; or they could form an alliance as a collective strategy during the Game, as explained by Eva:

> In the game, me and Mia were in an alliance. We weren't planning on it, but we decided to work together. And we shared like weapons. Like, I got thirst and she got water, and like, if she had hunger, I'd give her some food. Like, we'd share stuff. It helped because otherwise we'd have died probably. Or like, one of us would hide in a shelter while one of us would look out.

Alliances, however, did not guarantee survival:

> DAWN: Would making an alliance be a way of gaining more power?
> [noise signals general agreement among four boys]
> SAM: But it depends. Maybe not. Because if you don't have any weapons and you make an alliance, and then it turns out they don't have any weapons –
> ANTHONY: [jumps in] – then it's a band of people about to be killed.

Robert claimed that it is not simply a matter of weapons: "most of the time people were loyal to their alliances, and if someone decides – say, were a bit more selfish – they want to win this game, they can just kill the person, and the person wouldn't expect it at all." Through these kinds of experiences, one of the learning outcomes we identified in the group discussions concerned the role of trust in group dynamics, hence its importance in the exercise of power-with others.

While the operation of *power* was the key intended learning theme, we find it significant that the arbitrary distribution of weapons by the Capitol was not criticized to the same extent as the rules governing their use. By far, most complaints were levied against the differential effectiveness of weapons:

> The weapons you could've gotten by chance was a bow and a knife. And the knife is short range. It's just like close quarters. You could only go up to them and tap them on the shoulder and then they're dead. But the bow, it's like unstoppable. You can just like go up to someone two metres away, and if they have a knife it's – there's no chance. You can just say, "You're dead." (Emmett)

When Kirsten suggested that the game would be fairer with "less bows and more of the knives," Emmett retorted:

> Even if you give a lot of people knives, it doesn't match up to the bows. Because if there's like six people coming at you, you can say, "You're dead,

you're dead, you're dead." And then they're dead. And if they all have knives, it doesn't matter.

As hinted by Emmett, the bow and arrow received numerous complaints; members in every focus group discussion claimed that rules for the bow and arrow could invite cheating:

> The rule least followed was the rule within two metres to say, "You're dead" with the bow and arrow. Some people were discussing, like, "I'm not out," even though people were mostly sure they were out, but they could say "You're dead" when they were further away. (Robert)

During focus groups, ambiguity in the rules drew extensive criticism. Ambiguity could arise because of the rule requiring "two metres" for a kill with the bow and arrow, but also depending on whether people actually had a rope (which gave safety for 10 seconds) or whether people found a thirst card in the box retrieved from the cornucopia at the beginning of the Game but hid it, and because of the fact that the actual area covered by the fire started by Game Masters could not be exactly determined, so that no one in the quadrant had a chance to escape. Students in focus groups had a number of suggestions that would make the rules governing the use of weapons fairer: the knife could be thrown, there could be a limit on the number of arrows that participants with bows had to search for, there could be a shield to protect you from the bow and arrow, "soft red balls" could be used to send fire because they could be avoided. In this sense, while the rules governing play were subject to critique, the *process* through which the rules originated was not questioned. This latter outcome would require students to challenge the way the Capitol structured the nature of the activity (and perhaps the authority of their teacher, who led the entire activity). Students reflected on the process of rule making only when directly prompted in focus group discussions:

> DAWN: Do you think it's fair that somebody has that much power over the whole thing?
> BRANDON [who played a Game Master]: No. But it's kind of part of the game ... 'cause the Game Masters are meant to have power.
> EMMETT: If the Tributes just say, "We're not going to fight each other," then the Game Masters could say, "Well, you don't have to fight, but we'll just kill you." One by one. 'Cause they can do anything.

Following complaints about unfair rules from another group, and anticipating Jane's upcoming lessons on democracy, Dawn asked: "In the movie, a small group of people makes rules for everybody. Do you think that's fair?"

> ROBERT: I think it should be maybe like, more of a large group. So, more people can have their say, more heads thinking what the rules should be, how fair they should be. More people, with different experiences could contribute to that.
> EVA: Like the whole class could make up rules ... the teachers made it less fun. They made it like more, I guess, safe, but like – I think it would have been more fun if we had got to make up rules.

Following the focus groups, LJ and Dawn admitted to each other a "bit of disappointment" that student participants did not try to use an alliance to overturn, refuse, or rewrite the rules. The Tributes clearly recognized that "unfairness" was structured into the rules for the Game, and that these rules were issued by an "elite" (namely, adult teachers rather than the entire class), but remained committed to the predetermined script. As LJ reflected, the unquestioned acceptance of rules (especially those authored by their teacher) mirrors the experiential context of participants' everyday life as "students."

As noted above, the success of the Hunger Games Project can be attributed to the way it structured *felt experience* into learning. This experiential component is significant because politicization can be fostered when the operation of power – particularly in arbitrary ways – is a felt reality. Even though students did not question rule making, role play helped facilitate learning for understanding rules, laws, and government; developing personal responses to experiences of "unfair" rules and supporting them with opinions and judgments; and questioning a structured "reality" and modifying viewpoints to gain further understanding. This kind of learning may encourage students to question unfair situations in everyday life and develop politically aware responses. In this sense, the Hunger Games re-enactment supported learning about social justice. Below we discuss how role play can facilitate this outcome.

Student Learning from Role Play

This project connects students' experiences of agency to power through role play. For students to benefit from this experience, it was important for them to immerse themselves as deeply as possible into their assigned character. The creation and display of costumes were included in the project to facilitate immersion. In retrospect Jane concluded: "[If] I were going to do it again, I would actually spend more time developing the costumes and the characters." Drawing on mode of address, Jane organized class discussion following the costume parade to encourage students to think about how they presented themselves to the Audience and to draw connections to how they present themselves daily. During the activity self-presentation was motivated by a Tribute's commitment to survival during the re-enactment: it influenced their ability to garner provisions and receive special treatment during the Game.

We were initially surprised that several students embraced a cross-gender assignment (recall the enthusiasm for role play expressed by Kyle). Character cards offered subject positions that, when taken up by student actors, provided an opportunity – in a safe environment – to play with an "alternative" identity. In this way, role play can be used to challenge the seemingly fixed nature of social identities – with both gender and class structuring the "available design" of Collins's figured world.

To get students thinking about the nature of social identities early on, in debriefing the movie, the teacher could raise questions of racial representation by sharing points raised by critics of the film: "the production elements (camera work, lighting, etc.) continually emphasize [the heroine] Katniss's traditionally white-feminine beauty," and, by contrast, racialized minority "characters ... are cast in stereotypical and sacrificial supporting roles" (Kornfield, 2016, p. 6). If students are familiar with the books, the teacher could ask them to reflect on the casting of a White actor to play Katniss, when the book versions describe her as "a mixed race, Latina, or Middle Eastern individual" (Kornfield, 2016, p. 6).

In the re-enactment, engagement through role play enhanced the intensity of students' experiences, and thus their learning about power. While students "observed" the operation of power as they watched the film, their learning during the role play came through the embodied, rather than simply cognitive, identification with *Hunger Games* characters; learning was "active" rather than "passive," "felt" rather than "thought." As noted by Delwiche (2010) for video game play, Jane's students adapted aspects of their character and responded to the consequences of those choices (for example, about forming alliances). While participants in the Hunger Games Project did not exercise the degree of choice possible when playing video games, they nevertheless exercised the (limited) agency afforded by their prescribed role.

While not wanting to overstate the case, we can see parallels – in both board games and the role play structured into Jane's project – to the kind of learning promoted by video game play. In the world simulated by the game:

> The player must figure out the rule system (patterns) that constitutes the simulation (the rules that the simulation follows thanks to how it is

designed). The player must discover what is possible and impossible (and in what ways) within the simulation in order to solve problems and carry out goals. (Gee, 2008, p. 199)

Moreover, participation involves what Gee (2008) calls an "embodied empathy for a complex system" (p. 200), as the player seeks to participate within that system. While player agency was tightly regulated in the Hunger Games Project, structuring player agency through character cards enhanced student engagement in the activity, necessary for Jane's students to *experience* the operation of power.

The intense engagement of students in their character roles reflects the safety offered by a "required" classroom activity. But it might also reflect the fact that the students themselves "chose" their cards – albeit without knowing the associated character – and thus felt invested in the outcome. Along these lines, Lucey et al. (2013) suggest an interesting variation on Jane and LJ's approach – to involve the students *directly* in the creation of characters. "For example, using ethical situations from *The Hunger Games*, students can project characters who are composites of the people they know – including themselves – and then go on to play the characters that they created in the story they created" (p. 195). In keeping with her goal to link to her unit on government, Jane could have given students a set of questions to guide them in creating their own characters. What does it mean to be a good citizen? Will your character obey the laws of the land? Will they be guided by consensus? Or will they be somebody who questions conventional wisdom and takes a stand against perceived injustice? Will they question their beliefs and where those come from? Will they be a risk taker, a follower, or strategic about where and when to speak up or act? The point of such guidelines would be to encourage students to grapple with the complexities of citizenship in an unjust political system like Panem.

Whatever strategy is employed, the role play afforded by games illustrates how pleasure can be harnessed to learning. As Gee (2008) concludes, however, the result depends on the kinds of games and how they are used in the context of ongoing learning activities. Unlike the other cases in *Pop Culture and Power*, much of the learning from Jane's project was intended to take place well after the Game, as the students progressed through their unit on government. Jane wanted to provide them with a shared experience of rules as the operation of power to draw on during this unit. Activities became tangible examples of interactions with rules and power for the students to reference later. Class discussions were geared towards drawing out those topics and framing students' thinking within those terms. When they moved into a unit on government, Jane was able to refer to their "obsession" with fairness and the feelings that they had expressed about power during the debrief. In the final analysis, Jane's students experienced the exercise of power as situation-specific.

Alliances turned out to be a starting place to discuss politics. Almost every student was part of at least one alliance, with a couple secretly belonging to more than one. Jane remarked that alliances "could be similar to political parties, for example, in that there's more power in numbers, but at the same time you always have to maintain your own individuality in there, too, or you might be killed, right? Or in a political party you might be outcast." Consequently, Jane spent a lot of time talking about alliances during the class debrief. Many of the students believed alliances to have been an essential part of the Game, and a few even thought that those who broke alliances were the ones with the most power. This experience of betrayal – which was widely shared – gave Jane a basis for talking not only about party politics, but also about the misuse of power in general. In this way, the structured "unfairness" of the rules was a key to intended learning; this learning became an opportunity to discuss openly *how* rules are formulated in upcoming lessons because, as in Yvette's project, the "rules" that enable or constrain agency are the embodiment of social relations. Asking *how* rules are decided leads to the additional question of *who* gets to decide and whether some have been unjustly excluded from decision making.

Reflections on Learning from Violent Entertainment

Throughout the lessons for this project, Jane and LJ prioritized fun. Owing to the multifaceted structure of the activity, they were able to spend two weeks generating excitement for the Game through painting the hideouts, displaying costumes, and the role play itself. The students seemed to particularly enjoy this anticipation. Virtually all participants in the group discussions described the opening of the Game, which entailed choosing to run away or to the cornucopia, as "exhilarating." As a result, playing a Tribute offered the most fun: "I would say the Game Master, it was a bit boring. It's like you would walk around and maybe people [do] something and then maybe just like start a fire or kill a few people. It must've been more fun and more like exhilarating to be a Tribute" (Brandon). Mia agreed: "I don't think it would be very fun, 'cause you can't, like, run around and stuff and you don't have to – like, I think the fun part is trying not to get killed. But the Game Masters don't have to, because they know that they're not going to." When Dawn asked another group of four boys whether "they could make a game that would be as much fun, that didn't have killing in it," there was a resounding "No." Throughout the project, participants talked in a cavalier way about "killing" classmates – something Dawn found unsettling. During focus groups, Dawn and LJ prompted participants to reflect on the violence of *The Hunger Games*:

> DAWN: A lot of adults when they watch the film, they think it's too violent for kids like you. So, what do you think?
> BRANDON: Not at all. 'Cause I watch the *Walking Dead* at home, which is like really violent. So. But by the way, I'm not allowed to watch *The Simpsons*.
> DAWN: What do you think, Emmett?
> EMMETT: About the violence? Well, it – I don't think it's too much. 'Cause it's not – you don't see any blood ... Yeah, I read the book and, at the massacre of the cornucopia, everybody's just like killing each other, and it's kind of disgusting. But if – the only thing I didn't like is you know the guy, Cato? The big strong guy? The way he would kill most of his victims is he would go like this [grabs the side of his face with one hand and the back of his head with the other], and he would twist their neck ... and you can actually see one of those, and you can like hear the neck cracking and stuff and it's just disgusting.
> BRANDON: Well, at least they didn't show like the whole – well, I guess they did – like Cato's death. But at least they didn't show it like – 'cause that would've been really gross.

At this point, Dawn asked whether "not showing the gory stuff" makes portrayals of the story less violent. Mia and Kirsten both reasoned: "if you don't see it, then you don't really think about it a lot, 'cause you just *know* it happened." Brandon argued that the violence actually makes the role play more exhilarating: "It's kind of what makes the movie a bit more interesting, the violence, I would say. 'Cause if it was like cuddle bunnies and stuff, kids our age would never watch that." Other discussants shared these sentiments.

Despite our misgivings, in the end we conceded that "killing" actually enhanced learning. As Jane herself noted: "Because the Hunger Games are a matter of life and death, power is very visible." We concluded that the nonchalant attitude about media violence on the part of these students reflects the extent to which it is part of the everyday experience of what constitutes entertainment for youth (first-person shooter video games, for example, come to mind). Hoechsmann and Poyntz (2012) remind us: "what is important about the available research is that none of it demonstrates anything like a copycat relationship between media violence and young people's actions in the real world" (pp. 43–4).

As suggested by Brandon, at least some participants recognized that violence is used to market entertainment to them, a point that we think could be used to deepen critical media literacy through discussion about the film and game industries. Gee (2008) reminds us that "video games, like most popular culture media, reflect back to us, in part, the basic themes and even prejudices of our own society" (p. 197). Kellner (2009) points out that violence in movies can be either "emancipatory, when directed at forces of oppression, or reactionary, when directed at popular forces struggling against oppression" (p. 17). These remarks suggest that rather than sidestep violent entertainment for youth – or simply criticize it – in the safety of the classroom, it could be a useful venue for teaching about social justice.

Simmons (2012) makes a related point, arguing that "violence and brutality toward children are not fiction but fact" (p. 24). She goes on to use her extensive knowledge of *The Hunger Games* trilogy to imagine social-action project units organized around understanding and contesting social injustice and violence (e.g., involuntary labour, forced warriors, and the sex trade). Roxane Gay (2014) argues that the violence portrayed in *The Hunger Games* books and movies, crucially, is tempered by "hope – for a better world and a better people and, for one woman [the main character Katniss], a better life" (p. 130). Dystopias like *The Hunger Games* work as vehicles for teaching for social justice to the extent that they prompt readers (viewers) to consider injustice seriously and begin to imagine how the actual world might be made better. Along these lines, when presenting her project during our seminar, Jane remarked: "I hope the students come away with an experience of powerlessness, a sense of injustice, and some conclusions on how to change things." In keeping with her intentions, we arrived at the view that violence in pop culture can play an instructive role in exploring issues of power, as it operates from both "above" and "below."

In the final analysis, the Hunger Games Project provided a welcome break for students from other lessons that involved more obviously academic elements, like doing math or critical reading. Lessons from this project were a time for playing, when getting into your character was encouraged, and that might mean being a bit silly. As Jenkins et al. (2006) note, play is typically discouraged in the classroom, in part because it challenges a dichotomy between mind and body that, historically, has been seen as essential for "learning" (p. 23). The students helped create the project through their engagement in "play"; they asked questions that clarified role play and created costumes, deepening their experiential learning.[2] In this activity, play took the form of adopting fictive identities and then thinking through new scenarios from their adopted perspective (see Jenkins et al., 2006, p. 31). In this way, the Hunger Games project illustrates how teaching with popular culture can prepare students for active social citizenship.

Conclusion

Aside from music, film is probably the most commonly used medium in schools. Its history in the classroom reflects the use of documentary film in fields such as history and social studies. Film with the status of "popular culture" has made a more recent debut; as noted by LJ, popular film was likely to appear in the classroom prior to school breaks to provide "laid-back time" and, as a consequence, generated only superficial discussion. As expressed by LJ, the general sentiment among adults has been "There was *media* and then there was *education*." Against this sentiment, Jane's intention in using *The Hunger Games* was to provide her students with a shared understanding of "power" that later could be invoked when lessons focused on democratic government. The Hunger Games Project was an innovative way to introduce an alternative text – one of a dictatorship – for upcoming lessons on Canadian government. The novelty of her approach lies in a pedagogy based on role play; while students might gain an understanding of how governments can exercise power over citizens by watching and discussing the dystopia portrayed in *The Hunger Games*, role play enabled Jane's students to experience its operation. Jane and LJ maximized the potential for this learning by constructing character cards that arbitrarily located students in a power hierarchy. In short, the Hunger Games Project promoted embodied learning about the operation of power.

Embodied learning by Jane's students, however, was not limited to experiencing the operation of power. By re-enacting the cinematic version of *The Hunger Games*, student learning was harnessed to media literacy. As a group, the class experienced activities associated with movie making: staging a performance by casting characters, creating costumes for these characters, constructing props, considering what is appropriate for their audience, and taking up acting roles. More than one student carried out independent research on movie production by consulting a behind-the-scenes account of make-up and costumes used for filming. These kinds of activities visibly enhanced the pleasure of this learning.

Understanding whether, and how, the Hunger Games Project contributed to Jane's teaching about government would require research beyond our study. We do know she planned to connect what students had learned about alliances and power-with to party politics; she could also draw from their role-play experiences within a dictatorship to highlight the complex power relations present within interactions more typical of a parliamentary system of government. In the final analysis, we credit her project with enhancing our understanding of how pop culture can foster embodied learning in ways that support teaching for social justice.

6 Celebrity Marketing: Gender Performances in Popular Music

DAWN H. CURRIE, DEIRDRE M. KELLY, AND ZAVI SWAIN

Most of my students are very interested in music. Looking at celebrities or media influence or the power of one song – PSY's "Gangnam Style" has such a strong influence globally – would definitely intrigue them.

– Natalie, brainstorming prior to design of her unit (writing activity 4)

At the time of our project, Natalie was teaching Grade 11 and 12 Marketing classes, as well as Information Technology for Grade 10. She expressed interest in media literacy for youth

> because they are exposed to large amounts of information through the media and need to be equipped with the skills to critically synthesize this "knowledge" ... young people are targeted because they are at an age where their decision making is often influenced by external sources, such as their friends or pop culture.

Although Natalie believes that "pop culture manipulates children and youth," recalling her own teenage years, she argues: "Celebrities can also have a positive impact on teenagers." Natalie had idolized Miriam Yeung, a popular singer and actress in Hong Kong, where Natalie had family ties. Our seminar appealed to Natalie because she wanted to "learn more about how young people accept (or refuse) media influence." She expressed interest in the ways that celebrities market themselves to youth: "A pop star is wearing it, so it must be 'cool' ... For business, this is a way to capitalize on teenagers' obsessions with celebrities – using celebrities to endorse their brands, or having brands named after celebrities." As a Chinese Canadian born and raised in Vancouver, Natalie wrote in one seminar assignment: "I have often struggled to overcome stereotypes myself and certain values inflicted upon me." Interested in promoting social justice through critical media literacy, she asked: "How often do young people take a step back and realize what messages the media is trying to convey?"

Zavi (our research assistant who teamed up with Natalie) came to graduate studies with a background in teaching media literacy to high school students. His interest in critical media literacy for youth reflects his background of growing up

> with decidedly queer tendencies in a conservative, Southern Baptist family and as one of the only students from a white, middle-class background in a black, low-income school district ... I often experienced high levels of social discomfort and isolation, and escapism through books was something that was important to me as a young person.

Within this context, reading was an important, albeit temporary, distraction:

> We did not have cable television, only two or three local channels. My parents did not allow my sister or me to watch much television, and we rarely went to movies. Books, therefore, were my primary source for both entertainment and connection to the world at large ... I think for me the big draw was how easy they made it to become immersed in another world.

As a twenty-something educator working with youth, he does not find that "young people are 'mindlessly consuming' media as some theories of media education suggest." In his experience, "youth are already capable and actively critical of media ... young people are often very sceptical and aware of underlying messages in popular culture."

Research Setting

The setting for the activities described in this chapter was Island Secondary School (ISS) in Crawford, British Columbia. The school is in a quiet, suburban area of primarily single-family homes. It enrols about 1,250 "academically focused students" (ISS website). Many of the students attending ISS are from wealthy immigrant families; according to Natalie, they speak one or two languages besides English. She estimates that 80 per cent of the student body is Asian, with families originally from China, Hong Kong, and Taiwan. "We also have 50 to 60 international students from all over the world: Japan, Korea, some from Brazil."

ISS offers a wide variety of extracurricular activities that include art classes such as film photography and ceramics, as well as team swimming, tennis, and badminton. On-site amenities include three art studios, a new second-floor science wing, and a spacious music room. The school is digitally savvy in its operations, communicating with students and parents via the school website and with students about important upcoming dates and school events via Twitter.

The class that participated in this project consisted of 24 Grade 11/12 students and three Grade 10 students. Fifteen of the students identified as female and 12 as male. Most of the students were of Chinese or Filipino background, with one White student, one Black student, and several students of mixed descent. At times of casual interaction (e.g., on breaks, in the hallway), one could hear what Natalie jokingly referred to as "Chinglish": "a good mix of English and Chinese – Chinglish. It's what I speak, too."

Project Planning

Natalie and Zavi shared an interest in how gender identities are used to market music videos to youth; the fact that Zavi was finishing his Master's in Gender Studies was an asset. Together, they designed a project that integrated critical analysis into media production with content relevant to an elective marketing class (see Buckingham, 2003a). Treating popular music as an "invisible and unconscious" pedagogy (Kellner & Share, 2005, p. 372), they created the unit "Gender Representations in Popular Culture: Celebrity Marketing" to help students:

- Understand and analyse how gender and other social identities are constructed, what role different media platforms have in transmitting social messages, and what impact celebrity representations have on social perceptions of gender;
- Identify and discuss gender representations in popular music aimed at young people (e.g., LMFAO, PSY, Kelly Clarkson, Justin Bieber);
- Define and utilize social identity, gender identity, stereotype, representation, parody;
- Evaluate marketing strategies utilized by music celebrities and analyse how celebrities' social identities factor into their marketing of music videos. (unit lesson plan, April 2013)

This unit drew from Gee's (2011a) "identities building tool," introduced during the seminar:

> For any communication, ask what socially recognizable identity or identities the speaker is trying to enact or to get others to recognize. Ask also how the

speaker's language treats other people's identities, what sorts of identities the speaker recognizes for others in relationship to his or her own. Ask, too, how the speaker is positioning others, what identities the speaker is "inviting" them to take up. (p. 199)

Prior to this project, students had lessons on general business and marketing concepts, with a focus on digital media and commercial culture (discussed as "popular culture"). Early on, Natalie settled on showing and analysing a K-pop music video (like PSY's "Gangnam Style") as a "hook";[1] she felt that Korean pop, with its global audience, would appeal equally to the new immigrants and to the Canadian-born students in her class. Given that there had been no prior introduction to "social identities" or to "gender," two introductory lessons would be dedicated to these topics, followed by two lessons using identity concepts to analyse songs. The remainder of scheduled class time was to be devoted to in-class work on group projects. Natalie would grade the final projects based on students demonstrating what they had learned from the previous activities.

Natalie selected two popular music videos to be used as initial examples for students to analyse – one ("Ice Cream") by the K-pop artist Hyuna that featured PSY, the other ("Kiss You") by One Direction. Tools introduced in the seminar would be used to explore what social identity an artist is constructing (Gee's "Identities Building"); analyse the lyrics of songs (Gee's "Social Languages"); and identify how gender identities are being normalized (Gee's "Figured Worlds"). These tools were intended not only to guide analysis of songs but also to be used in the creation of alternative media through parody or mash-up videos as a form of redesign. Three relevant readings would be available online for students, as well as sample parody and mash-up videos.

A total of 11 class sessions were set aside for the Celebrity Marketing Project, each ranging from 30 to 75 minutes. Activities were designed to use the technology available in Natalie's classroom: a Smartboard, or digitally interactive white board, at the front of the room and iMac computers at each student seat. Multiple opportunities were structured into the project for students to practise and exhibit media literacy skills, for example through short writing assignments such as reflective journal entries and in-class group exercises that entailed analysis of song lyrics. The final assignment consisted of a digital media presentation accompanied by a 500-word essay on the topic "celebrity representations." Student learning was to be assessed on content, demonstration of critical analysis, and production quality (continuity editing, audio editing, graphics, acknowledgment of copyright).

Natalie describes her teaching style as "casual"; following a lesson overview, she facilitates group discussion or group work. Natalie encourages class discussion through group reports, which she uses to identify issues, raise questions, and solicit student opinion, often through a show of hands. Zavi observed "friendly competition among students in various classroom projects, with incentives such as being voted 'the best group skit' or winning a $15 iTunes gift card in a raffle." In keeping with Natalie's teaching style, "Gender Representations in Popular Music" was designed to be participatory more than lecture-based.

The Celebrity Marketing Project

Social Identities

Natalie opened the first session by asking students to consider "social identity," defined as "how you find a sense of membership and belonging in a group." She projected eight cartoon drawings of young people on the whiteboard, each with a different style. She asked students to identify which of the drawings they related to in terms of their own identity: "How would you define yourself? How would you describe your identity to other people? Can you associate yourself with any of these images or these identities on the slide?" The students laughed and chatted with one another, some pointing "That one!" They individually described their identities as Natalie called on them by name: "Who are you, James?" Students answered eagerly, often with mild humour – "beautiful [laughs]," "just normal," "a geek." "A student, 5'1 ... not fabulous," said one girl. The discussion continued as students enthusiastically raised their hands.

Natalie brought the discussion to a close by distinguishing between a personal identity and group identity. Drawing on mode of address, she elaborated how membership in a group can be used in marketing, pointing out how identity implicates categories such as gender, race, and age. For example, when Elizabeth indicated "I am a student," Natalie prompted the class: "Are you just a student? Doris, are you *just* a student? Or are you more than that?" In response, Doris replied "Asian," while a few classmates laughed. Natalie used this moment to emphasize how "social identity is very complicated ... The way you identify yourself has to do with gender, race, class, sexuality, and so on." A handout of relevant terms – including *social identity*, *representation*, and *stereotype* – was distributed.

The class then watched several clips from the documentary *Mickey Mouse Monopoly* (Picker, 2002). When asked how many students were Disney fans, about half of the class threw up their hands. When Natalie asked "why," one girl responded: "It's magical. It makes you feel good about yourself." Natalie prepared the class: "I have to warn you, those of you who *are* Disney fans, you may change your mind [light chuckle]." Students giggled as Natalie started the documentary, but watched intently. While they were very quiet during the clip that discusses racism in Disney films, the students were more talkative when it came to gender representations. Some laughed at the shots of feminine animals and others "awww-ed" at clips of *Snow White*. The documentary led to rich class discussion. Naomi claimed that the documentary "made me sad because you don't realize the subject's going on when you're a kid, but then now, when you watch it, you think, 'Oh, this is so bad.'" Natalie reminded her students that examining something critically "does not mean you cannot enjoy it, just that you are looking more deeply."

For homework, students wrote journal entries reflecting on their response to the film. Natalie asked them what effect the documentary had on their current perception of Disney and to compare the social identities of any two Disney characters (she gave as examples Tarzan versus Ariel, the Hunchback versus Cinderella). Some entries revealed that students were already aware of the ways that race and gender were presented in Disney films. For example, Dean wrote: "I remember distinctly when watching *Peter Pan* how the movie was racist to Native Americans." Other students expressed surprise. Elizabeth wrote in her homework:

> After I watched the documentary *Mickey Mouse Monopoly*, I felt my thoughts about Disney Movies had completely changed. The female characters in Disney movies present a distorted version of femininity – highly sexualized bodies, coy seductiveness, always needing to be rescued by a male ... [in] *Beauty and the Beast*, Belle endures an abusive and violent Beast in order to redeem him. I was shocked when I realized this, as my favourite movie was *Beauty and the Beast*.

The next lesson focused on gender as socially constructed through binaries and stereotyping. To encourage "more of the students' 'own' thoughts," a writing and drawing activity was introduced. Natalie projected instructions onto the white board: "You have just encountered an alien. It wants to know the difference between 'male' and 'female' humans. Use as many words and as much text as you need to describe a male versus female human." She suggested that if they liked, students could "draw them out." The students laughed and chatted among themselves as they worked. Four examples of output are shown in figure 6.1 through figure 6.4.

Celebrity Marketing and Popular Music 119

Figure 6.1. Student drawing to describe a male versus female human

Natalie asked the class to define gender identity; their thinking is reflected in the drawings they eventually produced. Several ideas were voiced in a brainstorming session: relative physical size and strength (see figure 6.1); female as the "opposite of male" (see, e.g., figure 6.2); "genetics" (see figure 6.3); and "what society says we are" (see, e.g., figure 6.4). The students laughed during this discussion, and Zavi noticed a lot of side chatter. One girl said that men have to have facial hair (see figures 6.1, 6.2, and 6.4). Dean asked why the lesson is called "Gender Identity," given that sex and gender are not the same.

As the students did a "gallery walk" to inspect everyone's drawings, Natalie asked if anyone was surprised by what they saw. Dean, who had already protested slippage between "gender" and "sex," continued to be vocal, responding to almost every question that Natalie asked the class. He said he was "disappointed, not surprised" that people don't understand the concept of male and female, a statement greeted by loud guffaws from other male students. Ahmed attempted to alter the sketch that Dean was holding up to show his classmates. After Natalie reprimanded

120 Pop Culture and Power

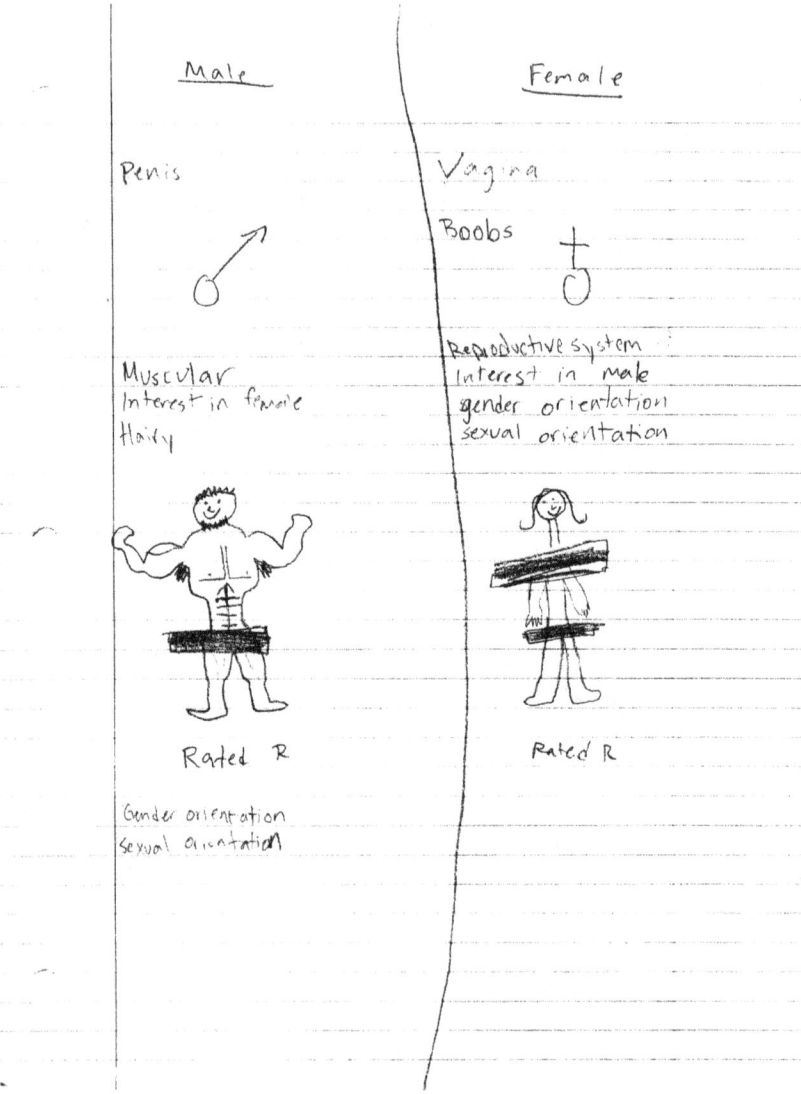

Figure 6.2. Student drawing to describe a male versus female human

the rowdy students, Dean continued, explaining that "male and female applies to all species, not just humans. 'Male' and 'female' means different DNA and, ah, genitals – you know, sexual organs. 'Man' and 'woman' is gender, it's not sex. Sex is about how you reproduce." He indicated that last year someone from a LGBTQ group visited the Grade 10 Planning classes to discuss the differences between sex and gender, but that

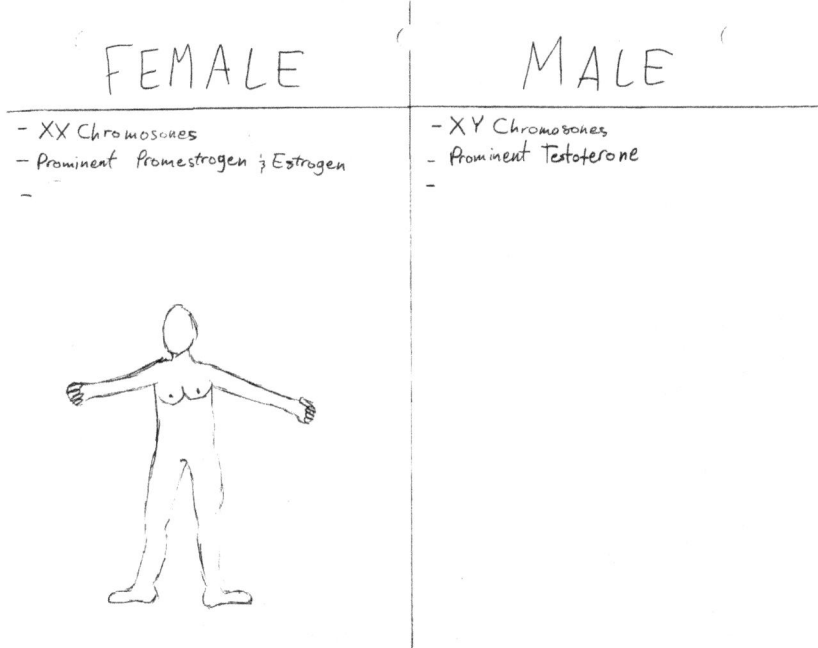

Figure 6.3. Student drawing to describe a male versus female human

"most people forgot." He then gave a spontaneous and lengthy explanation of the difference and went on to define *transsexual* and *transgender*. Natalie encouraged students to connect gender identity to the concept of *social identity*. After defining *gender identity* as one's "personal sense of being a man or a woman," she asked the class to think about the stereotypes they had used in their own work.

Two-minute clips from a children's movie and two documentaries dealing with gender were then shown: *Tangled, Tough Guise,* and *Miss Representation*. Disney's *Tangled* (Conli, Greno, & Howard, 2010) is a 3D computer-animated film about Rapunzel, a spirited teenage girl with an unlikely superpower: 70 feet of magical golden hair. Rapunzel uses her hair to perform many heroic feats that result in her eventual escape from captivity and marriage to the kingdom's most wanted, and most charming, bandit, Flynn Rider. *Tangled* generated class debate on whether the gender roles depicted in this film contradicted or reinforced stereotypes. Clips from *Tough Guise* (Ericsson, Talreja, & Jhally, 1999) connect gender representations in American commercial media to gender-based violence and a "crisis" in masculinity. Examining mass shootings, day-to-day

Figure 6.4. Student drawing to describe a male versus female human

gun violence, violence against women, bullying, gay bashing, and American militarism, lead writer and narrator Jackson Katz draws attention to the violent, sexist, and homophobic messages that boys and young men routinely receive from everyday culture, particularly entertainment media.[2] *Miss Representation* (Newsom, 2011) connects gender representations to issues of gender inequality, exploring how mainstream media contribute to the underrepresentation of women in influential positions by propagating limited and often disparaging portrayals of women. Students were assigned to groups to answer questions about gender identity based on one of the film clips: How is gender constructed by popular media? How does this affect you as a person? How does this influence consumer behaviour?

The results of this activity varied across groups, but there was much repetition, in part because students interpreted "how gender is constructed" as a descriptive rather than analytical question. Some of their descriptions were reminiscent of messages from *Mickey Mouse Monopoly*. Overall, student homework demonstrated comprehension of gender stereotyping. A smaller number of students were also able to discuss how femininity and masculinity, as social constructs, are connected to inequality. Cora and Stella wrote that *Tangled* "makes us feel that we must always be bright, bubbly, strong, and independent – not necessarily a bad thing but ALL the TIME! [Emoticon signifying dismay]." While the groups reporting on *Tangled* claimed that Disney is trying to construct a gender identity for women different from usual stereotypes, students gave little recognition of what we saw as obvious "contradictions" in Disney's effort, specifically, around heterosexual romance.

From Film to Popular Music

The following two lessons employed concepts from the earlier sessions to analyse popular music using "Ice Cream" by the Korean woman artist Hyuna and "Kiss You" by the pop boy band from London, One Direction. Natalie emphasized that the point of this activity was not "personal criticism." She posed a series of questions designed to help students analyse the content of lyrics and ways that celebrity artists represent themselves. These questions drew on the resources introduced for critical discourse analysis in our seminar, although neither Natalie nor Zavi specifically named this exercise as "critical discourse analysis." Instead, they encouraged students to consider:

1. What social identity is this artist trying to create and be recognized as?
2. How is the artist conveying this identity (through dress, language, media platforms used, etc.)?
3. What messages is this artist conveying about their identity in their song? (provide specific lyrical examples)
4. What representations and stereotypes do you see portrayed?
5. Who is the artist expecting their primary audience (target market) to be?
6. Explain why an artist might choose to use different types of social media or media platforms for different audiences.

Several students made sounds of recognition when Natalie showed a slide with the title of the first song, "Ice Cream." The original version (which is primarily in Korean, except for the line "I'll melt you down like ice cream") was compared to a version with English subtitles. Natalie asked the students what they thought the song was about. "So sexual!" cried one girl. "Girls are using their bodies to melt guys down like ice cream," said another girl. Natalie pointed out how sexuality is used as a form of power. She then introduced the video for "Kiss You" and instructed students to "read the imagery" as well as pay attention to the actual lyrics. There was a lot of talking. Natalie elaborated on the questions listed above as she assigned them as homework. Students worked intently in small groups. While the chatter made individual conversations difficult to follow, Dean could be heard criticizing One Direction ("Kiss You") because "they don't write their own songs. They are told what to sing by marketers." As previously, homework demonstrated a range of analytical thinking. There was widespread understanding of how the videos perpetuated stereotypical behaviour connected to gendered (hetero)sexuality.

All the groups interpreted Hyuna as using her sexuality to control men:

> She is trying to be recognized as a very sexual, seductive woman who is heterosexual. Also, she seems to be that one who is in control of any sexual relations she is trying to have through the use of her sexuality. (Naomi, Alice, and Dean)

About half of the groups described this behaviour as stereotyped:

> There is the stereotype that women have to dress provocatively or in a suggestive manner to get the attention of men. Hyuna wears very revealing dresses that show off her legs and shoulders, which grabs the attention of many people. Another one [stereotype] is that women are an object of pleasure because of the way she is dancing and moving her body around men.

All groups saw both men and young women as the intended audience and social media as a logical platform: "They would use YouTube and social networks to approach teens and maybe have links on iTunes and articles on the web to approach adults. Also, they would use their official website to approach diehard fans" (Naomi, Alice, Dean).

Other groups described "Kiss You" as "trying to create an image for guys that they are young, wild and have the power to do whatever they like. They are trying to be recognized as the ideal image for girls and that they can give the girls whatever they want" (Mun Yee, Vicki, Ammar). Although one group reported that "There was nothing stereotypical in this music video," Mun Yee, Vicki, and Ammar identified three stereotypes in the video: "guys are in command; girls listen to what the guys say; guys must be able to give girls everything shown in the video (car/bike/experiences)." As with "Ice Cream," students identified the target audience as "teens and young adults." Again, video was seen as a logical platform because "Everyone has time to go on their social media and check out what is happening with their favourite band/singer/performer/entertainer/celebrity/teachers" (Cora, Stella, Elizabeth).

In the following session, students were instructed to answer the six questions from the previous lesson, using any song that they liked. Groups were given 15 minutes to select songs and prepare answers. As music videos played, Natalie circulated through the room. The songs students chose included "California Gurls" by Katy Perry, "Fine China" by Chris Brown, "Gentlemen" by PSY, and "Thrift Shop" by Macklemore. Due to time constraints, only one group presented (Mun Yee, Ammar, Zian). When asked during their presentation why they had chosen "California Gurls," Mun Yee answered "for a really strong image [of women] ... very sexual, very provocative." When Natalie asked how males were represented, the group had more difficulty with their answers. "California Gurls" was described as perpetuating the view that "California girls are all 'toned, tanned, fit and ready' and only those girls are pretty and attractive." This group argued: "Everyone else is fat [by comparison] ... The message is that girls can attract guys by being provocative." This kind of answer was repeated across student homework. All groups identified stereotyping in the songs they had chosen, without always analysing how gender inequality is represented in pop music.

Celebrity Representations: Student Redesigns

Lessons culminated in the final assignment, "Celebrity Representations," with the remaining sessions dedicated to preparing and presenting group projects. Because Celebrity Marketing was designed to make the topic of media literacy relevant to the marketing curriculum, the questions designed for media analysis earlier had invited students to consider how the construction of a social identity might relate to marketing strategies, such as identifying and appealing to a target audience. Group projects would be the basis for assessing how well students had achieved the learning intended for the entire project: "understanding how gender and other social identities are constructed in popular culture; exploring the role that different media platforms have in transmitting social messages; and critically analysing the impact that celebrity representations have on social perceptions of gender." Students were given the following guidelines for their projects:

Choose one topic/strategy from 1–3 (or if you have another idea, have it approved by the teacher first):

1. Rewrite and/or re-film a parody to the song to include a new/different message about gender norms:

- Flip/subvert the gender norms being shown and/or
- Highlight something positive or important for teens to focus on
2. Create an interpretive music video using the same music (and lyrics)
   - Create a mash-up video (of different clips) to point out and discuss gender norms in music videos/music lyrics
   - Compare and critically examine images, music, and videos from a male artist and a female artist
   - Identify a common gender stereotype marketed in popular music and create a video that challenges it (e.g., challenge the representation of a woman as a "damsel in distress")
3. Create a fictitious celebrity who brings positive messages to his/her audience. Include a personal profile, an interview with him or her, and an example of a song/part of a song he/she has released.

Each group was required to turn in a 500-word essay discussing how gender differences are constructed in pop music and what impact these constructions might have on consumers. Students were reminded to use the media analysis tools that they had practised throughout the project.

Students worked in six self-selected groups, with four to five students per group. Except for one all-girl group, the groups were mixed gender. Most students chose Option 2 and female musicians, leading Zavi to worry that "the students are overly associating discussion of 'gender' with women, rather than recognizing that men and masculinity should also be examined and discussed." Students showed a high level of interest in the assignment as they chose their artists. Groups continued to play pop music on their computers throughout the remaining work sessions, even after they had selected songs for their final project. There were, however, several unexpected challenges. Both Natalie and Zavi had believed that giving students total freedom in selecting the artists and songs, as well as media to work with that they enjoyed, would encourage involvement, hence deepen learning. One unanticipated problem was that most groups struggled to commit to a specific song or artist.

Choosing the type of media presentation was also a challenge. In their original plan, Natalie and Zavi had envisioned that all groups would produce short videos. In her original lesson plan, Natalie had written: "The unit will culminate in a final creative project where groups of students create parody or 'mash-up' videos that examine and analyse gender representations in popular music." Natalie and Zavi both expected that students would most likely use video format because music videos are the main format for pop artists and because of the digitally advanced set-up of their classroom. They also assumed that students would find editing and making a video to be the most "fun" option. Contrary to these expectations, only one of the six groups produced a video. Three groups chose to create multimedia PowerPoint presentations that included text, photos, and embedded video clips. The other two groups chose to "flip" a song's meaning by rewriting the lyrics.

There were several factors that may have caused groups to opt out of video production for their final project. Despite all the in-class work sessions, selecting a topic and deciding how to focus analysis did not allow enough time to create a complex digital production. Students were much less tech-savvy than either Natalie or Zavi had anticipated. Because the students were all in an age range where they had grown up with computer and internet technology, and because they attended a school that offered advanced digital resources and classes, both Natalie and Zavi assumed that the students would not have any trouble making short videos. While the students were overall quite proficient in conducting online research, creating PowerPoint presentations, and using social media websites such as YouTube, the majority struggled to format and edit video material.

"Celebrity Representations" resulted in six group projects:

- Group 1: Beyoncé – produced two mash-up videos that feature feminist and non-feminist excerpts from various songs; their presentation compared the two types of messages (Zian, Maria, Audrey, Claire, Mun Yee);
- Group 2: Rihanna – a PowerPoint presentation of edited lyrics to challenge gender representations in the song "Take a Bow," shown against the original soundtrack (Cora, Amanda, Stella, Elizabeth);
- Group 3: Beyoncé versus Kanye West – a PowerPoint presentation contrasting male and female gender representations in "Run the World" and "That's My Girl" (note: students replaced the word "bitch" with "girl" in the song's original title, wanting to avoid "profanity") (Ben, William, Rose, Lana, Jason);
- Group 4: Usher versus Lady Gaga – a PowerPoint presentation contrasting male and female gender representations; their presentation raised questions about whether music videos have a "negative" or a "positive" effect on youth (Anna, Vicki, Andy, Dean);
- Group 5: Taylor Swift – a PowerPoint parody of "We Are Never Ever Getting Back Together" challenging gender representations in this song (Simon, Ammar, Alice, Naomi);
- Group 6: Justin Bieber versus Carly Rae Jepsen – a mash-up video of clips contrasting male and female gender representations in the music of these two artists (Ahmed, Raymond, Doris, Marco, James).

Both class presentations and homework essays were organized around the six questions introduced for media analysis. Presentations focused on how gender identities are constructed through the artists' dress and performance and the social significance of this construction for youth, while a few groups attempted to offer "alternative" lyrics that they claimed were more gender equal.

While initial planning had allocated 10 minutes for each final presentation, this plan did not anticipate difficulties students encountered with the technical aspects of their presentations. These difficulties had shown themselves during sessions when students were preparing their presentations. Many students did not understand how to digitally connect to or use the interactive Smartboard. Many also struggled with other basic technical skills, such as how to start and stop video and audio clips, or had difficulty adjusting the volume during their final presentations. Addressing technical problems was so time-consuming that the presentations took much longer than planned, resulting in less time for in-depth analysis.

Despite frustrations caused by these kinds of delays, students were intently engaged in their presentations. Several students in the audience made sounds of recognition as songs played. They could be observed bobbing their heads in time to the music, and two girls sang along to Beyoncé's "Love on Top." Overall, students had no difficulty describing how the self-presentations of artists in the videos contribute to gender stereotyping. Across different groups, stereotyping was described in terms of the artist's dress:

> The marketing of male and female artists is substantially different, although their target markets may be similar. In terms of appearance, female artists often dress outlandishly to flaunt their individuality and wealth (Nicki Minaj), or end up barely dressing at all (Beyoncé). Overall, standard conventions of what is proper or pretty are ignored by these artists; instead, they do what will attract the most attention and reinforce their uniqueness. Male artists are usually more moderate in the way they dress. They often stress their wealth and sense of adventure in the way they market themselves, which appeals greatly to youth. (Group 1)

As well as understanding how dress contributes to gender stereotyping, Group 4 discussed differences in song topics and lyrical content:

> Male artists tend to be shallow when they sing about women or when in love. They address women as an object and sing about how a female's appearance is what makes the males fall in love. Male artists rarely sing about

friendship or family because those topics do not do justice to their "image"; they would be considered unmanly.

… On the other hand, females would not just sing about a male's appearance but more of how they treat females. Occasionally, they produce a positive song that could be about a girl's self-esteem or about family. They would not go into great detail about a male's appearance like the way male artist do about females. In most of Lady Gaga's songs, she sings about herself or about God more than she does about males. In her song "Born This Way," Lady Gaga refers to men like an equal, "No matter gay, straight, or bi, lesbian, transgendered life, I'm on the right track baby, I was born to survive." Therefore, male artists are admired for their status while females are admired for their art.

This group wrote: "The songs and lyrics artists produce are narrowing the way people think."

Students also described how gendered relations, particularly romantic relationships, are represented in popular music: "Often, in song lyrics and videos, the female is portrayed as the one who is hurt in a relationship, or whose heart is broken. Also, for both genders, it seems like they need a girl or a guy to satisfy them and make them happy" (Group 1). This sentiment was common, as illustrated by Group 5:

Popular music constructs and enforces gender roles that males are usually aggressive in love while females are usually passive … I am told from popular music that males are aggressive in finding girlfriends, when a couple break up, the male will usually not do reflection and find a new girlfriend very soon. I think that these identities will make teenagers think that all males and all females are like that but actually it isn't. E.g. There are passive males and aggressive females actually.

Students also recognized that the double standard promoted in mainstream culture influences the marketability of artists:

Since female and male artists are marketed differently, it would also be different for the two different genders to achieve success. Male artists need to start off with a good image to maintain popularity in order to be successful; regardless if the male artist has a bad image while they are famous, the fans will still support them. For example, Justin Bieber started off with a good child image, but recently he has been seen smoking marijuana, which gives him a bad image. Even though his bad image has been revealed, his fans are still loyal to him … Similar to males, female artists become successful if they start with a good image. However, females have to keep a good image throughout their career or else their fan base will drop. For example, Britney Spears had a wide fan base when she first entered the entertainment industry; however, now she is known to be a drug abuser that enters and leaves rehab centres, giving her a small fan base. (Group 6)

Students agreed that music is a "huge part of our culture ... Many people look up to artists and celebrities as a standard and as trendsetters" (Group 1). As a result, "Media, especially music, has the power to [shape] how we view each other and ourselves" (Group 1). Group 5, who had chosen Taylor Swift, noted:

With all the different variety of singers and music, everyone has someone to look up to and inspire them. Although some of the new music artists are not a good example for our generation, Taylor Alison Swift, a country singer that has won over millions of people across the nation, is someone everyone can look up to.

In contrast to this view that celebrities can have a positive impact, there was a widespread sentiment across groups that the marketing of the kind of music videos explored in this project is "bad" for youth. As well as promoting consumption, popular music was seen to encourage harmful notions of gender and gender relations: "Young female teens are being told they are replaceable if they don't look like Victoria's Secret angels, and males are told they have to act a certain way to chase after girls" (Group 4).

Within the context of the earlier lessons, it is not surprising that students tended to focus on the "dangers" of gender stereotyping. The sexually provocative dress of female performers, especially, served to reinforce the kinds of comments we have seen in the students' earlier homework. Group 1 described Beyoncé's self-presentation as a contradiction to her avowed feminist identity. They reasoned that her "sexy clothes and stereotypical role of a woman in the kitchen [an image in one of the videos], giving her all to a man, contradicts this [identity]." Group 3, incorporating Beyoncé's "Run the World" into their presentation, argued that while "Beyoncé is promoting herself as a strong, independent woman in this song, her provocative clothes somewhat take away from the message."

Perhaps more telling is one group's interpretation of the project guidelines to construct a "parody" by "flip[ping]/subvert[ing] the gender norms being shown." Group 5 played a clip of the song "We Are Never Ever Getting Back Together," accompanied by a PowerPoint presentation. The intention of this group was to rewrite the Taylor Swift song to subvert gender norms. The audio for the song played the original version, but the group subtitled the clip with their new lyrics. As the music played, one group member explained that the new version of the song flips gender norms because the rewritten version is based on the perspective of a guy telling a girl that she is being creepy and over-controlling (as opposed to the original, where a girl explains this to a guy that she doesn't want to get back together with). In their rewritten version of the song, the girl wants to do whatever it takes to get back together. One girl in the group explained how they are accentuating a woman's powers over a man:

> The male is usually portrayed as the stronger, more powerful person in the relationship so, in this one, we have changed it so that the woman has more power over the guy by keeping him in her basement. So, overall, in the whole song we have changed it from a guy wanting to go back together with the girl, to the girl wanting to keep the guy forever and not letting him go.

The group did not provide any deeper analysis about the gender relations in the original or new song.[3]

Only one group took their analysis deeper than a "literal" reading of video representations. This group began by comparing Lady Gaga's look as "odd and different" to Usher, who they claimed looks like "a regular male artist." In the context of this difference, the group considered Usher's lyrics to be "shallow because all he sings about is a girl's physical appearance" (Dean). On the other hand, Vicki noted that Lady Gaga makes a positive difference through her foundation, "Born This Way," which empowers youth by "helping kids with self-confidence." In Usher's defence, Andy pointed out: "even though Usher's lyrics may not be meaningful, he still has a charity called Usher's New Hope Foundation." Dean concluded their presentation:

> The music industry changes regular and talented people into a package of what they do not seem to be. Even though this does not relate to gender representation, we wanted to show that no matter *who* you are, there is always good inside people, just like the cliché "don't judge a book by its cover." We shouldn't judge artists and celebrities because they are *told* what to do. (Group 4)

Their presentation thus offered an opportunity to take analysis further by questioning the practices through which music videos are produced; unfortunately, time constraints terminated the discussion.

In summary, student redesigns of music videos illustrate both the potential and the pitfalls of using pop music to foster critical media literacy.

Below we identify the challenges and opportunities experienced in the Celebrity Marketing Project specifically, and in exploring the gendered nature of pop culture more generally.

Promoting Critical Media Literacy through Gendered Pop Music

Gainer (2007) describes "complex literacy transactions" (p. 107) when youth engage with popular music. While his nine-year-old daughter easily identified the heterosexism in her favourite pop music, she subverted its message by simply replacing "he" with "she" (p. 111); rather than dismiss her response as "mistaken," Gainer draws attention to the pleasure that youth can experience in "righting a wrong." Like him, as an experience of exercising power-to, we see this pleasure as a potential invitation to engage youth in the politics of social change. The challenge is to harness this pleasure to an understanding of pop music as a venue for the operation of power.

The pleasure of working with famous artists was visible throughout the Celebrity Marketing Project: students could be observed singing along to lyrics or bobbing their heads in recognition of familiar tunes. While students easily identified gender stereotypes employed by various entertainers, with hindsight student focus on celebrities encouraged them to attend to the artists' self-presentation rather than the production practices demanded by music as a commodity. This focus may have been encouraged by Natalie's interest in celebrities (recall Miriam Yeung). After presenting PSY's "Gangnam Style" during our seminar, as a potential focus for her project, Natalie remarked:

> ... perhaps I'll use "Gangnam Style" or another song, and I'll analyse the messages in that song using these sorts of questions, inspired by Gee's identity building and mode of address tools: What sort of social identity is *the artist trying to create, and be recognized as? How is the artist conveying this identity? Through the way that they're dressed or the language they use* or the medium platforms? (Emphasis added)

In retrospect, because stereotyping takes the form of representation, the project was framed in ways that may have encouraged analysis of individual celebrity performances. Perhaps ironically, Natalie's original choice of K-pop could have helped redirect student attention towards issues that accompany music popularized through a commodity market. Describing celebrity culture as "an economic and social system," Gamson (2015), for example, points out that celebrity performances are the result of "the exigencies of controlling the production and marketing" of their music

(p. 276). Given its appeal among Natalie's students, K-pop would offer a compelling case study of the corporate control of pop stars, through its well-documented practices such as "slave contracts," 20-hour workdays, requirements for plastic surgery – among young women but, increasingly, among young men, too (CBC Docs, 2019) – sexual exploitation, and so on. This might include an exploration of *internalized racism*, because the beauty standards inspired by K-pop stars – wide eyes, small noses, and angled chins for women and "pretty boy" aesthetics for men (CBC Docs, 2019, para. 4) – are made possible through plastic surgery (Stone, 2013).[4]

At least a handful of students connected stereotyping to the demands of commercial production. Dean, for example, was heard criticizing One Direction because "they don't write their own songs. They are told what to sing by marketers." These kinds of comments suggest that although they did not explicitly analyse it, some students recognized how commercial culture normalizes and emphasizes the kind of stereotypes they identified as "problematic." An interrogation of media production could help students recognize how an emphasis on heterosexuality by studio producers shapes the agency of female performers exercising their power to challenge their marginalization (for further discussion, see Lieb, 2018).

While we do not dismiss stereotyping as an invitation to critical media literacy, below we explore the challenges that such a focus brought to the Celebrity Marketing Project as well as strategies for taking learning deeper than critique of media content, especially when that content is highly sexualized. We supplement data generated during learning activities with written unit evaluations by students and a focus group discussion that Dawn and Deirdre held with six participants – both completed after the project was concluded. Our plan was to include both male and female students in the focus groups. When students were invited to participate, only girls volunteered, however – a potential comment on the gendered dynamics of media activities such as those described in this chapter.

Lessons for the Celebrity Marketing Project were framed in terms of stereotyping to prompt critical reflection about the influence of pop music on youth. Keying off the documentaries shown to initiate this project, students had no difficulty in recognizing how stereotypes (specifically, gendered ones) are incorporated into celebrities' music performances:

> In the music industry males are being constructed and enforced as great dancers and being able to sing really well ... In comparison to the marketing strategy used for males, female artists are marketed through their body and sexual appearance. Female artists generally wear less clothes, in which the clothes they wear are more revealing than males. The clothes female

artists wear include mini skirts, tank tops, low-cut tops, and short-shorts. Female artists wear more colourful clothing that shows more skin because it attracts the eyes of men. (Group 6)

When asked what they had learned about the potential influence of pop music, students wrote in their evaluations of the unit:

Media gives us a narrow box to fit within. (Stella, Zian)
Women are undermined in media. (Anna, Naomi, Amanda)
Highly sexualized men and women are good marketing assets. (William)
We are actually very aware of these existing stereotypes and gender roles, yet sometimes we still conform to them. (Mun Yee)

We have seen above that Group 4 recognized the contrived nature of video performances. Little student work, however, moved beyond criticism of gender representations. Most of the students concluded that gender stereotyping was "bad" for young people, especially sexually provocative representations of women. Only Group 5 chose an artist for their final assignment whom they claimed young people can "look up to and [who can] inspire them" (Taylor Swift).[5] Individually, though, Zian – a first-generation immigrant and the only male member of Group 1 – connected his learning to social justice:

I also noticed artists (Beyoncé) who challenge the status quo of pop culture. They represent and in terms of media spearhead the growing numbers of people who believe in gender equality – both in terms of rights and power in relationships.

Students had much less, if anything, to say about racialized stereotypes or the racialization of feminine or masculine celebrity images, which is curious given the ethnic backgrounds of the students and their interest in the analysis of race in the documentary they had watched on Disney.

During discussion with Dawn and Deirdre, participants indicated that they had never had "anything like this" (discussions of gender in pop culture) in other classes. Nevertheless, when asked what might be "new," there was general agreement that focus group participants were already aware of how pop music perpetuates stereotyping. This knowledge was characterized as being "dormant" in their minds:

NAOMI: It makes you realize more about gender stereotyping in society, like sex appeal and stuff. You don't really think about it when you're just listening to it. But when you're actually analysing it, you realize what you missed.

ALICE: You don't learn anything new, you just realize it, 'cause I think we knew it before, but it's just in the back of your mind.

This response does not mean that class time spent on the project simply replicated what these girls already knew. Class activities offered an opportunity for critical reflection:

MUN YEE: This stereotyping we talked about in class, we just kind of accept it for what it is.

AUDREY: It's kind of shocking, though. We just kind of subconsciously absorb all of this in media and pop culture, and when you actually take a step back and analyse it – sexist and racist stereotypes in commercials and even in the news. It's shocking.

In this excerpt, we hear the girls saying that it is not stereotyping itself that is shocking, but rather the way that it had become normalized as a "fact" of dominant culture for them. In this way, troubling the everyday acceptance of stereotyping in pop music furthers one of the goals of critical media literacy: denaturalizing what has become taken for granted. The challenge is to promote an understanding of the *social* processes through which this naturalization happens. In effect, such an understanding would require students to question, and criticize, the market itself. Taking the topic of "stereotyping" beyond ideology critique, Natalie's initial idea – which was not very different from Yvette's – was for her young learners to connect what they saw as the negative impact of pop culture to marketing practices. Only one group took their analysis in this direction. We recognize the constraints imposed by the mandated curriculum of Natalie's class (Marketing). Putting that constraint aside for the moment, what lessons can we take from teaching about the gendered nature of pop culture – a topic that Liz, an experienced media educator, called her "biggest challenge ever"?

Given the lack of background in gender studies among most of the students in this project, introducing gender stereotyping was a useful entry point: it offers a tool to challenge biological essentialism, opening the door for social analysis. One problem, however, is that most student work correlated gender with sexed bodies (see figures 6.2 and 6.3, for examples). As evident in student drawings, while students recognized femininity and masculinity as social constructions, they did not question the association of femininity with female bodies and masculinity with male bodies, a move that normalizes heterosexuality and cisgender identity (i.e., that people express their gender according to their sex assigned at birth). The notable exception was Dean, who was able to draw on previous learning when guest speakers from a local LGBTQ community group visited the school. As he differentiated *sex* and *gender* for his classmates, the subtext of his intervention also addressed the way that sex and gender become blurred through the assumption of heterosexuality (made explicit in figure 6.2), what Judith Butler (1990) calls the *heterosexual matrix* (p. 208).[6] Much of what students described as "gender stereotyping" refers to the sexualization of gender, specifically femininity through women's bodies. Ingraham (1994) points out that this way of thinking conceals the normalization of heterosexuality, closing off critical analysis of sexuality as an organizing principle of social inequality (pp. 203–4). While we recognize that sexuality is not always a topic that teachers are prepared to discuss – or, indeed, administratively able to do – we suggest that much of the difficulty in teaching youth about gender by using pop culture stems from silence surrounding the topic of heterosexuality as socially, and not simply biologically, shaped. In Natalie's project, this silence foreclosed discussion of sexuality as a "mode of address" – a topic relevant to understanding how music videos "hail" young people as a marketing strategy.[7]

When sexuality operates but remains unanalysed in classroom discussion, students may fail to recognize that the feminist artists they are being asked to critique often play with the heterosexual matrix; their embodied performances can be a strategy to deconstruct femininity as the heterosexualized object of the male gaze. Exaggerated gender performances, such as those by Beyoncé, can be read as reversing conventional heterosexual roles as a strategy to bring the double standard of heterosexuality into view. While virtually all the student groups recognized – and criticized – this standard, they failed to recognize its parody in artistic performances, such as those by Beyoncé. Instead, both Group 3 and Group 4 maintained that Beyoncé's on-stage performance contradicts her claim to a feminist identity: Group 3 based this conclusion on Beyoncé's "provocative" clothing.

One lesson here is that unlike advertisements – discussed in the following chapter – music is more than simply a marketing product driven by the profit motive. Music is also a venue for political messaging, particularly for feminist musicians. To understand their messaging, a deeper analysis of their music requires knowledge of both the political biography of the artist and the political context that they address. From this perspective, analysis could be deepened through exploration of music as a venue of youth "rebellion" (e.g., a history of rock 'n' roll). Such an exploration could direct discussion away from the "bad influences" of pop culture by drawing attention to pop music as a venue for the exercise of power in support of social change. Listening to Beyoncé in a context that celebrates women's empowerment will result in a different decoding of her lyrics from listening with a conventional understanding of gender stereotyping. Such a reading might have perhaps been more in keeping with Natalie's own belief, stated in the opening of this chapter, that "celebrities can also have a positive impact on teenagers."

As we have seen, it is not so much that students in this project were unaware that sexuality is deployed in music videos: for example, written work by students typically described women artists (such as Hyuna in "Ice Cream") as "overly sexualized" (Claire, Doris, and Audrey). Naomi, Alice, and Dean argued that Hyuna is portrayed as "the one in control of any sexual relations she is trying to have through the use of her sexuality." They went on to claim that through her sexualized performance, Hyuna is "trying to be recognized as a modern and cool popular icon." These kinds of comments suggest that students recognized the female body as a cultural icon for sex. Interrogating how heterosexuality is normalized in this way would enable learners to recognize how marketing practices shape the agency of female performers. This recognition, in turn, draws attention to the struggle facing women performers who, through their artistry, attempt to challenge gender stereotyping in a context where commercial interests hold power-over music production.

During the focus group, we became aware of further examples of how gendered dynamics entered this project. Specifically, the girls we met with maintained that there were differences in what the boys, compared to the girls, took away from the class presentations:

> But what I noticed – what the boys noticed, and what the girls noticed in the presentations was different. Mostly the girls were looking at the message and what the video said and what the presenter said. But then from the guys, all I heard was comments about the nice car, or the pretty girl in the video [others laugh]. So, I don't know if they [the boys] paid attention, or realized the message. (Alice)

From this perspective, the gendered reception of popular music by students could be a jumping-off point to deepen media literacy through concepts such as *mode of address* and *interpellation* (employed in the following case study). We speculate that this kind of discussion could enhance the everyday relevance of this project by encouraging students to question more explicitly how music videos work to shape personal identities as well as shaping youth culture. It would also enable students to reflect on their affective investment in specific performers. Because these tools raise questions about *who* is being addressed, they draw attention to *how* lyrics might appeal to different listeners. Recognition of diversity in media reception has the potential to move students beyond monolithic claims about the universally "bad" influences of pop culture.[8]

At the same time, the gendered dynamic of the classroom itself provided a missed opportunity to forge links between media analysis and students' everyday experiences. In looking back at his field notes, Zavi became aware that the male students spoke up more than the female students, even though the girls slightly outnumbered the boys. (Researchers have been noticing this gendered pattern at least since Sadker and Sadker [1994] declared girls to be "missing in [classroom] interaction.") As a classroom guest, it was easier for Zavi to learn the names of the male than the female students. Despite Natalie's emphasis on inclusivity and Zavi's background as a feminist researcher, it is apparent from reviewing the videos that a handful (not all) of male students took up more "public space" during classroom discussions. This does not mean that the girls were silenced; rather, they tended to talk quietly among themselves a lot during the videoed sessions. The boys' relative monopolization of public space is not a classroom dynamic that is unique to the Marketing class (for an update of their earlier research and that of others, see Sadker, Sadker, & Zittleman, 2009); rather, it reflects existing gender privilege. Recognition of this privilege as it presents itself offers a "teachable moment." Such a moment emerged when Natalie asked for the names of the groups. Group 6 indicated that they were called "Raymond and the Boys." Natalie asked what this meant for Doris, the one girl in the group, and one of the boys yelled, "She's a boy, too!" The group debated among themselves and then changed their group name to "Doris and the Boys." Considering the project's focus on gender, in retrospect it would have been appropriate to examine these kinds of everyday dynamics in the classroom, as part of learning about the social context of meaning making.

The gender dynamics are likely even more complex than the above anecdote suggests. We reviewed all field notes and video clips again, after we had learned the names of all students, focusing on which boys dominated and how. It became clear that there were three patterns of interaction among the boys. First, there was a group of five sports-oriented boys who liked to joke around and occasionally shout out answers; their behaviour could be disruptive, and Natalie had to discipline them occasionally. James, for example, during a full-class discussion of gender identity, jokily exclaimed, "Mr. Kaur's [the student teacher's] my knight in shining armour!"

Two boys, Dean and Jason, appeared to be more academic and would frequently volunteer answers to questions posed by Natalie. A third group consisted of five boys with a quieter style, more akin to that of most girls in the class. They participated but did not tend to volunteer answers unless called upon.[9] Arguably, this latter group got the most out of the unit. In their final unit evaluations, Zian, the self-described "geek," wrote, "I liked this unit! ... The topic of celebrities should pertain to me [as a teen], but as a rather backwards and isolated individual, I didn't naturally know so much on the subject." Simon, who spoke English as an Additional Language (EAL), agreed, noting: "it reminds us that we should have our own thoughts when we deal with popular culture." Natalie had been concerned that first-generation immigrant students like Zian and Simon might not be familiar with North American pop culture and therefore she would have to "keep them engaged." Zian's and Simon's learning illustrates the complexity of media reception.

Deepening the learning components of the Celebrity Marketing Project in ways we suggest above would expand the analytical content of this project but also, admittedly, necessitate more class time. Given that time management can be a challenge for teachers, some aspects of the project as described in this chapter could be shortened. Time was lost because student groups had difficulty choosing topics for their final assignments and dealing with technology. The original reason for giving students complete freedom of choice of music was the belief that they would enjoy the project most if they were personally engaged with the songs or artist for their final assignment. Natalie and Zavi believed that pleasure would facilitate learning; that students would exhibit more curiosity and passion when engaging with media that "spoke" to them. While this belief may be common among teachers using pop culture in the classroom, it may be misplaced. Focus group discussion revealed that students in this study did not necessarily choose favourite artists and songs, as Natalie and Zavi might have expected:

> MUN YEE: For this project, I feel like we were completing it just for the sake of doing the project and getting the marks. We didn't realize we would have to think so deep. We just gave stereotypical answers [the room became quiet].
> NAOMI: We didn't pick favourites [others nod in agreement]. We just picked songs that had, like, really strong stereotypes.

These comments suggest that it might have been more productive to work with music that *resonates* with youth (by forming part of their everyday experience) but does not ask students to "criticize" favourite artists.

Although there was variety in the celebrity images and musical genres of the artists finally chosen – ranging from Lady Gaga to Kanye West – none of the student groups selected less well known or independent artists.[10] This may have happened because music preference is seen as a signifier of identity, particularly among young people. While it was apparent that students enjoyed and were familiar with the songs they examined, because final projects were conducted in groups and because students presented these projects to the entire class, it might have been difficult for a student to speak up about an "alternative" music choice for fear of judgment by their peers. Given the participatory format employed for class discussion, students publicly accounted for their choices and preferences. Natalie often encouraged class participation through, for example, an "opinion poll" with a show of hands. Students were also encouraged to applaud group reports. While we ourselves often employ such an informal teaching style, class approval potentially signals peer approval of individual student use of pop culture to construct their sense of self; in short, media choice can be construed as evaluation of one's "taste" and hence social standing. Choosing artists who are not "cool" among youth, for example, could mark one as "outside" peer culture.

This challenge demonstrates how media activities in the classroom must consider how cultural production by students might be received by an audience of peers. Having a list of artists for students to choose from would alleviate possible distress for any student concerned about what their musical choice might convey about their personal identity. A list could be compiled during a classroom brainstorm of current popular artists whose target audience is youth. We also suggest that projects requiring media production be informed by concepts used for audience analysis: *mode of address* (how social identity is used to address young people) and *interpellation* (how our personal identity is being "hailed"), for example. These tools, discussed in the following chapter, help connect the critic to the text, potentially enabling deeper reflexivity about *social identity* as not simply a generalized cultural construction but also our personal sense of "who we are." Such a line of inquiry highlights the political nature of music, something that was inadvertently bracketed by the focus on marketing.

A further recommendation would be to simplify the technological expectations of group projects. Even though ISS is a school that offers up-to-date technology and digital resources, it was evident that prerequisite skills were needed in technology use that most students in this project did not possess. Even as a teacher and a university student who both considered themselves to be tech-savvy, Natalie and Zavi struggled to assist students with video production; the technological limitations visibly frustrated students. Natalie decided that if she taught this project again, she would do so after a tutorial on using iMovie, and she would start with a younger group, such as her Grade 10 computer class. Otherwise, while it is necessary to have access to a computer with internet capabilities to research and view music videos, the final project could have employed simpler technology – such as making an infographic or PowerPoint slideshow – or take the form of a non-digital art project.

It was evident throughout this project that students took pleasure in listening to pop music in the classroom; they continuously played songs during the four workdays, bobbed their heads to the music, and sometimes sang along. Upon reflection, we all agreed that framing a project around music as a form of pop culture is an excellent way to open the door to youth media literacy. But we are aware of the difference between what is theoretically ideal and what is pedagogically possible in the context of public schooling. Although the gender work we hoped to see during the Celebrity Marketing Project did not always materialize, the cultural production required by the final assignment fostered students' sense of agency in meaning making – as the exercise of "power-to" and "power-with" – a desirable outcome in itself. At the same time, throughout this project students negotiated meaning from YouTube images, music, written lyrics, and bodily gestures. In this sense, they were engaged in the multiliteracies practised in their everyday, out-of-school lives.

Conclusion

The popularity of music videos as everyday entertainment for youth makes them a relevant venue for enhancing critical media literacy. The pleasure that these videos generated among students was evident throughout Natalie's project. Initially, both Natalie and Zavi expected that this pleasure would be harnessed to remixing videos as a "fun" learning experience. As active meaning makers, the students would learn through remix, as they blended "understandings based in prior knowledge and experience with new information as they construct new understandings from textual transactions" (Gainer & Lapp, 2010, p. 58). This expectation, however, did not always materialize. More than in other projects, we observed frustration as well as pleasure, much of it due to the technical nature of video production.

Difficulties in using technology were not the only challenge. Owing to their multimodal form, music videos are an excellent, but complex, venue for teaching critical media literacy. In Natalie's project, this complexity did not arise simply from the multimodal form or sexualized content of music videos, but also from the commodification of musical performance. Many students attributed the gendered practices they analysed to individual performers during class discussion, but, as voiced by Dean, these artists do not exercise total control over production of their videos: artists work within the confines of the music industry. In retrospect, the complexity of celebrity marketing cannot be captured by a focus on video performances as "representations." Such a focus brackets much of what happens "behind the scenes": the social relations of video production as exercising power-over artists, practices designed to address specific audiences identified by studio owners, conflict surrounding intellectual property rights, regulation of the music industry, and so on. These factors, and many more, mediate artistic creation and the artist's commodified performance. Discussion of them would have deepened student learning about how the artistic work of music celebrities is marketed.

A teachable moment for such a discussion was lost when Zian pointed out, during his group's presentation, that Beyoncé was also "Sasha Fierce" – her onstage alter ego – who he claimed is "not anything like she [Beyoncé] is portrayed in these videos." While this comment was not taken up during class discussion, his final assessment of the project evidenced learning that connected critical media literacy to social justice: Zian was among the few students who claimed that artists, such as Beyoncé, challenge the status quo, spearheading a growing movement for gender equality in the media industry. His comment, in particular, takes critical media literacy deeper than critique of gender representation.

In the final analysis, the Celebrity Marketing Project drew our attention to the backstage practices shaping music production as required for a critical analysis of video content. Giving visibility to these practices connects music videos, as discursive features of our cultural landscape, to the materiality of their economic and social production. The Celebrity Marketing Project thus helped deepen our thinking about the nature of a distinctly *social* approach for critical media literacy, elaborated in chapter 9.

7 Are You Being Hailed? Advertising as a Venue for Critical Media Literacy

DAWN H. CURRIE, DEIRDRE M. KELLY, AND AMY CLAUSEN

This generation seems so savvy with media creation and the web (YouTube, Photoshop, iMovie, and other easy media creation and dissemination tools) ... but what do these tools mean to them? Do they feel empowered by their savviness? Are they in a better/more powerful position than I was when I was a teenager in the mid-nineties?

– Amy, journalling before the seminar

When joining our seminar, Amy described "the biggest contradiction in my media life so far":

> When I feel particularly exhausted or drained or selfish, I enjoy watching hours of "guilty pleasures" and feeling my brain turn off completely ... It is a difficult thing to admit that I can watch hours of programming like *Say Yes to the Dress*, a parade of nervous brides-to-be spending thousands of dollars on big white dresses for traditional marriage ceremonies [that symbolize consumerism and heteronormativity].

Given her guilty pleasure in *Say Yes to the Dress*, it is perhaps instructive that, during the seminar, Amy identified Disney Princesses as a "particularly insipid example of the kind of multi-platform branding that targets very young children." Based on her awareness of the seductive power of media, Amy advocates media literacy among youth as a highly targeted audience. She believes that it is never too early to ask children about the media they see around them. While very young children may not be able to develop critical capacities, "asking a child to describe a picture helps them see all its parts, and can be a first step to visual literacy in other media."

Amy maintained that knowing when you are being targeted is an important life skill. Regardless of whether the message concerns consumption (e.g., a beauty product aimed at teen or "tween" girls), politics (e.g., a political party, a cause, or a charity speaking directly to young people aimed at influencing their parents' spending habits), or entertainment (e.g., music and film targeting youth), young people should be equipped to explore the message in order to understand its appeal. Attempting to "protect" youth by simply dismissing the kinds of texts they enjoy also dismisses the meaning, value, and pleasure they derive from these media. Like adults, young people do not mindlessly consume media; they *use* media (see Moje & van Helden, 2005). It is common for youth to display their own meaning making through appropriation and recycling of fashion and popular music, for example. Their displays are not necessarily evidence of manipulation, but a demonstration of their agency. In this spirit, Amy views contemporary youth as a generation with "brand new ways to enter into conversations with mass-market media." For her, teaching for social justice includes enhancing young people's recognition of the political role, broadly defined, that media play in the shaping of their worlds. The intention of her project was to help youth challenge that role through their media production.

Participants

Prior to our project, Amy co-founded and co-facilitated a Youth Art Initiative (YAI) at Vancouver Design Academy and the Vancouver Art Gallery. Unlike the previous three cases, Amy's project – which she titled "Are you being hailed?" – was held as a series of extracurricular workshops. Participants in YAI had been selected because of their interest in the role of the civic institution ("the art gallery" and "the art school") in Vancouver's cultural life: visual arts ability, artistic technique, or "talent" was not required. Through an eight-month, bimonthly program, conversation among 20 young people surfaced around race, gender identity, and power in popular visual culture, visual arts, and design. Amy anticipated that the content for her new project would require familiarity and trust among participants, qualities she would not have time to build with strangers. She therefore invited six YAI participants to work with her on the case study presented in this chapter. These participants, all girls, were aged 16 to 18. Two had graduated from high school, three were completing Grade 12, and one Grade 11. All of them excelled in self-directed art making and reflective writing, distinguishing them as "the most articulate and engaged" young women from the YAI group.

As the beginning of her project grew near, Amy recorded her growing excitement, fuelled by the fact that she had not had any contact with these girls during the previous year. In her journal she wrote:

> I am really excited to work with each of these young women again, but I realize I have not seen them in almost a year. At the end of YAI (May 2012), I was leaving Vancouver Design Academy to pursue my MA full time, and there were a lot of other changes going on in my life (I was newly pregnant, for instance!) ... I also know that a lot can change in a year, especially when you are 17, so it has occurred to me that the girls may have changed since I saw them last.

To reacquaint herself with participants, Amy sent out an informal survey to learn about their current pop culture preferences, social literacy in general, and subjectivities. Three questions were individually emailed to the group:

1. Name three current bands/musical artists that you like. Can you say a few words about their style, their fans, or their aesthetic?
2. Name a clothing brand whose advertising/brand appeals to you. What do you notice about their style? What do you like about their marketing? (e.g., photography, colours, lifestyle, etc.)
3. Please list 5–10 words that you think might describe YOU from an outsider's point of view – i.e., how might someone describe you who didn't actually know you, but could only guess based on your age, your size, your look/hair/makeup, race/ethnicity, your clothing style, your friends, your musical tastes, etc.

Amy studied the girls' responses before finalizing the plans for her project. The most revealing, hence interesting, information for her came from question 2. While the girls' answers showed pleasurable engagement with specific brands and fashion aesthetics, they also gave a sense that one "ought to be" critical of advertising:

> I enjoy Bench products mostly because of their fit, but also like their style and their marketing. Bench products have very large and noticeable logos on them. I don't like *this* so much. (Amanda)

> Though I buy most of my clothes from thrift and vintage stores, the easiest brand name for me to discuss would be American Apparel ... American Apparel's posters and photographs seem to say: "You don't have to be a supermodel to be better than everyone else." They market an "I-couldn't-care-less-what-happens-to-me-so-long-as-I-look-good-while-it's-happening" mindset that is essential to many sects of hipster culture. In their marketing they make a point of using provocative models in provocative poses, not always explicitly sexual, but with the kind of undercurrent that makes

one uncomfortable without knowing why. This, of course, makes their campaigns very striking. Though I don't necessarily respect their marketing strategies, it cannot be denied that they are effective. (Isla)

Although Amy's initial idea was to address critical media literacy through art and design, during the seminar she began leaning towards working with advertising texts. Amy asked herself how critical the girls would be about commercial media as a venue for the operation of power, the underlying theme of her case study:

> I remember reading *Adbusters* [when she was the age of her participants] and feeling both tickled, and also powerless, in the face of media juggernauts.[1] The whole system seemed designed to tear young women apart and force them into mindless, soulless consumptive roles, subordinate to both the patriarchy and the industrial complex. Do girls still feel this way? Or is it more complex now, with the rise of this "ironic" culture? Is the world-weary teen taking over from the bright-eyed idealism of the nineties and that wave of "media literacy"?

Lesson Planning and Preparation

As Amy settled on advertising as "popular culture,"[2] she wanted her workshop activities to seem fresh to participants, rather than a rehash of critical literacy or advertising critique that they might already have encountered. Given the ubiquity of advertising in our social landscape, it has been a mainstay in media education with youth. Research is accumulating that media literacy interventions aimed at advertising enable children and youth to recognize the selling intent of ads and how they work and, therefore, that young people learn to become more sceptical towards advertising tactics (e.g., Begoray et al., 2013 with Grade 7 students; Hobbs, 2004, 2007 with Grade 11 students; Nelson, 2016 with Grade 3 students). More work in this area is paying attention to affective responses (as opposed to only cognitive ones) and incorporating student production of ads (including creation of counter-ads and other activities). Nevertheless, an inoculation-from-harm frame (e.g., Pechmann et al., 2005) is still very noticeable when adults (researchers, parents, teachers) call for media education to counter the negative effects of marketing messages aimed at young people.

Amy argued that this approach betrays an underlying assumption: "young people are particularly vulnerable to media messages because they are in a state of development and *becoming*." While her pedagogical goal was to help learners see how social identities are used by advertisers to appeal to readers and, as a result, construct "certain kinds of people" and "certain kinds of worlds," Amy's interest concerns how young people *use* texts for their own complex purposes, including political ones. Her project would include tools for participants to use to "talk back" to advertising as the basis for political engagement with commercial media.

As an art instructor, Amy finds that critical literacy skills in art curriculum are underdeveloped in the public schooling system (for exceptions see Chung, 2005, 2007a, 2007b; Chung & Kirby, 2009; Duncum, 2001; Darts, 2004; Freedman, 1994). Depending on an individual teacher's interest and ability, art education at the senior secondary level *may* include a discussion of the political dimension of art and design, but few students Amy has met ever experience this. Rather, art and media education tends to focus on skill-based or career-focused art; graduates of secondary arts classes are coming away with increasingly impressive *technical* portfolios, but limited vocabulary in cultural studies topics, such as design history and theory, politics of identity and colonialism, and art as resistance. It is Amy's belief that familiarity with these topics in art and media education can promote awareness of social justice issues. Her plan was to facilitate activities that would culminate in creative "art work" by participants through reconfiguration of commercial texts in ways that would foster social consciousness among their audience.

Because youth are looking for evidence of their competence and acceptance in the social world, Amy recognized that they can experience pleasure through what we described in the seminar as "disciplined reading": pleasure arises when readers recognize themselves as belonging to the world configured by the text. Amy drew on Althusser's notion of "interpellation" because it helps us understand how we are "recruited" by advertising. It is the experience of being hailed as a subject that enables advertising to act as a venue for the operation of power (see Williamson, 1978). If an ad successfully hails a viewer, the viewer becomes the person whom the ad addresses. There is no logical reason to believe the ad was created with any "you" (as subject) in mind; the ad assumes an imaginary viewer. If hailed successfully, you take up the position of the intended spectator; it feels as if you and the ad "belong to the same world," the world *inside* the ad (Williamson, 1978, pp. 50–4). Advertising works in this way to construct what Gee (2011a) calls a "figured world," in this case a world organized around consumption. Pleasure arises through being spoken to as a member of that world: if we did not belong, we could not have been hailed. But this is a double movement: we did not exist in this figured world before being hailed. So, we are both recognized by and constructed by the ad. As we shall see, Amy's project brings this double movement into view.

The goal of Amy's workshops was for participants to be able to recognize how enjoyment of advertising can come from interactive positioning through interpellation, in order to then reverse the power of the text through reflexive repositioning. To promote this learning outcome, Amy took inspiration from Ellsworth's (1997) discussion of "mode of address." Simply put, this has to do with how a text "speaks" to an audience and influences them. In film studies, explains Ellsworth, "What it boils down to is this question: Who does this film think you are?" (p. 22). It cannot be discovered in the text, but rather in its reception, something that is not predictable; since people bring experiences as racialized, classed, and gendered readers to their meaning making, there is never only one possible reading for any text.

Following from Ellsworth, for an advertisement to do its work, the viewer must enter into a particular relationship with the image and its narrative. To do so, the ad must address its imagined audience in ways that invite entry into a particular position towards the text, from which the ad then works – it makes sense, gives pleasure, and sells itself and its products (Ellsworth, 1997, p. 28). As a relationship, mode of address is not visible; film scholars give it visibility by talking about the film's "hail." A successful hail illustrates the power of media; it is also what film scholars, like Ellsworth, want to subvert. Amy's approach to critical media literacy shares this goal. Once Amy's participants understood an ad's "hail," she wanted them to reposition themselves in a creatively reconfigured world, one of their own making. Amy's goal was to harness their redesigns to "culture jamming": "hacking" ads and "tweaking" messages in ways that surprise the reader, something both playful and political, what Harold (2004) calls "pranking" (see also Kenway & Bullen, 2001).

Combining her education in visual art with theoretical tools – interpellation (from social theory), mode of address (from film theory), situated meaning (from critical discourse analysis), social languages (from linguistics), intertextuality (from literary criticism), and figured world (from practice theory) – Amy designed workshop activities. Her goal was to enable participants to identify how social identity works in advertising, analyse how these identities are given meaning, and engage in political dialogue with commercial media. Through the workshop, participants would be able to (a) identify the target audience of a variety of media ads in print and online; (b) identify personal feelings in response to ads, particularly where ads are perceived as targeting viewers based on age, gender, sexuality, or race; and (c) articulate and share personal experiences of media advertising while referring to individual social identity markers and appreciate how these experiences influence the perception of texts. These "foundational" understandings of critical media literacy are interconnected and build upon one another, as will become apparent below.

The materials Amy needed for her workshops were minimal. They included a variety of contemporary commercial magazines, scissors, sticky notes, tracing paper and pens, a flip chart, and a laptop to access online materials. As part of the larger research project, she also gave participants small notebooks to record their responses and comments on workshop activities (these journals became part of the data set). In keeping with the informal nature of Amy's workshops, no evaluation criteria to assess learning were designed. Instead, Amy asked for participant feedback in the journals she had supplied and encouraged the girls to email queries individually and to dialogue with her online. Amy indicated that she would consider activities successful if participants (a) reflected on the connections between the media landscape and the construction of social identities; (b) acknowledged that other young women experience media texts differently from themselves, based on different social identities; and (c) demonstrated a desire to continue to dialogue about popular culture. She intended to hold a public showing of participants' final "art work" as a conclusion to this project.[3] Amy was sensitive to her dual role: in this project she would act as both teacher facilitator and researcher. Thoughtful discussion around personal issues – such as gendered identity, sexuality, and racism – requires a safe space. Inspired by Moje and van Helden (2005), Amy wrote that such discussion was most likely to happen "when participants invite the researcher into the role of learner." During final planning she "paid particular attention to the way that the researcher builds a relationship with participants, and allows conversations to unfold in both group settings and by personal correspondence." These types of considerations are reflected not only in the design of "Are you being hailed?" but also in Amy's decision to hold her workshops in a community-oriented café. Beginning on March 19, 2013, Amy met with participants for four sessions, each running for about three hours. Paulina (our research assistant) was present at most workshops to video record activities.

Research Setting

Because Amy's project took place outside of a formal classroom setting, participants and their parents considered the planned activities extracurricular. The site for workshops was a meeting room in a coffee shop located in the now gentrifying but working-class neighbourhood (affordable for artists) where Amy grew up. In her field notes, Amy described the venue as "a pleasant mix of hip vintage style and a DIY functional aesthetic":

> The café is decorated with a large mural proclaiming "community," "solidarity," and "truth" in a Latin American folk style, depicting scenes of political resistance and labour. A community bookshelf near the back contains a couple of hundred texts, organized into sections including "Women's Studies/LGBT," "Environment," and "Political Resistance." Users are encouraged to borrow and also donate texts. Bathroom facilities in the back hallway are labelled "People's Washroom." In keeping with the décor, even though menu prices are reasonable, lentil soup includes a "Pay what you feel" price listing. Matching the décor, the clientele is diverse.

Amy's choice of this venue reflected her desire for not only a safe space but also a nurturing space. Below we describe how Amy's activities played out during her workshops in order to explore how advertising can be used to promote critical media literacy.[4] As in the preceding chapters, our analysis accounts for the success of this project, while also discussing strategies that might take learning deeper.

Identifying Identities: Are You Being Hailed?

Amy opened the first workshop with a review of "social identities" as a key concept for her project. She presented participants with a list of categories that one might use to construct an identity – "gender, age, ethnicity, race, class or family background, religion, language spoken at home, sexual orientation, clothing style, body type/size, hairstyle, ability or disability." She asked participants to consider these prompts while they described their social identity in their journals. Her goal was to help them identify their subject positions as a reference for later discussions. Yasmine's entry illustrates her understanding of the contextual complexity of social identity:

> As a Muslim Persian girl who has sort of a "hip-hop life style" people think I'm weird! First impression of Persian people about me is "She's not a good girl!" because in my culture (which is really old fashion) a girl should act and look girly! And even though I like girly stuff, they think it's a bad thing to wear a hoodie and stuff like that!

Although none of the other girls expressed a similar tension from moving between conflicting cultures, all participants reflected on their race, sexual orientation, body type, and personal identity (using terms such as "nerd," "artsy," "athletic"). Amy reminded participants of the importance of identity as an analytical tool throughout all the workshops by affixing a poster to the wall with prompting questions for the girls to consider as they worked; the girls can be seen on video gesturing to the poster during discussions:

- What social identity is being constructed?
- How does my social identity influence how I interpret the image?
- How is my social identity constructed?
- How is my social identity manipulated?

Amy often steered conversation during the workshops to these questions to delve into her analytical topics. Once it was apparent that participants understood the concept of identity, Amy facilitated activities to help the girls see how advertisers use social identities to target specific readers.

Introducing Althusser's notion of "being hailed," Amy asked the girls whether they knew what it meant to hail a cab. In response, all the girls nodded and a few gestured by waving their arms. Amy continued:

> Some things in the [visual] world hail you. They want *you* to look at them. It's very true of advertising. Advertising is hailing people all the time. The readers of advertisements are being hailed, based on their social identity. So, an ad will be aimed at a housewife [for example], or men who watch football, and so on … "I *know* you. You want *this* because you are all of these things" [points to the identity prompts on the wall].

The girls could easily relate to the idea of being hailed by advertising texts, likening it to targeted marketing and social media on everyday venues such as Facebook.

Amy instructed the girls to identify whether ads in magazines she had supplied hailed them specifically (current and out-of-date fashion, design, and "lifestyle" magazines aimed at female readers). Each participant chose a print magazine and spent 15 minutes flipping through it, affixing a sticky note to each ad based on whether they felt interpellated by it. Amy explained the "rules": "If you feel the ad is hailing you, write YES on the post-it and a quick reasoning for why you feel hailed (for example, because I like bicycles, because I wear this brand of jeans, because I have long hair). If the answer is NO, write NO on the sticky note and move on." The atmosphere was casual. The girls chatted and pointed out ads to each other when they came across something they hadn't seen before or something that resonated with them. Once or twice Amy coached the girls not to "think about it too much" (in other words, "Don't start analysis just yet!"). She directed them to go with their first instinct – *what the ad does to them* (attract/resonate/repel/alienate). The activity was fast-paced, generating a shared energy.

After 15 minutes, Amy asked the girls to stop and swap magazines. The exercise continued, but the girls were to use a new colour of sticky notes as they flipped through a magazine that had already been flagged by another participant. This time, if the reader agreed with the previous assessment, she would simply flip the page. If she disagreed or felt she was being hailed for a different reason than the first reader, she affixed a new note with her response (a YES or NO and an explanation). After another 15 minutes, each magazine was now flagged with two colours of sticky notes. Ads with two differently coloured notes became the starting point for a discussion about differences in perception and in the identity constructed to hail readers. Girls were encouraged to speak up and explain their notes, although each note had somewhat of an anonymous quality, to the extent possible for this small group.

Ads that elicited opposite reactions from two participants became a fruitful stimulus for discussion. Examples include an ad for hair care products that featured a White woman with long straight hair. Isla felt that this ad was hailing someone she described as a "hair-conscious consumer" and did not identify herself this way. On the other hand, Rachel, who had long straight blonde hair, liked the ad. "I really like my hair," she said, unapologetically. She then laughed and admitted that perhaps she is exactly who Isla had identified as a "hair-conscious consumer," meaning that Isla had correctly predicted the hail of the ad. This identity ("hair conscious") was something that Rachel hadn't considered before, but she took ownership of it easily when it became apparent that this was something that set her apart from others in the group.[5] Eventually, Isla revealed that *even if she did* enjoy hair products, this wouldn't be the right product for her because she has African heritage and kinky hair.

A Chanel watch ad also triggered discussion; the ad featured an oversize watch face adorned with diamonds. Arielle indicated in her sticky note that the ad did not hail her: she did not use a watch, and she explained that she finds the diamonds to be "unappealing." Amy thought that she might be making a reference to practices and politics in the diamond mining industry, but did not pursue this possibility. Yasmine, on the other hand, claimed that she really liked the ad. She enjoys haute couture brands and likes to follow the fashion industry. She said, unapologetically, that although she also doesn't wear a watch, she "likes diamonds" and "likes bling." Here the diamonds themselves become the focus of the disagreement, not the ad, the watch, or the Chanel brand. It surprised but also delighted Amy that brief exchanges such as these turned quickly from a discussion of the brand or the product into a discussion of values, tastes, and affect. The girls were able to see that the ability for ads to hail a specific identity is associated with the viewer's subjectivity: how they feel about themselves and what they consider to be desirable.

While readings could result in different responses among the girls about the personal appeal of the ads, the ads also generated a shared humour, more often than not based on the ways in which gender was used to hail readers. Diana, for example, held up an ad for Moen. This ad featured a shirtless male splashing water on his face while leaning over a sink. Diana read the text: "It says like, 'No flowers. No potpourri. No knick-knacks.' There's nothing – just a sink. So, what does that say about how men are supposed to be perceived? Men just want the sink, that's it." Amy then asked, "Do you think that's [the man] the buyer of the sink? Or, is that the man that comes *with* the sink?" To laughter around the room, she continued: "Maybe I should buy the sink so that that hot, shirtless guy will come over [more laughter]." Discussion then connected the modern aesthetic of the setting to the construction of masculinity.

A further activity deepened discussion about the hail, focusing on two specific ads: one for American Apparel and one for Hollister. The American Apparel ad featured a woman wearing a red bodysuit, heeled black shoes, and knee-high black stockings. Her head was thrown back at an exaggerated angle. The setting was featureless. The Hollister ad contained a sepia-shaded shot of a male torso holding a surfboard. Isla, Diana, and Arielle formed a group to work on the American Apparel ad, while Amanda and Rachel worked together on the Hollister ad. Discussion started with each group member describing her individual reaction to the ad. Participants then wrote brief notes in their journals about the identity they believed was being constructed to hail readers. Sharing responses led to collaborative answers to the identity prompt questions that Amy had affixed to the wall.

In her personal reflections, Arielle described the identity being constructed in the American Apparel ad as "a thin White woman, tall and sexually charged." She commented: "It's teaching us to learn not to care as much and to be way sexier ... To be more 'out there' and to get more attention, wear less." Isla had a similar response, adding: "She's thin, she's style conscious. She's brave in a whole new world of how much leg you can show in public ... As a young woman it's telling me, 'You don't give a crap. Wear any scantily clad kind of thing you want.'" The girls agreed that they were being hailed by the ad's hipster style, based on their age and gender. They concluded that the bodysuit worked to normalize highly sexualized femininity. The girls also agreed that the overall "feel" was one of confidence and sexuality.

Amy used this ad to draw attention to visual elements, specifically the stark lighting and the high contrast of the red and black colours of the ad. She described the female model as placed "in a brightly lit box" and compared this setting to the male figure in the Hollister ad. The Hollister ad is set outdoors with light coming from all directions, making the overall image less harsh. Amy pointed out that effects created by lighting are deliberate choices: "They make the bright one-directional light [in many American Apparel ads] really obvious by showing a shadow outline. You see the shadow that her body casts [pointing to the image]. That might be photoshopped, added during post-processing ... It is lighting the model in a very specific way."

Amanda and Rachel then discussed the Hollister ad, describing it as constructing an identity that is "young, healthy, White" and also "upper class," based on the surfboard. Amanda commented that her social identity "is White and female and fit – but not *that* fit." Rachel added: "I am also White, healthy, and young, and I interpret the image as being someone that I identify with, so I feel like, if I buy this brand, maybe I will be up to this person's standards." Rachel described the model as representing "the ideal male figure." In an earlier email response to Amy's pre-workshop questionnaire, Rachel had described her fondness for the Hollister brand: "Hollister advertising includes lots of young shirtless men which appeals to many young people today. When we see teenagers like us having fun and being fit, we think that the brand can magically make us just like the people on the advertising posters. The odd thing is, even though I realize this advertising tactic, I still fall for the hunky half-naked guys on the posters."

Upon swapping ads and having each group reconsider the other group's responses, Isla, Diana, and Arielle concluded that the Hollister ad is, in fact, "selling abs." As Isla noted: "These shorts could be from anywhere. They don't say 'Hollister' on them. They don't look like particularly amazing shorts ... It's just selling this sexy man!" Amid laughter, she continued: "It seems kind of obvious. We always know that ads are selling sex. In the American Apparel ad, at least they're being specific ... Hollister is not. They're very ambiguous." The conversation turned to the notion of lifestyle brands and the sense in which advertisers are creating a social world, one of "summer, wealth, and leisure," what Arielle described as "The experience of being outside with your friends, at the beach all day ... Going to a party later."

To conclude learning about "the hail," Amy instructed the girls to tweak the two ads to make them more appealing. Each girl sketched her response using tracing paper, which could then be superimposed over the original image. After working on the American Apparel ad, Rachel held up her work. Her altered figure was wearing a bikini and flip flop sandals, with a towel draped over her arm; new text read "towel, bathing suit, and sun." Rachel explained: "I thought the posture in this one [pointing to the original ad] was very unappealing to me ... [Now] it looks like she could be in the sun and that kind of thing. I'm more drawn to it. It makes more sense to be in a bathing suit ad." Isla added a skirt and made the model stand "more upright," explaining: "I tried to make her standing upright just because that's a more empowered position. It's not so like incredibly sexualized. It's more like a well-dressed woman walking down the street." Isla went on to point out that because she is not too "drawing capable," the face on her rendition was "not totally feminine." Emphasizing that she was OK with that outcome, Isla added that, knowing American Apparel, she wouldn't doubt that there would be a man, or a gender queer person, wearing their clothes. "That would be OK, too." All the girls laughed, seemingly in agreement. In retrospect, this unprompted discussion among participants could have been taken up as a "teachable moment" about cultural heterocentrism.

Amy asked the girls to "take a moment" to write in their journals about their response to one of the altered ads (the Hollister or American Apparel). She asked: "What about this change appeals to you? If we are tweaking it to appeal to you, what is it about you that likes this person better [pointing to the altered American Apparel ad]?" In discussing their responses, Diana claimed that putting a shirt on the male torso in the Hollister ad made the man in the image "more approachable" for her: "They're trying to show you this is the ideal man. This is their version of it ... So, I just did what I thought would make him more casual and more approachable than a bare-chested man with a surfboard ... than a half-naked dude on the beach [laughs]."

How Is the Meaning That Hails Us Constructed?

For the next stage of analysis, Amy designed two activities, which she called "layering" and "mapping." She described these activities as enabling participants to (a) analyse contemporary advertising texts using a formal visual arts critique through attention to form, shape, line, texture, and other visual elements; and (b) isolate and identify discourses that combine written text and visual language in ways that convey meaning, influence the viewer, or both. Layering and mapping enabled participants to explore how the identities used to hail them as readers are constructed and how these identities promote specific values and attitudes (in other words, the ad's figured world). While this component of Amy's project drew on Gee's (2011b) tools for critical discourse analysis, she did not introduce the exercise as such; rather, she led the girls through her activity of first "layering" ads with tracing paper to identify themes and then "mapping" these themes according to the specific message they convey.

To launch into this exercise, Amy shared her own experience of being hailed by advertising and her creative response. While pregnant, she had come across a *Fit Pregnancy* magazine. Anticipating her project, Amy spent time analysing its cover, isolating the themes in its text by using tracing paper and picking out each "layer" of related themes on the cover. The most obvious theme was "Pregnancy." On this layer Amy pulled out words like "Pregnant," "Labour," and "Baby." On the second layer, which she called "Fit," she pulled out words like "Health," "Yoga," "Workout," and "Diet." On the third and final layer, Amy pulled all the remaining terms from the cover of the magazine: "Ache," "Pain," "Tips," "At Risk," "Avoid," "Blunders," "Rules," and "Fix." By examining this layer in isolation, she was able to see how the third (and perhaps most crucial) part of this textual composition is the construction of fear. That is, the ideal subject for buying this magazine is someone (a) pregnant, (b) concerned with health, and (c) fearful. Having seen these layers for herself and having isolated them manually with ink on paper, Amy had come to a deeper understanding of how the cover discursively promotes a specific subjectivity for a pregnant reader: someone anxious about pregnancy and thus a potential consumer of products advertised in the magazine.

She then recounted to participants the creative process through which she redesigned the cover, eliminating the third layer (fear) and tweaking the text so that it reflected Amy's own subjectivity about her pregnancy and her personal values. For example, Amy is sceptical of the medicalization of pregnancy and childbirth that frames these as risky rather than "normal" life events. Amy's analysis illustrated how the magazine (as a venue for advertising products for pregnant readers) appropriated diverse discourses (not all of which are historically associated with pregnancy) to configure pregnancy as a time of "worry" and increased self-regulation. This configuration is possible because of the intertextuality of meaning making: for example, absent but working through the cover of *Fit Pregnancy* is a discourse of the "good mother." Another discourse concerns individual women's personal responsibility for pregnancy outcomes through "proper" lifestyle choices. Although hidden, these discourses are essential to the meaning-making process.

Having described her art project, and after passing around the finished piece, Amy asked participants to individually select an ad and place a piece of tracing paper on top of it. Each girl ripped out a magazine ad

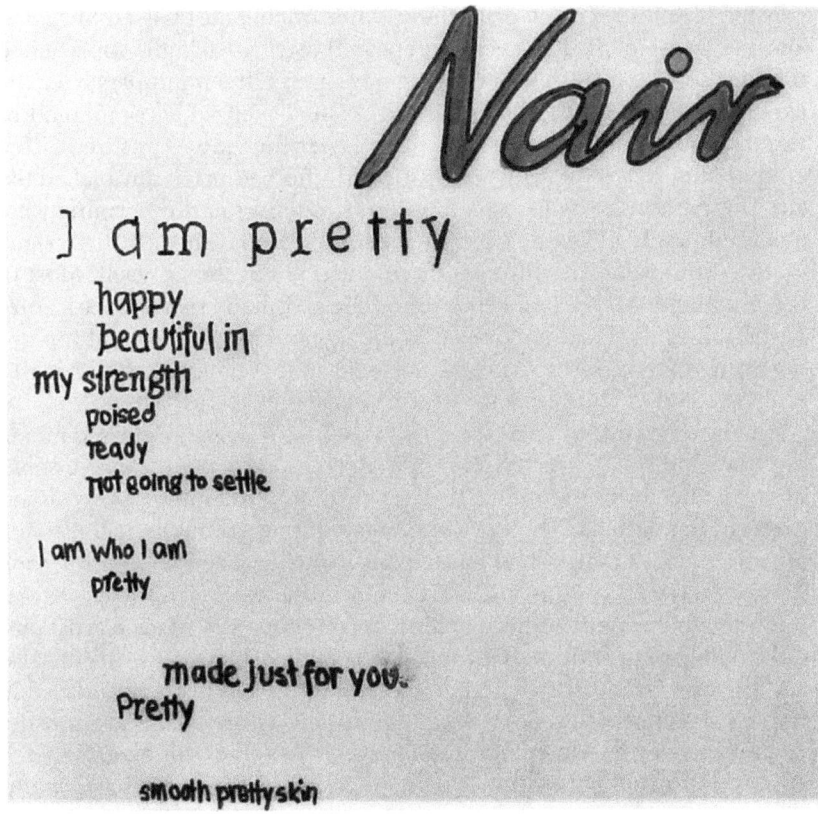

Figure 7.1. "Empowerment discourse" in a Nair ad identified by Isla

that either caught her attention or that she "wanted to work on." For 15 minutes, each girl traced one "theme" in her ad, which Amy now referred to as "discourses."

Again, Amy asked the girls not to "analyse things too much" but simply to peer through the tracing paper and see "what jumps out at them." The idea was not to create a work of art or a critique of the ad, but simply to see how the ad is composed and to identify one of the main elements in its composition. Many of the girls followed Amy's *Fit Pregnancy* example and picked out all the words or images in their chosen ad that they identified as belonging to the same theme. For example, in describing a Nair ad with the tag line "I am Pretty," Isla identified how themes come together in her ad to construct what she called an "empowerment discourse" (see figure 7.1).

After 15 minutes, each girl removed her tracing and passed her ad to another participant. The exercise repeated itself as each girl approached the new ad with a fresh sheet of tracing paper. Fifteen minutes later the exercise was repeated. The result was six ads, each ad accompanied by three layers of tracing paper. The three layers for the ad (by three different participants) were returned to the girl who had originally picked the ad. The next task was to place the layers together and determine what emerged. Each girl named her piece and created a short "artist's statement" about what the three layers revealed about the ad itself. Most of these statements had a mocking tone. The girls had created a caricature of the values they had uncovered in the ad, and they visibly had fun giving them a voice. In her journal and field notes, Amy began to refer to the participants' redesigns as "art work" and the girls as "artists."

The next activity enabled the girls to explore how the preferred meaning of the ad is constructed. It required each participant to make sense of the collectively identified themes through "mapping." Amy asked each girl to take an ad she was working on and post it on the wall. Passing out sticky notes, Amy asked participants to write three themes for each work, one on each note, and affix them to the work. This exercise was intended to draw out additional themes (discourses) that each artist may not be engaging with or that may have escaped her notice. It was also a litmus test to measure whether the emerging artwork was addressing themes that the other viewers had identified. Girls walked around the room, considering each piece in silence. At the end of this exercise, each piece now had nine sticky notes on it, three from each of the participants who were present for that session.

Each participant then sat with the nine notes that their work had inspired and grouped them in ways that made sense from the diverse themes. Most girls chose to arrange the sticky notes spatially, grouping them in common themes. An example is Isla's project, which she titled "Shape Shift" (see figure 7.2). The basis for this project was an ad for Triumph, a line of undergarments sold at The Bay. This ad featured the silhouettes of two women, both thin, scantily clad, assuming sexualized postures. Isla placed "Sex" themes on the left, "Change" themes on the right, and "How to be a woman" as the overlap. As Isla explained, themes were about "changing yourself, altering, transformation, betterment." They were all related to "satisfying yourself, changing yourself." She added, "All are about a lot of what advertising tells us as women – you need to change yourself for the better in order to be the 'best woman' you can be. A lot of that's linked to sexualization." In the conversation that followed, each participant explained how themes worked together in the various images to construct messages that analysts would call *discourses*.

Are You Being Hailed? 159

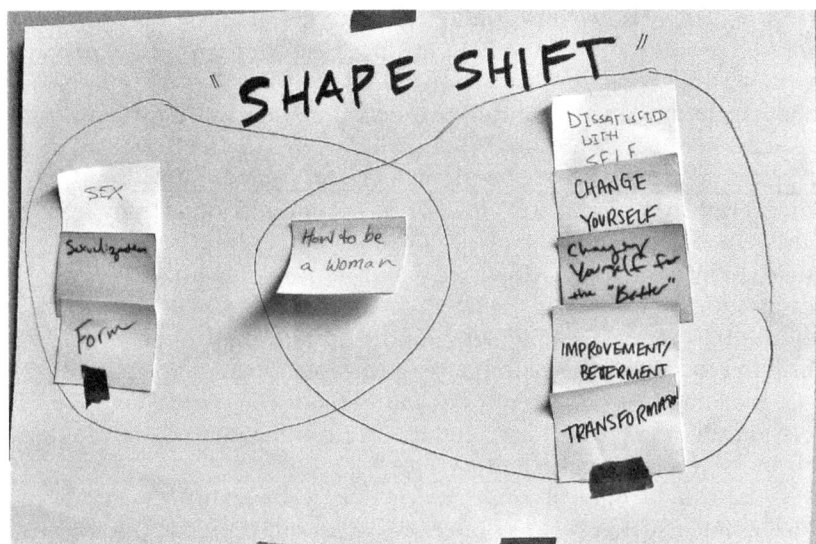

Figure 7.2. Isla's mapping of themes identified for Triumph undergarment ad

Gesturing to the artwork on the wall, Amy asked the group: "Does anyone have thoughts on how power comes into play?" As an example of power-over, Amy drew attention to the camera angle, which in most cases was pointing *up* to the women. Arielle connected this example to "the power of the point of view of the photographer," giving Amy the opportunity to introduce "the male gaze":

> The eyes that we are looking through are eyes of a heterosexual man. So, when we look at a female figure in these advertisements, what we're seeing is the view of womanhood as imagined, or as constructed, by a heterosexual White male ... When you see the female form, it's really highly sexualized.

None of the girls were familiar with the term *male gaze*, but all were interested in what it might mean and could recognize immediately how it might explain some of the images discussed in the workshop but also seen elsewhere.

Amy suggested: "perhaps it is telling that, generally speaking, we tend to assume the identity of the *photographer is male* when discussing photographic and composition choices about the *female object*." By considering how the images of women in ads are often constructed "as if" the viewer is male, the girls began to understand the gendered power imbalance in these photos. Amy elaborated on "the gaze" in terms of the dynamic between the viewer and the image. She noted that because the eyes of the female models are typically averted, as viewers we "have permission to stare because we are not being challenged." She used the American Apparel ad as an example; "we don't feel that we are invading her space"; the viewer has "permission" to stare at the model's body. Amy tells the girls: "In effect, *you* the viewer are the ones with power." She pointed out the similarity in the Hollister ad featuring only the (male) torso: "He can't see us staring at his body. Even though it is a male figure, there is still that power dynamic between the ad and the viewer." Diana was inspired to reflect, "It's definitely easy to objectify this man." All the girls seemed interested in finding out more about the gaze; Amy noted in her journal how pleased she felt that the girls seemed to be developing a curiosity about feminism and media.

Discussion included a consideration of how the texture, form, and colour of the images, as well as the written text, contributed to the construction of hidden, but active, discourses that supported a preferred reading. For the "Gendered Sink" project, Diana juxtaposed the Moen ad, featuring a man using a sink, with a different ad showing a woman using a kitchen sink. This strategy evoked a conversation, facilitated by Amy, about territory, gendered space, and normative, designed space (industrial spaces and clean lines are masculine, whereas feminine spaces take on a nurturing quality and employ "soft" pastel colours). Amy pointed out how these concepts are again related to the operation of power, stimulating a discussion about social class. Referring to the picture of a woman using a kitchen sink, Arielle noted: "I think that it's interesting that she's not preparing food. She's watering plants, which is very non-essential. Maybe she's wealthy and maybe she has people make food for her. So, I think there's class going on there." Diana then discussed how the "masculinized" ad, set in a rather aesthetically stark, but "high end," bathroom was also about social class. She remarked that reversing the gender of a person in an ad can alert us to the gendered operation of power.

Each girl titled the piece she had been working on and created a short statement about their ad's reinscribed message. Most of these statements had a quirky and sarcastic tone. For example, Arielle's project, based on an ad for a botanical-laced "green" anti-aging product, was titled "Wrinkles Aren't Natural!" Her statement read: "Wrinkles aren't natural, but this chemical product is! Aging isn't normal! Youthful plants on an old you" (Arielle's journal).[6] Similarly, the Nair ad recalled earlier talks about empowerment in relation to the beauty industry. Isla had grouped themes: on one side she placed themes concerning "What is feminine" and on the other "What is pretty." Isla explained that her goal was to explore and play with the way these two categories converge:

> The original ad has a lot about "... I'm not going to settle for anything but soft skin. I am who I am. I am pretty" [reading text]. So that's like – "She's a *girl*. She's happy with who she is." That's good. Awesome. But then it's in this context. It's, "I'm like this because I'm hairless." And also, "I'm thin. I'm White. I'm young." It's very twisted. I am who I am because I shave! [laughs] ... I'd love to see an ad that says, "I am hairy. And I am happy."

Amy used the girls' altered ads to deepen discussion about how texts operate as a venue of power. Her strategy was to get the girls to compare the ads, before and after their interventions, to illustrate how the viewer can also exercise power, as power-to. Examples come from the ads for American Apparel and Hollister, which the girls had "tweaked" in an earlier session. When Amy asked how power worked in the original American Apparel ad, Arielle initiated a discussion about using sexuality as a form of power-over viewers, identifying and connecting themes of sex, posturing, and identity. She pointed to the model's posture as a "version of women" that the ad wants the reader to be. Isla maintained: "There's a weird dynamic of trying to push sexualization as empowerment. But other parts of the ad, like her posture and everything, are not very empowering." Isla argued that the ad normalizes this contradictory message by presenting a contrived look and attitude as "everyday."

Amy then asked: "How does power work in the ads after they have been altered? Does power operate differently?" Pointing to two American Apparel ads that had been tweaked differently by participants – one that put the model on the beach in a swimsuit and the other that put her on stage – some girls decided that the model appeared to exercise more power-over the viewer. Diana said: "Maybe she is legitimately at the beach, enjoying the sun. It's still sexualized, but it makes sense for the occasion or context. There, she's on stage. She's showing herself off to everybody. She's performing something." Arielle disagreed, however, saying that the model has

> less power in the altered ads because it's more generalized and toned down in comparison to the original ad, where she is "out there." It may be seen as more of an extreme, but in the altered ones, you would see that every day in an ad. The images would be unremarkable. But a woman in a bodysuit walking down the street, you'd be, "What!"

Through these different readings of the representation of women's sexuality, each girl had begun to challenge the power of ads to address them as the reader imagined by ad designers. Participants were learning about media engagement as an exercise of power. In conclusion to this session, the girls discussed a number of online ads that Amy displayed on her laptop. The girls had no problems in transferring what they had learned from working with print to this digitized medium.

Reconfiguring Commercial Texts: What Do *You* Have to Say?

The final activity gave participants the opportunity to employ what they had learned about "reversing" the operation of power. Each girl chose one print ad to reconfigure by tweaking messages in playful ways that talk back to advertisers. As deliberative intervention, this form of culture jamming is an example of *power-to* operating as politicized agency. In the words of Amy Allen (1999/2018), it illustrates "resistance as the ability of an individual actor to attain an end or series of ends that serve to challenge and/or subvert domination" (p. 126).[7] Amy noted that culture jamming includes the ability to (a) identify and articulate representations of power in visual texts; (b) reflect upon media texts that sustain and/or challenge beliefs and traditions, particularly in regard to gender and sexuality; and (c) propose creative responses or resistances to advertising texts individually and collaboratively, and articulate intent in an artist's statement.

Amy instructed the girls to choose an ad they would like to rework with the aim of reconfiguring it in ways that would counter normalizing advertising practices. Because Isla had already been reworking the Nair ad, she wanted to make the piece more "palatable" by changing the look of the female figure to be a little curvier and making her ethnicity more open for interpretation. She added armpit hair to the figure and eliminated references in the text to "hair removal." The ad became a celebration of female body hair, inviting the reader to feel beautiful without removing it. For her finished piece, she made the hair darker, the model's eyes "more almond shaped," and the skin tone "light brown and ambiguous." In her journal Isla stated that her goal was to interrupt the idea that there is "this one form that you have to be." While her text used the same "empowerment discourse" that she had mapped in the original ad, her artwork reconfigured this "body hair removal" product into a "body hair grooming" product.

Diana chose the Hollister image and started playing with the construction of an identity for the torso in the frame. She described the male torso as "the idealized version of a man ... It's so exaggerated. It is a perfectly fit man who is wearing nothing. He's only there to be the object of your affection, or admiration, or whatever. It's kind of funny because – I wouldn't think it's marketed towards men, at least heterosexual men anyway." She decided that the ad is "selling lifestyle": "of being healthy, being tanned – just active." Diana's choice interested Amy: in the pre-workshop survey, Diana had described herself as "fat" and "frumpy," among other things. After the second workshop, Diana's journal notes revealed: "Surprisingly enough, one of the things I realized about the Hollister ad was in my face the whole time: the fantasy of being fit."

For her final project, Diana rendered the male torso a blank slate for the audience's projections of identity, including sexual fantasy. She wondered: "What if the torso were clothed in a particular style, for example?" She created layers that, when applied over the Hollister ad, transform the model into a range of other subjects – a young man with a laptop, a hipster with a journal (see figure 7.3). Her work thus fulfilled the interactive nature of final projects that Amy had envisioned: the viewer would select one of the outfits for the image and apply it to the figure, creating a man that reflects her (heterosexual) desire. Diana labelled each outfit as an identity type: Nerd, Hipster, Rocker. The viewer could select their "fantasy" man from the labels available and apply the overlay to the image. The act of playing with the man's clothing reminded the group of playing with paper dolls, a text-based activity traditionally associated with female figures and female users.

In their journals, the girls described how *power* operated, in either the original media text they had selected or their reworked piece. Amy left it to participants to define what they meant by power. For the Nair project, Isla's statement read: "I tried to take out the dynamic of 'you are an empowered woman because of this product' and change it to 'you are an empowered woman, and this product can help you show that.' Which is a much more palatable message for me. I also tried to make the image more inclusive to non-White, more realistically proportioned women." About the Hollister ad, Diana wrote:

> In the Hollister ad that I have chosen to work with, I feel that the power is in the hands of the viewer: the man is objectified to the point of being a paper doll. An object for the viewer to manipulate and modify into whatever they wish. It is interesting the model is male and being manipulated: it invokes the idea of humour, whereas if it were female, it might feel more malicious. Either way, I feel that the shift in power goes to the viewer. An idea for a title I have is Your Fantasy, or Choose Your Fantasy. Something about the viewer being in control. I suppose I see this as a parody of the Hollister ad, exaggerated to the point of being funny.

Figure 7.3. Diana's Hollister ad culture-jamming project in progress

Unlike some critical media literacy studies where participants critically examined ads and then created counter-ads (e.g., Harste & Albers, 2013), we found that the girls in Amy's case were able to "disrupt traditional discourses" rather than reproducing "them in their own ads," like the teachers in Albers et al. (2017, p. 226). We attribute Amy's relative success[8] to a number of factors. She asked the girls to reflect privately and in conversation with her about their social identities ahead of time, and she found ways to keep questions of power, media representation, and social group membership top of mind. Recall that from day one, Amy posted a list of social identity prompts on the wall for every workshop as well as key guiding questions such as "Who does this text want me to be?" She created several collaborative activities to encourage multiple readings of the various advertisement used, some initially semi-anonymous (e.g., use of stickies where girls could share their thoughts on an image and pass it along). These joint activities succeeded in surfacing and validating different individual interpretations based, in part, on the girls' various body types, family and peer cultures, and ethno-racial background. Crucially, Amy's layering and mapping demonstration and follow-up activities allowed the girls to visualize discourses as composed of words and images on distinct pieces of tracing paper that could be added or removed. In the case of her reworked *Fit Pregnancy* example, Amy was able to remove the "fear" layer and rework other layers to more closely reflect her own feelings and values around her pregnancy. As the girls each redesigned an ad to align more with their own sense of self, Amy addressed them as *artists* and called their journal reflections *artist statements*, underscoring the participants' creative *power-to*. She regularly prompted group discussion and individual reflection on how power operates.

In reflecting on the outcome of her project, Amy wrote in her journal: "Overall, I am proud, and feel connected with a new generation of feminists." Below we explore how this politicization was fostered by "Are you being hailed?" In chapter 9 we explore how critical social literacy would help to extend their political agency beyond the classroom.

Promoting Critical Media Literacy through Magazine Advertising

Duncum (2001) argues that images have become such a common feature of our daily landscape that they not only fuse with reality but have become a reality in themselves (p. 102). This fusion reflects the postmodern shift in economic production, from goods and services to the production of images and the styling of commodities through which we display our sense of self and our place in the social world. Ads are a ubiquitous feature of this contemporary visual culture; they are possibly the most pervasive pedagogical force in post-industrial capitalist societies. As such, they are a useful venue for promoting critical media literacy.[9]

We also note that because ads overstate their case, their textual constructions are more obvious than in less contrived texts. As argued by Love (2017), "the transparency of most advertisements' motives makes the medium a good training ground for students before teaching them to analyze other cultural artefacts, such as documentaries, (pulp) fiction, film, magazines, music, newspapers, television and social networking sites" (p. 3). The pedagogical effectiveness of the kinds of stereotypes promoted in advertising is easily observed when young children recycle their symbolic forms – such as using triangle skirts to indicate females in stick figure drawings (see Freedman, 1994, p. 162). This youthful tendency towards stereotyping invites "ideology critique" in the classroom: criticism of representations promoting social exclusion and hierarchies through semiotic emphasis of "difference." Ideology critique views these representations as constitutive of the attitudes, values, and behaviour of children and youth (for example, see Chung 2005, 2007a, b); it assumes that youth simply "internalize" media messaging. Hobbs, He, and Robbgrieco (2015) maintain: "the concept of media literacy was first formulated as a type of *cognitive defense* that could protect or inoculate young people from the persuasive power of advertising" (p. 453). To help young people learn to be sceptical and resistant to advertising, this approach to media literacy gives emphasis to misrepresentation and the manipulation of readers by the text. Perhaps ironically, it can sustain problematic binary thinking, through notions of "good" versus "bad," or "false" versus "real" imagery (for criticisms, see also Alvermann, Moon, & Hagood, 1999, p. 24; Kellner, 1990).

Not surprisingly, feminists (including Amy) have used advertising to show how stereotypical representations of femininity – portrayed through sexualized gender difference – subordinate women's interests and desires to those of men (see, for example, Chung, 2007a). In this context, critique helps to identify commercial culture as a site of political struggle; although ideology critique is often used in ways that are inadequately "social," we do not want to dismiss it too hastily. As we noted in chapter 2, using Chung (2005) as an example, ideology critique can potentially increase students' level of consciousness about the motivations of (in Chung's study) cigarette advertising. It can therefore offer a first step towards deeper interrogation of commercial culture. As illustrated in this chapter, "Are you being hailed?" connected textual manipulation to activities that moved discussion into an analysis of power, exercised not only by corporations but also by Amy's participants as consumers.[10]

As noted in earlier chapters, although we are critical of commercial culture, we reject the notion that young people need to be "inoculated" against harmful images, including advertisements. This assumption is typically informed by adult readings of the text, neglecting how it is taken up by young readers (see Currie, 1999). In contrast to "inoculation," Amy's project treats youth as agents of meaning making. Her project began in her *participants'* readings of ads, valorizing their reading pleasure. Participants experienced themselves as interpellated by the ad in ways that avoided implying that they were "duped" or "brainwashed" – responses that can encourage learners to "parrot" their instructor. Amy employed the pleasure of self-recognition in ways that validated the self-defined identities of the girls as ad readers.

In Amy's project, identity was explored as what makes the ad "work" (by successfully "hailing" us), while at the same time constituting those hailed as certain types of people (members of the ad's figured world). The goal of her workshops was to make this double movement obvious to participants, enabling redesigns that express their own embodied subjectivities. For example, Isla reconfigured a Nair hair removal ad in ways that revealed and rejected the dominant stereotype of femininity as not only hairless (that is, young) but also White. In doing so she reinscribed femininity to resonate with the non-dominant womanhood that she claimed for herself. This activity transformed the ad's power-over into participants' power-to resist and to parody advertising. We also note how Amy's project took advantage of the diversity of girls' responses to various ads, resulting in redesigns based on collaboration. By encouraging and accepting multiple readings of the same text as valid, Amy legitimated the diverse subjectivities of her participants (see Alvermann, 2002, p. 199) as a resource for meaning making. In this way, "Are you being hailed?" also afforded the exercise of power-with.

In the final analysis, rather than criticizing gender stereotypes and simply dismissing ads on the grounds that they "distort" reality, Amy introduced technical tools that gave the girls a voice to talk back to advertisers. Amy validated her participants' reading pleasures and, in doing so, harnessed this pleasure to playful rewriting of commercial culture through culture jamming or "subvertising" (see also Chung & Kirby, 2009; Gordon et al., 2018 on what they call "counter-advertising"). In this way, Amy's project encouraged girls to interrupt processes through which ads work to normalize what they represent, promoting alternative redesigns that challenged prescribed identities (such as femininity) as natural, hence stable, and universal.

Unique to Amy's case study is how she incorporated analysis of imagery into analysis of written text. Borrowing tools from visual arts, Amy enabled her participants to consider how colour, lighting, camera angle, image composition, and so on operate not only to normalize culturally and historically specific representations but also to activate the pleasure derived from a "disciplined" reading of the text. By encouraging reflexive self-examination about how identity and subjectivity are constituted in relation to the visual culture of commercial media, Amy's project enabled participants to experience commercial media as a venue for their exercise of power as well as to interrogate the power exercised by the text. While the manipulative character of advertising is by now so obvious as to risk remaining unremarkable, Amy played with her participants' affective investments to teach from "where the girls were at." Amy's participants were familiar with advertising and understood it as "motivated" text. We cannot help but speculate that their comfort level in admitting personal attraction to specific texts (an attraction that often contradicted that experienced by other readers) reflected, in part, the fact that Amy and not the girls chose the magazines that were subjected to critical inspection. This comfort gave Amy the opportunity to work *with* (not against) the girls' reading pleasure. Reading pleasure enables commercial interests to sell their audiences to advertisers (see Currie, 1999, pp. 304–5). This ability to appropriate everyday pleasure renders commercial media a powerful social force. Refusing to be positioned as a compliant consumer is a small, but nevertheless important, everyday political act. By inviting deeper interrogation of a social system organized to maximize consumption, "Are you being hailed?" supports teaching for social justice.

Adapting "Are You Being Hailed?" for the Classroom

Unlike previous case studies, Amy's project took place outside a formal classroom; unlike classroom projects, her small group of participants were self-selected. One unanswered question is how the activities that empowered Amy's learners might be adapted for classroom use. Amy's journal reflections on her project give us a partial answer; only classroom research can tell us more. From her previous work with youth in informal education, Amy knew that trust would be an important dynamic in fostering creative agency. Working at a community café fostered a relaxed atmosphere. It also allowed Amy to provide a food break during each workshop. These breaks served the project well; during breaks participants contemplated the art works from afar, chatted, and generally caught up on social conversations. Amy was pleased that the group gelled quickly and seemed at ease with one another: she claims that food breaks "nurtured" these dynamics. In this way, the context of activities helped to construct a safe space for participants to explore their media-related fantasies and their investments in advertising images that they otherwise identified as "problematic" (see Buckingham et al., 2005, pp. 44–5).

Amy noted that while the group size enhanced trust, working with a very small group also required flexibility. In her final report she noted:

> I also participated along with the students, often consciously attempting to work with the students on their projects, offering to help them cut out pictures, look for certain kinds of images, or offer feedback. This can be a tricky relationship in informal education; I do not want to be perceived as a *teacher* in the scholastic sense, but strive for something more egalitarian, equal parts mentor, facilitator, educator, and friend. This is my own style, and I would not use it in all contexts, or with other groups necessarily. But because of the nature of the workshops, I became somewhat of a co-participant in the art-making process.

Amy also wrote:

> When attempting similar workshops, educators should be familiar with composition issues in fine art and photography. Instructors should be prepared to discuss and demonstrate concepts like form, line, weight, hierarchy, repetition, etc. Experience conducting formal visual art critiques is also

crucial. Terry Barrett's *Criticizing Art* (1994) might be a useful entry point for others.[11] Instructors should also be broadly familiar with youth cultural references, including music, fashion, and social media habits of participants. Asking my group ahead of time to describe their personal tastes was a very useful exercise for me. I arrived having researched some of the cultural references they provided me and being familiar with their interests.

While attentive to the visual elements of commercial texts, Amy was able to structure her activity around cultural studies concepts in order for the girls to see how texts are more than "art objects"; these texts actively participate in the construction of the social world and its participants. As we have seen, key concepts she employed, often without naming or lecturing, included social identities, interpellation, mode of address, discourse, subjectivity, and figured worlds. These concepts enabled participants to understand how advertising works not simply as a system of symbolic communication that individual readers might enjoy, but also as a social venue promoting specific subjectivities and normalizing specific identities – those targeted by marketers. Rather than focus on the "harm" of constructed values and identities of advertising, Amy provided her young learners with tools that helped them critically investigate not only their visual landscape but also their affective responses to it: as in Jane's project, participants experienced the operation of power as an embodied experience, not through simply theoretical instruction.

At the same time as acknowledging how theoretical tools helped move participants' understanding beyond critique, in retrospect Amy decided that the theoretical "discussions-on-the-fly" that had enabled her to take advantage of "teachable moments" were often too unfocused, or that some "moments" had been missed. For example, given her participants' easy recognition of the racist subtext common in advertising, she could have introduced bell hooks's (2003) notion of "the oppositional gaze," a space of agency that enables oppressed people to "interrogate the gaze of the other but also to look back" (p. 95; see also Jacobs, 2016). In the end, like Yvette, Amy was not certain that participants always gained the benefit of take-away messages on theoretical constructs; in the future, she would be better prepared to deepen discussion on the hail, the gaze, the intersectional nature of identity, and discourse analysis. From girls' journals and informal feedback, Amy found that the girls were excited to learn a new metalanguage that they could apply to their ongoing engagement with popular culture.

In conclusion, by drawing attention to the political nature of everyday images, Amy's project fostered a way of seeing that we consider necessary for redesign that promotes social justice. Here we signal small p politics as acts of resistance, not to celebrate these individual acts as "empowerment," but to see them as a potential bridge to larger, more collective action. In chapter 9 we explore how raising questions about production of the magazines in which the ads appeared could promote capital P politics. Who decides on the content of magazines? How? Whose interests are served by harnessing reading pleasure to consumption? Is magazine production socially regulated? How and by whom? And so on. Answering these kinds of questions could move culture jamming and subvertising into the realm of politics beyond the classroom (recall our example in chapter 2).

In a society where "mass media is concentrated in only a few hands, and television news presentation is like a vaudeville act, the seriousness, clarity and even the perceived value of public discourse turns, as never before, on understanding visual images" (Duncum, 2001, p. 103). This is all the truer in these digital times (Albers, Vasquez, & Harste, 2017). Within this context, educating in and about images – digital and otherwise – has become an urgent matter. Like Natalie's project, we see "Are you being hailed?" as a bridge to the new hypermedia environment where youth can readily produce media incorporating not only written text but also images, movies, music, and the like. Still, Amy reminds us that critical discussion and reflection matter more than the technology used:

> Although their generation [youth] has invented the mash-up and played with every soundbite and meme *ad nauseum*, this workshop has invited us to mash-up ideas and images in hardcopy and collage, using glue sticks and paper and colour and scissors, and most importantly, *dialogue*. (Amy's journal notes)

Conclusion

Advertisements have long been a staple of media literacy education. Their use as a pedagogical venue reflects the view of ads as socializing viewers into the pleasures of consumption, with youth, in particular, vulnerable to their seduction. Within this context, critical media literacy emerged as a "solution"; it would inoculate young people from the harmful effects of advertising culture.

As noted in chapter 1, Liz (a media educator) liked to use ads because she could get everyone "on the same page anywhere from 30 to 60 seconds." Amy used the obviousness of their semiotic structure to introduce conceptual tools that enabled her participants to "talk back" to advertisers in their own language. As artists, the girls learned how to position viewers of their redesigned ads in ways that would subvert the advertiser's intentions. Their artwork challenged not only consumerism but also the sexism and racism rampant in advertising. In this way, Amy used critical media literacy to support her teaching for social justice.

The obviousness of ads also enabled girls to easily recognize the values promoted by advertising. Identifying how these values might – or might not – hail specific kinds of viewers shows how these values point to the interests that motivate these texts. The semiotic practices of ad designers, thus, provide a segue into analysis of the commercial world of media production, helping to connect the cultural and economic realms of meaning making.

8 Agency Revisited: Pop Culture in a Participatory Classroom

Students must be the ones to do the "thinking critically." All we're doing is giving them the tools to think critically with, or helping them to acquire and develop the tools to think critically with. But we're not telling them *what* to think.
– Dan, a retired media educator interviewed early in our study

In this chapter we return to questions that motivated our study: How can pop culture, as public pedagogy, be used by K-12 teachers to promote social justice? How does pleasure work through media engagement? And how might it be harnessed through popular culture when teaching critical media literacy to youth? In addressing these kinds of questions, university-based proponents of critical and anti-oppressive pedagogies too often fail to engage in ongoing conversations with school communities (teachers, students, administrators, parents) and, as a result, they can be long on theoretical abstractions and short on concrete examples and strategies grounded in lived experience within specific schools. This problem applies to the field of media literacy (see Buckingham, 1998c).

Teaching for social justice, regardless of subject area, requires a dialogic pedagogy. In theory, a participatory classroom culture supports equity-oriented learning by valorizing multiple student voices, enabling students to experience the "productive diversity" of "collective intelligence" while remaining mindful of power relations. But what does such a classroom look like "on the ground"? What does it mean, in practice, to promote independent meaning making by students? This chapter shares what we have learned about using pop culture to promote the kind of participatory classroom necessary when teaching for social justice. Such a classroom honours the agency of independent meaning making, and thus affords students the experience of exercising their power-to and power-with. This exercise of student power, however, does not always take class discussion where the teacher may have envisioned. While this chapter connects the pleasures of media production to intended learning, we begin by acknowledging the messiness that can emerge when student agency is given a (relatively) free rein. This messiness emerged during the Celebrity Marketing Project, sparked by unanticipated references to the highly publicized battering of Rihanna by Chris Brown, two well-known hip-hop artists.

In recounting this incident, we also address how unexpected outcomes can be transformed from a classroom "disturbance" into a teachable moment. Our analysis identifies processes that shaped student agency: affective investment by students in their interpretation of gendered violence; the implication of student identity in media engagement; the impact of classmates as an audience for student presentations; the intertextuality of meaning making; and the complexities of emergent pedagogy, where – at various moments and however provisionally – students become teachers and teachers become students in the face of multivocality. Because these processes are not unique to the Celebrity Marketing Project, we discuss how they shaped student agency across all our case studies, attending to strategies used by teacher participants that helped facilitate positive learning outcomes. We conclude by discussing teacher reflexivity in planning lessons that use pop culture to promote social justice and collaborative learning.

Unpredictable Affect: Coping with Unforeseen Moments

Our example of unforeseen messiness arose during a group presentation in Natalie's Celebrity Marketing Project. The all-girl group (Amanda, Cora, Stella, Elizabeth) was showing the video of Rihanna's hit song "Take a Bow" (released in 2007), in which the pop singer tells her unfaithful ex-boyfriend that she has no interest in reconciliation, despite his appearance outside her home, his apologetic texts, and his tears. The presenters had elected to rewrite the song lyrics. Rather than creating a new or different message about gender norms, their revisions had the effect of strengthening the female protagonist's message that the relationship was over and that she would not be fooled by his "show" of remorse (changing, e.g., "take a bow" to "don't come back," thus arguably moving from a mocking tone to a more directly angry one). The girls took turns pointing to signs of the music video protagonist's strength, which, they argued, challenged female stereotypes: her wearing black; her stronger, superior behaviour compared to her ex's begging and crying; and her setting his clothes on fire, which Amanda described as "a symbol of power and strength for the girl."

Raymond, one of the sporty boys who could be disruptive (see chapter 6), asked the first question of the group: "Was this song made after she [Rihanna] got beat by Chris Brown, or was it before?" Several girls in the audience immediately exclaimed, "Before! It's a really old song!" The class then fell silent, and it remained so in the long seconds after Natalie asked, "Any other questions for the group?" Turning her attention to the group itself, Natalie tried to redirect the discussion towards her intended learning outcome:

>NATALIE: What can you say about Rihanna as an artist? How does she promote herself, or what is her, sort of, representation?
>AMANDA: In this video?
>NATALIE: In this video, or overall, as a celebrity.
>   [Cora looks at Amanda, and both say together: "She is very strong." Elizabeth and Stella nod, while two girls in the audience say, "Yeah."]
>CORA: It's like her music becomes like that, "what up, girl," "so what" – like that sort of feeling when you're listening to it [the music video], yeah.
>NATALIE: OK.
>AMANDA: And, like Raymond said, even after getting beat up by Chris Brown, she didn't appear to be someone who was saying, "Oh, because of that, I'm going to stop my career for him" and everything. She still stood up, and she was still strong after all these difficult things that happened in her life.
>CORA: Apparently, she's back with Chris Brown, so, Whoa!
>   [Amanda laughs softly, shrugs her shoulders as if to say, "What can you do?"]
>NATALIE: Well, everyone has their own decision. It's hard to judge when you're not *in* the relationship. So, you don't know what goes on.
>   [Cora signals the end of their presentation by holding up both her hands.]
>NATALIE: Thank you [she starts clapping, and the class joins her].

In this excerpt, the presenters and some girls in the audience indicate that they perceive Rihanna and the woman in the song as powerful. Cora describes "that sort of feeling when you're listening" – an embodied affect associated with confident urban sassiness ("what up, girl"). Indeed, in the music video, Rihanna points and looks directly at the camera as she addresses her ex-boyfriend, sneers, turns her head away to signal she is done with him; she holds out her hand, opening and closing her fingers with a mocking expression on her face to indicate she no longer believes a word he says.

Raymond's question reminded the class that Rihanna's pop star boyfriend, Chris Brown, physically battered her in the car after a pre-Grammy

Awards party in 2009 (he was 19 at the time, she was 21). Girls in the audience responded spontaneously, uncertain perhaps where Raymond's question might lead; whatever their intent, the collective "Before!" did discourage Raymond from further comment. Natalie's open-ended question allowed Cora to voice her identification with the power of the video's protagonist, followed by Amanda's expression of admiration for Rihanna's strength in the aftermath of the assault.

Yet we know that not all girls admired Rihanna. According to Mary, interviewed at the beginning of our project:

> I know when I was teaching [in Ontario], that the girls loved Chris Brown. Like, they loved him! He could dance, he's sweet, he's young. And so, that he would be a violent man was not something that – or that Rihanna would leave him? ... they can't accept it. They still love him, and they're mad at her.

Reporting done for the *New York Times* and survey research showed many young people blamed Rihanna for the violence or felt that she bore responsibility along with Chris Brown (Hoffman, 2009).[1] Survey research done in 2013 (the same year as our case study) showed that some children and youth in Grades 4, 6, and 10 nominated *both* Chris Brown and Rihanna as people they most admired, while other age-mates nominated the two pop celebrities as people they most disliked (Power & Smith, 2017). In other words, one person's "hero" can be another person's "villain."

Given this widely publicized polarization, it is possible that Raymond's question aroused feelings of shame among some of the girls: in the early aftermath of the beating, when Rihanna reportedly did reunite briefly with Brown, some of her supportive fans turned on her with shaming messages (Hoffman, 2009). Pre-emptively, Cora acknowledged the ongoing rumours that Rihanna had returned to Chris Brown, and Amanda seemed to shrug it off as an embarrassment. Given time constraints, Natalie's comment may have been aimed at deflecting that shame. Unfortunately, her comments ("Well, everyone has their own decision. It's hard to judge when you're not *in* the relationship") foreclosed any discussion of the complexities of why many battered women in intimate relationships do return to their abusers (for a feminist analysis, see Rodier & Meagher, 2014).[2] This moment presented itself at the very end of Natalie's unit, but assuming time to respond, what might have been some ways for Natalie, as teacher, to convert this moment of unpredictable affect into a learning opportunity?

One possible springboard for critical analysis could have been the in-depth *New York Times* piece mentioned earlier (Hoffman, 2009; also see Hagood, Alvermann, & Heron-Hruby, 2010, pp. 48–9) because it provides numerous quotes from young people as well as multiple perspectives from adult authorities, ranging from African American studies experts to family violence prevention workers, public health officers, a pediatrician, educators, and counsellors. A teacher might ask students to explore the possible emotional investments revealed in quotes by ninth graders interviewed for the news article: "She [Rihanna] probably made him [Chris Brown] mad for him to react like that" (Hoffman, 2009, para. 3). The article also has the advantage of introducing feminist discourse on violence against women, amidst other discourses, all of which could be explored.

In the context of a first-year university women's studies course, for example, Rodier, Meagher, and Nixon (2012) detail a lesson on gendered violence, built around a music video, "Love the Way You Lie," featuring Eminem and Rihanna. One of their objectives is for students to see how pop culture implicitly condones sexual violence against women. While students in a women's studies class would be unsurprised by this direct focus on gendered inequality, in many K-12 school contexts, this approach would, more likely than not, provoke some strong student resistance.[3] The teacher would also be vulnerable to being dismissed as having a political agenda, which can impede a more open-ended analytic discussion, including consideration of the emotional stakes and power relations.

One strategy for pedagogically channelling unpredictable affect is to remind students of links to the course and its objectives. This was Natalie's first response, when she asked the presenters about how Rihanna, the celebrity, promoted herself. This question could have provided groundwork for an inquiry into how the dating violence incident affected the marketing of Rihanna and Chris Brown, the formal theme of the activity. Both stars had to grapple with the potential loss of sponsors. After a police photo of Rihanna's bruised face was published, CoverGirl makeup pulled an ad from TV featuring the singer but then reinstated the campaign days after Brown was sentenced to five years of probation and community service for the assault (Hardingham-Gill, 2009). In her first interview about the assault (nine months later), Rihanna explained to host Diane Sawyer on the TV news show *20/20* that she had put her CoverGirl sponsorship in jeopardy because she had briefly reunited with Brown. "I built this empire and the man that I love beat me and because I'm going back [to him], I'm going to lose it? No." Scholars Patterson and Sears (2011) here note how Rihanna "employs an economic rationale which illustrates a tacit recognition of herself as a powerful commodity in need of careful management and protection" (para. 32). Their analysis, thus, aligns with the intentions of Natalie's project.

Another way to address the objectives of Natalie's Marketing unit, while laying a foundation for critical analysis, would be to locate the Rihanna music video within an array of identity templates familiar to viewers of commercial music videos. Because music videos serve, in part, as marketing tools for celebrities as commodities, the stock characters in them extend to advertising more generally. For example, "Take a Bow," the music video that sparked the unforeseen emotional responses, embodies the "Vengeful Woman" figure which has become more prevalent in advertising in this postfeminist era (Gill 2008; Lieb 2018). According to Gill (2008), "A key theme of revenge adverts is the representation of a woman gaining the upper hand by punishing a man [always a sexual partner] who has transgressed in some way" (p. 46). Rihanna's revenge fantasy – not only in "Take a Bow" but in more recent and controversial music videos as well – invites "the female spectator to identify with the gleefully and unapologetically violent, charismatic and insatiable Angry Girl" (Ferreday 2017, p. 278). Perhaps the girls who reworked "Take a Bow," all of whom were Chinese Canadian, identified with the anger expressed by a woman of colour. Introducing students to the idea of intersectionality would give them an added tool to think about how the gendered identity templates never operate independently from other power dynamics such as race, culture, class, sexuality, ability, and age. They could compare and contrast the identity templates the music industry promotes for singers based on how they are positioned vis-à-vis dominant groups in society (for further discussion, see Kelly & Currie, 2020).

In this section, we analysed how unsolicited responses can be experienced by teachers as a "disturbance" to their planned lesson. While the incident involving Rihanna and Chris Brown may now seem dated, social issues surrounding violence against women and the treatment of women by the music industry remain salient (see Giorgis, 2020; Lieb, 2018): they are likely to emerge when students discuss youth music in an unconstrained context. We recount the example from our study because it illustrates how student agency in the classroom is shaped by the social nature of meaning making, bringing with it affective responses to media, as well as the importance of identity, audience, and the intertextuality of meaning making. Below we tease out these processes to show that they are not unique to the Celebrity Marketing Project. We conclude this chapter by discussing how teachers can use their authoritative power-over student learning to enhance intended learning.

Agency Informed by Affect

As seen above, classrooms engaged in critical media work can be messy spaces, full of contingencies and potential volatility. Teachers, of course, cannot foresee all matters arising from unpredictable affect; neither they nor their students "can always have command over discourse and over the various scenarios of urgency that arise out of grappling with difficult texts, especially those texts that implicitly engage trauma" (Marciniak, 2010, p. 889). Yet we know, as both teachers and learners ourselves, that some of the most powerful learning comes as a response to a disturbance, a response which then shows you who you are and where you stand (Biesta, 2006). For this reason, teachers need not fear affect and emotions; as we have argued, these can be used as entry points for analytical discussion and as conversation starters about matters of social injustice. Although often seen as interfering with rational thought, in fact, emotions give important "shoving power" to our "inner conversations"; they inform our commitments, personal identities, and, eventually, our social identities (Archer, 2000).[4]

Cora's reference (above) to "that sort of feeling" when you're listening to Rihanna attests to how embodiment is implicated in learning. It draws attention to *affect* as "bodily feelings that we experience when we read texts." Because these feelings typically "escape" language, we translate them into "emotions" (surprise, anger, fear, joy, disgust, and so on) in order to discuss them (Barthes, 1975, p. 17).[5] Once a feeling is labelled as an emotion, we can assign analytical significance to embodied encounters with pop culture. Barthes, for example, called the pleasurable feelings that emerge when we recognize ourselves in the text *plaisir*, characterizing these feelings as the result of "disciplined" reading because pleasure remains within the established order. Disciplined reading thus supports ideological meaning making because the meaning offered by the text "feels right." He contrasted this pleasure to *jouissance*, bodily feelings of bliss arising at "that moment when my body pursues its own ideas – for my body does not have the same ideas I do" (1975, p. 17). Such bliss can take us "outside" those responses prescribed by the established order. We are reminded of the young students in Mary's class (whom we interviewed early in our research), enchanted by rap lyrics about stigmatized behaviour (which they did not necessarily understand). When youthful pleasure escapes adult discipline in this way, it is often cited as evidence of the negative influence of media. In either form, pleasure is not to be found *in* the text itself; pleasure is produced when text and reader come together.

For both theoretical and pedagogical reasons, critical media literacy attends to affective as well as cognitive responses to media. Because affect results from the *relationship* between the individual and the text, it can only be experienced during media consumption; teachers cannot predict during lesson planning how their students will respond to pop introduced in the classroom as "educational" material. We return to this challenge in the conclusion to this chapter. Below we identify factors that can, unexpectedly, shape student agency.

Student Identities Matter: They Shape Agency

The notion of schooling as a meritocracy encourages teachers to ignore markers of student identity such as race, class, and gender, even as students are being taught the social significance of difference. One effect is to normalize heterosexual whiteness and able-bodiedness by locating "diversity" in marginalized bodies (see, e.g., Kelly, 2012, pp. 136–7). Teaching critical media literacy calls this practice into question because identity matters when media culture enters the classroom. Natalie's and Amy's activities foregrounded identities in the context of media consumption. Even when not the focus of a classroom activity, however, identity cannot be set aside: for example, while girls in Yvette's project produced board games based on shopping and school subjects, boys designed games around hockey and "war" (Dice Wars). Whether teaching about media consumption or its production, identities matter because they shape student agency.

While media targeting youth illustrate how commercial media work to construct a sense of who we are and where we belong, critical interrogation of such construction can bring students' sense of self into question. During Natalie's project, for example, watching *Mickey Mouse Monopoly* (Picker, 2002) did not simply change how students felt about Disney movies, but also how they felt about themselves: "[in] *Beauty and the Beast*, Belle endures an abusive and violent Beast in order to redeem him. I was shocked when I realized this – my favourite movie was *Beauty and the Beast*!" (Elizabeth, journal entry). It made another student, Naomi, feel "sad because you don't realize the subject's going on when you're a kid, but then now, when you watch it, you think, 'Oh, this is so bad'" (classroom observation). For both students, prior pleasure in what are reassessed to be "bad movies" is reinterpreted as conveying something negative about themselves or their past experiences.

Upon hearing Naomi's comment, Natalie tried to reframe the sadness and guilt that *Mickey Mouse Monopoly* elicited. She used four strategies. First, she raised questions about the experts featured in the film, noting that the filmmakers' perspective was not "neutral." Second, she noted that the task at hand was to examine "powerful brands to ask what power the brand might have over you." Third, she likened her own *initial* emotional reaction to the film to Naomi's:

> I was around 22 or 23 [years old]. I had been a Disney fan since *forever*. I have this many Disney VHS tapes [holds out her hands widely] – from *Aladdin*, to *Snow White*, to *Cinderella* – everything! … But after watching this, like Naomi, I was very upset. I didn't realize these things [racist, sexist representations].

Fourth, Natalie advised replacing emotional distress with critical analysis: "And now I have come to realize that I don't need to get upset, that I just need to look at things more critically" by "taking a step back" to identify "biases" and discourses in operation.

The challenge is to validate the integrity of personal identity as an entry point into critical interrogation of media without erasing the social. Amy's project, which was explicitly designed to validate her participants' individual identities, connected these identities to advertising practices taking place beyond the text. Amy's participants thus explored how personal identities are used in advertising to hail readers and, as a result, both confirm and construct the reader's sense of being a certain kind of person. Rather than compare themselves to idealized representations, a practice Currie (1999) found among young readers of fashion and beauty magazines, participants played with marketing identities to talk back to advertising; they constructed alternative meanings of womanhood. Isla used her African roots to redesign an ad employing White (European ancestry) signifiers for femininity. During the same activity Diana played with a Hollister ad to reverse the male gaze and, in doing so, render the male body an object of her desire. In this activity, alteration of ads to incorporate self-identities enabled girls to experience what Allen (1999/2018) calls their "power-to," by openly expressing their values and desires through redesign that either criticized or parodied established standards of femininity. By recognizing how their identities as (racialized) women are used by advertisers to hail them, participants were able to see how the power of media works through race, class, and gender as unmarked signifiers of idealized femininity. This recognition connected their *personal* identity – as a "hair-conscious consumer," for example – to a broader *social* group, one that is both constructed and subordinated by the text, that is, "women." In their final work, Amy saw an emergent interest in feminism. Amy's project thus promoted the experience of identity as affiliation rather than differentiation, an experience of "power-with" that is necessary for collective political action.

We can also see the potential to promote an experience of affiliation in the role play used in Jane's project; character cards disciplined the behavioural repertoires available to her young students. Apart from initial groaning as some read their character cards, students, overall, took up the role play enthusiastically, despite often being assigned a gender not connected to their sexed body. In Jane's project, students thus challenged the available design of gender in ways that Natalie's students could not. Role play offered Jane's students an opportunity to act out alternative ways of being in the world without censure, giving them the embodied experience of what Davies (1993) calls "the constitutive force of text" (p. 158).

In summary, one goal of critical literacy is to investigate how identity categories are deployed in media in ways that impart a sense of authentic selfhood, a process that can shut down critical interrogation because our identities *feel* as if they come from within ourselves. Classroom activities can disturb this feeling, affording students an opportunity to question established meanings of selfhood – reified through media representations – as well as to validate alternative ways of being through redesign. As we elaborate in the following chapter, one challenge is to avoid reconstituting neoliberal individualism, a pitfall Amy deftly met by prompting participants to understand themselves in relation to social markers of power (e.g., race, gender, class) rather than notions of competition, entrepreneurship, and consumer choices. Such a connection is the beginning of an inquiry that explores how the selfhood that we are encouraged to construct, and accept as authentic, can work to sustain relations of inequality. It can be a first step, therefore, in *experiencing* how power operates through media.

The Audience Is Everything

Much has been written about young people as the audience for media texts; less is available about children and youth as the audience for media activities in the classroom. The teachers in our case studies, of course, all brought knowledge of their students into the planning and execution of their lessons; they had to think about how best to engage students in activities, considering their diverse social identities and the various power asymmetries shaping classroom interaction – a challenging prospect, particularly at the secondary level. While planning the Celebrity Marketing Project, Natalie identified her "top concern" as

> meeting the diverse needs of all students, when you have a full range of abilities, from students who are gifted and want a challenge, and at the other end of the spectrum, new immigrants who may not speak the language [of instruction] well and may be experiencing culture shock. If I design a classroom activity that has to do with pop culture, to them [the new immigrants], that might not be something that they are familiar with. So, how do you keep them engaged?

Indeed, Natalie's concern has been borne out by research showing that recent immigrants to Canada who speak English as an Additional Language (EAL) often lack current knowledge of North American pop culture, which can hamper their participation in class discussions (Duff, 2001). In response to this challenge, Natalie selected popular songs and artists to initiate her project that she thought her EAL students would recognize. This decision had the unintended consequence of steering students towards mega pop stars and away from independent artists who appealed more to non-EAL students.

As illustrated in our research, especially by Natalie's project, students routinely express strong opinions about celebrity culture, about what is "trending," what is not, and why. Teachers may welcome this expression as an opportunity to enhance the relevance of material used in the classroom. Because personal taste is implicated in opinions on pop culture, one challenge is that media activities can amplify the performativity of student identities in the classroom. Dyson (1997), for example, found that while in the classroom (but not necessarily after school hours), middle-class children differentiated themselves from their lower-income and working-class peers by disavowing their interest in specific media culture.[6] In other words, asking students to work with favourite media texts is asking them to reveal what matters to them in front of an audience of their peers. During media activities it is necessary to consider whether students are performing for themselves (as we might intend when exploring how media facilitates constructions of selfhood, for example in Amy's study), for their teacher (as was the case for some of Natalie's students), or for their classmates (as intended in Jane's project). While the sharing encouraged by a participatory pedagogy can productively shift expertise from the teacher to the students, it can also exacerbate marginalization that already exists; peer judgment can be especially harsh for students performing identities outside normative gender, sexuality, or both. The challenge is to transform peers from an audience for self-expression into partners for collaborative learning; while small group work and peer feedback inevitably risk exposing students to peer evaluation, in our case studies they also gave students the opportunity to learn from each other.

Yvette's students learned how to revise their board games for different ages when a senior class was invited to play them. Similarly, a class of same-aged students played the role of Audience in the re-enactment of *The Hunger Games*. In Jane's activity, Ms. Knight's students gave responses to a pre-game presentation of characters. In both cases, "guest" students became meaningful participants, enabling them to give relevant feedback. Collaborative learning was also central to Amy's project; artwork by individual girls was frequently handed around the group, resulting in composite output. In all three cases, there is no evidence that students were at risk of negative judgment from their peers. The reaction of several male classmates to Dean's gender drawing in Natalie's project, however, reminds us that this may not always be the case. Conventional secondary schools like Natalie's, of course, are structured in ways that can generate more peer conflict compared to elementary schools (e.g., more curriculum differentiation, multiple teachers and classes with a different set of peers in each one, an increase in competitive and high-stakes testing, etc.). In addition, the fact that Jane's classroom was governed by the principles of "fairness" reflected in her school's official mandate likely facilitated the positive reception of classmates' work, reminding us that the school culture itself is part of the bigger learning context that cannot be ignored.

When promoting students' exercise of power-with, it can be a challenge to ensure the relatively safe environment needed for open discussion based on self-disclosure. Both Yvette and Jane, in an elementary school setting, indicated that they often orchestrate group composition or assign specific roles based on their familiarity with student potential to promote a desired learning outcome. For example, Jane knew her students well enough to make an appropriate assignment for Game Master, a role that she determined required a level of maturity. A further strategy is to provide an opportunity for personal expressions of media preferences and analyses through journalling (as in the case of Amy's activity) or individual writing of "exit memos" (as in Natalie's activity) that can be used by the teacher without subjecting the author to more public judgment. Whatever strategy is employed, using pop culture to promote media literacy brings personal tastes and values into public discussion.

In summary, students typically perform many different identities for a classroom audience, such as the "good student" – performed for their teacher – and, at times, the "class clown," the "popular" girl, the "jock," and so on for their peers. At times, these roles conflict with that of "learner." The challenge is to help students take up a "teaching" role, as Olivia (a teacher participant in our seminar) explained, reflecting on conversations with her students, ages 9–13 years:

> Once the discussions started going, students were eager to discuss and debate a wide variety of topics. They openly shared their opinions and were able to articulate reasons behind their thinking. Often their peers would ask clarifying questions that would push them to look at things differently. After a while they weren't at all hesitant to say, "I'm not sure about that," "What about …?" and "Why …?" The fact that those questions were most often directed at each other rather than myself or my teaching partner made for some of the most uplifting moments of my day!

Texts as Context: Intertexuality in Meaning Making

While literacy as meaning making begins from the text, it is not limited by meaning *in* the text: every social text is in conversation with already-existing texts that offer interpretative repertoires for new readings. Referred to as *intertextuality* and originating in literary analysis, this conversation takes place not only through obvious, direct references to other texts (for example, those of overt instruction) but also indirectly, through unspoken codes of established meaning. An example of the latter is the ad for an anti-aging product that appealed to Arielle because of an implicit "green" theme. The association of "green" with the imputed "naturalness" of the product's botanical ingredients led Arielle to sarcastically title her piece "Wrinkles aren't natural!" The association of "green" with nature is not explicitly found *in* the ad itself; advertisers rely on a knowledgeable reader to make this association. The implied association is possible because we bring to our reading and viewing of social texts cultural resources that include what we already know, making the intended message "feel right." Such a feeling can mask the need to critically engage with the text. This is because intertextuality, which does not always happen at a conscious level, helps sustain the hegemony of discourses that dominate social dialogue (see Currie, Kelly, & Pomerantz, 2007). One goal of critical media literacy is to bring into view unwritten but active texts that scaffold dominant meaning making. Amy's project illustrates how this goal can be pursued.

In her activity Amy used layering and mapping themes in magazine images to informally introduce critical discourse analysis, as one way to bring unspoken but active meaning into view. She illustrated this activity by revealing hidden meanings associated with pregnancy – as a "time of worry" and "heightened female responsibility" – in a cover of *Fit Pregnancy*, a magazine purportedly promising to empower expectant mothers. Although not explicitly referenced, discourses supporting pregnancy as a time of heightened management and personal responsibility constructed the reader as someone predisposed to consume products displayed throughout the magazine. Amy's activity brought the "preferred" but veiled meaning constructed by the text into media critique. Through exchange of responses, the girls collaboratively identified the hidden but active meanings embedded in various commercial texts. This activity could, thus, segue into a deeper level of analysis that connects the power of the text to hail readers to the context of its production (an issue we take up in chapter 9). We can also see how layering and mapping would be a useful exercise for other types of texts, including news articles and political campaigns.

Redesign in the classroom entails an ongoing dialogue between what students implicitly know already and what they encounter in class lessons. During the Monopoly Project, for example, young students drew on what they knew to design their own games. While some students claimed that creating rules was fun, many found it challenging and, as a result, fell back on what they knew from *Monopoly*. Isabel, for example, overcame frustration by asking herself: "Like, how do the *Monopoly* people do it?" By relying on a game that they already knew (and that the teacher had introduced as a "model"), one result was that student games sustained the dominant logic of economic competition, rather than challenge it as Yvette had intended; student meaning making unintentionally engaged students in a process of naturalizing monetary relations. Some of this outcome can be traced to students' lack of alternative experiences of – hence ways to think about – winning or, indeed, of moving away from competition altogether to enjoy engaging in a fun, convivial joint endeavour.

The challenge is to encourage student creativity, as an exercise of power-to, by validating what they know while at the same time broadening the range of texts available for their meaning making. Jane's project is an instructive example of how intertextuality can be incorporated into lesson planning to increase texts available for meaning making. The Hunger Games was not a stand-alone project as were the other media projects in our study. The activity that Jane designed was intended to generate a shared experience that could be referenced later during lessons on government. During a debrief of the alliances that formed during the role play, she made a point to mark the topics of party politics and abuse of power, anticipating social studies units already planned. "When we finish Canadian government," explained Jane, "we go to Ancient Greece," because the students will "compare an ancient civilization with our government, right? And *The Hunger Games* is loosely based on the story of Perseus and the Minotaur and the Athenian youth that were sacrificed to the Minotaur." The concrete experience of role play was designed to give meaning to otherwise abstract notions of power-over and the "relations of ruling" that sustain its operation. Jane's activity illustrates how intertextuality offers novel opportunities for integrating pop culture into formal curriculum.

At the same time, what happens when necessary texts are not available to students is illustrated in the Celebrity Marketing Project. Stereotyping offered an obvious tool to analyse music videos; marketers can rely on young consumers to easily recognize assumed associations between sexuality and female bodies. Many students chose artists who played with this association while lacking an understanding of how feminism has affected the music industry. Beyoncé, for example, has been characterized variously as a feminist, an anti-feminist, and a post-feminist artist by media critics, owing to the way she performs these associations (see, e.g., Zeisler, 2016). In our study, one group described Beyoncé's sexualized self-presentation as a contradiction to her avowed feminist identity. They reasoned that her "sexy clothes and stereotypical role of a woman in the kitchen [an image in one of the videos], giving her all to a man, contradicts this [identity]." Another group that incorporated Beyoncé's "Run the World" into their presentation argued that while "Beyoncé is promoting herself as a strong, independent woman in this song, her provocative clothes somewhat take away from the message." In our feminist reading of Beyoncé, in contrast, we saw a parody of traditional femininity. Only Dean – who reminded classmates about a previous guest talk from the LGBTQ community – was able (and perhaps willing) to recognize (but not necessarily name) Butler's heterosexual matrix. For the most part, his spontaneous and detailed explanation of the difference not only between sex and gender but also between transsexualism and transgendered identities was met with silence. Across most of the class discussion and homework, gender was conflated with sexuality, as read from female celebrities' provocative dress and antics, something not obvious for male performers. In this way, unrecognized intertextuality helps account for the difficulties that students may encounter when exploring gender in media culture; without being able to unpack the complex, unspoken relationships of sex-gender-sexuality, students did not interpret their reconfiguration as parody (for further analysis, see Kelly & Currie, 2020).

In summary, in the current context where youth have access to a virtually unlimited range of social texts, intertextuality can result in meaning making not anticipated by the teacher. Intertextuality, however, also presents an opportunity for new learning. Lessons can be structured into media activities in ways that broaden the range of texts students can bring to their meaning making. In Jane's project, new "texts" on power and government were added during debriefing of the activities, a strategy that allows the teacher to respond to what transpired (see Pompe, 1996). While Amy may have wished, in retrospect, to have planned a more detailed discussion of the male gaze, her ability to introduce it spontaneously draws attention to the need for teacher reflexivity when using media in activities promoting independent meaning making. We elaborate this point below.

Affect Reclaimed as Agency: The Pleasure of Redesign

Once normalized, available meaning can be experienced as "common sense" and, as a result, easily overlooked in the kind of investigation that critical media literacy is designed to promote. One facilitator of normalization is our embodied, affective response to the text. As noted above, this response can make its meaning "feel" right and, thus, place the text beyond question. But our feelings can also take us outside established culture, disrupting dominant conventions in unexpected ways. Referred to as "the politics of pleasure" (see Luke, 1994; Alvermann, Moon, & Hagood, 1999), the teacher must negotiate embodied affect. While we understand why teachers may want to avoid topics that invoke emotionally charged, potentially polarized responses among students, such avoidance forecloses an opportunity for critical reflection. An alternative response has been to valorize – rather than avoid or dismiss – the affective investment students have in pop culture. As Buckingham (2003b) warns, however, in seeking positive engagement with student affect, teachers may inadvertently colonize students' knowledge, reinscribing what the teacher says as the only valid knowledge. The challenge is to encourage student pleasure (because it presumably motivates learning) while fostering a stance that promotes self-reflection on personal media practices, an issue we take up in chapter 9.

Because pleasure is a result of meaning making through engagement with the text, it cannot be read off the text, in advance, during lesson planning. Early in this chapter, we attended to affect as "disruptive." Here, we return to a question that motivated our research focus on pop culture: How can the pleasure of media engagement be harnessed to learning? To answer this question, we returned to our case studies, where we observed five expressions of student pleasure generated during activities designed to promote critical media literacy. Identifying these expressions and the learning they embody enables us to subsequently identify the kinds of activities that can harness pleasure to media engagement.

The Disciplined Pleasure of Recognizing Oneself as Figured World Participant

Following Barthes (1975), we observed what we call *disciplined pleasure* in Jane's activity in particular. Through role play, her students participated in a reality constructed by *The Hunger Games*. We characterize the pleasure generated by this activity as "disciplined" because, by staying in role, student Tributes followed rules governing their use of weapons – as the key resource available to them. Because these rules were not always "fair," this scripted outcome would enable Jane, later, to discuss the social relations that structured the world they re-enacted. Included in the experiences Jane could draw on were student responses to the arbitrary chances of survival through the formation of alliances (albeit short lived) and attempts by some students to bribe Sponsors. These two outcomes, in particular, offered lessons on the operation of power in a context of unequal relations; these lessons did not come from what could have been (simply) a shared experience of viewing the film but, rather, as in video games, from the shared experience of "being" in the game's figured world. This experience resulted in many suggestions by students about how the rules could be revised, although only one student spontaneously took issue with the hierarchical relations through which rules were established. This kind of discussion came in later lessons on government, after completion of our study.

As seen in chapter 5, students clamoured for an opportunity to re-enact *The Hunger Games* again. Their pleasure can be attributed to the way they immersed themselves in their assigned roles. Their creative costumes and thoughtful elocution of fictional characters illustrate pleasure that came from recognizing themselves as players in an imagined world, one orchestrated by the teacher. The innovative nature of this activity lies in the opportunity that was created for young learners to try out unfamiliar roles. While the structured nature of the activity disciplined student pleasure, it also provided the safety needed to perform these roles: re-enactment generated an experience through which to question what might otherwise be presented by the teacher as simply an idea (for example, the operation of "power") or taken for granted as "normal" (as in the case of gendered identities). While students might be able to envision alternative realities while watching film as a classroom activity, role play enables them to experience those possibilities firsthand. It enables them to experience the constructed nature of what might otherwise be treated as "given." Because Jane was later able to draw on student experiences in a comparison of a dictatorship to democratic government, this activity can be claimed to support teaching for social justice.

The Pleasure of Negotiation: Rendering the World Familiar

The second type of pleasure we observed during classroom activities was *negotiated pleasure*: participants altered the figured world of media culture to better resonate with what they already knew. Students drew on their lived experience to redesign media texts: in one instance, board games, in another, magazine advertisements. In both cases, students can be characterized as negotiating new meanings – but not necessarily alternative realities – by reconfiguring media texts. While Yvette was initially disappointed in the production of games that replicated basic principles of *Monopoly*, her students did not simply reiterate identical texts; they reshaped features of the game to reflect their everyday worlds. In describing their shopping game, for example, Isabel told Dawn that they chose their theme because "we both like shopping." While she and Hannah "kind of took half of it [rules for their game] from *Monopoly*," they also innovated: "We had this idea. Instead of houses – you know in *Monopoly* how you get three of the same colours, you get to put a house on it. But we were thinking about putting a 'closed' sign on it, so if you landed on it, it would be like you were stealing from a shop that was closed. And you would have to pay double the rent."

In this way, the games produced by Yvette's young students were not imitation but entailed negotiation: as game creators, students drew on what they already knew to render the figured world of *Monopoly* familiar. Negotiated pleasure, such as that expressed when redesigning *Monopoly*, enables students to recognize that the constructed worlds of media are not fixed. Discovering that social texts are open to reconstruction can be a first step in independent redesign. Importantly, their redesigns valorized experiential knowledge as a resource for meaning making that, historically, has been excluded from the classroom by being denied the status of "knowledge."

How valorization of experiential knowledge can support student exercise of their power-to in politically aware ways is perhaps more obvious in Amy's workshops. Like the students in Yvette's activity, participants personalized the figured world of media culture – in this case, magazine texts – renegotiating the mediated sphere of womanhood and sexual relations. Participants drew upon their own identities to reappropriate messages about femininity. For example, Isla described as funny the Nair ad with the tag line "I am Pretty," given that it promotes a painful method of removing natural hair. Describing herself as "queer/allied," she tweaked both the text and the image, making the female figure curvier and darker skinned (like herself). Isla's redesign illustrates how those marginalized in established culture can validate their experiential knowledge. The caution is that familiarity can harbour unacknowledged elements of the established order. Clothes shopping was a "natural" activity for girls in Yvette's project, for example. It is also worth noting that while Isla played with the racialization of femininity in women's magazines, the predominance of White imagery was not questioned by other participants.

The Pleasure of Resistance: Talking Back to Power

The third type of pleasure we observed emerged through rejection of the figured world of the text; we call it *resistant pleasure*. By resistance we refer to "opposition with a social and political purpose" (Knight Abowitz, quoted in Stack & Kelly, 2006, p. 12). That opposition includes redesign that explicitly challenges the intended, or preferred, reading. Resistance thus goes beyond critique; by going against established meaning, the pleasure of resistance is based on a consciously political subtext. In Amy's case, pleasure was generated when established meaning was deconstructed and parodied. For her final piece, Isla asked viewers to reconsider what is "pretty" and what is "feminine." She explained that her goal was to play with the way these two themes converge in an ad for hair removal in order to transform Nair – a product promoting hairless femininity – into a "body hair grooming" product. By adding armpit hair, she made the ad a celebration of female body hair, inviting the female reader to feel beautiful without hair removal. Isla's playful parody challenges signification that supports specific meanings of femininity while marginalizing alternatives. This move enabled her to take her pleasure beyond renegotiation to reinscription of the discourse embedded in the text. In contrast to negotiated meaning that accepts premises embedded in the original text (as in the Monopoly Project), Isla's text offers new meaning, illustrating how change is possible in meaning making (Alvermann & Hagood, 2000, p. 199). Because playful reinscription challenges reified categories of available design, it could encourage learners to question how official definitions of reality become "fixed," opening the door to becoming political aware and active.

The Pleasure of Creation: Designing Something New

The fourth form of pleasure is that of *creative expression*, readily observed during activities for all four projects. Despite the "disciplined" nature of role play, the pleasure of creative expression was evident in the costume parade by Jane's young students. As seen especially in Yvette's and Amy's projects, the pleasure of production does not require access to expensive, or highly technical, resources, something that Dan claimed could intimidate interested teachers. In fact, dealing with technical glitches that unexpectedly emerged in Natalie's project limited potential learning. The use of "simple" materials can direct attention to the creative elements of media production. For example, students in Yvette's Monopoly Project used everyday materials, such as pizza boxes, crayons, and glue. Taylor, who expressed some frustration while using everyday materials on hand to design a complex game called *Resources*, told Dawn that, when his project was finished, he "felt good": "There's like that moment when it's all done, and you get to appreciate your work." A further example comes from the girls who "foodified" *Monopoly*: "We created it, and it's *our* game [gestures to her chest] ... Nobody else can say 'We made it.' Only us can say, 'We made it ... we *made* it!'" (Isabel).

At the same time, creative expression in itself does not give rise to alternative redesign. In Natalie's Celebrity Marketing Project, Naomi told Deirdre and Dawn how much "fun" she had when her group rewrote the lyrics to the Taylor Swift song "We Are Never Ever Getting Back Together." Their revised song, "I will make you love me forever and ever," transformed a sassy pop tune into a tale of horror, where the female protagonist is determined to hold onto her guy by keeping him locked in her basement. "That's where my creative side comes in," explained Naomi. "I'm not good at making things or ... writing lyrics, but if I can just take lyrics and change them into something really creepy, then that was fun!" For these students, resisting the dominant discourse meant a simple reversal, using whatever is opposite (see Davies, 1993). Naomi's redesign illustrates that creative pleasure, in itself, cannot be read as "empowerment"; the pleasure of designing media can promise, but does not guarantee, "shoving power" towards redesign offering alternative futures.

During all activities, creative pleasure for students came from giving material expression to their own ideas and experiences that could then be shared with classmates. Analytically speaking, their pleasure speaks to the fact that we confront a cultural world that, for the most part, is not of our making. Historically, corporate control of media production leads to the ready availability of cultural resources that work to subordinate our needs and desires to the interests and ideas of an "invisible other." Media production provides the experience of creative agency, supporting the exercise of power-to by giving expression to one's own social vision, albeit with no assurance that the vision can be realized.

The Pleasure of Collaboration

Finally, we observed pleasure generated by the collaborative nature of media activities. Most noticeable in Yvette's, Jane's, and Amy's projects, engaging others in their final product could enhance students' creative pleasure. The Hunger Games Project provided a welcome break for students from other lessons that involved more obviously academic elements; in Neil's words, "like in math, you can't really work together with your friends." In fact, the students in Yvette's class afterwards thanked her for "letting us have so much free time!" Amy attributes the success of her project to the social connections established among the girls in her workshops, facilitated by generous breaks for finger food and socializing. The resulting comfort level enhanced the sharing of personal media responses and reflection on each other's artwork; it facilitated experiences of "power-with."

We do not claim to have captured all the possible expressions of pleasure that come through youthful engagement with media. While the instructions from *Truth or Dare* to "pull hair lightly" or "hug the teacher" may, on the surface, seem innocuous, they illustrate how young people can find pleasure in violating expected classroom behaviour and the authority of adult teachers (also see Buckingham, 2003b, p. 313). Moreover, we do not intend to imply that pleasure was the only affective response; infrequent as they were, we noted moments of student displeasure (for example, "frustration"). Student responses – whether frustration, pleasure, or anger – remind us of the important role that affect plays in learning. Stifling these responses can send the message that student subjectivities (how they feel about the text but also about themselves) are not legitimate or lack authority, an outcome working in opposition to the intention of critical literacy.

In summary, each of the expressions of affect as pleasure in our study comes from the experience of agency, through redesign that promoted (a) recognition of self as a legitimate participant in a figured world endorsed by (adult) others; (b) reconfiguration or alteration of the world as endorsed by (adult) others in order to include aspects of self; (c) reinscription as "talking back" to a figured world that students recognize as not in their interests; (d) the creation of shared media that gives material expression to the student's subjectivity; and (e) participation in the collective redesign of the social world. In each case, pleasure arises from the opportunity for students to reconfigure their cultural world in ways that incorporate (hence validate) their identities, lived experiences, and desires. Media production by youth can generate a pleasure that the cultural artifacts (toys, books, games, TV programming, and so on) already available to children as resources for meaning making may not provide. As noted especially by gender scholars, these commercial resources may not capture children's subjective (read: "felt") definitions of themselves or the world they inhabit, no matter how dedicated adults may be to socializing them into the established order. Children (as do adults) confront a world of already-made (read: "alien") meaning; media production can be a venue for children and youth to design what is important to their subjective life. Noticeable for Isla and Diana, it offers an opportunity to challenge the colonization of our subjectivity by corporate culture.

While pleasurable, creative agency in itself is not the "empowerment" we have in mind. Liz, for example, alluded to "one school in particular that I will leave unnamed that consistently produces violent and misogynistic film material every year." Valorizing student enjoyment of media production cannot mean "anything goes" (Alvermann, Moon, &

Hagood, 1999, p. 35; see also Rymes, 2011). When teaching for social justice, redesign must challenge the power of media to promote practices with harmful consequences for the social and natural world. Student redesign during our case studies engaged students in small p politics: student agency was exercised within the microcosm of the classroom. In the following chapter we explore how critical media literacy can foster capital P politics – active social citizenship in the world beyond the classroom. As noted in chapter 1, such politics include, but extend beyond, electoral politics to grassroots activism, "engagement in associations or civic organizations, egalitarianism, and dialogue across differences to solve collective problems" (Kelly, 2014, p. 389). Promoting this kind of outcome transforms critical media literacy into critical *social* literacy, elaborated in chapter 9. In the remainder of this chapter, we turn to teacher agency in planning lessons to be implemented in a participatory learning environment.

The Teacher as the Learner

Pompe (1996) argues that in previous generations, teachers held a much more influential role than today. She argues:

> children coming to school might have had new worlds opened up to them which they had no way of coming upon otherwise: great stories, a knowledge of other fascinating times and places, things to thrill and dream of. Nowadays, all the magic seems to be firmly *outside* [the classroom] ... (pp. 94–5)

While teachers might intend to use media as a strategy to restore "the magic" of discovering new things, introducing pop culture into the classroom brings with it an everyday world that is not always shared by adults. Unlike academic curriculum based on topics that are chosen and introduced by the teacher-as-expert, there is a good chance that media culture relevant to youth will be more familiar to most students than to their teacher. Using media that targets youth or is produced by youth means that the teacher, along with the students, is positioned as learner, a challenge that is magnified by the rapidly changing nature of what is popular among youth. This challenge is also magnified in a participatory classroom where the agency of creative meaning making is welcomed. As voiced by Dan in the quote that opened this chapter, media literacy not only encourages, but *requires*, independent meaning making: "Although there's lots of nasty stuff out there – no question about that – from my perspective it's really important that we do not do the students' thinking for them."

As illustrated by Yvette and Amy (and discussed by Alvermann, Moon, & Hagood, 1999, pp. 39–40), fostering agency through media engagement requires the teacher to be able to continually renegotiate her multiple roles as authority figure, guide, and learner. Given that there will be different levels of engagement among students in the same class (most noticeable, perhaps, in Natalie's class), teachers must move in and out of their multiple roles to flexibly address individual student learning, while at the same time identifying facilitators of deepened reflection for everyone. In this context Yvette wondered: When does the teacher need to relinquish control to valorize her students' knowledge? When does she interfere with student media engagement to offer guidance?

For Yvette, not interfering with student creations resulted in output that initially disappointed her as "imitation." Even though *Truth or Dare* was one of the few games that did not strictly follow the *Monopoly* template, the group's game still normalized, rather than challenged, the capitalist market (because the students creating this game decided that the winner would be the player with the most money), counter to Yvette's intended learning outcome. In retrospect, however, Yvette reasoned that innovation requires an understanding of the mechanics of available design. As an activity promoting collective meaning making, she was satisfied that her students demonstrated what is required for collaborative redesign as an exercise of power-with: sharing tasks in the production of media, collective decision making, resolving disputes without conflict, taking turns during game play.

Because media production requires independent decision making and engages students in a shared culture in ways that mandated classroom learning does not generally allow,[7] we have seen how meaning making can escape the adult teacher's control. How does the teacher exercise their authoritative power-over to enhance learning? Despite her many years of teaching, Yvette still questioned the right balance between "giving free rein" and "interfering to provide guidance." Thus, learning how to use pop culture in the classroom is an ongoing process. Jane, Yvette, and Natalie concluded their participation in our study with enthusiasm to revise and repeat their projects with their next group of students. In support of their ongoing learning, and using what we learned from the case studies, we return to the question raised by Yvette: How can teachers exercise their power-over classroom dynamics in ways that give students "free rein" in meaning making, yet guide them in their learning? In addressing this question, we have deepened the notion of teacher reflexivity that we initially developed for our seminar. Our revised framework is presented below in table 8.1.

In summary, because literacy entails meaning making by the learner, students must be given the freedom of trial and error. By giving students relatively free rein, there can be multiple responses by different students during any media activity. Their readings of media texts, however, may not simply be different; they may contradict each other or even offend some students or their teacher. Teachers need to be prepared for this multivocality: there is no single, coherent meaning of any text, no matter how expertly the preferred reading is constructed. As we have seen, using pop culture in the classroom can take meaning making in unexpected directions. For some teachers, it may seem that the tables are reversed: the teacher becomes a student of youth culture. Exactly how the educator becomes educated is open to further exploration. While Liz was able to draw on years of experience that enabled her to know what would work "when she saw it," she also emphasized that good intentions alone do not ensure desired learning outcomes.

Multidimensional Reflexivity in Lesson Planning

As materialists, we would be remiss to leave the reader with the impression that the "correct" pedagogy alone can guarantee positive learning outcomes. In both our initial interviews and throughout our project, we were reminded of how the teaching conditions in BC schools shape what can, and cannot, be done in the classroom. Dan summarized some of these conditions during his interview:

> Being a classroom teacher for 30 years, I know the sort of gruelling routine it is, and the demands of administration, the demands of the Ministry of Education, the demands of parents. A lot of these people have a very limited horizon when it comes to what they conceive as education. You know, it's "reading, writing, arithmetic" – so when you start to talk [to teachers] about something that doesn't appear to immediately belong, then they just say, "I don't know. I don't really have time for that [media literacy]. I'd love to do it. It sounds great. But I don't have time to do it. How am I going to fit it in? What am I going to take out?"

In answering these kinds of questions, it matters whether the surrounding community is urban, suburban, or rural; key, also, are its level of affluence or poverty; the diversity of its student body and staff; the predominant political and religious ideologies; school size, history, and micro-politics; the nature of accountability practices and assessment measures; class sizes; and school type (elementary, secondary, alternative, traditional). It matters that the attendance of most children and youth in classrooms is compulsory and administered by timetable and curricular mandates. It matters that schools are arenas of conflict where groups (inside and outside schools) vie for status and control over resources and ideas (Kelly & Brandes, 2010, p. 393). These contextual factors mediate the translation of any one teacher's plans for bringing critical literacy into the complex realities of classroom practice. Suffice it to say that these conditions do not impinge solely on teaching media literacy; as working conditions for schoolteachers, they can only be addressed through collective action by teachers and their supporters.

As illustrated especially in Mary's and Yvette's activities, home culture plays an important role when using media for teaching (see, e.g., Mills & Levido, 2011; Morrell, 2017). Demonstrated by the parental inquiry into our study, parents and guardians can be vocal advocates for what their children encounter at school; what they advocate may collide with media literacy as it plays out in the classroom. Complicating the role of home culture is that meaning making is a context-specific practice; what students may say about a text in the classroom can be at odds with how they engage with the identical text after school hours. Students learn to adapt their behaviour to the implicit and explicit rules and regulations (as well as audience) that govern classrooms. Within a context of such unpredictability, how can teachers plan to shape their students' meaning making in ways that enhance intended learning? Clearly, there are no guarantees.

In short, there are many factors that make it challenging for teachers to undertake critical media literacy. To simply ignore or censure the media young people consume or what they produce, however, feeds a larger impulse to protect children from media culture, based on a belief about the innocence of childhood. An alternative approach, which we advocate, is the practice of teacher reflexivity. By *reflexivity* we refer to self-awareness on the part of teachers as to their power-over, and how it can be exercised when promoting a participatory classroom culture as an ongoing accomplishment. It requires the ability to locate self within the relations of collective activity. As everyday participants in the accomplishment of a shared reality, all people exercise agency through reflexivity within the immediacy of the given situation. Evidence, for example, can be found in the way that people adjust their behaviour according to their definition of the situation. Adjustment to the everyday contingencies of social situations, however, may not take place at a conscious level. In contrast, teacher reflexivity is a self-conscious activity, based on awareness that meaning making in the classroom is a social accomplishment, in which they are a participant.

As teachers, we can never predict student responses to lesson content, especially when that content includes pop culture. Reflection on awkward moments – such as the one involving Rihanna and Chris

Brown – is the hallmark of the teacher as learner. Teacher reflexivity shares the goals of what the NLG (1996) calls "critical framing": "learners can gain the necessary personal and theoretical distance from what they have learned, constructively critique it, account for its cultural location, creatively extend and apply it, and eventually innovate on their own" (p. 87). In our work, framing takes the form of critical interrogation that helps us explore the multidimensional investments we hold in our own teaching practices and desired outcomes. These investments can be magnified when using pop culture to promote a participatory ethos of inclusivity and multivocal interpretation of media texts. From our study we identify five dimensions of reflexivity and organize prompting questions thematically as an aid to teacher reflexivity (see table 8.1 on page 199). Exercised during lesson planning, teacher reflexivity can help us prepare – to the extent possible – for unanticipated student responses.

Personal reflexivity interrogates the ways that we are implicated in the media we choose to teach with. It requires us to ask, for example: How are my life experiences reflected in my interest in media literacy? What have these experiences taught me about popular culture? How does my identity (e.g., my social class, gender, and age) influence my own understanding of media? Why have I chosen this particular media text? Am I open to unexpected meaning making by my students who might criticize – or reject – media I have selected? And so on.

Analytical reflexivity is about the theoretical categories and tools that we bring to media education and our understanding of media engagement. As Alvermann, Moon, and Hagood (1999) argue, choosing theory is a political act (p. 136). It requires us to ask, for example: How does my understanding of the social world influence how I have chosen to teach about media, including how I think about "children" and "youth" and their media engagement (e.g., children as "vulnerable" and easily misled, or as experienced consumers)? Hagood, Alvermann, and Heron-Hruby (2010) describe three views of pop culture that teachers might hold – as mass, folk, and/or everyday culture – and the implications of these different views for teaching youth using media texts (pp. 9–12).[8] How might I identify my theoretical orientation, if asked? How do the categories of analysis that I introduce in the classroom affect student responses (e.g., does an emphasis on sexism or racial stereotyping silence learners, or encourage them to simply mimic my critique)? And so on. When teaching for social justice, interrogation extends to one's understanding of social change. In our study, we asked: How does power operate through media engagement by students, as a force for promoting change? Our materialism required us to think beyond the discursive realm in order to connect media engagement to social change in the world of embodied practice.

Affective reflexivity recognizes the emotional investment we make in teaching media literacy, as well as awareness of our own responses to specific media. Affective reflexivity asks, for example: How does my emotional investment in media affect what I have chosen to use in my classroom? How I present new ideas to my students? What about my emotional reaction to my students' media responses – how might my affective investment in my prepared lesson prevent me from "hearing" my students' responses? From understanding what their responses could tell me about the lives of my students? From taking their learning deeper, beyond emotional responses? And so on.

Political reflexivity refers to awareness of the political nature of media engagement, hence of teaching media literacy. Janks (2018) distinguishes between the small p politics of teaching – issues that emerge in local settings, such as a classroom – and the capital P politics that arise when media engagement is taken beyond the classroom, to a more global level (pp. 30–2; also see Janks, 2010, p. 188; Kellner & Share, 2007). By our own confession, our seminar failed to emphasize this level of engagement that asks students to consider the political implications of their learning (for examples of working at this level, see Vasquez, 2004; Friedman, 2011; Janks et al., 2014). Political reflexivity is what connects media literacy to the politics of social change that can promote a more equitable future for today's children and youth. What kinds of politics, as well as pleasure, are implicit in the media I choose to use? Are implied by the way I present media as the operation of power? How does my approach to media literacy help to prepare young people for engagement in the politics of meaning making (especially as media producers using social media)? For designing a more equitable future? How can my lesson direct students towards the politics of social change? In chapter 9 we take this kind of reflexivity further, through interrogation of the institutional context of teaching media literacy.

Ethical reflexivity interrogates the need to use popular culture in ways that ensure inclusivity by acknowledging and respecting the diverse backgrounds of students. When teaching, it considers how you treat each learner, who you pay attention to, and who you ignore. It asks: Whose experiences are legitimated by the media I choose? Whose values are legitimated? Whose might be devalued? Does my pedagogy recognize and valorize the knowledge that young learners bring to the classroom? Whose experiential knowledge do I tend to value most? Why? Whose do I not, and how might it be addressed in ways that do not silence learners? And so on. Ethical reflexivity embraces both what is taught and how teaching is practised.

Table 8.1. Teacher reflexivity when using popular culture in the classroom

Dimension of reflexivity	Sample questions
Personal	• What is my own history of media engagement? What did I enjoy when the same age as my students? Why? What enhanced my enjoyment? How? • How does my personal history influence my current thinking? For example, why have I chosen this specific medium? • How am I positioned by the text? To what effect?
Affective	• What emotional investment do I have in teaching media literacy? For example, what are my expectations? • What emotional investment do I have in using this specific text? • How might youth respond to this text? Can I be non-judgmental about their responses? • Is what I have chosen likely to generate pleasure among students? Which students? Will it offend any students? Which students? Why? How might I turn their responses into a "teachable moment"? • What emotional investment do I have in students' responses to this text? To my lesson?
Analytical	• What categories do I use to understand or analyse the media I have chosen? • What difference do these make? For example, are these categories likely to resonate with my students? • How are my students likely to be positioned by the media I have chosen? Which ones? How? • Are there alternative ways to analyse this text? Why (or why not) use them? How might I encourage my students to acknowledge the validity of other readings of the text? • How do I understand "power" as a force for change?
Political	• What kind of politics is promoted by using the media activity I have chosen? • What kind of follow-up activities might politicize the media production by my students (e.g., a public display)? • Does my media activity help students understand social inequalities and exclusions, for example by encouraging class discussion? Alternatively, do the media I have chosen "naturalize" the kinds of processes that foster inequalities and exclusions? • Is my choice of media likely to upset my colleagues? Parents or guardians of my students? How might I anticipate and respond to their concerns?
Ethical	• Does my choice of media or media activity promote negative thinking about any social group (e.g., through stereotyping)? Of which group(s)? How can I counter it? • Is the specific media text I chose relevant to the everyday experiences of students? Does it valorize or devalue the knowledge students bring to my classroom? • Will my media or media activity discount the family values of any of my students? Which ones? How? • Does the media or media activity that I have chosen present an opportunity to promote thinking about social and ecological justice?

In sum, teacher reflexivity recognizes, and considers, the power that teachers exercise over youth in their classrooms; it is a necessary element when teaching for social justice. One important goal of teacher reflexivity is to foster student experiences of inclusivity based on respect for difference. The types of questions we outline above are summarized in table 8.1; they were at the forefront of our own seminar preparation. We intended to model reflexivity in our own teaching during Phase 1, while being aware of the limitations of self-interrogation. Inevitably, some of the influences on our teaching practices will "remain beyond the reflexive grasp" (see Reay, 2012, p. 637). We consider reflexivity to be characteristic of effective teaching, no matter what subject area. Because the investments we address typically operate at a pre-conscious level, teaching for social justice requires self-questioning that brings these investments into conscious interrogation. While teachers can practise reflexivity through "reflection-*on*-past-action," it is "reflection-*in*-action" that enables them to take advantage of unexpected "teachable moments" in their classroom (see Schön, 1995). An example, discussed in chapter 7, is when Amy spontaneously introduced "the male gaze" during her activity. Though this was not a topic in Amy's original lesson plan, Diana drew on Amy's impromptu discussion to construct a female gaze that reversed the operation of power: Diana transformed media power-over into consumer power-to.

The questions we pose in table 8.1 are only suggestive and not meant to be prescriptive. The kind of interrogation we advise is context-specific; the age and learning history of students, for example, will prompt specific kinds of questions. In the final analysis, we view reflexivity as a form of self-study, as a practice associated with continual learning about using popular culture when teaching for social justice. In this sense, self-reflexivity is what the NLG calls "learning how to learn" (1996, p. 67). In chapter 9, we extend the exercise of reflexivity to student redesign.

9 Power Revisited: Harnessing Media Engagement to Social Change

Perhaps the key philosophical and political issue in this millennium is this relationship between cultural systems of representation – traditional print texts, writing, mass media, journalism, advertisements, web pages, texts, instant messages, digital communications – and social and economic reality.
– Allan Luke (2013, p. 137)

Developments since the inception of our project have dramatically altered the media landscape. As media engagement increasingly takes place online, media users are as likely to encounter "fake news," "alternative facts," and disinformation as they are an opportunity to redesign a better future. Negotiating this digital environment adds urgency to the call for media literacy informed by an understanding of the power vested in media. As we argue in this chapter, literacy that treats media as a cultural artifact separated from its production cannot offer an adequate understanding. In its place, we elaborate a materialist approach to media literacy that uncovers the relations of media production and the practices those relations afford.

In this chapter we revisit the operation of power through media, elaborating how it can be incorporated into teaching critical social literacy. Keying off our case studies, we explore how the framework employed for our seminar can be used to interrogate digital and social media as well as pop culture taking the form of print, television, games, film, and so on (on this point, see Buckingham, 2020, p. 235). We begin by outlining what a materialist ontology of media might look like, describing how it differs from the treatment of media texts as discourse. To illustrate how our layered ontology supports teaching for social justice, we describe how fairy tales, as an example of everyday entertainment, can be interrogated as a venue for the hidden operation of power. By emphasizing the social nature of both media and media engagement, we reject the notion that critical literacy can be taught as a skill. Instead, we offer CSL as an analytical sensibility that can support informed judgment during, and as an outcome of, media engagement. From our case studies we identify how this support comes through distinct, but interrelated, modes of student reflexivity. We conclude with a contemporary example of youth exercising their collaborative power in response to the racist use of social media. This example illustrates the power of youth to redesign the social world in ways that promote social justice.

Teaching Media Literacy as Social Change

Case study chapters enabled us to share what we learned about teaching literacy in the context of a participatory pedagogy encouraging independent meaning making (chapter 8). Such a context affords young people the experience of meaning making, as the exercise of agency, within the microcosm of the classroom. Within this context teachers can authorize experiential knowing as legitimate knowledge, giving students the opportunity to exercise their "power-to" create media and their "power-with" as collaboration with classmates. We refer to this exercise of power within the classroom as small p politics.

While our case studies were not designed to take students' exercise of power beyond the classroom, they are part of our larger project, designed to explore how critical media literacy can support social change. This goal informed our teaching during the seminar. As noted in chapter 3, this seminar was developed to address the lack of opportunities for practising teachers to enhance their capacity for media analysis. While a growing literature shares practical examples and theoretical frameworks for teaching CML with youth, a smaller number of educators have turned their attention to teaching teachers (Kellner & Share, 2019; Share et al., 2019; Buckingham, 2019; A. Butler, 2020). We add our work to this emerging literature by sharing what we learned from our study. As noted earlier, the first challenge we faced was how to prepare teacher participants to use pop culture to support their teaching for social justice. Student learning during the classroom activities inspired by our seminar offers an assessment of critical social literacy as a framework for teaching teachers.[1] Following the tenets of design research, in this chapter we revisit the question that our seminar was designed to explore: How can critical media literacy support teaching for social justice?

We designed our seminar from the view that teachers cannot offer CML in support of civic engagement without an understanding of *power*. During the seminar we treated media as a *venue* for the operation of power, to consider how media engagement can be harnessed to social change through the coordination of meaning making – hence practice – across diverse sites of media consumption. Understanding how media work in this way required us to problematize what is typically taken for granted in teaching media literacy: the *ontological status of media*. How is power vested in media? How can our answer help teachers harness that power to their teaching for social justice?

As materialists, below we analyse how the power operating through media ultimately resides in social relations and practices that, while embodied by the text, originate outside the text because they precede the text. Our materialist ontology addresses the challenge raised by Luke (2013): how to connect media, as a "cultural system of representation," to its "social and economic reality" (p. 137). It thus supports a distinctly *social* approach to media literacy: media texts invite practices that work to (re)constitute the social order by offering readily available resources for meaning making. Teaching literacy that harnesses media engagement to a more just world must challenge the use of meanings that reproduce the status quo if it is to connect the small p politics enacted in the classroom to social practices beyond the classroom. *Critical social literacy* is a step in that direction by promoting media engagement that interrogates power exercised through media. In the remainder of this chapter, we revisit how CSL offers tools for teaching that can support such a goal.

A Social Ontology of Media

As discussed in chapter 2, the power of media as social texts is reflected in their ability to coordinate meaning making – hence action – across diverse audiences in disparate sites of local media consumption. This coordination works through the textually mediated discourse of media messaging. For this reason, researchers interested in pop culture as a pedagogical resource typically analyse the power of media as *discourse*: collections of statements – written, visual, or spoken – that invite knowledge making about their subject matter. As argued by Kress (1989), discourses "define, describe and delimit what it is possible to say and not possible to say (and by extension what it is possible to do or not to do) with respect to an area of concern" (quoted in Bartlett & Holland, 2002, p. 11). In this way, discourse is seen as a

> regulatory framework that shapes knowledge and gives language and text meaning in a given sociohistorical context. Discourse can be understood as the negotiated sets of epistemological rules that a given society uses to

produce and endorse truth claims and normative behaviours. (Rogers, 2017, p. 204, drawing on Foucault)

Critical discourse analysis explores how discourse signifies "truth" through its discursive operations and how certain discourses become authoritative. The idea is that by challenging truth claims embedded in the text, we open spaces for resistance and discursive renegotiation through redesign (Rogers, 2017, p. 206). Critical discourse analysis supports such a goal by revealing the epistemological rules at work in media texts.

In general, we find critical discourse analysis (cda) useful.[2] As we have seen in chapter 3, for the media education seminar we used cda tools to interrogate the constructed nature of everyday categories of meaning making. During class discussion we questioned, for example, how thinking and talking about "adolescents" and "stages" of cognitive development inform beliefs – hence practices – among educators about the appropriate age for introducing media literacy. As noted by Hall (1986) and Smith (1990b), once the meanings and values promoted by established discourse become a "normal" aspect of everyday practice, they operate at a level below ordinary consciousness; they "feel" right because their meaning seems to reflect what, in actuality, is being constructed. The social origins of the meanings we employ to understand and navigate the social (and natural) world remain submerged, while nevertheless being active. By revealing the socially constructed nature of taken-for-granted meaning, critical discourse analysis gives us the beginning of – but not complete – understanding of how power operates through media.

The problem remains that in much of the discourse analysis inspired by Foucault's (1980) configuration of "power/knowledge," power operates everywhere but seemingly comes from nowhere (Smith, 1990a, p. 70). On this point, Smith acknowledges that Foucault's work tells us something important about how power is dispersed throughout the everyday world; nevertheless, in some discourse analysis inspired by Foucault, the origin of hegemonic discourse – hence power – can be mystified. We have no way to grasp its origins in human action taking place through social relations and the practices these relations afford. The danger is that this mystification can limit political agency, by rendering it simply a discursive practice. This can lead commentators to conflate semiotic redesign with social change. In contrast, we view redesign as, potentially, a *vehicle* to support social change: discourse analysis on its own cannot connect discourse, as a system of representation, to the social and economic reality that produced it.[3] Because our research interest as educators is in using media to promote change, within but beyond the text, we need media literacy that locates power in human action: such literacy requires a materialist ontology of the power operating through media texts.

Our ontology, represented in table 9.1, treats media texts as a *venue* for the operation of power; media texts themselves, as "things," do not exercise power, but rather afford its exercise by humans. Inspired by Smith's notion of textually mediated discourse and critical realism (Fleetwood, 2005; Archer, 2010; Creaven, 2015), each level in table 9.1 identifies a moment during which power operates through media engagement. While everyday meaning making begins when we encounter the text as a cultural artifact (experienced at the "empirical" level), media gain power socially when the meaning in the text coordinates meaning making (taking place at the level of "the actual") in ways that embody the values and interests of its producer (revealed at the level of "the deep real").[4] In this way, our ontology connects media, as a cultural system of representation, to social and economic reality. The power of media is attributed to human practices; political agency is directed towards changing practices that sustain an unjust social order. In doing so, our approach supports capital P political agency. Because our approach to critical media literacy emphasizes the social nature of both media texts and media engagement, we call it *critical social literacy* (CSL), a term Davies (1997) introduced some time ago.[5]

While the elements of table 9.1 have been identified by others, what is new is theorization of how the three moments of meaning making interrelate, offering a framework for designing classroom activities that promote a distinctly *social* literacy. Because each level is embodied by the text, hence a characteristic of the text, media analysis based on CSL traces the origin of the text to the specific human activities that produced it. Based on our ontology, critical social literacy supports teaching for social justice by showing the operation of power through media as a property of social relations and the practices these relations afford. To uncritically accept the categories of meaning embedded in the text as resources for meaning making is to imply that they naturally "reflect" the social (and natural) order, as originating in "things" in themselves outside the intentional action of humans. Such meaning making naturalizes the given social order, something that critical social literacy aims to disrupt.

Our seminar was designed to inspire activities that interrogate how media texts work to naturalize the given order. As we have seen, teacher participants chose one seminar theme (Amy, for example, chose "Who does this text want me to be?") and one or two seminar tools to explore their theme (mode of address, the hail). Here we describe how fairy tales could be used in teacher education to inspire a fuller range of classroom

Table 9.1. A social ontology of media texts

Level	Case	Description
The empirical	Media text	• In the everyday world, media texts provide resources for meaning making • These resources can become taken for granted, naturalized
The actual	Media text as a form of communication	• As a form of communication, the meaning in the text embodies values, attitudes, desires of its creator, operating as resources for everyday meaning making, hence practice • *Analytical significance*: shifts focus from semiotics to meaning making by media consumers; media represent the social order as an object of consciousness • Power operates through construction of selfhoods as well as figured worlds • *Political significance*: textual fetishism can (mis)direct political struggle towards the content of media, for example the "truth value" or simple "effects" of its representations
The deep real	Media text as a venue for the operation of power	• Meaning embedded in the text embodies specific social relations of production and dissemination and their vested interests • Historically, media industries had more or less exclusive access to and control over the means of producing media culture that becomes a site of struggle over representations, especially for media targeting youth; struggle engages parents and teachers but also the state through regulation of both corporate ownership of media and content of media • Power is revealed as control over access to media production and dissemination • Contemporarily, new technologies of communication give increased access to everyday people as a venue for the production and dissemination of meaning • *Analytical significance*: capitalist production becomes embedded in corporate cultural production expressed through media – communication technologies for everyday cultural production (computers, smartphones, camcorders, etc.) themselves result from their commodification; they embody the vested interests of their creators • *Political significance*: struggle emerges over the commodification of everyday cultural production, facilitated by corporate control over the means of cultural production (e.g., through computer programming and apps) and ownership of media content as "intellectual property" (whether produced by the culture industry or by everyday media producers)

activities.[6] While conventional literacy tools show learners how a preferred reading is structured by semiotic elements in the text, interrogation of this reading draws attention to the values, desires, and practices embodied by the text and, ultimately, to the nature of the relations that motivate its production. In short, CSL locates the power of media in specific human actions that give media texts their power in the first place.

Into the Classroom: Promoting CSL through Fairy Tales

Despite their seemingly innocuous nature as bedtime stories for children, fairy tales reveal how power works through such everyday media.[7] The widespread use of fairy tales to entertain children ensures that this genre will be familiar to most students. Fairy tales can thus be incorporated into a number of subject areas beyond media studies – literature, creative writing, art, drama, history, social studies, and marketing, for example.[8] The imaginative representation of characters makes these texts accessible to very young learners, while the acceptance of magic helps to steer class discussion away from issues of misrepresentation and discussions of whether they are "harmful" or "beneficial," as might be encouraged by media critique. As we will argue, the magic of fairy tales can stimulate children's imaginations about alternative worlds.

The classroom activities suggested below are based on a pedagogy of interrogation that treats students as active knowers rather than receivers of knowledge. Interrogation is fostered by instruction on "thinking devices" (Gee, 2011b, pp. 11–12), used in our seminar and outlined in table 3.1, that guide inquiry by posing certain kinds of questions. For purposes of illustrating table 9.1, below we describe activities addressing the text as a *cultural object*, the text as *symbolic communication*, and the text as *a social product*. Each theme is accompanied by a number of suggested activities that prompt critical reflection on the ways that power works through media.

The Text as Cultural Object: How Is Meaning Inscribed in the Text?

The intent of this theme is to explore how the text, as a cultural artifact, constructs a "preferred reading" (Hall, 2004). This theme takes literacy beyond conventional rules of language use by revealing processes that are hidden, but active, in the text. One obvious process in fairy tales is how the acceptance of magic suspends disbelief. Students could be asked how this suspension happens, to then explore how fairy tales also encourage readers to accept their sexism and racism. Disney films, in particular, have inspired extensive analyses of how fairy tales naturalize femininity as compliance to male power (see Jorgensen, 2019). One result is the normalization of romantic love through which a female protagonist lives "happily ever after" in a heterosexual marriage, typically after being rescued by a prince (Mollet, 2019). As noted by Schickel (1968), Watts (1997), and Wasko (2001), only certain kinds of people are given full access to the figured world of Disney – White, middle-class, cisgendered, and heterosexual people. To explore how stereotyping sustains this process, students can be asked to consider: Who lives in the text's figured world? Who is missing? Which character has the most power? The least power? How do you know this? What might happen if the identities of characters in these roles were changed? And so on. Comparing Eurocentric fairy tales to Indigenous storytelling would draw further attention to the cultural specificity of meaning constructed by popular texts (see Hearne, 2017), raising further questions about power exercised through cultural domination.

The multimodal nature of contemporary storytelling enables students to compare classic narratives in a printed version to animated or live film versions. This comparison could consider how variations in costumes, song, music, animation, and so on influence the meaning that can be constructed. Students could trace the transformation of fairy tales over time through online research. Beauchamp (2010) describes how *Cinderella*, for example, originated in the Chinese story of Ye Xian during the Tang Dynasty. She argues that the now familiar story took shape in China during the ninth century, influenced by both Hindu and Buddhist traditions, and was transmitted to Europe during the 17th century. For a more contemporary example, Mollet (2019) describes how Disney's *Snow White and the Seven Dwarfs* was born out of Depression culture in the 1930s and reflects changing American ideology (p. 228). By identifying what kind of world is constructed by the text during different historical epochs, along with the values and social relations that constitute its figured world (see Gee, 2011b; Holland et al., 1998), students can explore what these texts reveal about social change more generally.

Along these lines, the female characters of contemporary Disney films – Mulan, Belle, Moana – could be discussed in relation to changing gender roles, taking racialization into account (for examples, see Lacroix, 2004; Wohlwend, 2014; England, Descartes, & Collier-Meek, 2011; Dundes & Streiff, 2016). Students could design new characters and storylines that embody their experiences of the current context. Such an activity could draw attention to contradictory messaging that often characterizes children's literature. Bellas (2017), as an example, analyses how contemporary "teen screen" tales (for example, *The Princess Diaries* and *Pretty Little Liars*) incorporate discourses of "girl power," all the while sustaining a traditional representation of youthful femininity that is not only idealized but offered as an "essence" that makes girlhood "special" (also see Huang, 2019). These kinds of activities take media literacy beyond critique by helping students imagine themselves as the authors of new, different stories (see Yeoman, 1999).

In short, activities that denaturalize the meanings embedded in popular culture enable students to recognize the constructed nature of media texts. The often whimsical nature of fairy tales helps to avoid framing interrogation in terms of the "authenticity" of representation, inviting instead a critical analysis of available design while at the same time fostering creative reimagining of what exists.

The Text as Symbolic Communication: How Does the Text Engage Readers?

This theme connects the text to its reception by embodied readers, highlighting reader agency: the operation of power is revealed by connecting the text, as a cultural object, to social practice beyond the text. The intent here is to foster recognition that the reading of any text, as a situated practice, has social consequences, dependent upon the context of reading and the identity of readers. A key consequence is a sense of selfhood activated by our affective response to the text.

Because reading is an embodied activity, affective connection to the text can be explored by beginning with personal engagement: Which character do you enjoy most? Why? What might you change about this fairy tale? Why? Group discussion provides an opportunity for students to understand why different readers may make different meanings from – hence hold different affective attachments to – the same text. A fruitful line of inquiry would be opened if gendered patterns emerge through class discussion. Within this context students can explore how the text hails its readers: Who does the text imagine *you*, the reader, to be? Want you to be? How do you know this? Who is not addressed by the text? Fan fiction published online provides an opportunity to discuss how tales engage diverse audiences (see Kustritz, 2019). Students could explore fairy tales that have been rewritten by audiences excluded from, or caricaturized in, "classic" tales of mainstream culture. Tiffin (2015), for example, describes Indigenous African stories that resist colonization (also see Lester, 2019; Zipes, Greenhill, & Magnus-Johnston, 2015).

Role play, as an embodied activity successfully employed in Jane's project, enables students to experience for themselves how social practices associated with specific identities can be limiting and are perpetuated through the scripts of popular culture. This play could include the design of costumes, masks, and other prompts for tales such as *Snow*

White, *Rapunzel*, or *Sleeping Beauty*. Assigning roles by lottery (rather than choice) would result in students randomly enacting situations of being either powerful or powerless, according to character scripts. As seen in Jane's activity, role play in the classroom can potentially offer a safe space to challenge the rigidity of gendered binaries, for example (see Wohlwend, 2012). The resulting experience could encourage rewritten scripts where student authors describe how they have changed the storyline, for what audience, and how this audience has been addressed.

In short, these kinds of activities foster media engagement as an embodied activity that brings affective investments, as well as cognitive processing, into meaning making. It affords students the opportunity to experience their power-to question media construction and, potentially, to rewrite media texts together as an exercise of power-with. Introspection about personal responses can be encouraged through journalling, while group discussion offers an opportunity for students to learn from the responses of others. Teacher endorsement of the diversity of student media responses that emerges can lend legitimacy to alternative meaning making.

The Origins of Media: Who Produced the Text? For What Purpose?

The goal here is to recognize how media texts embody the social relations and practices that enable media production, particularly in commodity form. An instructive case is Walt Disney Company, one of the world's largest media conglomerates and producer of contemporary fairy tales (Wasko, 2016). Because it has generated academic interest, extensive teaching resources are available (see, for example, Giroux & Pollock, 2010; Wasko, 2016; Medina & Wohlwend, 2014; Watts, 1997). Given that Disney targets a "family audience," its products are familiar to most North American children. At the time of writing, the conglomerate owned and operated the ABC broadcast television network; cable television networks such as Disney Channel, ESPN, A&E Networks, and ABC Family; publishing, merchandising, music, and theatre divisions; and 14 theme parks around the world. Its global reach includes contracts with sweatshops that enable North American children to vicariously experience the "Disney dream" through purchase of clothing, accessories, school supplies, and so on fashioned after Disney characters.

Hines (2010) documents how fairy tales from around the world have been collected, translated, and edited in ways to consolidate European cultural authority (see also Sun, 2011; Makdisi & Nussbaum, 2008). Disney offers a particularly rich example of the power of media production to consolidate, as well as normalize, the power of corporate America.

Following the lead of Medina and Wohlwend (2014), students could "map" the Disney empire (p. 46), tracing what Orenstein (2011) calls the "Princess Industrial Complex." Medina and Wohlwend (2014) describe this Complex in terms of:

> franchises, anchored by films, television shows, or video games, with a reach that extends beyond multimedia to toys, books, video games, collectibles, apparel, and all sorts of household goods. These products link and circulate through identity texts embedded in the familiar narratives, characters, and logos that cover the products. (p. 44)

Research into the working conditions of its offshore production provides a basis to explore the origins of Disney products in countries like Haiti, Honduras, Indonesia, Thailand, and China (Friedman, 2011, p. 254), where labour regulations favour capitalist producers. While Disney films have naturalized the association of "girlhood" with Disney Princess culture in countries such as Canada (see Mollet, 2019; Wohlwend, 2009, 2014), the material products that support this culture often embody child labour. Friedman (2011) describes how his students took their criticisms of Disney beyond the classroom. After showing a documentary on Disney sweatshops, he suggested that students could write letters to Disney headquarters. Instead, a sizeable group of students (and their parents) joined a rally by the National Labor Committee, held outside the local Disney store.

Disney's empire also outsources animation for films and TV shows to countries like Korea (Lee, 2019), India (Crosby, 2011), and France (Hopewell & Keslassy, 2016). Students could locate these production practices in the context of government regulation, particularly of commercial culture for children and youth. This regulation includes the Canadian Radio-Television and Telecommunications Commission (CRTC), for example, inviting discussion of the political struggle to foster distinctly Canadian culture that resists American colonization.

In conclusion, activities inspired by CSL, keying off table 9.1, connect the power of entertainment culture not only to the everyday meaning-making practices of children but also to media production and distribution by those who benefit from the commodification of youthful imaginations. Of course, we recognize that in actual classroom settings, learning will not likely unfold as easily as our hypothetical examples imply. The point is, an exploration of the social relations that regulate this commodification, ultimately, prepares students for a politics beyond the classroom through grassroots activism (for examples, see Petrecca, 2008; Friedman, 2011; Hanbury, 2018) as well as democratic participation in media regulation.

Digital Capitalism Poses New Challenges, Deepens Older Ones

Above we described activities that show how power works *through*, not *as*, media. As shown in table 9.1, this power can be traced to human relations and practices that produce media as textually mediated discourse, because these relations and practices are embodied by the text. One challenge is that print and audio messaging is being displaced by the omnipresent superimposition of visual images and sounds, making the origins of this messaging difficult to trace. Media scholars have coined the term *mediatization*, in part to capture "the pervasive spread of media contents and platforms through all types of context and practice" (Couldry & Hepp, 2013, p. 191). The result is that our experience of media engagement is also being transformed:

> Growing up living a partially simulated life of screens, earbuds, and joysticks is now a normal experience, so much so in fact that there is an increasingly fuzzy line that divides what one knows from where one has learned it, or what one has experienced from where it actually happened. (Hoechsmann & Poyntz, 2012, p. 17)

An added factor is the speed with which information and misinformation alike spread through digital media, as well as the sheer number of people and organizations creating and circulating multimodal texts. This transformation has been accompanied by hidden practices that new technologies enable. While the current context makes it ever more urgent for youth to determine the social origins of their mediated knowing, making this determination is becoming ever harder, placing new demands on media education. These demands are illustrated by our own experience of researching a "fake news" story during a local by-election.

Tracking Power in a Networked World of "Fake News"

We became intrigued by an online story about a controversial national politician. On its face, the headline for the story appeared dubious: a left-leaning politician from a "minority" social group showcasing his multi-million-dollar mansion. We began our search for the origins of this story at what we call *Level 1, the media text* itself, which appeared in the online version of the *Vancouver Courier*, a credible local news source. The story of interest appeared in the middle of three "hot-linked" ads appearing just below the *Courier*'s news content, with a heading "You may like" on the left side of the screen and, in smaller type, "Sponsored links by Taboola" on the right side. The ads are designed to entice the reader to click on them by issuing a challenge ("Almost Nobody Aces This 1970s Car Quiz – Can You?"), offering a chance at love ("Lonely in Vancouver? Try These Dating Sites"), or allowing a voyeuristic peek into wealth and celebrity ("Jagmeet Singh Shows Off His New Mansion" – our story of interest). As readers *engage with these texts* – at what we call *Level 2* – the curious reader may be enticed to click onto these intriguing links. Alternatively, they may see these ads as equivalent to wallpaper, something trivial to pass over quickly to avoid wasting time or worse (e.g., encountering adware, malware, ransomware). To avoid these distractions, in pursuit of our story of interest, Deirdre had to endure 145 more clicks – evidence that our story of interest is a clickbait site.

While the *Tyee* reporters who broke this story were able to reveal it as fake news, the question remained: Who was behind this fake news? A politically motivated hacker? The clickbait site? The network sponsoring the ad? Unlike some examples we might have selected, this one is relatively complex in terms of understanding the motivations behind its creation – or even who the creator is. In an attempt to trace the latter, our interrogation took us to the *deep real* – *Level 3* – asking how this media text was produced and how its production hid the operation of power.

In part, the answer rests on understanding that online advertising today often involves layers of subcontracting, which can make it difficult or impossible to hold corporations to account. Credible news sites like the *Courier* agree to post sponsored ads to earn money. In this case, it contracted with Taboola, a major third-party company that connects advertisers with publishers (i.e., the *Courier*). The *Courier* (like other publishers) can indicate *types* of ads they don't want to appear (say, sex ads), but Taboola decides on the *specific* ads that will appear. If a reader on the publisher's website clicks on an ad, that advertiser will pay the network. The network then pays a share of that money to the publisher. Given the economic incentives, it is not in the interest of the ad network or the publisher to ask too many hard questions of advertisers. And, indeed, Taboola – when contacted by *The Tyee* – reported that its client was the one who selected and posted the story and, like all clients, was responsible for content (Beers & Carney, 2019a). Yet repeated efforts by reporters to contact the client proved fruitless. Taboola refused to provide the reporters contact information for its client (Beers & Carney, 2019b) but did eventually remove the ad that contained the falsehood (Beers & Carney, 2019a).

The *Tyee* reporters discovered that a "deliberately hidden registrant" purchased the story's domain name, which pointed "to a server in California on Cloudflare, a company that can obscure the location of web servers from the public" (Beers & Carney, 2019b, para. 30). Current laws in place do not require Canada's federal government to hold Taboola or its client accountable for the fake ad and story (Beers & Carney, 2019b). The client may have just been out to make money: clickbait website owners typically earn cash based on the number of clicks or views their ad gets. The site could knowingly or unknowingly have hosted a "cloaker," which the CEO of Taboola described as "advertisers who submit content that looks legitimate at first but is later replaced with fake content" (quoted in Beers & Carney, 2019b, para. 25). What is clear from this example is that the structure of the global online advertising industry significantly diffuses responsibility for circulation of fake news about political candidates, which, left unchecked, threatens our current democratic system of governance (for further discussion, see Boler, 2008; Kozolanka & Orlowski, 2018; McChesney, 2013; Mason, Krutka, & Stoddard, 2018). Our interrogation, which began with our encounter with the text, raises issues that direct us to the politics of media production and dissemination.

Our point in describing this extended example is to illustrate how the *social relations and cultural practices* that are active in new multimodal forms of information can remain hidden from media consumers. Goering and Thomas (2018) summarize the situation: "Not only are we seeing more emotionally manipulative online content, but it is also more challenging to find and validate the source of information we consume" (p. 3, citing Hobbs, 2017). Unlike conventional media texts that leave an audit trail of editors, publishers, film directors, and so on that make authors accountable to their readers, the authorship of online texts can be rendered virtually unknowable, giving new meaning to what we call "the hidden operation of power." While the origin of media texts continues to be embodied by the text, contemporary technologies make it possible to intentionally cloak authorship. Even as the technological skill to navigate the multitude of new textual practices and the ability to decode multimodal messages are both necessary for literacy in an "age of information," they are not sufficient for our purposes; they cannot, on their own, account for the text. This new, multimodal networked world of media messaging led us to reconsider how we think about "literacy."

We recount the above experience (of a seasoned media critic) to illustrate some of the challenges of literacy for the twenty-first century. As illustrated above, new challenges include the loss of accountability because of technology that enables deliberate cloaking of authorship, hence intent. Another set of challenges posed by digital capitalism stems from how algorithms promote corporate interests by monetizing personal information (see Fuchs, 2014), encouraging media engagement in ways that perpetuate systemic biases (see Mansell, 2017, p. 155; Bakir & McStay, 2018;

boyd, 2014; Kantayya, 2020).⁹ The monetization of media engagement is perhaps most pernicious in the emergence of digitized selfhoods.

Data Colonialism and Digitized Selfhood

A full decade has gone by since we first conceived of our study. During that time, the contours of a new social order have begun to emerge more clearly from a sea change that started as early as 2005, when Google's search results started to be personalized; critical media scholars began noting the importance of how the so-called semantic web aggregates user data to learn more about each user, mainly for commercial purposes (Hoechsmann & Poyntz, 2012; boyd, 2014). Today, many, if not most, North Americans view television and movies and listen to music through streaming services like Netflix and Spotify. We watch music videos online through video aggregators like YouTube and VEVO or via other corporate-owned social media platforms like Facebook. Online gaming has become a multi-billion-dollar industry. Whether we access popular culture through fee-paying services or ostensibly use them for free, corporations have found multiple ways to earn money from users, including the generation of data about audiences. Data brokers, such as Taboola (the third-party company that connects advertisers with publishers, described earlier), now "specialize in collecting information from medical, financial, criminal, and other records for categorizing individuals through algorithmic means" (Couldry & Mejias, 2019, p. 340). While corporations may assure us that the location and personal data generated from using their devices (e.g., to help monitor our health and fitness) will not be used in advertising, they often still sell these data to brokers. Under the guise of "customer convenience" and "customization," our digital usage patterns are being systematically harvested and processed for current or future use by corporations and governments.

Thus, today, media not only saturate our everyday life but have deepened their reach. As we described above, to navigate the internet and use corporate-owned social media platforms, we must inure ourselves to a constant barrage of pop-up ads and submit to data-mining techniques. Our online social media activities "become accessible, traceable, analyzable in real time to institutions with whom we do not necessarily have a relationship of trust" (Albers, Vasquez, & Harste, 2017, p. 230; for an example of the privacy risks associated with school districts in British Columbia using a Google-owned Learning Management System, see Levine, 2020). Couldry and Mejias (2019) have theorized these new social relations, including technologically enhanced data-mining practices, as "data colonialism":

the colonial appropriation of life in general and its annexation to capital, through various mechanisms of which one is the digital platform. The platform, we argue, produces the social for capital, that is, a form of "social" that is ready for appropriation and exploitation for value as data, when combined with other data similarly appropriated. (p. 338; also see Fuchs, 2014)

Data colonialism involves the "vast reorganization of human life" (Couldry & Mejias, 2019, p. 341). Included in that reorganization is the emergence of digitized selfhood. The "freedom" promised by online connection to a world of others engages us in everyday practices that connect our meaning making, as a localized practice, to processes of commodification that can remain invisible to – hence often unquestioned by – social actors. De Lissovoy (2018) argues that digitized selfhood emerges from neoliberal capitalism, a context that actively "reframes the discursive and symbolic organization of subjectivity" (p. 188). This reorganization takes place, in part, through practices demanded by new social media – Facebook, Instagram, Snapchat, Twitter, TikTok, and other venues of monitored self-presentation. One becomes a participant in these virtual worlds by digitizing selfhood. The pleasure of media production on these sites can be transformed into a relentless cycle of updating and disseminating our identity profiles. As we have argued, engaging with these platforms renders us vulnerable to corporate exploitation, while locating the new, digitized subjectivity within demands facing a generation of workers denied a social safety net as they attempt to establish a foothold, however tenuous, in the highly precarious "communicative" economy of neoliberal capitalism (De Lissovoy, 2018, p. 198).

The neoliberal mandate – that individuals assume responsibility for dealing with the increasingly uncertain conditions of their existence – has become commonplace (see, e.g., Vassallo, 2013 on the rise of "self-regulated learning"). In the highly competitive market, youth need customized self-presentation to make themselves stand out for the most desirable jobs; the outcome of their self-production becomes experienced as a consequence of personal decision making. Davies and Bansel (2007) point out that the "diffuse and largely invisible" nature of the technologies that enable this neoliberal subjecthood makes it increasingly difficult to open this process to critical interrogation (p. 249). This difficulty has been magnified by the digitization of selfhood; new social media can work against the kind of reflexive interrogation that promotes social change.

One response has been the suggestion to restrict youth's online activities. While we see some merit in such a suggestion, we do not see it as a "solution"; indeed, restricting online media engagement can curtail the political potential of the internet.[10] We see digitized selfhood as an embodiment of textually mediated ruling that operates as local meaning making, through processes originating in extra-local social relations and practices (Smith, 1990a). The challenge is to replace the connectivity that fragments selfhood over multiple sites with political agency through recognition of shared interests in social justice issues with dispersed others. There is ample evidence that this collective exercise of power-with and power-to can facilitate social change: #MeToo and #Black Lives Matter are good examples. Commenting on #BlackLivesMatter, Jenkins (in Andersen, 2017) notes: "What might at one time have been treated as a series of isolated incidents ... is now understood in relation to systemic racism in large part because that hashtag helped diverse and scattered participants to link their perspectives and experiences together" (p. 9).

To be sure, we do not see media literacy as the answer to the power that media exercise over their users; rather, we maintain that adults have a responsibility to foster young people's ability to question both the content *and* the processes that accompany media messaging. This responsibility is an example of how adults can exercise their power-over youth to help effect a positive outcome.

To recap, while everyday media users are now able to expand their technological capital and thus use social media to create new opportunities for social and political organization, they do so in a context where unequal power relations remain unchanged (Schäfer, 2011). The challenge is that media engagement occurs through digital technologies that are not designed by everyday media users; they do not come under the control of either the user or the teacher. An emerging literature is beginning to include these conditions as a necessary component of CML (see Bakir & McStay, 2018; Buckingham, 2019; de Roock, 2021; Kohnen et al., 2020; Mason & Metzger, 2012; Mason, Krutka, & Stoddard, 2018; McDougall, 2019; Pangrazio, 2018).

As our relationship to reality is becoming increasingly digitally mediatized, de Roock (2021) argues that "under-theorizing technology means overlooking power" (p. 185). He notes: "Several decades into the internet revolution, digital technologies have neither leveled the educational playing field nor opened up democratic possibilities as they once were expected to" (p. 4). Critical media literacy needs to interrogate the production of media technology as well as the production of media content. As we illustrate below, by directing attention to social relations that control the production of information and communication technologies, the layered ontology of CSL supports such an approach.

CSL as Informed Judgment through Reflexive Interrogation

Within our increasingly mediatized context, CSL is about educating young people to make informed decisions as social agents. Drawing on research in adolescent development, Middaugh (2019) suggests that youth often contribute to the spread of misinformation by sharing false media stories (p. 45). While acknowledging that more research is needed, she suggests that because many young people tend to prefer "sensational or emotionally evocative" media, they can be attracted to (and thus share) what has been dubbed "outrage media" (discourses using language intended to provoke strong emotional responses, such as anger, disgust, moral indignation, and so on) (p. 47). She offers teaching strategies to address this challenge (pp. 53–6). As Share, Mamikonyan, and Lopez (2019) note, given that gatekeeping of digital information is minimal or absent, we need to attend to how young people make judgments when online (p. 2); while misinformation may not originate in media produced by youth, media practices lacking sound judgment have the potential to amplify the problem.

Hobbs (2010) identifies "a constellation of life skills that are necessary for full participation in our media-saturated, information-rich society," including the ability to do the following: "make responsible choices" while "locating and sharing materials"; "analyze messages in a variety of forms"; create multimodal content; "reflect on one's own conduct and communication behavior"; and "take social action by working individually and collaboratively" (pp. vii–viii). While our thinking about CSL shares these kinds of goals, to us, thinking about literacy as a "skill" fails to consider power. Emphasis on "skill" reflects the institutional context of literacy education: educators have long been required to measure literacy formally. In the context of "fake news," McGrew et al. (2019) developed "easy-to-use scoring guides" informed by practices of professional fact checkers to evaluate online information. Based on three questions,[11] educators can quickly determine "whether students possess[ed] the skills needed to make sound judgments" (p. 62). When literacy is operationalized as a finalized accomplishment in this way, it becomes what Barrow (1990) describes as a "mechanical skill" that "can be trained by extensive practice without regard to particular context" (p. 282).[12]

In the place of skill, we propose critical social literacy as an analytical sensibility promoting informed judgment during, and as an outcome of, media engagement. *Informed judgment* refers to decision making based on the understanding of media as a venue for the operation of power. It enables youth to make responsible choices as media consumers, while reflecting on their own conduct during media engagement. As described by Jenkins et al. (2006): "Sampling intelligently from the existing cultural reservoir requires a close analysis of the existing structures and uses of this material; remixing requires an appreciation of emerging structures and latent potential meanings" (p. 33; also see Gainer & Lapp, 2010).

Through CSL, informed judgment is promoted by reflexive interrogation. To be *reflexive* is to be aware of one's role in the re/constitution of social reality as an ongoing collective activity. It includes the ability to locate self, as a user and producer of meaning, within the relations of meaning making as a social practice. As participants in the accomplishment of a shared reality, all people engage in reflexivity within the given contexts of their everyday lives. This *reflexivity* is a running "mental commentary which always precedes, accompanies and reflects upon our actions" (Archer, 2000, p. 319). In this way, Archer (2007) argues: "*The subjective powers of reflexivity mediate the role that objective structural or cultural powers play in influencing social action and are thus indispensable to explaining social outcomes*" (p. 5, emphasis in original). She maintains that reflexivity is "exercised through people holding internal conversations" (Archer, 2007, p. 63). "The key feature of *reflexive* inner dialogue is silently to pose questions to ourselves and to answer them, to speculate about ourselves, any aspect of our environment and, above all, about the relationship between them" (Archer, 2007, p. 63). During media engagement, reflexivity mediates between what we call agency and power; reflexive interrogation shapes media engagement by bringing what is typically taken for granted into consideration.

Adjustment to the everyday contingencies of social situations, however, may not take place at a conscious level. While we have described reflexive practices as an "internal" conversation, this type of criticality is not, as Burbules and Berk (1999) argue, "a purely individual trait":

> Because criticality is a function of collective questioning, criticism, and creativity, it is *always* social in character, partly because relations to others influence the individual, and partly because certain of these activities (particularly thinking in new ways) arise from an interaction with challenging alternative views. (p. 62, emphasis in original)

While other educators may employ the term *critical thinking*,[13] reflexive interrogation connects this thinking to self-conscious activity in the social world; it engages learners in the exercise of judgment as

> forming opinions *with* and *through* our encounters with others ... To judge is to form points of view or positions regarding others, and to do this requires that we involve ourselves in "a talking through, a bringing forth,

a constant engagement with one's own thought and that of others" (Silverstone, 2007, p. 44). This requires us to act in the world, to go out and engage with others in order to understand others. Through this, judging involves risk-taking and, often, a challenge to the status quo, because to judge is to see things from many sides and thus to understand perspectives not yet taken. (Hoechsmann & Poyntz, 2012, pp. 198–9)

Media activities that require students to participate in, and reflect upon, various media practices with others enable them to hone their judgment, which, in turn, prepares them for media engagement beyond the classroom.

Our experiences as teachers have taught us that although all people have the capacity for reflexive interrogation, this capacity is underdeveloped in a corporate culture such as ours. As consumers of commercial media, we are discouraged from recognizing, let alone challenging, how commodified entertainment, for example, sustains social inequality and marginalization. "Individuals are often not aware that they are being educated and constructed by media culture [such as 'pop culture'], as its pedagogy is frequently invisible and unconscious" (Kellner & Share, 2005, p. 372). Prompted by the teacher, reflexive interrogation brings the pedagogical nature of media into view, disrupting the normalization of what students encounter as already given. It does so by examining whether, and how, the available meanings work to naturalize the current social order and, in doing so, secure the power operating through media (see McGregor, 2000, p. 222).

Reflexive Practices during Media Engagement

Youth are necessarily designers of the future; we believe that critical social literacy has the potential to encourage youth to design more equitable alternatives to what exists. The operative word here is *potential*; in our view, not all "critical" approaches[14] to media literacy achieve this potential. Literacy supporting positive social change must encourage reflexive interrogation not only of what already exists but also of what is being brought into existence during media engagement as redesign. From our project we identify five modes of reflexive interrogation associated with student media engagement (analogous to the dimensions of teacher reflexivity we discussed in chapter 8). We use the term *mode* to signal a "quality of mind"; modes do not correspond to different "types of people" or different "learning styles," although we believe they can inform teaching strategies. While each represents a distinct moment when students might become or be made politically aware, these modes do not follow a linear progression and are not meant as hierarchal. They are, however, interconnected by their relationship to critical social literacy as an analytical sensibility.

Our thinking has been influenced by Margaret Archer's account of "being human," in which a person is "an active and reflective agent" who is sometimes required to respond creatively, alone or with others, to "unscripted circumstances" (Archer, 2000, p. 221; see also 2007). Employed by teacher participants in our larger study (see Kelly & Currie, 2021), each mode of reflexive interrogation encourages different types of questioning, as "forms of dialogue" (Archer, 2003) with self and others. As an ongoing process, reflexive interrogation is both the means and the end for politicization. The process of becoming politically aware does not come through the "correct" answers to reflexive interrogation as much as it does through the subsequent evaluation, by students, of their own answers. As Archer (2000) notes, "we are quintessentially evaluative beings," and this means "It is we human beings who determine our priorities and define our personal identities in terms of what we care about" (p. 318).

Giving Students Opportunities to Reflect on What They Care About

To support informed judgment, we suggest that teachers attend to three facets of student self-evaluation of their media responses: the *relevance* of the issues brought into consideration; personal *commitment* to these issues, based on the individual's value system; and the perceived *urgency* of action. To illustrate, we draw from the fruitful use of hip-hop in a spoken word poetry unit that Mary, an educator whom we interviewed early in our study, described.

Mary (herself White) was teaching Grade 6 in a relatively low-income, racially diverse suburb of Toronto, where Black people were the single largest "visible minority" group. Regardless of race, gender, or class, the most popular genre of music among her students was hip-hop. Mary, an avowed fan, wanted to honour the inner-city Black origins of the music while addressing anti-Black racism. Thus, part of the unit involved her playing a different clip every day from the *Def Poetry Jam* TV series, making sure that her students saw "women, different races represented, different people doing different things." The unit culminated in students writing a poem focused on "something they were passionate about," memorizing it, and then performing it for classmates. "Think about the thing that matters most to you right now," Mary prompted her students. In the end, one of the Black students focused on racism, another on slavery, while many across ethno-racial groups explored the "importance of being a good friend." Reading their choices through the lens of race, we can see that, for some Black students, not only were the experiences and origins of racism relevant to their daily lives, but – based on their values – they named the injustice and made that a priority. Racism may not seem as relevant to many White students; experience is important here. Yet, relevance can also be learned. Acknowledging that people sometimes try to dismiss all hip-hop as misogynist or consumerist, Mary made her students aware that "hip-hop actually has roots in social activism," sharing examples that "do not degrade women" and that are "not all about money." Another opportunity for learning relevance came when students each performed their spoken word poem. These performances were videotaped and edited into a single show that the class watched together; Mary also gave each student a digital copy to keep and share with others.

We cannot help but think that this activity enhanced the relevance of racism as a social issue to students, including those from the dominant White culture. By knowing the Other through the shared passion for hip-hop, this activity has the potential to enhance commitment to a shared political goal – that of challenging racism, in both the mainstream reception of Black music and the social conditions voiced by hip-hop. Within this pedagogical context, recognition of the urgency for action might be enhanced when students recognize hip-hop as anti-racist protest. Of course, we acknowledge that the outcome of reflexive interrogation cannot so easily be guaranteed by any specific classroom activity, and it will vary across any group of learners. We provide this example to illustrate that hip-hop, as pop culture enjoyed by youth, has the potential to be used in the classroom to engage individual students in an "inner conversation" (Archer, 2003), or, through class discussion, dialogue with others (for more on hip-hop education and CML, see Graves et al., 2020; Hill & Petchauer, 2013). This experience could segue into political action beyond the classroom, such as participating in the anti-racist protests that were underway at time of writing.

Prompts for such conversations were structured into the media activities designed by teachers during our project and are summarized in table 9.2; they remain to be explored in diverse teaching contexts. The prompts in our table were used to promote reflexive interrogation through personal journal writing and, at other times, were structured into group discussion. In both cases, the goal was to facilitate deeper learning by encouraging students to consider the *relevance* of social issues brought into consideration; the *commitment* to social change, based on the individual's or their group's value system; and the *urgency* for action based on shared experience. Within the context of these kinds of considerations, we identify modes of individual and collaborative interrogation that can support informed judgment during media engagement.

Promoting Student Reflexivity

Practised during media production, reflexive interrogation begins at the individual level by stimulating consideration of how the identity, experiences, beliefs, and values of the author are embedded in their text. Following Archer (2003, 2007, 2014), *personal reflexivity* takes the form of an internal interrogation through which the selfhood of the author is brought into investigation. In Amy's activity, participants drew on their gendered and racialized identities as legitimate resources for redesigning ads. As agents of meaning making through media production, students from marginalized groups can similarly have their experiences – hence selfhoods – recognized by classmates. Power is experienced and exercised as the "power to" by Archer's (2000) "I" (i.e., the subject of self-consciousness).[15] Through this mode, Amy's project, notably, also promoted *analytical reflexivity*, when she introduced participants to tools for critical discourse analysis, interpellation, mode of address, and the gaze. Girls redeployed these tools to talk back to advertisers – an activity that led them to recognize the relevance of feminism as a political movement for gender inclusion and equality. In short, Amy's activity promoted *political reflexivity* as participants identified political interests accompanying their social identities as racialized "women."

Meaning making, however, is not carried out by isolated individuals; it is necessarily a social practice, even when carried out alone. The social nature of this practice becomes obvious during group work. When working with classmates, students in our study engaged in collaborative interrogation that enabled them to experience how any text can have different meanings, resulting in different relevance for readers with different social identities (for example, by gender, race, age, and ability). Thus, collaborative interrogation can help students recognize that texts that they might not otherwise question can be harmful to groups of which they may not be members. It can encourage affiliation with others, through recognition of shared interests (such as love of music, sports, other activities) and, as a result, commitment to collective action.

An example that unfolded at the time of writing was the collective action by youth following the school shooting in Parkland, Florida. Survivors of the high school shooting called on advertisers to pull support from a Fox News show, after host Laura Ingraham mocked student and gun control advocate David Hogg as a "whiner" and later compared child migrant detention centres to "summer camps" (see Hanbury, 2018). In their challenge to Fox media, students exercised power collectively, in terms of "us" rather than "me" – as "power-with." In this example, they demonstrated *political reflexivity* that directed their action towards corporate ownership of, and access to, the means of meaning making. This collective action was a response to student experiences of school violence. In our study, open dialogue among classmates in Natalie's activity produced an unexpected opportunity for student learning about gendered violence. These kinds of opportunities underline the importance of teacher as well as student reflexivity (see chapter 8).

As observed in especially Natalie's project, the role of affect cannot be ignored. While it can act as a positive force by pushing learners to take political action (as in the Parkland case), it can also be a barrier to political affiliation. Recall that the all-girl group presenting on the powerful protagonist of Rihanna's "Take a Bow" was taken aback when Raymond reminded them that Rihanna was beaten up by her then boyfriend, Chris Brown. Some of the girls appeared to feel embarrassed by the suggestion that Rihanna may have reunited with Brown after the beating. Perhaps they felt shame that the protagonist of "Take a Bow" – whom they had presented as powerful and independent – had been seen by others, instead, as weak, both physically and emotionally. Complex feelings of shame, or anger turned towards the social group to which she belonged, may have distanced Stella, a member of the group presenting on Rihanna, from feminism as a political movement to end gendered violence. In her final evaluation she wrote:

> I would add a section to the unit that focuses on the hypocrisy and double standards that arise when people are trying to step out of the shadow of stereotypes and societal standards. For example, some women may wish for society to view them as equals to men, to perceive them as strong and capable, yet when in a dangerous situation, expect to be protected by a male.

Not coincidentally, in his final evaluation Marco (a member of Raymond's group) wrote: "Women are not what they seem" – like Stella, he levelled a charge of hypocrisy at women as a group; his displeasure with the unit seemed to mute the kind of introspection Natalie's project was designed to stimulate (recall the showing of *Tough Guise*). Critical social literacy thus recognizes the need for *affective reflexivity*. Interrogation brings to light emotional investments the students have in their media responses, as well as in anticipated audience responses to their own media production. Recognition of these investments lays the ground for *ethical reflexivity*. Ethical reflexivity considers how you treat other people: who do you pay attention to, and who do you ignore during media engagement?

Just as for other unscripted learning, there are no certain outcomes when learning includes the experiential and emotional aspects of students' lives. Nevertheless, reflexive interrogation encourages – but does not guarantee – more inclusive media engagement or more equitable redesign. We illustrate our notion of reflexive interrogation in table 9.2. This table captures our optimism about youth as designers of a potentially better future. By recognizing that available design embodies and supports certain practices and values while discounting others, reflexive interrogation prompts students to consider how existing practices and values – instantiated in any given media text, including their own – might be transformed (Janks, 2018). Within the context of this optimism, table 9.2 identifies practices that can support re/design of a more equitable, inclusive, and sustainable future. We note that the principles of these practices, particularly those related to ethics, correspond to the guidelines that Yvette employed during the Monopoly Project. While she may have been disappointed with her students' redesigns, her project engaged learners in taking turns, making collective decisions, considering fairness, resolving conflict, and so on. In the final analysis, we conclude that Yvette's emphasis on the *ethics of designing* was, for her young students, as important as the media they produced.

To recap, reflexive interrogation can be encouraged by the types of prompts summarized in table 9.2, promoting informed judgment that supports social justice. These prompts employ the tools outlined in table 3.1. In effect, reflexive interrogation is a practice that recognizes one's media engagement as an exercise of power. Because these modes of reflexive interrogation locate the production of media in specific human actions that give media texts their power in the first place and in the re/constitution of the social world through their reception, we have been referring to the overarching approach as *critical social literacy* (CSL) (see figures 9.1 and 9.2). Reflexive interrogation in service of CSL involves questioning categories that sustain inequalities and exclusions, as well as media practices that circulate these categories as "natural" (e.g., by clicking "likes" or sharing media based on affective, rather than reasoned, responses to texts).

As illustrated by our case studies, the kinds of questions in table 9.2 can be incorporated into lesson planning by teachers to prompt class discussion or journal writing. As with our other tables, these questions are suggestions; they offer tools that teachers can employ to shape student agency during media activities in the classroom. They remind us that while media confront us as a fait accompli, they originate in intentional human activities. The point is to harness interrogation not only to already given design but also to the process of redesigning the social

Table 9.2. Student reflexivity during media engagement

Modes of reflexivity	Sample questions
Personal	*For individual media engagement:* • Why have I constructed this text or decided to share it? For or with whom? Why? • What motivates me? • What does this text say about me, as author? Does it convey what I intended? • How does my personal identity shape my thinking about media I produce or encounter? *For collaborative media engagement:* • What other viewpoints surfaced? How did I respond to viewpoints that contradicted mine? Why? • Did my responses silence others, or did they encourage others? • What did we learn from the exchange of views? What have I learned from the exchange of views?
Affective	*For individual media engagement:* • How does this text make me feel? Why? • What emotional investment do I have in producing or sharing this text? • How might others respond to this text? • What emotional investment do I have in responses by others? Why? *For collaborative media engagement:* • What emotional exchanges, if any, among group members or in response to audience members occurred? Can we name the emotions? • Did the exchange prompt me or members of my group to reconsider positions or opinions? How?
Analytical	*For individual media engagement:* • What kind of world does this text construct? • What categories and language do I use? Are they appropriate in light of my intended meaning? • What difference does my choice of language make in terms of the meaning that could be constructed by others? • Are there alternative ways to express this message? Should I use them (or not)? • What kinds of social values are promoted by the text? *For collaborative media engagement:* • How does our text compare to existing media genres that we know about? • Do we each, individually and across our group, feel that the social groups we belong to are represented or missing? What patterns of belonging or absence do we detect?

(Continued)

Table 9.2. (*continued*)

Modes of reflexivity	Sample questions
Political	*For individual media engagement:* • What kind of actions or inactions are promoted by messages in the text, both intended and unintended? • Does the text support a particular group or marginalize a particular group? A particular person? • Does the message challenge what I believe to be unfair? What kind of action or inaction does it encourage? *For collaborative media engagement:* • How might people from diverse backgrounds engage with our text? • What are the consequences of missing voices? • How might we change the text to enhance its appeal to diverse people? With what implications for how power works through our text?
Ethical	*For individual media engagement:* • Are representations in the text fair? • Will this text offend anyone? Who? Why? • Does the text promote stereotypes? • Does the text valorize or devalue the experience of others? • Should I share this text? *For collaborative media engagement:* • Did all group members have equal opportunities to express their ideas? • Did audience members' descriptions of our group's text (what they thought it was about) make us aware of harmful meanings we had not intended? • How was our message perceived by others and with what impact on them? How did we respond?

world. While reflexive interrogation is introduced in the classroom, the long-term goal is to foster reflexivity-in-action (see Schön, 1995) among young people, as practice that, eventually, will no longer depend on teachers' prompting questions. The principal aim is to spark conversation, debate, thinking, and action – informed judgment – about how to live together and resolve future societal concerns.

"What Kind of World Do You Want to Live In?"

At the conclusion to our seminar during Phase 1, one teacher participant wrote: "The road ahead for critical educators is long, but the work is worth doing" (Yue). To this we add, "The work is urgent." Contributing

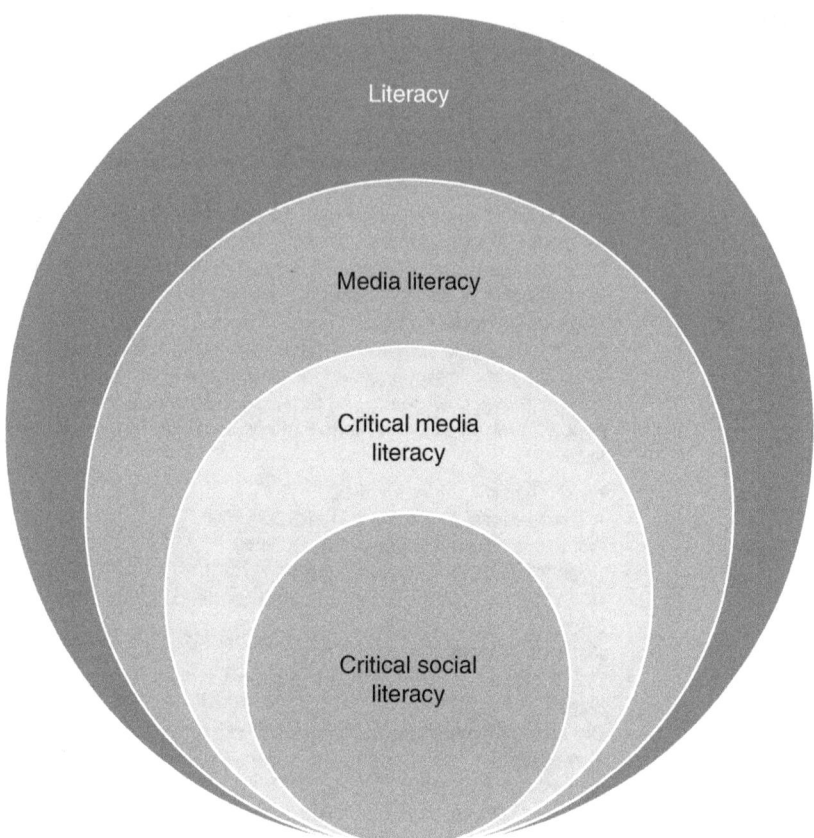

Figure 9.1. Concept map of critical social literacy and related terms

to this urgency is the current context where media production has become an everyday practice for youth. Such a context presents challenges, but also opportunities, for youth to collectively engage in constructing the kind of world they want to live in.

How teachers can support such an outcome is illustrated by a collaborative activity at inner-city John Oliver Secondary School (JOSS) in Vancouver, British Columbia. In response to racist comments posted on Twitter, students co-created with teachers, over the course of an academic year, their own Digital Code of Conduct (Rossi, 2013, 2014). JOSS hosted school-wide assemblies and smaller student groups to discuss the problem of online hate and what kindness online might look like. "All 1,100

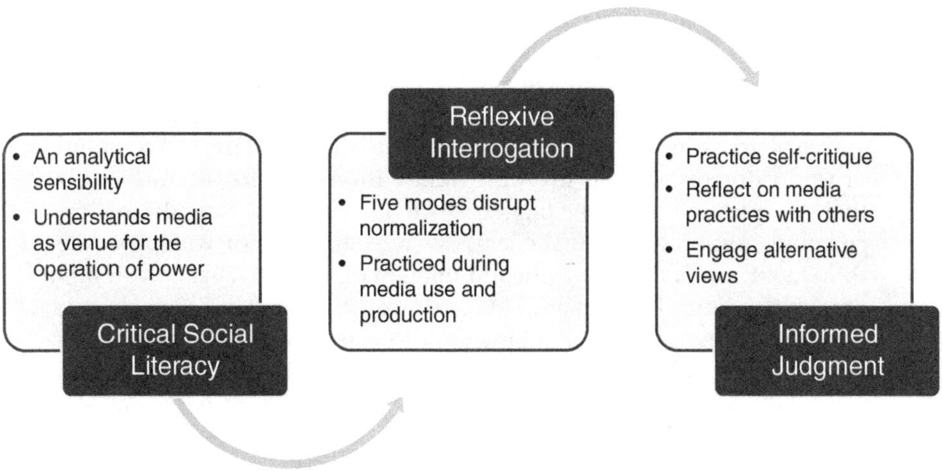

Power Revisited 229

Critical Social Literacy
- An analytical sensibility
- Understands media as venue for the operation of power

Reflexive Interrogation
- Five modes disrupt normalization
- Practiced during media use and production

Informed Judgment
- Practice self-critique
- Reflect on media practices with others
- Engage alternative views

Figure 9.2. The relation of CSL to reflexive interrogation and informed judgment

students at the school wrote 10 statements about how they would act online. Each classroom submitted its top 10 statements, and student leaders and teachers synthesized the final statements for the code" (Rossi, 2014, para. 9). Based on journalist reports, we see evidence of the sort of personal, ethical, and political modes of reflexive interrogation we summarize in table 9.2. Some students and teachers alike said they felt, upon reflection, a "disconnect ... between their online and offline personalities." "When you realize that" these two personalities "are both the same thing," explained one student, then "it's much easier not to bully online, not to harass people, not to do those things. It's much easier to realize 'that's me'" (Rossi, 2014, para. 6). In other words, the process of negotiating a code of conduct provided an experience of texts as social products: it placed student authors as embodied subjects in a textual object of their making. As a student leader at JOSS told a reporter, "When the students created the code of conduct, the students said 'I choose to be a better citizen online,' 'I choose to not bully people online' and I think it's much more powerful when students choose to do it because it's a voluntary thing, and they're not being forced to participate in this" (Singh-Joseph, 2014, para. 11).

In this example, we see how school leaders recognized secondary students as already knowing subjects and political actors. They created opportunities for youth to act together to construct the kind of environment they want to live in. They exhibited solidarity against racism and other forms of cyber harassment to practise democracy within the school. We see this as a powerful rejoinder to the ongoing erosion of the democratic political imaginary. We believe that the opportunities to engage students in this kind of activity are endless: engagement in social and ecological justice concerns can start by simply asking, "What kind of world do you want to live in?" Wendy Brown (2018) acknowledges that this question poses the biggest challenge when teaching those most currently advantaged. But she suggests it as a frame for young people thinking through their "biggest and smallest decisions. What do you support, with whom do you stand? What do you oppose? And what do you do when challenges come, unbidden, into your midst?" (para. 10). The point, she says, "is to mix the questions of what you want to be and do with what you want this world to be, and let that mixture pave your way in the adult world" (para. 8).

Within this context, critical social literacy aims to support children and youth in their practices of meaning making as the vehicle for redesigning an alternative future. Critical social literacy involves the development of human capacities for an array of practices supporting social change, exercised both individually and collectively. This array includes self-reflexivity, creativity, relationship building, identity building, analysis of language choices and sign systems, attunement to the play of power and the consequences for dis/advantaged groups, and thinking about the ethics of human communications. Critical social literacy directs attention to moments where youth, as agents, can exercise these capacities to design the future world they want to live in.

APPENDICES

Appendix A: Course Syllabus for CSL Seminar

Popular Culture in the Classroom:
Teaching for Critical Social Literacy
Fall, 2012
EDST 580A, section 081; SOCI 598A, section 002; WMST 505A, section 001

Seminar Coordinators:

Dr. Dawn Currie, Sociology   Dr. Deirdre Kelly, Educational Studies
dawn.currie@ubc.ca 604-822-3576   deirdre.kelly@ubc.ca, 604-822-3952

Seminar Description

This seminar explores the use of popular culture as a resource for teaching critical social literacy (CSL). *Social* literacy entails an understanding of how media (both commercial and student authored) are implicated in everyday life as a venue of power (in terms of both media production and media reception). The seminar begins by outlining a framework for analysis of media texts. The emphasis of the seminar, however, is practical: assigned readings, group discussion, and class activities are designed to help participants connect theoretical issues to their everyday professional practices. Our intended outcome is the enhanced ability of participants to design CSL exercises for public school classrooms. The intended audience is public school teachers and researchers interested in designing and assessing classroom activities to promote CSL.

We will teach this seminar from a social justice perspective. It is being piloted as part of the coordinators' larger research project, titled *Classroom Use of Popular Culture as a Vehicle for Critical Social Literacy*. This research is funded by the Social Sciences and Humanities Research Council of Canada and has received approval from UBC's Behavioural Research Ethics Board.

This seminar will be held Wednesdays from 4:30 to 7:30 p.m., beginning September 12, 2012 and ending November 28, 2012. We will meet at the Vancouver Board of Education, 1580 West Broadway, Vancouver, Room TBA [for details, see WebCT Vista: *CSL seminar meeting location, VSB 2012.docx*].

Participants

This seminar is open to both interested graduate students enrolled at UBC (who will receive three academic credits) and teachers practising in Vancouver and the Lower Mainland who would like to enhance their ability to design and implement classroom activities employing popular culture. There are no formal academic prerequisites.

Format

This seminar employs a student-centred, participatory format; while the instructors will introduce and discuss key analytical frameworks and issues, emphasis will be given to group discussion and small group activities that employ these analytical tools. Students will sign up (solo or in pairs) to facilitate group discussion of assigned readings. Students taking the seminar for academic credit will be assigned supplemental readings; they will be expected to help deepen class discussion by amplifying analytical points in the assigned readings. A Reading Package will be distributed (at no cost) to participants. While we have "finalized" a schedule of readings and seminar topics, the seminar will unfold according to the learning progress of participants.

Intended Learning Outcomes

It is our intention that teachers will gain insight into their current teaching practices, while becoming better prepared to design classroom activities using public media. Students taking the seminar for academic credit will gain an overview of current theory and research on critical media/cultural studies. They will be required to design a classroom activity based on seminar learning.

Schedule of Topics

September 12th – Introduction to the Seminar and to Seminar Participants.

In this first session, we will identify what brought each of us to this seminar and share our expectations. Readings include:

Sensoy, Ozlem. (2007). Social education and critical media literacy: Can Mr. Potato Head help challenge binaries, essentialism, and Orientalism? In D. Macedo & S.R. Steinberg (Eds.), *Media literacy: A reader* (pp. 593–602). New York: Peter Lang.

For credit students:

Vadeboncoeur, Jennifer A. (2005). Naturalised, restricted, packaged, and sold: Reifying the fictions of "adolescent" and "adolescence." In J. Vadeboncoeur & L.P. Stevens (Eds.), *Re/constructing "the adolescent": Sign, symbol and body* (Vol. 33, pp. 1–24). New York: Peter Lang.

September 19th – What Is Critical Social Literacy?

In this session we will lay common ground for class discussion by defining key terms and identifying key issues in media education (for example, what do we mean by "text," what is the difference between "popular culture" and commercial culture, and why does this difference matter; what does social justice have to do with analysis of media, and so on). We will also discuss "critical reflection" and explore how and why it is a necessary skill for CSL teaching. Readings include:

Hagood, Margaret C., Alvermann, Donna E., & Heron-Hruby, Alison. (2010). Introduction: What's in your backpack? In *Bring it to class: Unpacking pop culture in literacy learning* (pp. 1–12). New York: Teachers College Press.

Pungente, John J., Duncan, Barry, & Andersen, Neil. (2005). The Canadian experience: Leading the way. *Yearbook of the National Society for the Study of Education, 104* (140–60).

Read pages 374–77 and skim the rest according to interest:

Kellner, Douglas, & Share, Jeff. (2005). Toward critical media literacy: Core concepts, debates, organizations, and policy. *Discourse: Studies in the Cultural Politics of Education, 26*(3), 369–86.

Gainer, Jesse S. (2010). Critical media literacy in middle school: Exploring the politics of representation. *Journal of Adolescent & Adult Literacy, 53*(5), 364–73.

For credit students:

Alvermann, Donna E., Moon, Jennifer S., & Hagood, Margaret C. (1999). Approaches to teaching using popular culture and the politics of pleasure. In *Popular culture in the classroom: Teaching and researching critical media literacy* (pp. 22–40). Newark, DE: International Reading Association.

Buckingham, David. (2003). Media education and the end of the critical consumer. *Harvard Educational Review, 73*(3), 309–27.

Share, Jeff. (2009). Young children and critical media literacy. In R. Hammer & D. Kellner (Eds.), *Media/cultural studies: Critical approaches* (pp. 126–51). New York: Peter Lang.

September 26th – How Can We Study "Texts" as Part of the Social (Rather Than Only Cultural) World?

In this session we will lay out a framework for analysing media texts that connects media texts to everyday practices through which the social world is re/constituted. Readings include:

Young, Josephine P. (2000). Boy talk: Critical literacy and masculinities. *Reading Research Quarterly, 35*(3), 312–37.

Jenkins, Henry. (2007). Chap. 3: Death-defying heroes. In *The wow climax: Tracing the emotional impact of popular culture* (pp. 65–74). New York: New York University Press.

For credit students:

Brock, Deborah. (2012). Thinking about power: Exploring theories of domination and governance. In D. Brock, R. Raby, & M.P. Thomas (Eds.), *Power and everyday practices* (pp. 11–32). Toronto: Nelson Education.
Gee, James P. (2011). Theoretical tools. In *How to do discourse analysis: A toolkit* (pp. 149–84). New York: Routledge.
Phillips, Louise, & Jørgensen, Marianne W. (2002). Chap. 3: Critical discourse analysis. In *Discourse analysis as theory and method* (pp. 60–95). Thousand Oaks, CA: Sage.

October 3rd – How Is Meaning Making an Exercise of Power?

Building on our understanding of power, we will explore a perhaps too obvious expression of the power of the media: Walt Disney and the commodification of childhood. In this session we will introduce and practise media analysis, and reflect on the lingering impact of media we enjoyed as children. Readings include:

Holson, Laura M. (2004, October 4). A finishing school for all, Disney style. *New York Times*, pp. C1, 11.
Hall, Stuart. (2000). Heroes or villains? and Stereotyping as a signifying practice. In J.M. Iseke-Barnes and N.N. Wane (Eds.), *Equity in schools and society* (pp. 97–109). Toronto: Canadian Scholars' Press.
Friedman, Steven. (2011). Taking action against Disney: A teacher struggles with encouraging direct student action. In E. Marshall & Ö. Sensoy (Eds.), *Rethinking popular culture and media* (pp. 253–7). Milwaukee: Rethinking Schools.

Optional homework to create or adapt a lesson plan:

Padva, Gilad. (2008). Educating the Simpsons: Teaching queer representations in contemporary visual media. *Journal of LGBT Youth*, 5(3), 57–73.
MediaSmarts. Canada's Centre for Digital and Media Literacy. http://mediasmarts.ca/teacher-resources/find-lesson

For credit students:

Buckingham, David, & Sefton-Green, Julian. (2003). Gotta catch 'em all: Structure, agency and pedagogy in children's media culture. *Media, Culture & Society*, 25(3), 379–400.

Saukko, Paula. (2003). Reading ideology. In *Doing research in cultural studies: An introduction to classical and new methodological approaches* (pp. 99–114). Thousand Oaks, CA: Sage.

Wasko, Janet. (2008).The commodification of youth culture. In K. Drotner & S. Livingstone (Eds.), *The international handbook of children, media and culture* (pp. 461–75). Thousand Oaks, CA: Sage.

October 10th – How Does the Media Give Us Pleasure?

As follow-up to the previous session, we will discuss the way that "reading" media is not simply a cognitive process; media engages us through our "feelings," especially feelings of pleasure. We will deepen our understanding of teaching media studies through recognition that pleasure can take various forms, including that of refusing the intended message. In the remainder of the seminar, we explore how to harness the pleasure of refusal (talking back to power), as well as the pleasures of creativity, media competence, and critical analysis for CSL teaching. Readings include:

Fiske, John. (1989). The jeaning of America. In *Understanding popular culture* (pp. 1–21). Boston: Unwin Hyman.

Gainer, Jesse S. (2007). Social critique *and* pleasure: Critical media literacy with popular culture texts. *Language Arts, 85*(2), 106–14.

For credit students:

Grossberg, Lawrence. (1992). Is there a fan in the house? The affective sensibility of fandom. In L.A. Lewis (Ed.), *The adoring audience: Fan culture and popular media* (pp. 50–65). London: Routledge.

Rymes, Betsy. (2011). Deference, denial, and beyond: A repertoire approach to mass media and schooling. *Review of Research in Education, 35*, 208–38.

October 17th – Who Does This Text Think I Am?

In order to help understand the power of especially commercial media, we will explore how texts appeal to readers and introduce some tools for analysing this appeal. Readings include:

Ellsworth, Elizabeth. (1997). Mode of address: It's a film thing. In *Teaching positions: Difference, pedagogy, and the power of address* (pp. 21–36). New York: Teachers College Press.

Moje, Elizabeth B., & van Helden, Caspar. (2005). Doing popular culture: Troubling discourses about youth. In J. Vadeboncoeur & L.P. Stevens (Eds.),

Re/constructing "the adolescent": Sign, symbol and body (Vol. 33, pp. 211–47). New York: Peter Lang.

For credit students:

Alvermann, Donna E., & Hagood, Margaret C. (2000). Critical media literacy: Research, theory, and practice in "New Times." *Journal of Educational Research*, *93*(3), 193–205.

Davies, Bronwyn. (1994). Reading fictional texts. In *Poststructuralist theory and classroom practice* (pp. 101–23). Geelong, Australia: Deakin University.

October 24th – Who Does the Text Want Me to Be?

Building on the previous session, we will explore how the text attempts to construct particular kinds of readers/viewers. This happens through the construction of particular kinds of "subjectivities" – ways of feeling and thinking about the social world constructed by the media. Readings include:

Please read the section titled "Research on mapping subject positions and its implications," pp. 197–199 in:

Alvermann & Hagood, 2000 – for full citation, see Week 6 (for credit students)

Gee, James P. (2002). Millennials and Bobos, *Blue's Clues* and *Sesame Street*: A story for our times. In D.E. Alvermann (Ed.), *Adolescents and literacies in a digital world* (pp. 51–67). New York: Peter Lang.
Read one of the following for a jigsaw activity (to be assigned in class):
Bennett, Andy. (1999). Rappin' on the Tyne: White hip hop culture in Northeast England – an ethnographic study. *Sociological Review*, *47*(1), 1–24.
Durham, Meenakshi Gigi. (2004). Constructing the "new ethnicities": Media, sexuality, and the diaspora identity in the lives of Asian immigrant girls. *Critical Studies in Media Communication*, *21*(2), 210–29.
Leistyna, Pepi, & Alper, Loretta. (2007). Critical media literacy for the twenty-first century: Taking our entertainment seriously [class matters]. In D. Macedo & S.R. Steinberg (Eds.), *Media literacy: A reader* (pp. 54–78). New York: Peter Lang.
Marshall, Elizabeth, & Sensoy, Özlem. (2009). The same old hocus-pocus: Pedagogies of gender and sexuality in *Shrek 2*. *Discourse: Studies in the Cultural Politics of Education*, *30*(2), 151–64.

For credit students:

Davies, Bronwyn. (1997). Constructing and deconstructing masculinities through critical literacy. *Gender and Education*, *9*(1), 9–30.

Weedon, Chris. (1987). Chap. 4: Language and subjectivity. In *Feminist practice and poststructuralist theory* (pp. 74–106). New York: Basil Blackwell.

October 31st – Are We All Media "Dupes"?

In this session we will argue not. Specifically, we will explore how audiences actively negotiate their own meanings. One result is a multitude of constructed meanings and of media affects. Here, the analytical task is to reveal the range of meanings available in any text and to interrogate how our social identity – intersected by age, gender, "racialization," class location, our sexualized identity, and so on – complicates meaning making. Readings include:

Excerpts from (to be assigned later in the term):

Jenkins, Henry, et al. (2006). *Confronting the challenges of participatory culture: Media education for the 21st century.* Chicago: The John D. and Catherine T. MacArthur Foundation.

Alvermann, Donna E., & Hagood, Margaret C. (2000). Fandom and critical media literacy. *Journal of Adolescent and Adult Literacy, 43*(5), 436–47.

Black, Rebecca W. (2005). Access and affiliation: The literacy and composition practices of English-Language Learners in an online fanfiction community. *Journal of Adolescent and Adult Literacy, 49*(2), 118–28.

For credit students:

Burwell, Catherine. (2010). Rewriting the script: Toward a politics of young people's digital media participation. *Review of Education, Pedagogy, and Cultural Studies, 32,* 382–402.

Saukko, Paula. (2003). Studying lived resistance. In *Doing research in cultural studies: An introduction to classical and new methodological approaches* (pp. 39–54). Thousand Oaks, CA: Sage.

November 7th – How Is the Classroom a Site for the Production of Texts?

In this session we will apply what we have learned about analysis of texts to our classrooms. This application has a dual task: the first is to think about the kinds of media that can be used in the classroom, the second to analyse student reception of these media, especially when this reception is not what we anticipated when designing a teaching activity. Readings include:

Kenway, Jane, & Bullen, Elizabeth. (2006). Pedagogies that bite/byte back. In H. Lauder, P. Brown, J.-A. Dillabough & A.H. Halsey (Eds.), *Education, globalization and social change* (pp. 524–36). Oxford: Oxford University Press.

Hill, Marc Lamont. (2009). Wounded healing: Forming a community through storytelling in hip-hop lit. *Teachers College Record, 111*(1), 248–93.
Read one of the following, depending on your interest:
MacGillivray, Laurie, & Martinez, Anna Maritza. (1998). Princesses who commit suicide: Primary children writing within and against gender stereotypes. *Journal of Literacy Research, 30*(1), 53–84.
Reed, Andrew. (2011). Stenciling dissent: Political graffiti engages students in the history of protest for social justice. In E. Marshall & Ö. Sensoy (Eds.), *Rethinking popular culture and media* (pp. 298–303). Milwaukee: Rethinking Schools.

For credit students:

Buckingham, David (2003). Classroom strategies. In *Media education: Literacy, learning and contemporary culture* (pp. 70–85). Cambridge: Polity Press.
Lankshear, Colin, & Knobel, Michele. (2007). Sampling "the new" in new literacies. In M. Knobel & C. Lankshear (Eds.), *A new literacies sampler* (pp. 1–24). New York: Peter Lang.

November 14th and 21st – The Final Sessions Will Take the Form of Workshops.

Participants who choose this option will design classroom activities to share with seminar participants for group feedback and refinement.

November 28th – Wrap-up.

Responsibilities for all participants (for academic credit, also see below).

Weekly Readings:

It is the instructors' responsibility to facilitate learning. They will do so by amplifying analytical points introduced by the readings and providing constructive commentary on student ideas. Lecturing will be kept to a minimum, based on the needs of the group. The success of the seminar depends on everyone coming to sessions prepared to discuss the assigned readings. Class members will learn as much from the exchange of views inside the classroom as we will from analysing the readings on our own. To enrich class discussion, participants will take responsibility for facilitating class discussion. We will assign responsibility for each week during our first session.

Writing Activities:

This seminar is a component of Dawn and Deirdre's larger research project, *Classroom Use of Popular Culture as a Vehicle for Critical Social Literacy.*

During the initiating phase of the research, both teachers who were interviewed and published scholars indicated that one of the challenges to using public media in the classroom is that youth often take pleasure from the media that teachers want to use to stimulate critique. This pleasure can stifle rather than facilitate classroom discussion. The goal of our research is to understand how pleasure works through media, particularly commercial entertainment. This understanding will enable teachers to harness media pleasures in their teaching.

Your participation in this seminar includes the completion of writing activities that will help us explore how pleasure works through commercial media. These activities entail the submission of a series of short written responses to weekly questions posed by the seminar coordinators. These questions will entail the use of the media analysis tools introduced during our seminar meetings. Because we are asking you to explore issues of your own media pleasure, we hope that the writing activities will be enjoyable.

Instructions for each activity will be elaborated at the close of each session. Some of your writing will be shared with classmates; we will also endeavour to give you regular feedback. We appreciate receiving an electronic version of your written activities. You may like to submit a "seminar journal" of these writing activities at the conclusion of the seminar. We expect to publish our research and, in doing so, draw upon materials written by seminar participants. We encourage you to choose a pseudonym for your writing, although some participants may like to have their contributions to the research visible through use of their actual names. We will discuss the pros and cons of using your actual name during the first session.

Designing a Classroom Activity: Optional for Non-credit Participants:

We assume that you are taking this seminar in order to enhance your ability to design classroom activities promoting critical social literacy through the use of public media. The final seminar meetings will give you the opportunity to design such an activity; detailed instructions on this activity will be available on the full syllabus (distributed during our first session). We will also discuss this activity in detail during seminar sessions. We will devote time during our concluding sessions for peer feedback on these designs.

Required Assignments for Participants Receiving Academic Credit

As well as completing the above activities, to receive academic credit you will be graded on three required assignments. Dawn and Deirdre will each independently assess your work; in other words, your final grade will reflect their collaborative assessment. You will need to submit two copies of your assignments.

Synthesis-Response-Question Paper:

Each participant will be responsible for facilitating class discussion of assigned readings. Participants receiving academic credit are required to prepare one Synthesis-Response-Question (SRQ) piece. The SRQ should be written as a narrative rather than a bulleted summary. It should (1) synthesize the reading in approximately one paragraph; (2) provide your response to the reading in one-half page (e.g., add a new idea or example, discuss a point you agree or disagree with and why, take up an idea that relates to your experience, discuss the implications for teaching, etc.); (3) pose critical questions about the reading that will enhance our understanding of course themes. Strong SRQs will illuminate the arguments being made by the author(s) by drawing connections to previous class readings. The SRQ should fit on one page of paper (font size 12; maximum 500 words). Email your SRQ to both Dawn and Deirdre no later than the Sunday before the Wednesday that your reading is to be discussed in class. Your SRQ will be used to stimulate class discussion. You will receive 10% of your final grade for your SRQ.

>Name your SRQ as: SRQ_Author last name.Your Name.doc
>(e.g., SRQ_Levinson.Deirdre Kelly.doc).

Two Reading Response Papers:

These papers should be based on two assigned readings of your choice (these should be chosen from the section on the syllabus marked "for credit students"). Papers should be about three pages (double spaced, 12 pitch) in length. Identify the key argument by the author(s) or the analytical tool introduced by the author(s). More importantly, your essay should assess the utility of the article for designing a classroom activity to promote critical social literacy. One purpose for this assignment is to facilitate your design of a classroom activity, so direct your discussion to thinking about your own project. These papers are worth 15% each of your final grade; in other words, **30% of your final grade** is based on reading response essays. In order for us to give you feedback, hand in these essays as you complete them.

Design for a Classroom Activity:

Based on what you have learned in the seminar, create a lesson or unit that you might like to teach in the future, bearing in mind a particular audience (e.g., a media education unit for middle-school children). During the final meetings of the seminar, you will present your classroom activity for peer feedback. In order to receive peer feedback:

(a) name the lesson or unit;
(b) indicate the learning objectives;
(c) provide an overview of, and a rationale for, the content and organization of topics;
(d) identify materials and resources you will use (e.g., readings, websites); and
(e) discuss educational activities, assignments (if relevant), and evaluation criteria in light of your learning objectives. If relevant, identify which courses (or learning outcomes within an IRP) your lesson or unit will fit into.

In order to help Dawn and Deirdre assess the utility of the seminar, identify how you will incorporate one or more of the inquiry tools we have discussed in the seminar (e.g., you incorporate it into a planned activity and explain how learners might use it). In your discussion, include your reflections on the pedagogical and curricular choices that you made as you designed the learning activity (i.e., why the name, why the objectives, why the topics, why the readings, why the assignments and evaluation criteria). Also think about the group of people (present or in the future) you will be teaching. How do their identities (e.g., age, socioeconomic status, race/ethnic background, gender, sexuality, etc.) affect how you create this lesson or unit – the activities, evaluation, resources, and so on? What knowledge are you expecting the learners to have before you teach this? What kinds of follow-up activities or lessons might be appropriate? Non-teaching students may want to consider partnering with one of the teacher participants. On the day one partner is scheduled to present, the other partner might take responsibility for leading off the commentary. Partners might also exchange and review drafts of each other's written work. If ready and in order to get the highest quality of peer feedback, you may want to distribute via email a written preface to your project (e.g., learning objectives, some salient details of the lesson or unit) along with any requests and expectations (what you want the group's help with). On the actual day of your presentation:

- Plan to present for 10–15 minutes
- Consider the following elements:
  - An overview of your learning activity (lesson, unit);
  - An explanation of how it uses what you have learned in the seminar;
  - Identification of areas or dilemmas where you want feedback.

While all participants are encouraged to design a classroom activity, students taking the seminar for academic credit are required to complete this activity, as 60% of their final grade will be based on this activity. Collaboration with a practising teacher will not impact on your grade. A final version of your classroom activity is due one week after the final seminar meeting. Please submit hardcopies to both Dawn and Deirdre (if this is difficult, we will accept electronic attachments of final assignments).

Appendix B: Writing and Other Homework Activities – CSL Seminar 2012

Week 1:

- Why is media literacy important for young people?
- At what age do you think it is appropriate to begin teaching media literacy? Why?
- Please give examples.

Week 2:

- After reading each other's paper [on Writing Activity 1; Week 1], interview your partner in order to help them deepen their reflexivity.
  - "Interview" means prompting your partner to deepen their thinking by reflecting on how they have come to "know" the topic of "media and youth" (give concrete examples) and by encouraging them to explore how they feel about the issue of media and youth.
- Based on your interview experience, rewrite your answer to the questions we posed for Writing Activity 1:
  - "Why is media literacy important for young people? At what age do you think it is appropriate to begin teaching media literacy? Why? Refer to the kinds of questions in the PowerPoint presentation."

The PowerPoint questions were grouped into three categories, as follows:

- What categories (and thinking devices) we think with
- How you interact in social encounters
- How you feel (about what you think you know and how you interact with others)

Week 3:

- Think of a movie or book that you still really remember from your childhood; describe it.
- How did you interact with this cultural artifact? What context were you in?
- How did it make you feel?
- What was so striking about it that lingers in your memory so long?

Week 4:

- Describe a film or TV show that you currently enjoy.
- Compare this to your favourite film or book [from childhood] that you wrote about last week. What has changed? How?
- How does thinking about these changes influence what you might use for CSL with the young students you teach?

Week 5:

- Think back to a time when a classroom activity (or working with young people) resulted in an emotional response you did not anticipate.
- How did you deal with it at that time (reflection **in** action)?
- How might you deal with it now (reflection **on** action)?

Week 6:

- In lieu of writing, participants were assigned to read one of four optional readings for a jigsaw activity centred on the question: How do young people make sense of pop culture?
  - What subject position/s were spotlighted in your assigned reading?
  - What difference did those markers of identity (e.g., gender, class, etc.) make in terms of how young people negotiated meanings of the commercial or pop culture text/s being studied?
  - [In small groups, across the four readings] Identify how intersectionality is illustrated in your article.
  - Discuss the implications for designing a classroom activity to enhance CSL.

Week 7:

- In lieu of writing, participants were asked to visit *fanfiction.net*.
- Choose a topic that interests you (your options will include movies, TV programs, books, and so on).
- Explore the kinds of texts produced by fans on this topic; be prepared to describe what you have found to the class.
- What kinds of skills are being demonstrated?
- What kind of learning is taking place?
- Keep in mind the CDA tool that is written on your card and be prepared to discuss it in relation to your site; you can review these tools in our PowerPoint slideshows from previous seminars posted online.

Week 8:

- Please pick one theme from the seminar up to this point that you think will be useful in your teaching.
- How might it inform your teaching practice? Or …
- How might it inform your inquiry (research) on critical social literacy?

Weeks 9 and 10:

- Participants taking the seminar for credit will work on their final projects (to design classroom activities).

Weeks 11 and 12:

- Participants will share their final projects with seminar classmates for group feedback and refinement.

Appendix C: Ethics and Example of Parent/Guardian Informed Consent Letter

This multiple case study took place in seminar rooms in a school board office after hours, two school districts, three public schools (two elementary, one secondary), and one privately owned community café. It involved people ranging from nine years old to retirement age. In chapter 3 we detailed some of our challenges taking this multi-phased, complex project through the Behavioural Research Ethics Board process. The protracted series of exchanges with the Board resulted in significant delays; in certain moments, we experienced the ethical review process as a bureaucratic nightmare rather than an encouragement to thoughtful, morally informed research. Like Hammersley (2009) and Corbin and Morse (2003), we believe some of the questions and demands put to us implicitly and inappropriately assumed project assessment criteria developed for biomedical research, and we question the legitimacy of such regulation on ethical grounds. Nevertheless, we respect and support the idea of an ethical review process and believe that researchers need to be accountable for what they research and how they carry out their inquiries. The ethical review process is among the first steps researchers take to be as transparent as possible in their ongoing conduct and relationships with research participants and to avoid or minimize harm. For us, respecting our participants was paramount.

Informed consent – and assent, in the case of people under age 19 – is an essential part of ethical research. At our university (and many others), such consent is often given via a letter and a signed and dated form. Generally, the various versions of our form included:

- The purpose of our study and details of procedures involving participants as well as their total time commitment;
- The rights of participants, such as the right to withdraw from the study at any point without having to provide a reason and the right not to answer specific questions;

- The risks and benefits of participation, if any, that were foreseen;
- The ways that we planned to protect the participants' confidentiality; and
- Reassurance that, for the classroom study phase of our research project, while student participants were obliged to participate in regularly scheduled pedagogical activities, they were under no obligation to participate in interviews, to be videotaped, or to have any classwork or homework used as data.

Below, we include the approved template we created for parent or guardian consent. We adapted this depending on the research phase, the age, and the role of the participant. For example, in the case of teacher participants, we provided them the option of using their real names, because we felt it was an important way to credit them for their ideas, if they so desired. Here is the relevant passage from the teacher consent letter:

> You will have a choice either to be identified by name in the reports of the completed study or to have your identity kept strictly confidential through the use of a pseudonym. You can change your mind about how to be identified at any point in the study. If you want us to use your real name, you will have the option of indicating that you want specific quotes attributed anonymously. No schools will be identified by name in the study.

In keeping with this promise, when we had a complete version of each case study chapter, we sent this to the teacher and graduate research assistant involved in that case for their feedback. Teachers did not request that we make any changes; instead, they emailed comments like this:

> It was nice to read through this while on maternity leave since I miss my classroom (during the quiet times when the baby's sleeping). I don't have any changes to make; it was interesting to read the reflections and your analyses on the project. (Natalie)
>
> Thank you for the draft, it was very interesting to read and remember that activity. You seem to have documented it very thoroughly ... Connecting learning to the lived experience of students continues to be a challenge and focus for my teaching. I am always looking for new and exciting ways to engage the enthusiasm they come to school with every day. Thank you for the opportunity to learn! (Jane)
>
> Whew! I did, I finally was able to complete a reading of the chapter uninterrupted and enjoy the conclusion of this project! I have no comments re: the accuracy ... the chapter brought up many memories of things I said/wrote and then forgot about! (Amy)

At this stage, they let us know whether they wanted to use their real name or a pseudonym; one teacher requested a pseudonym and selected it herself.

The University Of British Columbia

Department of Sociology
6303 N.W. Marine Drive
Vancouver, BC, Canada V6T 1Z1
Tel: (604) 822-6683
Fax: (604) 822-6161

PARENTAL/GUARDIAN CONSENT FORM

Popular Culture in the Classroom: Teaching for Critical Social Literacy

Dr. Dawn Currie	Dr. Deirdre Kelly
Principal Investigator	Co-Investigator
Department of Sociology	Department of Educational Studies
Phone: 604-822-3576	Phone: 604-822-3952

Date_____

Dear Parent/Guardian:

I am currently working on my master's degree/doctorate at the University of British Columbia. I have been hired by Professors Dawn Currie and Deirdre Kelly, who are conducting a study titled "Popular Culture in the Classroom: Teaching for Critical Social Literacy." The study is being funded by the Social Sciences and Humanities Research Council of Canada (SSHRCC).

PURPOSE OF THE STUDY:
The purpose of this study is to develop learning activities for teachers to use in their classrooms to promote media literacy. An activity has been designed by your child's teacher, NAME, as part of the larger study. We are seeking your permission to include your child's participation in our assessment of this learning activity.

STUDY PROCEDURES:
Our assessment will be based on classroom observations I will make along with a second Graduate Assistant hired on the study. These observations will take the form of field notes and video recordings. The purpose of the video recordings is to ensure accuracy in classroom observations. The recordings will be viewed only by Professors Currie and

Kelly and their Research Assistants for the purpose of assessing learning. Professors Currie and Kelly may also like to talk with the children after the activity and observations have been completed. They would not talk individually with children, but rather with a small group of children.

CONFIENTIALITY:
Both field notes and video recordings will be stored on a password-protected research computer kept at UBC for at least five years. After completion of all publications from the study, all data will be destroyed. Neither the real names of any students or of the school will be identified in published reports of the study. As interviews will be conducted in pairs or small groups in this study, there is limited confidentiality in that the researcher and co-investigator cannot control what another student with whom your child would be interviewed may or may not share outside of the interview. At the same time, the discussions with children will be focused on the learning activity; no personal questions will be asked. We anticipate that the discussions would be very similar to ordinary talk about school.

POTENTIAL RISKS:
There are no known risks for your child's participation in our assessment study. While all children will participate in the learning activity, only children who have been given parental/guardian permission will be included in our assessment, including video recording; children who do not have parental consent or who have agreed themselves to participate in our study will not be video-taped.

POTENTIAL BENEFITS:
This assessment has the potential to enhance insight into the classroom practices of your child's teacher and help increase their repertoire of teaching skills.

YOUR CHILD'S ASSENT:
We will be asking your child's assent along with your consent. Our Research Assistant, NAME, will explain what "assent" means to the children and distribute the forms. Your child's teacher, TEACHER'S NAME, will oversee collection of these forms. I assure you that there is no pressure on your child to participate; there will be no negative repercussions should either you or your child decide not to participate in our study.

CONTACT FOR FURTHER INFORMATION:
If you have any questions regarding the project or our request for your child's participation, please contact either Dr. Currie at (604) 822-3576 or Dr. Kelly at (604) 822-3952.

CONTACT FOR CONCERNS ABOUT THE RIGHTS OF RESEARCH SUBJECTS:
If you have any concerns about the treatment or rights of research subjects, you may contact the Research Subject Information line in the UBC Research Services Office at (604) 822-8598.

Please complete the attached forms as soon as possible. Return one signed copy to the school and retain the second copy for your personal records. We thank you for your consideration of this request.

Sincerely,
NAME
Graduate Research Assistant
Masters/Doctoral Student
University of British Columbia
Contact Information _____

The University Of British Columbia

Department of Sociology
6303 N.W. Marine Drive
Vancouver, BC Canada V6T 1Z1
Tel: (604) 822-6683
Fax: (604) 822-6161

CONSENT:
I have received and read a copy of the letter that describes a study called "Popular Culture in the Classroom: Teaching for Critical Social Literacy." I understand that participation of my child in this research is entirely voluntary, and that non-participation or withdrawal from the project will in no way affect my child.

PLEASE CHECK, AS APPROPRIATE:
___ I consent to my child's participation in the assessment study
___ I consent to my child being video-taped as part of this assessment study
___ I consent to having Drs. Currie and Kelly talk with my child
Student's Name (Please print in full) _____
Parent/Guardian's Name (Please print in full) _____
Parent/Guardian's Signature _____
Date _____
PLEASE RETURN TO [TEACHER'S NAME] BY _____

Appendix D: Details from the Hunger Games Project Lesson Plan

The Hunger Games Project (see chapter 5) used the movie and books as a springboard for a role play experience intended to help students explore conventional conceptions of power. For those interested in learning more, this appendix provides details on (a) the game's basic rules and resource cards and (b) how learning was assessed. Survival is key to the game. Well in advance, students will draw at random a unique character card (not based on the book or movie) listing their Tribute's background information (motivations, fears), skills, and weaknesses. Their character card will influence their participation in the game. Important, also, will be the resources they receive at the start of the game. On the day the role play is enacted, teachers place boxes of varying sizes on the playground "arena"; each box contains a random assortment of resource cards. The food and water cards, attached to strings, must be worn around the Tributes' necks. Every 10 minutes the Peacekeepers (teachers) will do a lap to make sure every Tribute has both food and water. If they do not, they are "dead" from either starvation or thirst. As seen in table A.1, embedded within the resource cards are rules about how the Hunger Game will play out (e.g., a rope card would give its Tribute the possibility of a three-minute time-out) and who has what power (e.g., the Capitol's Game Masters and President have the power to inflict obstacles such as a flood, "killing" any Tribute in a designated sector).

As mentioned in chapter 5, Jane and LJ used a variety of ways to assess students' learning throughout the Hunger Games Project. The text table below provides details. One particularly important assessment tool was the out-of-role reflection. Jane asked students to write about the following questions: (a) What did you like about the game? (b) What did you dislike about the game? (c) When you found out your role, how did you feel? (d) How did it feel when you killed someone, or when someone was killed? (e) What role did appearance play in the game? (f) How did

Table A.1. Hunger Games Project resource cards

Where distributed or by whom	Type of card	Number of cards	Directions (meaning of the card)
At The Cornucopia	Slingshot	8	You can steal a card from someone
	Knife	8	You can kill someone if you can touch their shoulder
	Rope	8	You can safely tie yourself in a tree for 3 minutes (time-out)
	Bow & arrow	6	You can kill someone if you are within 2 metres
	Canteen	4	You can steal someone else's water
	Knapsack	3	You can steal someone's food
	Illness	4	You have 5 minutes to get medicine before you die
	Blanket	4	You can keep warm
The Game Masters	Thirst & starvation	10	You have 5 minutes to find a food or water card and return it to the Game Master before you die
	Food & water	10	You must wear this card (with string attached) around your neck
The Peacekeepers (teachers)	Exhaustion	4	You have 3 minutes to find a blanket and return it to a Peacekeeper or you die
Audience members	Beauty	4	Someone likes you and gives you medicine
The Capitol (powers)	Thunderbolt	–	Kills anyone who goes out of bounds
	Flood	–	Kills anyone in a designated sector
	Fire	–	Kills anyone in a designated sector
	Mutant hornet	–	Kills anyone tagged
	Rabid dog	–	Kills anyone tagged

appearances give power? (g) Who had the most power in the game? (h) How was it used? (i) Who also had power? (j) How did you get a sense of power? (k) When did you feel powerlessness?

Details from the Hunger Games Project Lesson Plan 255

Table A.2. Assessment of learning in the Hunger Games Project

Timeline	Activities	Assessment measures *Students will ...*
Pre-game	☐ In-role reflections ☐ Costume development	• Express thoughts, feelings, intentions, and attitudes of their assigned character • Reflect to make connections between drama work and self • Ask and respond to questions in role • Create costume to enhance drama work
Pre-game	☐ Presentation to audience	• Demonstrate audience interaction • Use body and voice effectively to convey meaning • Use persuasive techniques to sway audience opinion
During game	☐ Role play	• Explore tension and conflict in role • Demonstrate an ability to stay in character • Follow rules and guidelines for safe use of props and equipment • Demonstrate audience interaction • Apply critical thinking skills to a range of problems and issues
Post-game	☐ Out-of-role reflections ☐ Group debrief	• Reflect to make connections between drama work and the experiences of self and others • Explore the issues of power and powerlessness as experienced in the role play • Ask and respond to questions out-of-role to help create meaning from the drama • Reflect to make connections between the fictional world and the real world • Consistently demonstrate respect for peers' ideas and contributions
Post-game	☐ Classroom follow-up	• Compare the concept of power in *The Hunger Games* and *The Giver* • Brainstorm to identify student understandings of power structures in Canada

Notes

1 Teaching for Social Justice: Pop Culture in the Classroom

1. We agree with David Morley that all interaction is mediated (in Christensen & Morley, 2014, p. 215), even when face to face. And, as Scott (1992) notes, how we interpret our individual (read: private) experience of the world is mediated by culture. Given these complications, Couldry and Hepp (2013) claim that the term *mediatization* is needed, to supplement "mediation." They clarify: "While 'mediation' refers to the process of communication in general – that is, how communication has to be understood as involving the ongoing mediation of meaning construction, 'mediatization' is a category designed to describe change" (p. 197). In keeping with its common usage in published literature, in *Pop Culture and Power* we use the shorthand term *mediation* to capture the social role of media texts.
2. As explained in chapter 2, for analytical purposes we differentiate between commercial media and everyday cultural production. Although our empirical focus is what is generally referred to as "popular culture," our analysis of media texts applies to cultural artifacts that extend beyond entertainment, including news reporting, policy and legal documents, political campaigns, and so on.
3. We acknowledge that all youth do not have equal access to the internet; indeed, beyond access, the use of digital media is stratified. This stratification of access and usage has come to be known as the *digital divide*. Despite claims to the contrary, internet access is not universal. "While composite estimates are that 89% of North Americans and 73% of Europeans and Australians have Internet access, global access continues to be below 50%" (Luke et al., 2017, p. 261, n. 4). Using data from the 2010 Canadian Internet Use Survey, Haight, Quan-Haase, and Corbett (2014) further "demonstrate that the digital divide not only persists, but has expanded to include inequality in the level of online activity and SNS [Social Networking Site]

usage" (p. 503). While many policy makers and researchers associate the digital divide with such issues of stratified *access* and *usage*, it can also refer to differential *outcomes*. In this approach, critical scholars focus on "measuring the differential economic, social, cultural and individual *outcomes* of Internet use" to aid in understanding "why digital technology innovation yields persistent unequal outcomes in society" (Mansell, 2017, pp. 149, 150).

4 According to Statistics Canada (2019), youth aged 5 to 17 self-reported, on average, 3 hours of screen time per day; the screen time was lower for children (2.5 hours) compared to youth (4 hours) (p. 6). Girls were more likely to report time spent on a computer, tablet, or smartphone doing activities such as browsing the internet, emailing, accessing social media, or doing homework, while boys were more likely to play video games (p. 7).

5 The New London Group took its name from its meeting place in New London, New Hampshire. Group members – based in Australia, the USA, and the UK – included Courtney Cazden, Bill Cope, Norman Fairclough, James Gee, Mary Kalantzis, Allan Luke, Carmen Luke, Sarah Michaels, and Martin Nakata. The ideas introduced in their 1996 article were developed in a book edited by Cope and Kalantzis (2000).

6 See, for example, the special issue of *Theory into Practice* marking the twentieth anniversary of the NLG's "now foundational article" (Garcia & Seglem, 2018, p. 1), assessing its impact, and looking ahead to future developments in multiliteracies scholarship and practice (Garcia, Luke, & Seglem, 2018).

7 Given that multiliteracies is a pedagogy, the convention is to treat "multiliteracies" as a singular noun.

8 In more recent years, scholars also use digital remix as a metaphor for new literacy. Gainer and Lapp (2010) draw an explicit link between remix and redesign: "Much like the New London Group's concept of literacy as redesign, literacy as remix positions readers as active meaning-makers who blend understandings based in prior knowledge and experience with new information as they construct new understandings from textual transactions" (p. 58).

9 For an analysis of Donald Trump's use of the term *fake news* to manipulate inconvenient facts for political ends and the implications for critical media literacy, see Kozolanka and Orlowski (2018).

10 For a critique of this Google program, see the Media Education Foundation Newsletter, November 6, 2018. In a discussion of consumption and surveillance in their chapter titled "Media Literacy 2.0," Hoechsmann and Poyntz (2012) make clear that Google is part of the problem, not the solution: "Making the situation all the more complex, on social networking sites and in online game spaces, children are increasingly targeted with demographic-specific advertising. One of the many interesting innovations of Google,

the world's number-one website, is intuitive advertising, a Web 3.0 innovation that responds to the user's online profile, the sites they visit, and the clicks they make on individual sites. (Web 3.0 is the semantic web that aggregates user data to learn more about each user for primarily commercial purposes.) Thus, part of the social networking experience, and web trolling in general, is to view ads that have been specifically chosen to knit in with users' online habits and concerns so as to maximize purchasing messages" (p. 162).

11 Originating in the activism and published work by women of colour, "intersectionality" signals that we always occupy numerous identity positions. Following from this, a person can be oppressed by others (for example, a woman can be oppressed by men because of their gender privilege) while also being an oppressor (for example, a White woman can be the oppressor of Black women because of her racialized privilege). Social context dictates how our identities are salient in a specific situation. For further reading see Yuval-Davis (2006); Clegg (2016); and Walby, Armstrong, & Strid (2012).

12 We want to inject a note of caution, particularly in light of recent events that reveal how social media practices in some cases are actually helping to erode public debate and deliberation. Scepticism about digital media being able to promote civic engagement is highly warranted as long as the platforms and other technology remain under corporate domination (see Fuchs, 2014; de Roock, 2021). We return to this topic in chapter 9.

13 Neoliberalism is based in economic policies that promote the political and cultural treatment of individuals as entrepreneurial actors, exercising a market rationale in every sphere of life (Brown, 2003). Because neoliberalism is associated with "less government," individuals are increasingly deemed to be responsible for their own fate, characterized as a consequence of personal decision making. Within this context, Gee (2002) describes a mandate for millennials to self-manage their future possibilities as "shape-shifting portfolio people" who must continually customize their self-presentation according to the current demands of a competitive market.

14 For a discussion of the commercial appropriation of hip-hop, see Morrell and Duncan-Andrade (2005/6).

15 See Kelly and Pomerantz (2009) for an analysis of "how pervasive and 'natural' postfeminism has become in popular cinematic representations of teenage girls, as well as how easily and 'naturally' feminism is lampooned" (p. 4).

16 Mary also told us that this incident contributed to her decision to give up her teaching position to return to graduate studies.

17 Janks (2010) connects small p politics to Politics: "the socio-historical and economic contexts in which we live produce different conditions of possibility and constraint that we all have to negotiate as meaningfully as we can.

While the social constructs who we are, so do we construct the social. This dialectic relationship is fluid and dynamic, creating possibilities for social action and change. Working with the politics of the local enables us to engage in a different kind of transformative redesign" (p. 188).

18 It interests us that the MediaSmarts site (http://mediasmarts.ca/), updated in September 2018, states that, in BC: "The curriculum framework for English Language Arts and Social Studies contains a strong media education component" (Media Education in British Columbia: Curricular Overview, para. 2). Also: "*All curriculum areas provide learning opportunities for media education. It is not taught as a separate curriculum*" (Value of Integrating Media Education, para. 2, italics in original). At the same time, Hoechsmann and Poyntz (2012) state that, typically, teachers' preparation lags behind school districts' desire to respond to demands for using the latest technologies (p. 146).

19 Dan indicated that while a Vancouver-based group, CAME (Canadian Association of Media Educators), produced useful material throughout the 1990s, when the founder retired, "nobody else picked it up, so it hasn't really put anything out I would think for about 20 years." Toronto also had an advocacy group, Ontario's Association for Media Literacy (AML). See Rennie (2015) for a history of the media literacy "scene" in Vancouver, British Columbia in relation to the development of media education in Ontario (and Toronto, in particular).

20 Twitter would make a relevant study in regard to the relationship between form and content of media.

21 The definitions of *popular culture* that Storey (1993) describes include culture having a large audience; culture that is outside "high culture"; mass culture; culture originating "from the people"; the "site of struggle between the forces of resistance of subordinate groups in society, and the forces of incorporation of dominant groups in society" (pp. 6–17). Our commitment to using pop culture to teach for social justice makes the latter definition most relevant to our work, although our interest in how power operates through media directs our analytical attention to the relations of media production.

22 Given the increasing commodification of new media, enabling the appropriation of commercial media content for the production of what we call popular culture, issues of copyright are becoming increasingly relevant for youth. At the same time, given the commercialization of media production by everyday people (on YouTube, for example), copyright issues apply not only to ownership of media produced by corporations but also to the income-generating media production by everyday users. In this context, some educators include copyright as a topic in literacy education (see Amidon, Stedman, & DeVoss, 2018; also Burwell, 2013, 2018). In *Pop Culture and*

Power, we include copyright issues in the regulation of media production (for example, in table 9.1).

23 As we describe in chapter 9, these venues of everyday media production have also been monetized by corporations that "harvest" and sell user data, enabling advertisers to personalize their advertising practices.

2 Agency and Power as Media Engagement

1 For an exception, see the special issue of the *Journal of Media Literacy* on "Agency," especially the contribution by Andersen (2017).
2 Mason and Metzger (2012) critique the *Position Statement on Media Literacy* by the US-based National Council for the Social Studies for its uncritical argument that media literacy can facilitate participatory democracy if students' interest in media is simply harnessed.
3 Inspired by Foucault, poststructuralists discuss "subjectification" as that process through which we continually remake ourselves as thinking, feeling subjects. We do so by subjecting ourselves to dominant forces that shape us in specific ways, to become specific kinds of persons. Subjectification thus captures how "One is both subject to power and at the same time able to take up the position of a subject in and through power ... the domination and the empowerment of an individual are complexly intertwined" (Allen, 1999/2018, p. 119). What is at stake is how to theorize agency (see Davies, 2006). Because we become subjects through the regulatory mechanisms of discourse, in some interpretations influenced by literary theory, discourse is given the determinant role, a position that denies individuals agency.
4 An important exception is Janks (2010), who has an extended discussion of what she means by *power*, drawing on two concepts of power, one from neo-Marxist theories (particularly John Thompson's [1987] critical theory of ideology), the other from Foucault.
5 "Ideology" is generally used to signal ideas that distort our everyday understanding of social reality; specifically, ideology prevents people from recognizing capitalism as systematic exploitation. Dahlgren (2015, p. 729) locates the intellectual roots of ideology critique in media studies in the work of Karl Marx and traces its development through the neo-Marxism of Althusser, the Frankfurt School, and work on hegemony by Gramsci. Early assumptions about "false consciousness" increasingly gave way to more sophisticated epistemologies, some of which link media representation to the political economy of media industries. Although we are critical of how "ideology critique" is often used in media education, we concede that it has the potential to take learning "deeper" by connecting representation to the social relations and practices of media production. See chapter 9.

6 A perhaps odious example of cultural reification is the way that the construct "personality" is used, in everyday parlance, to express the essence of an individual – a truth that captures the core of their being. Because "personality" decontextualizes agency, it depoliticizes human behaviour.
7 As noted in chapter 1, what we call fully "critical" media literacy must connect critique to practice.
8 The appropriation of commercial culture by everyday media users is not always the free-for-all that our examples may suggest. Meaning can be a site of struggle about the ownership of ideas, taking place over intellectual property rights. Some television producers, film studios, and book publishers have been aggressive in issuing "cease and desist" letters to fan websites that incorporate their material without permission. For example, Fox television closed *Simpsons* fansites. One result is the trend by entertainment corporations to commodify what has been long-tolerated fan activity (Sunder, 2019). The Recording Industry Association of America, in particular, has been on the front lines of the fight against copyright infringement, which the industry calls "piracy." These types of examples illustrate how the exercise of "power-to" entails a struggle against the power that corporations wield in terms of the production of media by everyday people.
9 More recently, a mashup also refers to a web application that combines multiple services into a single application.
10 We are mindful, however, that groups excluded historically from making mainstream culture may not have a vocabulary that enables them to express their experiences. When interviewing women, for example, DeVault (1999, chap. 4) found that they often lacked the language to describe what was important to them. She had to learn how to "listen" to the silences, uncertainties, and hesitations that characterized these interviews. Rather than treating these irruptions as "technical errors" due to a faulty interview technique, DeVault analysed them as limitations in the language available to her participants speaking as women in a "man's world."
11 The conditions of Liz's work make this understandable. She did not know her students ahead of time, faced tight time constraints, and so on.
12 The political consequences of new communication technologies have fostered what Coyne (1999) calls "technoromanticism" – utopian optimism that the internet will have a positive impact on the involvement of ordinary citizens in direct democracy. This optimism is based in digital technologies as a mechanism facilitating alternative channels of civic engagement such as political chat rooms, electronic voting, and mobilization of virtual communities, all of which can revitalize mass participation in public affairs. In contrast, cyber-pessimists regard digital technology as "a Pandora's box unleashing inequalities of power and wealth, reinforcing deeper divisions between the information rich and poor, the tuned-in and the tuned-out, the

activists and the disengaged" (Norris, 2015, p. 348). This account contends that internet politics will disproportionately benefit the elite (also see Dean, 2005). As for all politics, the impact of communication technologies in promoting a more participatory democracy in Canada is a historical and not theoretical question.

13 Of course, we recognize that political conditions vary by province, by school district, and even by individual school. Teachers sometimes face resistance to teaching for social and ecological justice. Relevant examples include the conservative opposition from parents and religious organizations to Ontario's revised sexuality education curriculum (see, e.g., Bialystok & Wright, 2019). Conservative political alliances have stalled anti-bullying policies in BC school districts, intended to support LGBTQ2A+/gender diverse communities (see, e.g., Herriot, Burns, & Yeung, 2018; Loutzenheiser, 2015). When the United Conservative Party (UCP) regained power in Alberta in 2019, they began to roll back policies put in place by the previous NDP government that aimed to protect the rights of queer youth and school staff and authorize Gay-Straight Alliances in schools. In a province polarized over its oil industry, conservative leaders as well as parents have attacked social studies teachers for simply attempting to highlight more than one perspective on the issue of fossil fuels (see Keller, 2019). To this point, UCP leader Jason Kenney initiated a provincial curriculum review, led by a panel that has recommended that the social studies curriculum "reflect the importance of natural resources to Alberta's economy" (K. Butler, 2020, para. 5).

3 *Pop Culture and Power*: Teaching as Research

1 This lack of resources reflects, to some degree, the marginal status of media studies in general. Although the Ministry of Education in Ontario was among the first in the provinces to introduce media studies as a subject area in 2003, it was promoted as a pedagogical tool for "reluctant readers" (Ferguson, 2011, p. 137; also see Dehli, 2009). As Mary (another educator interviewed early in our study) experienced, such a belief can lead parents as well as teachers to discount pop culture (e.g., rap music) as possible curriculum, even as they might otherwise claim that children need to learn "skills" to "protect" them from media.

2 This dual role subsequently presented challenges in crafting a coherent account of our study. *Pop Culture and Power* simultaneously theorizes how power operates through media in ways that can be harnessed to teaching for social justice, while exploring critical media literacy as a teaching strategy to support such a goal, recognizing that CML itself is a theoretical undertaking.

3 "'Visible minority' refers to whether a person belongs to a visible minority group as defined by the Employment Equity Act and, if so, the visible minority group to which the person belongs. The Employment Equity Act defines visible minorities as 'persons, other than Aboriginal peoples, who are non-Caucasian in race or non-white in colour.' The visible minority population consists mainly of the following groups: South Asian, Chinese, Black, Filipino, Latin American, Arab, Southeast Asian, West Asian, Korean and Japanese" (Statistics Canada, 2017). While relying on Statistics Canada to inform our demographic profile of our research setting, we are disturbed by how phrases like "non-Caucasian in race" perpetuate a belief in biologically fixed and discrete human races, "rather than highly complex, changing and contested *social* constructions" (Gillborn, 2016, p. 383, n. 4).

4 The brochure indicated that participants would receive a $200 honorarium in recognition of their contribution to our study as well as travel expenses.

5 In the end, although close to a dozen teachers expressed interest in our project as relevant to their teaching, only five teachers could commit to the project.

6 Children occupy a subordinate position and exercise less influence over their own lives than do adults, including when they participate in ethnographic research. Aarsand and Forsberg (2010, p. 255) point out that ethnographic video recording – a common research practice and one that we employed – raises a number of ethical issues when research concerns children. They outline a number of strategies to honour the corporeal privacy of children, many of which we incorporated into our data generation (also see Christensen, 2004).

7 Our letters of informed consent for parents and guardians (included in Appendix B) sought permission for their child to (a) participate in the study; (b) be videoed during the classroom activities; and (c) talk with Professors Currie and Kelly. Overall, the return rate of consent letters and assent forms was very high, although permission for the different aspects of participation varied; some students participated in the research without being video recorded, for example, while others participated and were videoed, but did not receive parental permission to speak with Currie or Kelly. We appreciate the challenge this configuration of participation presented for our research assistants who videoed sessions; some classes consisted of as many as 29 students.

8 We are aware of critiques of Althusser's argument about interpellation. Feminists have pointed out that the subject interpellated by the text must already experience themselves as a subject in order to be hailed (Hey you!).

9 This logic has been used as the basis for claiming a "materialist analysis" of ideology.

10 In Ellsworth's (1997) case, "text" refers to the delivery of curriculum to a student audience.
11 While we employed advertising – because of the obviousness of its textual constructions – virtually all media texts address their intended audience in similar ways.
12 This claim assumes that there will be an audience; of course, this assumption is not always warranted.
13 We stipulate "felt" to signal that experiential knowledge giving rise to a disjuncture may not be able to be articulated – put into words – because no vocabulary may yet exist. Examples include sexual harassment and date rape; both were experienced by women but could not be named before the Women's Liberation Movement.

4 The Monopoly Project: Meaning Making through Board Game Production

1 For background on the history of *Monopoly*, see Pilon (2015).
2 In contrast to other case studies (see chapters 5 and 6), Yvette developed the Monopoly Project alone in the seminar. Then, when it came time to implement the unit, Paulina joined to support Yvette and document the lessons.
3 For a discussion of feminist responses to the "girl question" in gaming, see Cassell & Jenkins (1998); Jenson & de Castell (2011); Fisher & Jenson (2017).
4 Games not described in detail here include *School's Out* (a *Monopoly*-style game where players buy school subjects), *Hamunopoly* (a *Monopoly*-style game using Japanese cartoon characters), *Business Monopoly* (where players buy companies), *Resources* (a complex game styled after *Settlers of Catan*), *Trivia* (resembling *Trivial Pursuit*), and *Dice Wars* (resembling the dice game called *Yahtzee*).
5 "Teens spend $155 billion a year, children younger than 12 spend another $25 billion, and both groups influence perhaps another $200 billion of their parents' spending each year (Ohayon, 2011; Quart, 2003)" (Harste & Albers, 2013, p. 383).
6 We note that the original version of *Monopoly*, as well as its many spinoff versions, did not intend to be a critique of capitalism itself. In Magie's case, it was designed as a critique of a capitalist economy with few constraints on monopolization of land.
7 To be sure, digital games differ from board games in certain ways (e.g., computer mediation allowing players to be in different physical locations), but they are similar in many other ways; namely, being governed by a process or set of rules to be followed, which, in turn, shapes how the game occurs, how the players interact, and how each game unfolds through the

distinctive actions of various players. As Beavis (2014) notes about video games: "Games might be texts, but they also depended on forms of knowledge right at the boundaries of what might be thought of as literacy. They were as much about action as reading, and they stretched well beyond what we had hitherto thought of in these terms" (p. 435).

5 *The Hunger Games*: Using Popular Film to Learn about Power

1 *The Giver* (Lowry, 1993) is a book about a dystopia like the one featured in *The Hunger Games*. Although popular among middle-school teachers, various schools in the USA have banned it, or attempted to do so, citing violence and unsuitability for the age group (Blatt, 2014).
2 There were two students who did not participate in the same way as the others. One of these students was the boy with high-functioning autism. During most of the lessons, this boy spent time reading on his own. He did, however, join in during the role play as a Game Master. The other student who had a very difficult time participating was the boy who barely spoke English. LJ noticed other boys making fun of his difficulties with language on several occasions. LJ often observed this boy hunched over, looking down, shuffling around, and seeming to be struggling through the lesson. It was not clear, however, that this project was more difficult for him than school was generally.

6 Celebrity Marketing: Gender Performances in Popular Music

1 Just as Natalie was co-designing her unit plan (December 2012), PSY's "Gangnam Style" became the first YouTube video to reach one billion views.
2 As argued in the previous chapter, violence in youth entertainment can be a productive venue for discussing issues of social justice. In chapter 8 we will see how the issue of male violence unexpectedly emerged in the Celebrity Marketing Project, although it was not followed up, owing to time constraints.
3 Group 5, arguably, had selected a song where the *original* could be interpreted as already (liberal) feminist; it voices the thoughts of a girl who is resolved to set firm boundaries, putting a definitive end to her on-again, off-again relationship with a fickle and manipulative boyfriend. The assignment option that Group 5 selected asked them to "flip or subvert gender norms." Their *revision* of the lyrics aimed to show the female as stronger than the male in the relationship, by changing the title from "We Are Never Ever Getting Back Together" to "I Will Make You Love Me Forever and Ever." The female narrator refuses to accept that she and her boyfriend have broken up; she peers into her boyfriend's window, watches him while

he sleeps, locks him in her basement, and refuses him food. The revised song becomes a horror story, where the female is, as one member summed it up, "creepy and unstable." We were struck by the way the independent-minded female of the original Taylor Swift song was transformed into a "psycho," echoing the anti-feminist film *Fatal Attraction*, where the mentally unstable "other woman," as played by Glenn Close, stalks the married Michael Douglas character and, infamously, boils the family pet bunny when he spurns her.

4 Without intending to sensationalize the extent of suicide among K-pop stars, we suggest that researching the death by suicide of K-pop singer – and feminist – Sulli (aka Choi Jin-ri) at age 25 would have enabled Natalie to raise questions about the power of the music industry. This approach offers the potential to shift discussion away from the motivations of individual performers. On the death of Sulli, see Ahmed (2019); Hollingsworth and Seo (2019).

5 Although not the focus of their final essay, Group 4's oral presentation, collectively, made the case that Lady Gaga was a positive force in the world, as noted earlier.

6 Butler (1990) writes that she uses the term *heterosexual matrix* "to designate that grid of cultural intelligibility through which bodies, genders, and desires are naturalized. I am drawing from Monique Wittig's notion of the 'heterosexual contract' and, to a lesser extent, on Adrienne Rich's notion of 'compulsory heterosexuality' to characterize a discursive epistemic model of gender intelligibility that assumes that for bodies to cohere and make sense there must be stable sex expressed through a stable gender (masculine expresses male, feminine expresses female) that is oppositionally and hierarchically defined through the compulsory practice of heterosexuality" (p. 208).

7 Unlike the situations in the previous two chapters, as well as the following one, students were not invited by their teacher to participate in the videos' figured worlds; their learning took place by analysing that world as "outsiders."

8 We recognize that this kind of response was encouraged by the documentaries introduced in early lessons. Although these documentaries offer ready-to-use teaching resources that usefully illustrate stereotyping, for us they have the potential to stifle the kind of deeper, social analysis needed for critical interrogation.

9 An unanswered – but intriguing – question for us concerns the reluctance of boys to participate in post-project focus groups.

10 Further to this point, in Lesson 4 (analysis of a social identity in a song) Vicki worked *alone* on independent (alternative) rapper Macklemore's song "Thrift Shop." She did not explicitly name *class* (or conspicuous

consumption as its marker) as the social identity that Macklemore constructed in his lyrics and accompanying music video, but this seemed to be what she meant. Vicki wrote: "Macklemore is trying to show that you can get good clothes for a low price. He shows that you don't need to spend $50 on a t shirt to be stylish. The song also displays that the thrift shop isn't lame, unlike how it's represented in pop culture."

7 Are You Being Hailed? Advertising as a Venue for Critical Media Literacy

1 Duncan (2007) criticizes *Adbusters* for "establishing a pedagogy which is reinforced throughout that the mass media are all bad for you, that the simple life is best" (p. 204). Heath and Potter (2004), in their book *The Rebel Sell: Why the Culture Can't Be Jammed*, argue that contributors to *Adbusters* and others have misled an entire generation into believing that alternative consumption and observing "buy nothing day" are efficacious political actions. In an interview, Potter elaborated: "It's had huge pernicious effects: it's reduced faith across the board in the ability of government to effect positive social changes. There's this entire generation of kids now who think that government's a waste of time, thanks to [Naomi Klein's] *No Logo*" (quoted in Ince, 2004, para. 13). If their assessment of youth's take-home message is accurate, that message is contrary to the goal of teaching for social justice. We return to culture jamming in chapter 8.
2 In this project, Amy employed the definition of "popular culture" as "mass culture" (see Storey, 1993).
3 For reasons beyond the scope of the current discussion, this public showing could not be held.
4 The actual project did not unfold exactly according to the narrative that follows; for example, some activities occurred over several sessions, and online advertising was also analysed, albeit to a lesser extent than print ads. For the sake of clarity and coherence, we have organized our narrative in ways to highlight the learning themes that shaped each activity.
5 In Freedman's study (1994), some of her female participants responded to ads by integrating their personality with their idealized conceptions of the characters, creating ideal identities for themselves (p. 164).
6 In this way, Arielle identified a contradictory juxtaposition typical of advertisements for beauty products: that of nature opposed to culture.
7 We elaborate on redesign as resistance in chapter 8.
8 Diana's reworked ad arguably reproduced heteronormativity, while disrupting femininity as passive.
9 Advertising is also a useful venue for researching how commercial media works as public pedagogy.
10 Of course, age and grade level are key here.

11 Further to Amy's point about teachers needing to be able to name and understand visual elements of ads (and other visual texts), Harste and Albers (2013) use visual discourse analysis (VDA) as their main theoretical framework in preparing classroom teachers to do critical literacy curriculum using ads and counter-ads. See also Ostenson (2012), who discusses criteria from the fields of visual and film art that teachers could adapt when assessing students' multimedia production work.

8 Agency Revisited: Pop Culture in a Participatory Classroom

1 Lazar (2007) draws attention to the contemporary context of postfeminism. This ideology "paints a world in which power relations have become reversed: it is women who, through their sexual prowess, wield power and control over men" (p. 157). Davies (1993) notes how this reversal is facilitated by the everyday embeddedness of binary thinking about gender (also see Markowitz & Puchner, 2016).
2 We write this in early 2018, as the #MeToo movement is in full force, demonstrating via social media the prevalence of sexual assault and harassment, mostly by men against women, in workplace and other settings. It seems likely that even a few years later, this changed historical context, a specific moment in sexual politics, might perhaps have led Natalie to respond differently to the Rihanna–Chris Brown case.
3 As mentioned in chapter 1, Liz, a media educator, told us that feminism is the present-day "F" word.
4 At the same time, in the context of using a film showing that "wars are gendered activities," Marciniak (2010) has argued that an "excess of affect" (pp. 872, 874) can also interfere with learning.
5 We are aware of the pitfalls of too neatly separating affect from emotions; cultural studies scholar Sara Ahmed notes how in everyday life, they are inseparable: "While you can separate an affective response from an emotion that is attributed as such (the bodily sensations from the feeling of being afraid), this does not mean that in practice, or in everyday life, they are separate. In fact, they are contiguous; they slide into each other; they stick, and cohere, even when they are separated" (quoted in Anwaruddin, 2016, p. 387).
6 In another research project that illustrates how youth appropriate as well as produce media texts to foster specific self-identifications and generate allegiances, Stack (2010) showed how – in a media education class where students produced their own videos – some White boys traded on hegemonic masculinity and whiteness to legitimate their subjectivity vis-à-vis the Other.
7 The exception, of course, is arts-based curriculum.
8 Rymes (2011) provides a typology of researcher stances to the study of mass media and schooling – what she calls the deference, denial, or repertoire

approaches. This typology could easily be adapted to describe a range of possible teacher attitudes to pop culture in the classroom, a consideration of which could serve to deepen educator reflexivity. One type of teacher response gives too much *deference* to students' preferences by muting the teacher's critique of mass-mediated youth cultural practices; another response *denies* the complexity of practices that characterize youth media consumption by harnessing them to mainstream, institutionalized educational goals. Rymes advocates, instead, an approach that recognizes how "mass-mediated signs" (e.g., youth cultural texts such as rap lyrics) are meaningful only when embedded in social practice. Rymes employs a *repertoire approach* that acknowledges meaning making as a situated practice: "For example, when a teacher uses a familiar hip-hop beat (a mass-mediated youth cultural sign) to teach a math formula (a different practice), the sign takes on a different role. The sign may still be recognizable to youth, but the meaning it holds in a teacher's repertoire is very different" (p. 210).

9 Power Revisited: Harnessing Media Engagement to Social Change

1 Share et al. (2019) offered a four-unit teacher education seminar to prepare in-service and pre-service K-12 teachers to teach their students how to critically analyse and create all types of media. Beginning with a theoretical overview, the course treated media education as a framework of conceptual understandings rather than as a body of knowledge or set of skills. As follow-up, they assessed their framework through an online survey of teacher participants, employing primarily quantitative measures. In contrast, in this chapter we assess the utility of our seminar curriculum through analysis of student learning and focus group discussions with our teacher participants' students after the various units had been completed.
2 We use the lower-case acronym for critical discourse analysis (cda) to signal various forms under a common umbrella rather than adherence to Norman Fairclough's specific approach, usually spelled as "CDA."
3 For alternative views on the political efficacy of Foucault's work, see Heller (1996); Al-Amoudi (2007); Allen (2002). In a feminist reading, Amy Allen (2002) argues: "And although I would agree that the account of subjectivity and agency that Foucault offers is not fully adequate ... I would nonetheless insist that the claim that Foucault embraces the death of the subject and a denial of agency is incorrect and based on an over-reaction to things he actually said" (p. 136).
4 Much current research on teaching literacy focuses on what we call Level 2, where power is activated as youth engage with media. This focus carries the danger of perpetuating the view of media power as "domination" and youth as media consumers, rather than also producers. Discourse analysis implies

that power operates *as* discourse as when the existence of the media text is an analytical given. Because we view power as exercised by people and not things, CSL connects power to the relations and practices of media production that afford the exercise of power, an approach that supports teaching for social justice.

5 To our knowledge, Davies first used the term *critical social literacy* in 1997. Across several classroom projects, she encouraged young students to question the constructed nature of gender. Her pedagogical goal was in keeping with the idea of youth as redesigning their futures; she wanted them to open new possibilities for the way they thought about, hence enacted, their social identities (see Davies, 1993). Her strategy was to give students the ability to catch "language in the act of formation" of their identities in order to critically renegotiate their language use once aware of its social effects (1997, p. 29). "With *critical social literacy* oneself becomes a shifting, multiple text to be read. The construction of that self through discourse, through positioning within particular contexts and moments and through relations of power, is both recognized and made revisable. Critical social literacy involves the development of a playful ability to move between and amongst discourses, to move in and out of them, to mix them, to break their spell when necessary. It involves the capacity reflexively to critique text and context and to act on that reflection" (p. 29, emphasis in original).

6 Fairy tales were not discussed in our critical media education seminar; neither were they taken up by teacher participants.

7 For a critique of fairy tales (and cartoons), see Christensen (2017). As will become apparent below, CSL includes the kinds of interrogation she encouraged with her students; however, our layered ontology extends questioning to "deeper" levels of analysis.

8 Given Fairy Tale Studies as an area of academic investigation, extensive scholarship in these subject areas is available to inspire and guide lesson preparation.

9 In addition to social media's implication in algorithmic social sorting and discrimination, Fuchs and Trottier (2015) discuss the problem of corporate and state "surveillance creep": "As powerful new surveillance tactics are developed, the range of their legitimate and illegitimate use is likely to spread" (p. 129, quoting Gary Marx).

10 We like the approach taken by Child and Youth Studies Professor Shauna Pomerantz, who started a research project on TikTok with her 11-year-old daughter while both were in lockdown during the COVID-19 pandemic. The popular web-based app enables users to create 60-second videos intended to entertain. Pomerantz described TikTok as "a lingua franca for young people" that can help teachers connect to students by opening

conversations, showing interest in learning about students' worlds, and talking with them about the platform (Tutt, 2021).
11 Students are scored on whether they can answer three questions: who is behind this information; what is the evidence; what do other sources say? (McGrew et al., 2019, p. 61).
12 Ruitenberg (2019) builds on Barrow's work and explores how his critique of "skill talk" applies equally well to the present-day focus on "competencies" in many educational jurisdictions across Canada, including British Columbia, and around the world.
13 See chapter 1, where we discuss the multiple and contrasting meanings of the word *critical*.
14 We have in mind approaches that focus on "critical" as in inferential thinking, taking a sceptical stance, or logical and analytical "skills."
15 Archer delineates three interlocutors in our inner conversations: the "I," one's current self and the "agent of action"; the "You," one's future self; and the "Me," one's past self (see Archer, 2000, esp. chap. 7).

References

Aarsand, Pal, & Forsberg, Lucas. (2010). Producing children's corporeal privacy: Ethnographic video recording as material-discursive practice. *Qualitative Research, 10*(2), 249–68. https://doi.org/10.1177/1468794109356744

Ahmed, Tufayel. (2019, October 14). K-pop singer Sulli, who spoke out against cyberbullies, dead at 25. *Newsweek.* Retrieved from https://www.newsweek.com/sulli-k-pop-singer-dead-choi-jin-ri-sm-entertainment-1464962

Al-Amoudi, Ismael. (2007). Redrawing Foucault's social ontology. *Organization: The Interdisciplinary Journal of Organization, Theory and Society, 14*(4), 543–63. https://doi.org/10.1177/1350508407078052

Albers, Peggy (Ed.). (2018). *Global conversations in literacy research: Digital and critical literacies.* New York: Routledge.

Albers, Peggy, Vasquez, Vivian, & Harste, Jerome C. (2017). Critically reading image in digital spaces and digital times. In Kathy A. Mills, Amy Stornaiuolo, Anna Smith, & Jessica Pandya Zacher (Eds.), *Handbook of writing, literacies and education in digital culture* (pp. 223–34). New York: Routledge.

Allen, Amy. (1999/2018). *The power of feminist theory: Domination, resistance, solidarity.* Boulder, CO: Westview Press.

Allen, Amy. (2002). Power, subjectivity and agency: Between Arendt and Foucault. *International Journal of Philosophical Studies, 10*(2), 131–49. https://doi.org/10.1080/09672550210121432

Althusser, Louis. (2004). Ideology and the ideological state apparatuses. In Charles Lemert (Ed.), *Social theory: The multicultural and classic readings* (3rd ed., pp. 317–21). Boulder, CO: Westview Publishing Company. (Original work published in 1971).

Alvermann, Donna E. (2002). Effective literacy instruction for adolescents. *Journal of Literacy Research, 34*(2), 189–208. https://doi.org/10.1207/s15548430jlr3402_4

Alvermann, Donna E. (2018). A critical untangling of adolescents' literacy practices and popular culture. In Peggy Albers (Ed.), *Global conversations in literacy research: Digital and critical literacies* (pp. 178–90). New York: Routledge.

Alvermann, Donna E., & Hagood, Margaret C. (2000). Critical media literacy: Research, theory, and practice in "New Times." *Journal of Educational Research*, 93(3), 193–205. https://doi.org/10.1080/00220670009598707

Alvermann, Donna E., & Hinchman, Kathleen A. (Eds.). (2012). *Reconceptualizing the literacies in adolescents' lives: Bridging the everyday/academic divide* (3rd ed.). New York and London: Routledge.

Alvermann, Donna E., Moon, Jennifer S., & Hagood, Margaret C. (1999). *Popular culture in the classroom: Teaching and researching critical media literacy.* Newark, NJ: International Reading Association.

Amidon, Timothy R., Stedman, Kyle, & DeVoss, Dànielle Nicole. (2018). Remix and unchill: Remaking pedagogies to support ethical fair use. In Renee Hobbs (Ed.), *Routledge companion to media education, copyright, and fair use* (pp. 65–80). New York: Routledge.

Andersen, Neil. (2017). Henry Jenkins interviewed by Neil Andersen. *Journal of Media Literacy*, 64(1–2), 4–11.

Anwaruddin, Sardar M. (2016). Why critical literacy should turn to "the affective turn": Making a case for critical affective literacy. *Discourse: Studies in the Cultural Politics of Education*, 37(3), 381–96. https://doi.org/10.1080/01596306.2015.1042429

Archer, Margaret S. (2000). *Being human: The problem of agency.* Cambridge: Cambridge University Press.

Archer, Margaret S. (2003). *Structure, agency and the internal conversation.* Cambridge: Cambridge University Press.

Archer, Margaret S. (2007). *Making our way through the world: Human reflexivity and social mobility.* New York: Cambridge University Press.

Archer, Margaret S. (2010). Routine, reflexivity, and realism. *Sociological Theory*, 28(3), 272–303. https://doi.org/10.1111/j.1467-9558.2010.01375.x

Archer, Margaret S. (2014). Structural conditioning and personal reflexivity: Sources of market complicity, critique, and change. In Daniel Finn (Ed.), *Distant markets, distant harms: Economic complicity and Christian ethics* (pp. 26–50). Oxford: Oxford University Press.

Bakir, Vian, & McStay, Andrew. (2018). Fake news and the economy of emotions. *Digital Journalism*, 6(2), 154–75. https://doi.org/10.1080/21670811.2017.1345645

Barboza, David. (2014, July 10). Despite a pledge by Samsung, child labor proves resilient. *New York Times*. Retrieved from https://www.nytimes.com/2014/07/11/business/international/children-found-working-at-samsung-supplier-in-china.html

Barrett, Terry. (1994). *Criticizing art: Understanding the contemporary*. Mountain View, CA: Mayfield Publishing Company.

Barrow, Robin. (1990). Skills. In Robin Barrow & Geoffrey Milburn (Eds.), *A critical dictionary of educational concepts: An appraisal of selected ideas and issues in educational theory and practice* (2nd ed., pp. 281–3). New York and London: Harvester Wheatsheaf.

Barthes, Roland. (1975). *The pleasure of the text* (Richard Miller, Trans.). New York: Noonday Press.

Bartlett, Lesley, & Holland, Dorothy. (2002). Theorizing the space of literacy practices. *Ways of Knowing*, 2(1), 10–22.

Beauchamp, Fay. (2010). Asian origins of Cinderella: The Zhuang storyteller of Guangxi. *Oral Tradition*, 25(2), 447–96. https://doi.org/10.1353/ort.2010.0023

Beavis, Catherine. (2014). Games as text, games as action: Video games in the English classroom. *Journal of Adolescent & Adult Literacy*, 57(6), 433–9. https://doi.org/10.1002/jaal.275

Beers, David, & Carney, Bryan. (2019a, February 5). Fake story about Jagmeet Singh pops up on *Vancouver Courier* site, others. *The Tyee*. Retrieved from https://thetyee.ca/News/2019/02/05/Singh-Mansion-Fake-News/?utm_source=daily&utm_medium=email&utm_campaign=060219

Beers, David, & Carney, Bryan. (2019b, February 11). Site that lied about NDP leader during election lives in web's shadows. *The Tyee*. Retrieved from https://thetyee.ca/News/2019/02/11/Website-Jagmeet-Singh-Lie/?utm_source=daily&utm_medium=email&utm_campaign=110219

Begoray, Deborah, Wharf Higgins, Joan, Harrison, Janie, & Collins-Emery, Amy. (2013). Adolescent reading/viewing of advertisements: Understandings from transactional and positioning theory. *Journal of Adolescent & Adult Literacy*, 57(2), 121–30. https://doi.org/10.1002/JAAL.202

Bellas, Athena. (2017). *Fairy tales on the teen screen: Rituals of girlhood*. New York: Palgrave Macmillan.

Berliner, Lauren S. (2018). *Producing queer youth and the paradox of digital media empowerment*. New York: Routledge.

Bialystok, Lauren, & Wright, Jessica. (2019). "Just say no": Public dissent over sexuality education and the Canadian national imaginary. *Discourse: Studies in the Cultural Politics of Education*, 40(3), 343–57. https://doi.org/10.1080/01596306.2017.1333085

Biesta, Gert J.J. (2006). *Beyond learning: Democratic education for a human future*. London: Paradigm Publishers.

Blatt, Ben. (2014, August 14). Why do so many schools try to ban *The Giver*? *Slate*. Retrieved from http://www.slate.com/blogs/browbeat/2014/08/14/the_giver_banned_why_do_so_many_parents_try_to_remove_lois_lowry_s_book.html

Boler, Megan (Ed.). (2008). *Digital media and democracy: Tactics in hard times.* Cambridge, MA: MIT Press.

boyd, danah. (2014). *It's complicated: The social lives of networked teens.* New Haven, CT: Yale University Press.

Brown, Wendy. (2003). Neo-liberalism and the end of liberal democracy. *Theory and Event,* 7(1). https://doi.org/10.1353/tae.2003.0020

Brown, Wendy. (2018, May 14). *What kind of world do you want to live in? Remaking the University.* Retrieved from http://utotherescue.blogspot.com/2018/05/what-kind-of-world-do-you-want-to-live.html

Buckingham, David. (1998a). Introduction: Fantasies of empowerment? Radical pedagogy and popular culture. In David Buckingham (Ed.), *Teaching popular culture: Beyond radical pedagogy* (pp. 1–17). London: Routledge.

Buckingham, David. (1998b). Pedagogy, parody and political correctness. In David Buckingham (Ed.), *Teaching popular culture: Beyond radical pedagogy* (pp. 63–87). London: Routledge.

Buckingham, David (Ed.). (1998c). *Teaching popular culture: Beyond radical pedagogy.* London: Routledge.

Buckingham, David. (2003a). *Media education: Literacy, learning, and contemporary culture.* Cambridge: Polity Press.

Buckingham, David. (2003b). Media education and the end of the critical consumer. *Harvard Educational Review,* 73(3), 309–27. https://doi.org/10.17763/haer.73.3.c149w3g81t381p67

Buckingham, David. (2008). Children and media: A cultural studies approach. In Kirsten Drotner & Sonia Livingstone (Eds.), *The international handbook of children, media and culture* (pp. 219–37). Thousand Oaks, CA: Sage.

Buckingham, David. (2016). Do we really need media education 2.0? Teaching media in the age of participatory culture. In Christine Greenhow, Julia Sonnevend & Colin Agur (Eds.), *Education and social media: Toward a digital future* (pp. 1–15 (online)). Cambridge, MA: MIT Press.

Buckingham, David. (2019). *The media education manifesto.* Cambridge: Polity Press.

Buckingham, David. (2020). Epilogue: Rethinking digital literacy: Media education in the age of digital capitalism. *Digital Education Review,* 37, 230–9. https://doi.org/10.1344/der.2020.37.230-239

Buckingham, David, with Banaji, Shakuntala, Burn, Andrew, Carr, Diane, Cranmer, Sue, & Willett, Rebekah. (2005). *The media literacy of children and young people: A review of the academic research.* London: Ofcom.

Buckingham, David, & Burn, Andrew. (2007). Game literacy in theory and practice. *Journal of Educational Multimedia and Hypermedia,* 16(3), 323–49.

Buckingham, David, & Sefton-Green, Julian. (1994). *Cultural studies goes to school: Reading and teaching popular media.* London: Taylor & Francis.

Bullock, Katherine, & Zhou, Steven. (2017). Entertainment or blackface? Decoding Orientalism in a post-9/11 era: Audience views on *Aladdin*. *Review of Education, Pedagogy and Cultural Studies, 39*(5), 446–69. https://doi.org/10.1080/10714413.2017.1344512

Burbules, Nicholas C., & Berk, Rupert. (1999). Critical thinking and critical pedagogy: Relations, differences, and limits. In Thomas S. Popkewitz & Lynn Fendler (Eds.), *Critical theories in education: Changing terrains of knowledge and politics* (pp. 45–65). New York: Routledge.

Burwell, Catherine. (2010). Rewriting the script: Toward a politics of young people's digital media participation. *Review of Education, Pedagogy, and Cultural Studies, 32*, 382–402. https://doi.org/10.1080/10714413.2010.510354

Burwell, Catherine. (2013). The pedagogical potential of video remix: Critical conversations about culture, creativity and copyright. *Journal of Adolescent & Adult Literacy, 57*(3), 205–13. https://doi.org/10.1002/JAAL.205

Burwell, Catherine. (2018). Youth, bytes, copyright: Talking to young Canadian creators about digital copyright. In Renee Hobbs (Ed.), *Routledge companion to media education, copyright, and fair use* (pp. 155–68). New York: Routledge.

Butler, Allison T. (2020). *Educating media literacy: The need for critical media literacy in teacher education.* Boston and Leiden: Brill.

Butler, Judith. (1990). *Gender trouble: Feminism and the subversion of identity.* New York: Routledge.

Butler, Kayla. (2020, January 29). Alberta curriculum review urges focus on basic learning, standardized tests. *Edmonton CityNews.* Retrieved from https://edmonton.citynews.ca/2020/01/29/alberta-curriculum-review-urges-focus-on-basic-learning-standardized-tests/

Cassell, Justine, & Jenkins, Henry. (1998). Chess for girls? Feminism and computer games. In Justine Cassell & Henry Jenkins (Eds.), *From Barbie to Mortal Kombat: Gender and computer games* (pp. 2–45). Cambridge, MA: MIT Press.

CBC Docs. (2019). Changing face: Plastic is fantastic in South Korea. Retrieved from https://www.cbc.ca/passionateeye/features/plastic-is-fantastic-in-south-korea

Cheung, Christopher. (2020, January 21). Need a break from real rental nightmares? Try this game. *The Tyee.* Retrieved from https://thetyee.ca/Culture/2020/01/21/Play-The-Vancouver-Housing-Game-On-Your-Phone/?utm_source=daily&utm_medium=email&utm_campaign=210120

Christensen, Linda. (2017). Unlearning the myths that bind us: Critiquing cartoons and society. *Rethinking Schools, 31*(3), 22–7.

Christensen, Miyase, & Morley, David. (2014). New media, new crises, new theories? An interview with David Morley. *Popular Communication, 12*(4), 208–22. https://doi.org/10.1080/15405702.2014.960572

Christensen, Pia Haudrup. (2004). Children's participation in ethnographic research: Issues of power and representation. *Children and Society, 18*(2), 165–76. https://doi.org/10.1002/chi.823

Chung, Sheng Kuan. (2005). Media/visual literacy art education: Cigarette ad deconstruction. *Art Education, 58*(3), 19–24. https://doi.org/10.2307/27696072

Chung, Sheng Kuan. (2007a). Media/visual literacy art education: Sexism in hip-hop music videos. *Art Education, 60*(3), 33–8. https://doi.org/10.2307/27696214

Chung, Sheng Kuan. (2007b). Media literacy art education: Deconstructing lesbian and gay stereotypes in the media. *International Journal of Art and Design Education, 26*(1), 98–107.

Chung, Sheng Kuan, & Kirby, Michael S. (2009). Media literacy art education: Logos, culture jamming, and activism. *Art Education, 62*(1), 34–9.

Clegg, Sue. (2016). Agency and ontology within intersectional analysis: A critical realist contribution. *Journal of Critical Realism, 15*(5), 494–510. https://doi.org/10.1080/14767430.2016.1210470

Conli, Roy (Producer), Greno, Nathan, & Howard, Byron (Directors). (2010). *Tangled* [motion picture]. Buena Vista Home Entertainment.

Connell, R.W. (1987). *Gender and power.* Stanford, CA: Stanford University Press.

Cope, Bill, & Kalantzis, Mary (Eds.). (2000). *Multiliteracies: Literacy learning and the design of social futures.* London: Routledge.

Corbin, Juliet, & Morse, Janice M. (2003). The unstructured interactive interview: Issues of reciprocity and risks when dealing with sensitive topics. *Qualitative Inquiry, 9*(3), 335–54.

Couldry, Nick, & Hepp, Andreas. (2013). Conceptualizing mediatization: Contexts, traditions, arguments [editorial]. *Communication Theory, 23,* 191–202. https://doi.org/10.1111/comt.12019

Couldry, Nick, & Mejias, Ulises A. (2019). Making data colonialism liveable: How might data's social order be regulated? *Internet Policy Review, 8*(2), online. https://doi.org/10.14763/2019.2.1411

Coyne, Richard. (1999). *Technoromanticism: Digital narrative, holism, and the romance of the real.* Cambridge, MA: MIT Press.

Creaven, Sean. (2015). The "two Marxisms" revisited: Humanism, structuralism, and realism in Marxist social theory. *Journal of Critical Realism, 14*(1), 7–53. https://doi.org/10.1179/1572513814Y.0000000008

Crosby, Tim. (2011). How outsourcing works. *How Stuff Works.* Retrieved from https://money.howstuffworks.com/outsourcing4.htm

Currie, Dawn H. (1997). Violence against women: Confronting the limits of legal solutions to social problems. In George Rigakos & Kevyn Bonnycastle (Eds.), *Battered women: Law, state and contemporary research in Canada* (pp. 41–51). Vancouver: Collective Press.

Currie, Dawn H. (1999). *Girl talk: Adolescent magazines and their readers.* Toronto: University of Toronto Press.

Currie, Dawn H. (2001). Dear Abby: Advice pages as a site for the operation of power. *Feminist Theory, 2*(3), 259–81. https://doi.org/10.1177/14647000122229523

Currie, Dawn, Kelly, Deirdre M., & Pomerantz, Shauna. (2007). Listening to girls: Discursive positioning and the construction of self. *International Journal of Qualitative Studies in Education, 20*(4), 377–400.

Currie, Dawn H., Kelly, Deirdre M., & Pomerantz, Shauna. (2009). *"Girl power": Girls reinventing girlhood.* New York: Peter Lang.

Dahlgren, Peter (2015). Mass media: Introduction and schools of thought. In James D. Wright (Ed.), *International Encyclopedia of the Social and Behavioral Sciences* (2nd ed., Vol. 14, pp. 726–32): Amsterdam: Elsevier.

Darts, David. (2004). Visual culture jam: Art, pedagogy, and creative resistance. *Studies in Art Education, 45*(4), 313–27. https://doi.org/10.1080/00393541.2004.11651778

Davies, Bronwyn. (1989). *Frogs and snails and feminist tales: Preschool children and gender.* St Leonards, Australia: Allen & Unwin.

Davies, Bronwyn. (1993). *Shards of glass: Children reading and writing beyond gendered identities.* Cresskill, NJ: Hampton Press.

Davies, Bronwyn. (1997). Constructing and deconstructing masculinities through critical literacy. *Gender and Education, 9*(1), 9–30. https://doi.org/10.1080/09540259721420

Davies, Bronwyn. (2006). Subjectification: The relevance of Butler's analysis for education. *British Journal of Sociology of Education, 27*(4), 425–38. https://doi.org/10.1080/01425690600802907

Davies, Bronwyn, & Bansel, Peter. (2007). Neoliberalism and education. *International Journal of Qualitative Studies in Education, 20*(3), 247–59. https://doi.org/10.1080/09518390701281751

Dean, Jodi. (2005). Communicative capitalism: Circulation and the foreclosure of politics. *Cultural Politics, 1*(1), 51–74. https://doi.org/10.2752/174321905778054845

Dehli, Kari. (2009). Media literacy and neo-liberal government: Pedagogies of freedom and constraint. *Pedagogy, Culture & Society, 17*(1), 57–73. https://doi.org/10.1080/14681360902742860

De Lissovoy, Noah. (2018). Pedagogy of the anxious: Rethinking critical pedagogy in the context of neoliberal autonomy and responsibilization. *Journal of Education Policy, 33*(2), 187–205. https://doi.org/10.1080/02680939.2017.1352031

Delwiche, Aaron. (2010). Media literacy 2.0: Unique characteristics of video games. In Kathleen Tyner (Ed.), *Media literacy: New agendas in communication* (pp. 175–91). New York: Routledge.

Denworth, Lydia. (2019, November 1). Social media has not destroyed a generation. *Scientific American*. Retrieved from https://www.scientificamerican.com/article/social-media-has-not-destroyed-a-generation/

de Roock, Roberto Santiago. (2021). On the material consequences of (digital) literacy: Digital writing with, for, and against racial capitalism. *Theory into Practice*, *60*(2), 183–93. https://doi.org/10.1080/00405841.2020.1857128

DeVault, Marjorie L. (1999). *Liberating method: Feminist social research*. Philadelphia: Temple University Press.

Domonoske, Camila. (2016). Students have "dismaying" inability to tell fake news from real, study finds. *The Two-Way*. Retrieved from https://www.npr.org/sections/thetwo-way/2016/11/23/503129818/study-finds-students-have-dismaying-inability-to-tell-fake-news-from-real

Duff, Patricia A. (2001). Language, literacy, content, and (pop) culture: Challenges for ESL students in mainstream courses. *Canadian Modern Language Review/Revue canadienne des langues vivantes*, *58*(1), 103–32. https://doi.org/10.3138/cmlr.58.1.103

Duncan, Barry. (2007). Looking for the empowerment in Adbusters' Media Empowerment Kit. *Our Schools/Our Selves*, *17*(1), 203–5.

Duncum, Paul. (2001). Visual culture: Developments, definitions, and directions for art education. *Studies in Art Education*, *42*(2), 101–12. https://doi.org/10.2307/1321027

Dundes, Lauren, & Streiff, Madeline. (2016). Reel royal diversity? The glass ceiling in Disney's *Mulan* and *Princess and the Frog*. *Societies*, *6*(35), 1–14. https://doi.org/10.3390/soc6040035

Dyson, Anne H. (1997). *Writing superheroes: Contemporary childhood, popular culture, and classroom literacy*. New York: Teachers College Press.

Eklund, Ken. (2020). World without oil. Retrieved January 16, 2020, from http://writerguy.com/wwo/metahome.htm

Ellsworth, Elizabeth. (1989). Why doesn't this feel empowering? Working through the oppressive myths of critical pedagogy. *Harvard Educational Review*, *59*(3), 297–324. https://doi.org/10.17763/haer.59.3.058342114k266250

Ellsworth, Elizabeth. (1997). *Teaching positions: Difference, pedagogy, and the power of address*. New York: Teachers College Press.

England, Dawn Elizabeth, Descartes, Lara, & Collier-Meek, Melissa A.. (2011). Gender role portrayal and the Disney princesses. *Sex Roles*, *64*, 555–67. https://doi.org/10.1007/s11199-011-9930-7

Ericsson, Susan, Talreja, Sanjay (Producers), & Jhally, Sut (Director). (1999). *Tough guise: Violence, media, and the crisis in masculinity* [DVD]. Media Education Foundation.

Ferguson, Susan. (2011). Classroom contradictions: Popular media in Ontario schools' literacy and citizenship education policies. *Education, Citizenship & Social Justice*, *6*(2), 137–51. https://doi.org/10.1177/1746197911410371

Ferreday, Debra. (2017). "Only the bad gyal could do this": Rihanna, rape-revenge narratives and the cultural politics of white feminism. *Feminist Theory*, *18*(3), 263–80. https://doi.org/10.1177/1464700117721879

Fisher, Stephanie, & Jenson, Jennifer. (2017). Producing alternative gender orders: A critical look at girls and gaming. *Learning, Media and Technology*, *42*(1), 87–99. https://doi.org/10.1080/17439884.2016.1132729

Fiske, John. (1989). *Understanding popular culture*. Boston: Unwin Hyman.

Fleetwood, Steve. (2005). The ontology of organization and management studies: A critical realist approach. *Organization: The Interdisciplinary Journal of Organization, Theory and Society*, *12*(2), 197–222. https://doi.org/10.1177/1350508405051188

Flores-Koulish, Stephanie A., & Smith-D'Arezzo, Wendy Marie. (2016). The Three Pigs: Can they blow us into critical media literacy old school style? *Journal of Research in Childhood Education*, *30*(3), 349–60. https://doi.org/10.1080/02568543.2016.1178673

Foucault, Michel. (1980). *Power/knowledge: Selected interviews and other writings, 1972–1977* (C. Gordon, L. Marshall, J. Mepham, & K. Soper, Trans.). New York: Pantheon Books.

Fraser, Nancy. (1989). *Unruly practices: Power, discourse, and gender in contemporary social theory*. Minneapolis: University of Minnesota Press.

Fraser, Nancy. (2009). Feminism, capitalism and the cunning of history. *New Left Review*, *56*, 97–117.

Fraser, Nancy. (2015). Legitimation crisis? On the political contradictions of financialized capitalism. *Critical Historical Studies*, *2*(2), 157–89. https://doi.org/10.1086/683054

Freedman, Kerry. (1994). Interpreting gender and visual culture in art classrooms. *Studies in Art Education*, *35*(3), 157–70. https://doi.org/10.2307/1320217

Freire, Paulo. (1972). *Pedagogy of the oppressed*. Harmondsworth: Penguin.

Friedman, Steven. (2011). Taking action against Disney: A teacher struggles with encouraging direct student action. In Elizabeth Marshall & Özlem Sensoy (Eds.), *Rethinking popular culture and media* (pp. 253–7). Milwaukee: Rethinking Schools.

Fuchs, Christian. (2014). *Social media: A critical introduction*. London: Sage Publishing.

Fuchs, Christian, & Trottier, Daniel. (2015). Towards a theoretical model of social media surveillance in contemporary society. *Communications*, *40*(1), 113–35. https://doi.org/10.1515/commun-2014-0029

Fujino, Diane C., Gomez, Jonathan D., Lezra, Esther, Lipsitz, George, Mitchell, Jordan, & Fonseca, James. (2018). A transformative pedagogy for a decolonial world. *Review of Education, Pedagogy, and Cultural Studies*, *40*(2), 69–95. https://doi.org/10.1080/10714413.2018.1442080

Gainer, Jesse S. (2007). Social critique *and* pleasure: Critical media literacy with popular culture texts. *Language Arts, 85*(2), 106–14.

Gainer, Jesse S. (2010). Critical media literacy in middle school: Exploring the politics of representation. *Journal of Adolescent & Adult Literacy, 53*(5), 364–73. https://doi.org/10.1598/JAAL.53.5.2

Gainer, Jesse S., & Lapp, Diane. (2010). Remixing old and new literacies = motivated students. *English Journal, 100*(1), 58–64.

Gamson, Joshua. (2015). Celebrity. In James D. Wright (Ed.), *International encyclopedia of the social and behavioral sciences* (2nd ed., Vol. 3, pp. 274–8). Amsterdam: Elsevier.

Garcia, Antero, Luke, Allan, & Seglem, Robyn. (2018). Looking at the next 20 years of multiliteracies: A discussion with Allan Luke. *Theory into Practice, 57*(1), 72–8. https://doi.org/10.1080/00405841.2017.1390330

Garcia, Antero, & Seglem, Robyn. (2018). This issue. *Theory into Practice, 57*(1), 1–4. https://doi.org/10.1080/00405841.2017.1411721

Gay, Roxane. (2014). What we hunger for. In Gay, *Bad feminist: Essays* (pp. 122–30). New York: HarperCollins.

Gee, James Paul. (2002). Millennials and Bobos, *Blue's Clues* and *Sesame Street*: A story for our times. In Donna E. Alvermann (Ed.), *Adolescents and literacies in a digital world* (pp. 51–67). New York: Peter Lang.

Gee, James Paul. (2004). Discourse analysis: What makes it critical? In Rebecca Rogers (Ed.), *An introduction to critical discourse analysis in education* (pp. 19–50). Mahwah, NJ: Lawrence Erlbaum Associates.

Gee, James Paul. (2008). Learning theory, video games, and popular culture. In Kirsten Drotner & Sonia Livingstone (Eds.), *The international handbook of children, media and culture* (pp. 196–212). London: Sage Publishing.

Gee, James Paul. (2011a). *How to do discourse analysis: A toolkit*. New York: Routledge.

Gee, James Paul. (2011b). *An introduction to discourse analysis: Theory and method* (3rd ed.). New York: Routledge.

Gee, James Paul. (2018). Books and games. In Peggy Albers (Ed.), *Global conversations in literacy research: Digital and critical literacies* (pp. 132–43). New York: Routledge.

Gill, Rosalind. (2008). Empowerment/sexism: Figuring female sexual agency in contemporary advertising. *Feminism and Psychology, 18*(1), 35–60. https://doi.org/10.1177/0959353507084950

Gillborn, David. (2016). Softly, softly: Genetics, intelligence and the hidden racism of the new geneism. *Journal of Education Policy, 31*(4), 365–88. https://doi.org/10.1080/02680939.2016.1139189

Giorgis, Hannah. (2020, July). Hip-Hop won't stop protecting alleged abusers. *The Atlantic*. Retrieved from https://www.theatlantic.com/culture/archive/2020/07/the-women-who-still-dont-matter-to-hip-hop/613681/

Giroux, Henry A. (1987). Citizenship, public philosophy, and the struggle for democracy. *Educational Theory, 37*(2), 103–20. https://doi.org/10.1111/j.1741-5446.1987.00103.x

Giroux, Henry A. (2004). Cultural studies and the politics of public pedagogy: Making the political more pedagogical. *Parallax, 10*(2), 73–89. https://doi.org/10.1080/1353464042000208530

Giroux, Henry A., & Pollock, Grace. (2010). *The mouse that roared: Disney and the end of innocence* (2nd ed.). Lanham, MD: Rowman & Littlefield Publishers.

Giroux, Henry A., & Simon, Roger I. (1989). *Popular culture, schooling, and everyday life*. Granby, MA: Bergin & Garvey.

Goering, C.Z., & Thomas, P.L. (2018). An introduction: Can critical media literacy save us? In C.Z. Goering & P.L. Thomas (Eds.), *Critical media literacy and fake news in post-truth America* (pp. 1–6). Leiden/Boston: Brill Sense.

Gonick, Marnina. (2003). *Between femininities: Ambivalence, identity, and the education of girls*. Albany: State University of New York Press.

Gonzalez-Bailon, Sandra. (2015). Social protest and new media. In James D. Wright (Ed.), *International encyclopedia of the social and behavioral sciences* (2nd ed., Vol. 22, pp. 512–17). Amsterdam: Elsevier.

Gordon, Chloe S., Jones, Sandra C., Kervin, Lisa K., & Howard, Steven J. (2018). "You could get sick, disgusting": An analysis of alcohol counter-advertisements created by children. *Health Education Research, 33*(5), 337–50. https://doi.org/10.1093/her/cyy022

Graves, Daren A., Kelly, Lauren Leigh, & McArthur, Sherell A. (2020). Introduction: Teaching for critical consciousness at the intersection of critical media literacy and hip hop education. *International Journal of Critical Media Literacy, 2*(1), 1–8. https://doi.org/10.1163/25900110-00201001

Green, Bill. (1988). Subject-specific literacy and school learning: A focus on writing. *Australian Journal of Education, 32*(2), 156–79. https://doi.org/10.1177/000494418803200203

Greenpeace International (Producer). (2008, April 21). Dove onslaught(er) [video] Retrieved from https://www.youtube.com/watch?v=odI7pQFyjso

Grossberg, Lawrence. (2009). Cultural studies: What's in a name? (one more time). In Rhonda Hammer & Douglas Kellner (Eds.), *Media/cultural studies: Critical approaches* (pp. 25–48). New York: Peter Lang.

Guzzetti, Barbara J., Elliott, Kate, & Welsch, Diana. (2010). *DIY media in the classroom: New literacies across content areas*. New York: Teachers College Press.

Hagood, Margaret C., Alvermann, Donna E., & Heron-Hruby, Alison. (2010). *Bring it to class: Unpacking pop culture in literacy learning (Grades 4 through 12)*. New York: Teachers College Press.

Haight, Michael, Quan-Haase, Anabel, & Corbett, Bradley A. (2014). Revisiting the digital divide in Canada: The impact of demographic factors on access to the internet, level of online activity, and social networking site usage.

Information, Communication & Society, 17(4), 503–19. https://doi.org/10.1080/1369118X.2014.891633

Hall, Stuart. (1986). The problem of ideology: Marxism without guarantees. *Journal of Communication Inquiry, 10*(2), 28–44. https://doi.org/10.1177/019685998601000203

Hall, Stuart. (1992). The West and the rest: Discourse and power. In Stuart Hall & Bram Gieben (Eds.), *The formations of modernity* (pp. 185–227). Cambridge: Polity Press.

Hall, Stuart. (2000). Heroes or villains?; and Stereotyping as a signifying practice. In Judy M. Iseke-Barnes & Njoki Nathani Wane (Eds.), *Equity in schools and society* (pp. 97–109). Toronto: Canadian Scholars' Press.

Hall, Stuart. (2004). Encoding/decoding. In Stuart Hall, Dorothy Hobson, Andrew Lowe, & Paul Willis (Eds.), *Culture, media, language: Working papers in cultural studies 1972–79* (pp. 117–27). London: Routledge. (Original work published in 1980).

Hammer, Rhonda, & Kellner, Douglas (Eds.). (2009). *Media/cultural studies: Critical approaches.* New York: Peter Lang.

Hammersley, Martyn. (2009). Against the ethicists: On the evils of ethical regulation. *International Journal of Social Research Methodology, 12*(3), 211–25. https://doi.org/10.1080/13645570802170288

Hanbury, Mark. (2018, June 18). A Parkland shooting survivor is reigniting his war against Laura Ingraham. Here are all of the advertisers that cut ties with her show during their last battle. *Business Insider.* Retrieved from https://www.businessinsider.com/fox-news-advertisers-respond-david-hogg-boycott-2018-3/#nutrish-1

Hardingham-Gill, Tamara. (2009, June 25). Easy breezy CoverGirl Rihanna is reinstated as face of make up brand days after former lover pleads guilty to assaulting her. *Daily Mail.* Retrieved from http://www.dailymail.co.uk/tvshowbiz/article-1195407/CoverGirl-Rihanna-reinstated-face-make-brand-just-days-lover-pleads-guilty-assaulting-her.html

Harold, Christine. (2004). Pranking rhetoric: "Culture jamming" as media activism. *Critical Studies in Media Communication, 21*(3), 189–211. https://doi.org/10.1080/0739318042000212693

Harste, Jerome C., & Albers, Peggy. (2013). "I'm riskin' it": Teachers take on consumerism [feature article]. *Journal of Adolescent & Adult Literacy, 56*(5), 381–90. https://doi.org/10.1002/JAAL.00149

Hearne, Joanna. (2017). "I am not a fairy tale": Indigenous storytelling on Canadian television. *Marvels & Tales, 31*(1), 126–46. https://doi.org/10.13110/marvelstales.31.1.0126

Heath, Joseph, & Potter, Andrew. (2004). *The rebel sell: Why the culture can't be jammed.* Toronto: HarperCollins.

Hebdige, Dick. (1979). *Subculture: The meaning of style.* London: Routledge.

Heller, Kevin Jon. (1996). Power, subjectification and resistance in Foucault. *SubStance*, *25*(1), 78–110. https://doi.org/10.2307/3685230

Hemmings, Annette. (2006). Great ethical divides: Bridging the gap between institutional review boards and researchers. *Educational Researcher*, *35*(4), 12–18. https://doi.org/10.3102/0013189X035004012

Herriot, Lindsay, Burns, David P., & Yeung, Betty. (2018). Contested spaces: Trans-inclusive school policies and parental sovereignty in Canada. *Gender and Education*, *30*(6), 695–714. https://doi.org/10.1080/09540253.2017.1396291

Hill, Marc Lamont. (2009). Wounded healing: Forming a community through storytelling in hip-hop lit. *Teachers College Record*, *111*(1), 248–93.

Hill, Marc Lamont, & Petchauer, Emery (Eds.). (2013). *Schooling hip-hop: Expanding hip-hop based education across the curriculum*. New York: Teachers College Press.

Hines, Sara. (2010). Collecting the empire: Andrew Lang's fairy books (1889–1910). *Marvels & Tales*, *24*(1), 39–56.

Hitchcock, David. (2018, Fall). Critical thinking. In Edward N. Zalta (Ed.), *Stanford encyclopedia of philosophy*. Retrieved from https://plato.stanford.edu/entries/critical-thinking/

Hobbs, Renee. (2004). Analyzing advertising in the English language arts classroom: A quasi-experimental study. *Studies in Media & Information Literacy Education [SIMILE]*, *4*(2).

Hobbs, Renee. (2007). *Reading the media: Media literacy in high school English*. New York: Teachers College Press.

Hobbs, Renee. (2010). *Digital and media literacy: A plan of action*. Washington, DC: Aspen Institute Communications and Society Program and the John S. and James L. Knight Foundation.

Hobbs, Renee. (2017). Teaching and learning in a post-truth world. *Educational Leadership*, *75*(3). Retrieved from http://www.ascd.org/publications/educational_leadership/nov17/vol75/num03/Teaching_and_Learning_in_a_Post-Truth_World.aspx

Hobbs, Renee, He, Haixia, & Robbgrieco, Michael. (2015). Seeing, believing, and learning to be skeptical: Supporting language learning through advertising analysis activities. *TESOL Journal*, *6*(3), 447–75. https://doi.org/10.1002/tesj.153

Hoechsmann, Michael, & Poyntz, Stuart R. (2012). *Media literacies: A critical introduction*. Malden, MA: Wiley-Blackwell.

Hoffman, Jan. (2009, March 19). Teenage girls stand by their man. *New York Times*. Retrieved from http://www.nytimes.com/2009/03/19/fashion/19brown.html

Holland, Dorothy C., Lachicotte, William, Jr., Skinner, Debra, & Cain, Carole. (1998). *Identity and agency in cultural worlds*. Cambridge, MA: Harvard University Press.

Hollingsworth, Julia, & Seo, Yoonjung. (2019, October 15). Death of K-pop star Sulli prompts outpouring of grief and questions over cyber-bullying. CNN. Retrieved from https://www.cnn.com/2019/10/15/asia/kpop-sulli-death-aftermath-intl-hnk-scli/index.html

hooks, bell. (2003). The oppositional gaze: Black female spectators. In Alison Jones (Ed.), *The feminism and visual culture reader* (pp. 94–105). New York: Routledge.

Hopewell, John, & Keslassy, Elsa. (2016, June 15). French animators lure U.S. studios with tax rebates, diverse talent. *Variety*. Retrieved from https://variety.com/2016/film/global/disney-sends-animation-projects-to-france-1201795423

Huang, Shin-ying. (2019). Postfeminist influences on fairy tales, real and imagined: A critical media literacy classroom investigation. *Gender and Education, 31*(6), 688–704. https://doi.org/10.1080/09540253.2018.1467002

Hyslop, Katie. (2017, August 14). How do we ready kids for the next generation of fake news? *The Tyee*. Retrieved from https://thetyee.ca/Mediacheck/2017/08/14/Ready-Kids-Next-Gen-Fake-News/?utm_source=daily&utm_medium=email&utm_campaign=140817

Ince, Judith. (2004, November 15). All culture jammed up. *The Tyee*. Retrieved from https://thetyee.ca/Mediacheck/2004/11/15/AllCultureJammed/

Ingraham, Chrys. (1994). The heterosexual imaginary: Feminist sociology and theories of gender. *Sociological Theory, 12*(2), 203–19.

Iyer, Radha, & Luke, Carmen. (2011). Gender representations in the media and the importance of critical media literacy. In Steven Tozer, Bernardo P. Gallegos, Annette Henry, Mary Bushnell Greiner, & Paula Groves Price (Eds.), *Handbook of research in the social foundations of education* (pp. 434–49): Routledge.

Jacobs, Charlotte E. (2016). Developing the "oppositional gaze": Using critical media pedagogy and Black feminist thought to promote Black girls' identity development. *Journal of Negro Education, 85*(3), 225–38. https://doi.org/10.7709/jnegroeducation.85.3.0225

Jacobson, Nina, Kilik, Jon (Producers), & Ross, Gary (Director). (2012). *The Hunger Games* [motion picture]. Lionsgate Films.

Janks, Hilary. (2010). *Literacy and power*. New York: Routledge.

Janks, Hilary. (2013a). Critical literacy in teaching and research. *Education Inquiry, 4*(2), 225–42. https://doi.org/10.3402/edui.v4i2.22071

Janks, Hilary. (2013b). The importance of critical literacy. In Jessica Pandya & JuliAnna Ávila (Eds.), *Moving critical literacies forward: A new look at praxis across contexts* (pp. 32–44). New York: Routledge.

Janks, Hilary. (2018). Doing critical literacy. In Peggy Albers (Ed.), *Global conversations in literacy research: Digital and critical literacies* (pp. 29–40). New York: Routledge.

Janks, Hilary, with Dixon, Kerryn, Ferreira, Ana, Granville, Stella, & Newfield, Denise. (2014). *Doing critical literacy: Texts and activities for students and teachers.* New York: Routledge.

Jenkins, Henry. (2006). *Convergence culture: Where old and new media collide.* New York: New York University Press.

Jenkins, Henry, with Clinton, Katie, Purushotma, Ravi, Robinson, Alice J., & Weigel, Margaret. (2006). *Confronting the challenges of participatory culture: Media education for the 21st century.* Chicago: The John D. and Catherine T. MacArthur Foundation.

Jenkins, Henry. (2007). *The wow climax: Tracing the emotional impact of popular culture.* New York: New York University Press.

Jenkins, Henry, Shresthova, Sangita, Gamber-Thompson, Liana, Kligler-Vilenchik, Neta, & Zimmerman, Arely. (2016). *By any media necessary: The new activism of American youth.* New York: New York University Press.

Jenson, Jennifer, & de Castell, Suzanne. (2011). Girsl@Play. *Feminist Media Studies, 11*(2), 167–79. https://doi.org/10.1080/14680777.2010.521625

Jorba, Marta, & Rodó-Zárate, Maria. (2019). Beyond mutual constitution: The properties framework for intersectionality studies. *Signs: Journal of Women in Culture and Society, 45*(1), 175–200. https://doi.org/10.1086/703499

Jorgensen, Jeana. (2019). Gender, sexuality and the fairy tale in contemporary American literature. In Andrew Teverson (Ed.), *The fairy tale world* (pp. 260–72). London and New York: Routledge.

Kahn, Richard, & Kellner, Douglas. (2004). New media and Internet activism: From the "Battle of Seattle" to blogging. *New Media & Society, 6,* 87–95. https://doi.org/10.1177/146144480403990

Kahn, Richard, & Kellner, Douglas. (2006). Oppositional politics and the Internet: A critical/reconstructionist approach. In Meenakshi Gigi Durham & Douglas Kellner (Eds.), *Media and cultural studies: Key works* (pp. 703–25). Malden, MA: Blackwell.

Kantayya, Shalini (Director). (2020). *Coded bias* [motion picture]. Netflix.

Keller, James. (2019, December 10). Alberta school lesson on oil sands prompts threats from parents amid sensitivity over industry's image. *Globe and Mail.* Retrieved from https://www.theglobeandmail.com/canada/alberta/article-rcmp-intervene-after-school-lesson-on-albertas-oil-industry-prompts/

Kellner, Douglas. (1990). Critical theory and the crisis of social theory. *Sociological Perspectives, 33*(1), 11–33. https://doi.org/10.2307/1388975

Kellner, Douglas. (1998). Multiple literacies and critical pedagogy in a multicultural society. *Educational Theory, 48*(1), 103–22. https://doi.org/10.1111/j.1741-5446.1998.00103.x

Kellner, Douglas. (2009). Toward a critical media/cultural studies. In Rhonda Hammer & Douglas Kellner (Eds.), *Media/cultural studies: Critical approaches* (pp. 5–24). New York: Peter Lang.

Kellner, Douglas, & Gooyong, Kim. (2010). YouTube, critical pedagogy, and media activism. *Review of Education, Pedagogy, and Cultural Studies, 32*(1), 3–36. https://doi.org/10.1080/10714410903482658

Kellner, Douglas, & Share, Jeff. (2005). Toward critical media literacy: Core concepts, debates, organizations, and policy. *Discourse: Studies in the Cultural Politics of Education, 26*(3), 369–86. https://doi.org/10.1080/01596300500200169

Kellner, Douglas, & Share, Jeff. (2007). Critical media literacy, democracy, and the reconstruction of education. In Donaldo Macedo & Shirley R. Steinberg (Eds.), *Media literacy: A reader* (pp. 3–23). New York: Peter Lang.

Kellner, Douglas, & Share, Jeff. (2009). Critical media education and radical democracy. In Michael W. Apple, Wayne Au, & Luis Armando Gandin (Eds.), *The Routledge international handbook of critical education* (pp. 281–95). New York: Routledge.

Kellner, Douglas, & Share, Jeff. (2019). *The critical media literacy guide: Engaging media and transforming education.* Leiden and Boston: Brill/Sense.

Kelly, Deirdre M. (2010). Media representation and the case for critical media education. In Mary Clare Courtland & Trevor Gambell (Eds.), *Literature, media, and multiliteracies in adolescent language arts* (pp. 277–303). Vancouver: Pacific Education Press.

Kelly, Deirdre M. (2012). Teaching for social justice: Translating an anti-oppression approach into practice. *Our Schools/Our Selves, 21*(2), 135–54. Retrieved from http://www.policyalternatives.ca/sites/default/files/uploads/publications/National%20Office/2012/02/osos106_Teaching_Social_Justice.pdf

Kelly, Deirdre M. (2014). Alternative learning contexts and the goals of democracy in education. *Teachers College Record, 116*(14), 383–410.

Kelly, Deirdre M., & Arnold, Chrissie. (2016). Cyberbullying and Internet safety. In Barbara Guzzetti & Mellinee Lesley (Eds.), *Handbook of research on the societal impact of digital media* (pp. 529–59). Hershey, PA: IGI Global.

Kelly, Deirdre M., & Brandes, Gabriella Minnes. (2010). "Social justice needs to be everywhere": Anti-oppression education in teacher preparation. *Alberta Journal of Educational Research, 56*(4), 388–402.

Kelly, Deirdre M., & Currie, Dawn H. (2020). Beyond stereotype analysis in critical media literacy: Case study of reading and writing gender in pop music videos. *Gender and Education.* https://doi.org/10.1080/09540253.2020.1831443

Kelly, Deirdre M., & Currie, Dawn H. (2021). Teacher reflexivity when using pop culture in the classroom. *International Journal of Critical Media Literacy, 2*(2), 121–47. https://doi.org/10.1163/25900110-02020001

Kelly, Deirdre M., & Pomerantz, Shauna. (2009). Mean, wild, and alienated: Girls and the state of feminism in popular culture. *Girlhood Studies, 2*(1), 1–19. https://doi.org/10.3167/ghs.2009.020102

Kenway, Jane, & Bullen, Elizabeth. (2001). *Consuming children: Education, entertainment, advertising.* Buckingham: Open University Press.

Kenway, Jane, & Bullen, Elizabeth. (2006). Pedagogies that bite/byte back. In Hugh Lauder, Phillip Brown, Jo-Anne Dillabough, & A.H. Halsey (Eds.), *Education, globalization and social change* (pp. 524–36). Oxford: Oxford University Press.

Kilbourne, Jean (Writer). (2010). *Killing us softly 4: Advertising's image of women* [motion picture]. Media Education Foundation.

Knobel, Michele, & Lankshear, Colin. (2008). Remix: The art and craft of endless hybridization. *Journal of Adolescent & Adult Literacy, 52*(1), 22–33. https://doi.org/10.1598/JAAL.52.1.3

Kohnen, Angela M., Mertens, Gillian E., & Boehm, Shelby M. (2020). Can middle schoolers learn to read the web like experts? Possibilities and limits of a strategy-based intervention. *Journal of Media Literacy Education, 12*(2), 64–79. https://doi.org/10.23860/JMLE-2020-12-2-6

Kornfield, Sarah. (2016). *The Hunger Games*: Understanding postfeminist and postracial ideologies. *Teaching Media Quarterly, 4*(4), 1–10.

Kozolanka, Kirsten, & Orlowski, Paul. (2018). Media literacy in an era of fake news and alternative facts. *Media literacy for citizenship: A Canadian perspective.* Toronto: Canadian Scholars' Press.

Kress, Gunther. (1989). *Linguistic processes in sociocultural practice.* Oxford: Oxford University Press.

Kress, Gunther. (2000). Design and transformation: New theories of meaning. In Bill Cope & Mary Kalantzis (Eds.), *Multiliteracies: Literacy learning and the design of social futures* (pp. 149–58). London: Routledge.

Kupiainen, Reijo. (2013). *Media and digital literacies in secondary school.* New York: Peter Lang.

Kustritz, Anne. (2019). Fairy tale, fan fiction, and popular media. In Andrew Teverson (Ed.), *The fairy tale world* (pp. 284–96). London and New York: Routledge.

Lacroix, Celeste. (2004). Images of animated others: The orientalization of Disney's cartoon heroines from *The Little Mermaid* to *The Hunchback of Notre Dame. Popular Communication, 2*(4), 213–29. https://doi.org/10.1207/s15405710pc0204_2

Lankshear, Colin, & Knobel, Michele. (2007). Sampling "the new" in new literacies. In Michele Knobel & Colin Lankshear (Eds.), *A new literacies sampler* (pp. 1–24). New York: Peter Lang.

Laughter, Judson. (2015). ELA teacher preparation 2.0: Critical media literacy, action research, and mashups. *Contemporary Issues in Technology & Teacher Education, 15*(3), 265–82.

Lazar, Michelle M. (2007). Feminist critical discourse analysis: Articulating a feminist discourse praxis. *Critical Discourse Studies, 4*(2), 141–64. https://doi.org/10.1080/17405900701464816

Lee, Joonkoo. (2019). Three worlds of global value chains: Multiple governance and upgrading paths in the Korean animation industry. *International Journal of Cultural Policy, 25*(6), 684–700. https://doi.org/10.1080/10286632.2017.1353605

Lester, Neal A. (2019). African-American adaptations of fairy tales. In Andrew Teverson (Ed.), *The fairy tale world* (pp. 232–47). London and New York: Routledge.

Levine, Matthew A.J. (2020). *Troubling clouds: Gaps affecting privacy protection in British Columbia's K-12 education system.* Vancouver: BC Freedom of Information and Privacy Association. Retrieved from https://fipa.bc.ca/wp-content/uploads/2020/09/2020_troubling_clouds_LMS_report.pdf

Lévi-Strauss, Claude. (1966). *The savage mind.* Chicago: University of Chicago Press.

Levy, Pierre. (2010). From social computing to reflexive collective intelligence: The IEML research program. *Information Sciences, 180*(1–2), 71–94. https://doi.org/10.1016/j.ins.2009.08.001

Lieb, Kristin J. (2018). *Gender, branding, and the modern music industry: The social construction of female popular music stars* (2nd ed.). New York: Routledge.

Loutzenheiser, Lisa W. (2015). "Who are you calling a problem?": Addressing transphobia and homophobia through school policy. *Critical Studies in Education, 56*(1), 99–115. https://doi.org/10.1080/17508487.2015.990473

Love, Mark. (2017). Problematizing videogames: Teaching students to be critical players. *Teaching English with Technology, 17*(4), 3–24.

Lowry, Lois. (1993). *The giver.* New York: Delacorte Press, Random House.

Lu, Jingyan, Hao, Qiang, & Jing, Mengguo. (2016). Consuming, sharing, and creating content: How young students use new social media in and outside school. *Computers in Human Behavior, 64*, 55–64. https://doi.org/10.1016/j.chb.2016.06.019

Lucey, Thomas A., Lycke, Kara, Laney, James, & Connelly, Christopher. (2013). Dimensions of citizenship through the lens of *The Hunger Games*: Fiction and the visual and performing arts as springboards for citizenship education. *Social Studies, 104*(5), 190–9. https://doi.org/10.1080/00377996.2012.725110

Luckin, Rosemary, Clark, Wilma, Graber, Rebecca, Logan, Kit, Mee, Adrian, & Oliver, Martin. (2009). Do Web 2.0 tools really open the door to learning? Practices, perceptions and profiles of 11–16-year-old students. *Learning, Media and Technology, 34*(2), 87–104. https://doi.org/10.1080/17439880902921949

Luke, Allan. (2013). Regrounding critical literacy: Representation, facts and reality. In Margaret R. Hawkins (Ed.), *Framing languages and literacies: Socially situated views and perspectives* (pp. 136–48). New York: Routledge.

Luke, Allan. (2018). Critical literacy, school improvement, and the four resources model. In Peggy Albers (Ed.), *Global conversations in literacy research: Digital and critical literacies* (pp. 1–13). New York: Routledge.

Luke, Allan, & Freebody, Peter. (1999). Further notes on the Four Resources Model. *Reading Online*, 1–7.
Luke, Allan, Sefton-Green, Julian, Graham, Phil, Kellner, Douglas, & Ladwig, James. (2017). Digital ethics, political economy and the curriculum: This changes everything. In Kathy A. Mills, Amy Stornaiuolo, Anna Smith, & Jessica Pandya Zacher (Eds.), *Handbook of writing, literacies and education in digital culture* (pp. 252–62). New York: Routledge.
Luke, Carmen. (1994). Feminist pedagogy and critical media literacy. *Journal of Communication Inquiry*, 18(2), 30–47. https://doi.org/10.1177/019685999401800200
Luke, Carmen. (1997). Media literacy and cultural studies. In Sandy Muspratt, Allan Luke, & Peter Freebody (Eds.), *Constructing critical literacies: Teaching and learning textual practice* (pp. 19–47). Cresskill, NJ: Hampton Press.
Luke, Carmen, & Gore, Jennifer (Eds.). (1992). *Feminisms and critical pedagogy*. New York: Routledge.
Lukes, Steven. (2005). *Power: A radical view* (2nd ed.). New York: Palgrave Macmillan.
Lukes, Steven. (2018). Noumenal power: Concept and explanation. *Journal of Political Power*, 11(1), 46–55. https://doi.org/10.1080/2158379X.2018.1433755
Makdisi, Saree, & Nussbaum, Felicity. (2008). *The Arabian Nights in historical context: Between east and west*. Oxford: Oxford University Press.
Mansell, Robin. (2017). Inequality and digitally mediated communication: Divides, contradictions and consequences. *Javnost – The Public*, 24(2), 141–61. https://doi.org/10.1080/13183222.2017.1287966
Marciniak, Katarzyna. (2010). Pedagogy of anxiety. *Signs*, 35(4), 869–92.
Markowitz, Linda, & Puchner, Laurel. (2016). Troubling the ontological bubble: Middle school students challenging gender stereotypes. *Journal of Gender Studies*, 25(4), 413–26. https://doi.org/10.1080/09589236.2014.987657
Marshall, Elizabeth, & Rosati, Matthew. (2014). "May the odds be ever in your favor": Teaching class and collective action with *The Hunger Games*. *Rethinking Schools*, 28(4), 20–5.
Marshall, Elizabeth, & Sensoy, Özlem. (2013). One world: Understanding the discourse of benevolent girlhood through critical media literacy. In Barbara J. Guzzetti & Thomas W. Bean (Eds.), *Adolescent literacies and the gendered self: (Re)constructing identities through multimodal literacy practices* (pp. 31–9). New York: Routledge.
Mason, Jennifer. (2002). *Qualitative researching*. London: Sage Publications.
Mason, Lance E., Krutka, Dan G., & Stoddard, Jeremy. (2018). Media literacy, democracy, and the challenge of fake news. *Journal of Media Literacy Education*, 10(2), 1–10. https://doi.org/10.23860/JMLE-2018-10-2-1
Mason, Lance E., & Metzger, Scott A. (2012). Reconceptualizing media literacy in the social studies: A pragmatist critique of the NCSS position statement on

media literacy. *Theory & Research in Social Education, 40*(4), 436–55. https://doi.org/10.1080/00933104.2012.724630

McChesney, Robert W. (2013). *Digital disconnect: How capitalism is turning the Internet against democracy*. New York: New Press.

McDougall, Julian. (2019). *Fake news vs media studies: Travels in a false binary*. Cham, Switzerland: Palgrave Macmillan.

McGregor, Glenda. (2000). Kids who "talk back": Critically literate or disruptive youth? *Journal of Adolescent & Adult Literacy, 44*(3), 220–8.

McGrew, Sarah, Breakstone, Joel, Ortega, Teresa, Smith, M., & Wineburg, Sam. (2019). How students evaluate digital news sources. In Wayne Journell (Ed.), *Unpacking fake news: An educator's guide to navigating the media with students* (pp. 60–73). New York and London: Teachers College Press.

McRobbie, Angela. (1991). *Feminism and youth culture*. London: Macmillan.

Media Education Foundation. (2018, November 6). Seriously? Google wants to teach our kids about internet privacy and safety? Retrieved from https://www.mediaed.org/google-teaching-kids-about-privacy/

Medina, Carmen Liliana, & Wohlwend, Karen E. (2014). *Literacy, play and globalization: Converging imaginaries in children's critical and cultural performances*. New York: Routledge.

Mehan, Hugh. (2008). Engaging the sociological imagination: My journey into design research and public sociology. *Anthropology & Education Quarterly, 39*(1), 77–91. https://doi.org/10.1111/j.1548-1492.2008.00006.x

Metro, Rosalie. (2014). From the form to the face to face: IRBs, ethnographic researchers, and human subjects translate consent. *Anthropology & Education Quarterly, 45*(2), 167–84. https://doi.org/10.1111/aeq.12057

Middaugh, Ellen. (2019). Teens, social media, and fake news. In W. Journell (Ed.), *Unpacking fake news: An educator's guide to navigating the media with students* (pp. 42–59). New York and London: Teachers College Press.

Mills, Kathy Ann, & Levido, Amanda. (2011). iPed: Pedagogy for digital text production. *Reading Teacher, 65*(1), 80–91. https://doi.org/10.1598/rt.65.1.11

Minh Hang, Pham Thi, & DiGangi, Joseph. (2018, March 14). Your cool new Samsung smartphone brought to you by noise, pain and miscarriages. Opinion, *USA Today*. Retrieved from https://www.usatoday.com/story/opinion/2018/03/14/your-cool-new-samsung-smartphone-brought-you-noise-pain-miscarriages-pham-digangi-column/397173002/

Mirra, Nicole, Morrell, Ernest, & Filipak, Danielle. (2018). From digital consumption to digital invention: Toward a new critical theory and practice of multiliteracies. *Theory into Practice, 57*(1), 12–19. https://doi.org/10.1080/00405841.2017.1390336

Moje, Elizabeth Birr. (2007). Developing socially just subject-matter instructions: A review of literature on disciplinary literacy teaching.

Review of Research in Education, 31, 1–44. https://doi.org/10.3102/0091732X07300046001

Moje, Elizabeth Birr, & Luke, Allan. (2009). Literacy and identity: Examining the metaphors in history and contemporary education. *Reading Research Quarterly, 44*(4), 415–37. https://doi.org/10.1598/RRQ.44.4.7

Moje, Elizabeth Birr, & van Helden, Caspar. (2005). Doing popular culture: Troubling discourses about youth. In Jennifer Vadeboncoeur & Lisa Patel Stevens (Eds.), *Re/constructing "the adolescent": Sign, symbol and body* (pp. 211–47). New York: Peter Lang.

Mollet, Tracey. (2019). The American dream: Walt Disney's fairy tales. In Andrew Teverson (Ed.), *The fairy tale world* (pp. 221–31). London and New York: Routledge.

Morrell, Ernest. (2017). Toward equity and diversity in literacy research, policy, and practice: A critical, global approach. *Journal of Literacy Research, 49*(3), 454–63. https://doi.org/10.1177/1086296x17720963

Morrell, Ernest, & Duncan-Andrade, Jeffrey. (2005/6). Popular culture and critical media pedagogy in secondary literacy classrooms. *International Journal of Learning, 12* (9), 273–80. https://doi.org/10.18848/1447-9494/CGP/v12i09/48068

Morriss, Peter. (2006). Steven Lukes on the concept of power. *Political Studies Review, 4*, 124–35. https://doi.org/10.1111/j.1478-9299.2006.000104.x

Nelson, Michelle R. (2016). Developing persuasion knowledge by teaching advertising literacy in primary school. *Journal of Advertising, 45*(2), 169–82. https://doi.org/10.1080/00913367.2015.1107871

Newsom, Jennifer Siebel. (Producer). (2011). *Miss representation* [DVD]. Girls' Club Entertainment.

NLG (The New London Group). (1996). A pedagogy of multiliteracies: Designing social futures. *Harvard Educational Review, 66*(1), 60–92. https://doi.org/10.17763/haer.66.1.17370n67v22j160u

NLG (The New London Group). (2000). A pedagogy of multiliteracies: Designing social futures. In Bill Cope & Mary Kalantzis (Eds.), *Multiliteracies: Literacy learning and the design of social futures* (pp. 9–36). London: Routledge.

Norris, Pippa. (2015). Political communication. In James D. Wright (Ed.), *International encyclopedia of the social and behavioral sciences* (2nd ed., Vol. 18, pp. 342–9): Amsterdam: Elsevier.

Ogilvy & Mather (Producer). (2007, December 5). *Onslaught* [video] Retrieved from https://www.youtube.com/watch?v=gNo29Z_Mqok

Ohayon, L. (July, 2011). *I need it, Mommy!* In *That Money Show*. Accessed February 28, 2012, from www.pbs.org/wnet/moneyshow/cover/111000.html

Orenstein, Peggy. (2011). *Cinderella ate my daughter: Dispatches from the front lines of the new girlie-girl culture.* New York: HarperCollins.

Ostenson, Jonathan William. (2012). Connecting assessment and instruction to help students become more critical producers of multimedia. *Journal of Media Literacy Education*, 4(2), 167–78.

Pangrazio, Luci. (2018). What's new about "fake news"? Critical digital literacies in an era of fake news, post-truth and clickbait. *Páginas de Educación*, 11(1). https://doi.org/10.22235/pe.v11i1.1551

Patterson, Natasha, & Sears, Camilla A. (2011). Letting men off the hook?: Domestic violence and postfeminist celebrity culture. *Genders* (53), 1–16.

Pechmann, Cornelia, Levine, Linda, Loughlin, Sandra, & Leslie, Frances. (2005). Impulsive and self-conscious: Adolescents' vulnerability to advertising and promotion. *Journal of Public Policy & Marketing*, 24(2), 202–21. https://doi.org/10.1509/jppm.2005.24.2.202

Pelo, Ann, & Pelojoaquin, Kendra. (2006–7, Winter). Why we banned Legos. *Rethinking Schools*, 21.

Penuel, William R., & O'Connor, Kevin. (2018). From designing to organizing new social futures: Multiliteracies pedagogies for today. *Theory into Practice*, 57(1), 64–71. https://doi.org/10.1080/00405841.2017.1411715

Petrecca, Laura. (2008, November 19). Moms offended by Motrin ads get tweet revenge through Twitter. *USA Today*. Retrieved from http://www.usatoday.com/tech/products/2008-11-18-motrin-ads-twitter_N.htm

Picker, Miguel (Director). (2002). *Mickey Mouse monopoly* [DVD]. Media Education Foundation.

Pilon, Mary. (2015). Lizzie Magie invented *Monopoly*, so why haven't we heard of her? *The Guardian*. Retrieved from http://www.theguardian.com/commentisfree/2015/apr/10/lizzie-magie-invented-monopoly-landlords-game

Pomerantz, Shauna, & Field, Miriam. (2021). A TikTok assemblage: Girlhood, radical media engagement, and parent-child generativity. In Fiona Blaikie (Ed.), *Visual and cultural identity constructs of global youth and young adults: Situated, embodied and performed ways of being, engaging and belonging* (pp. 139–57). London: Routledge.

Pompe, Cathy. (1996). "But they're pink!" – "Who cares!": Popular culture in the primary years. In Mary Hilton (Ed.), *Potent fictions: Children's literacy and the challenge of popular culture* (pp. 92–125). London: Routledge.

Power, Sally, & Smith, Kevin. (2017). "Heroes" and "villains" in the lives of children and young people. *Discourse: Studies in the Cultural Politics of Education*, 38(4), 590–602. https://doi.org/10.1080/01596306.2015.1129311

Prensky, Marc. (2001). Digital natives, digital immigrants: Part 1. *On the Horizon*, 9(5), 1–6. https://doi.org/10.1108/10748120110424816

Quart, Alissa. (2003). *Branded: The buying and selling of teenagers*. New York: Basic.

Reay, Diane. (2012). Future directions in difference research. In Sharlene Nagy Hesse-Biber (Ed.), *Handbook of feminist research: Theory and praxis* (2nd ed., pp. 627–40). Thousand Oaks, CA: Sage.

Reitman, Ivan (Writer). (1990). *Kindergarten cop* [motion picture]. In Ivan Reitman & Brian Grazer (Producer). Universal Pictures.

Rennie, James Joseph. (2015). *Making a scene: Producing media literacy narratives in Canada*. Doctoral dissertation, University of Toronto, Toronto. Retrieved from http://hdl.handle.net/1807/71312

Rodier, Kristin, & Meagher, Michelle. (2014). In her own time: Rihanna, post-feminism, and domestic violence. *Women: A Cultural Review, 25*(3), 176–93. https://doi.org/10.1080/09574042.2014.944416

Rodier, Kristin, Meagher, Michelle, & Nixon, Randelle. (2012). Cultivating a critical classroom for viewing gendered violence in music video. *Feminist Teacher, 23*(1), 63–70. https://doi.org/10.5406/femteacher.23.1.0063

Rogers, Matt. (2016). Problematising participatory video with youth in Canada: The intersection of therapeutic, deficit and individualising discourses. *Area, 48*(4), 427–34. https://doi.org/10.1111/area.12141

Rogers, Matt. (2017). Participatory filmmaking pedagogies in schools: Tensions between critical representation and perpetuating gendered and heterosexist discourses. *Studies in Social Justice [Windsor], 11*(2), 195–220. https://doi.org/10.26522/ssj.v11i2.1522

Rossi, Cheryl. (2013, September 18). High school gets social media 101 course: Disturbing Twitter trend prompted lesson. *Vancouver Courier*, pp. 1, 4. Retrieved from https://www.vancourier.com/news/john-oliver-secondary-school-gets-social-media-101-course-1.627902

Rossi, Cheryl. (2014, February 27). School creates digital code. *Vancouver Courier*. Retrieved from http://www.vancourier.com/news/school-creates-digital-code-1.869932

Ruitenberg, Claudia. (2019). Plus ça change: The persistence of "skill talk" in competency discourse. *Philosophical Inquiry in Education, 26*(2), 124–36. https://doi.org/10.7202/1071435ar

Rymes, Betsy. (2011). Deference, denial, and beyond: A repertoire approach to mass media and schooling. *Review of Research in Education, 35*, 208–38. https://doi.org/10.3102/0091732X10389428

Sadker, David M., Sadker, Myra, & Zittleman, Karen (2009). *Still failing at fairness: How gender bias cheats girls and boys in school and what we can do about it* (rev. ed.). New York: Scribner.

Sadker, Myra, & Sadker, David M. (1994). *Failing at fairness: How America's schools cheat girls*. Toronto: Maxwell Macmillan Canada.

Schäfer, Mirko Tobias. (2011). *Bastard culture! How user participation transforms cultural production*. Amsterdam: Amsterdam University Press.

Schickel, Richard. (1968). *The Disney version: The life, times, art and commerce of Walt Disney*. New York: Simon and Schuster.

Schön, Donald A. (1995). Knowing-in-action: The new scholarship requires a new epistemology. *Change, 27*(6), 26–34. https://doi.org/10.1080/00091383.1995.10544673

Scott, Joan W. (1992). Experience. In Judith Butler & Joan W. Scott (Eds.), *Feminists theorize the political.* (pp. 22–40). New York: Routledge.

Share, Jeff, Mamikonyan, Tatevik, & Lopez, Eduardo. (2019). Critical media literacy in teacher education, theory, and practice. *Oxford research encyclopedia, education* (pp. 1–30). Oxford: Oxford University Press.

Sholle, David. (1994). The theory of critical media pedagogy. *Journal of Communication Inquiry, 18*(2), 8–29. https://doi.org/10.1177/019685999401800202

Silverstone, Roger. (2007). *Media and morality: On the rise of the mediapolis.* Cambridge: Polity Press.

Simmons, Amber M. (2012). Class on fire: Using *The Hunger Games* trilogy to encourage social action. *Journal of Adolescent & Adult Literacy, 56*(1), 22–34. https://doi.org/10.1002/JAAL.00099

Singh-Joseph, Renu. (2014). Technology: The good, the bad & the ugly. *Darpan: Reflecting South Asian Lifestyle.* Retrieved from http://www.darpanmagazine.com/lifestyle/tech/technology-the-good-the-bad-the-ugly/

Smith, Dorothy E. (1987). *The everyday world as problematic: A feminist sociology.* Boston: Northeastern University Press.

Smith, Dorothy E. (1990a). *The conceptual practices of power: A feminist sociology of knowledge.* Toronto: University of Toronto Press.

Smith, Dorothy E. (1990b). *Texts, facts, and femininity: Exploring the relations of ruling.* London: Routledge.

Smith, Dorothy E. (1999). *Writing the social: Critique, theory and investigations.* Toronto: University of Toronto Press.

Souto-Manning, Mariana, & Price-Dennis, Detra. (2012). Critically redefining and repositioning media texts in early childhood teacher education: What if? And why? *Journal of Early Childhood Teacher Education, 33*(4), 304–21. https://doi.org/10.1080/10901027.2012.732669

Stack, Michelle. (2008). Spectacle and symbolic subversion: Canadian youth-adult video collaborations on war and commodification. *Journal of Children and Media, 2*(2), 114–28. https://doi.org/10.1080/17482790802078615

Stack, Michelle. (2009). Video production and youth-educator collaboration: Openings and dilemmas. *McGill Journal of Education, 44*(2), 299–318. https://doi.org/10.7202/039038ar

Stack, Michelle. (2010). "In movies, someone always has to play the bad guy": Mediatized subjectivities and youth media production. *Nordic Journal of English Studies, 9*(3), 197–217. https://doi.org/10.35360/njes.236

Stack, Michelle, & Kelly, Deirdre M. (2006). The popular media, education, and resistance. *Canadian Journal of Education, 29*(1), 5–26. https://doi.org/10.2307/20054144

Stake, Robert E. (2006). *Multiple case study analysis.* New York: Guilford Press.

Statistics Canada. (2013). *Immigration and ethnocultural diversity in Canada: 2011 national household survey.* Retrieved from http://www12.statcan.gc.ca/nhs-enm/2011/as-sa/99-010-x/99-010-x2011001-eng.cfm.

Statistics Canada. (2017). *Immigration and ethnocultural diversity: Key results from the 2016 Census. The Daily.* Retrieved from http://www.statcan.gc.ca/daily-quotidien/171025/dq171025b-eng.htm.

Statistics Canada. (2019). *Physical activity and screen time among Canadian children and youth, 2016 and 2017.* (Catalogue no.82-625-X). Retrieved from https://www150.statcan.gc.ca/n1/pub/82-625-x/2019001/article/00003-eng.htm.

Steeves, Valerie. (2014). *Young Canadians in a wired world, phase III: Life online.* Ottawa: MediaSmarts.

Stone, Zara. (2013, May 24). The K-pop plastic surgery obsession. *The Atlantic.* Retrieved from https://www.theatlantic.com/health/archive/2013/05/the-k-pop-plastic-surgery-obsession/276215/

Storey, John. (1993). *Cultural theory and popular culture.* Athens: University of Georgia Press.

Sun, Chyng-Feng. (2011). Mulan's mixed messages: Disney's film drags Chinese civilization through the mud. In Elizabeth Marshall & Özlem Sensoy (Eds.), *Rethinking popular culture and media* (pp. 106–9). Milwaukee: Rethinking Schools.

Sunder, Madhavi. (2019, July 23). Intellectual property: When fandom clashes with IP law. *Harvard Business Review.* Retrieved from https://hbr.org/2019/07/when-fandom-clashes-with-ip-law

Szucs, Eszter. (2013). Sex talk online: Sexual self-construction in adolescent Internet spaces. *Girlhood Studies: An International Journal, 6*(1), 117–34. https://doi.org/10.3167/ghs.2013.060109

Thompson, John B. (1987). Language and ideology: A framework for analysis. *Sociological Review, 35*(3), 516–36. https://doi.org/10.1111/j.1467-954X.1987.tb00554.x

Tiffin, Jessica. (2015). Stick becoming crocodile: African fairy-tale film. In Jack Zipes, Pauline Greenhill, & Kendra Magnus-Johnston (Eds.), *Fairy-tale films beyond Disney: International perspectives* (pp. 222–32). London: Routledge.

Tutt, Paige. (2021, March 19). From headache to helpful – Teachers on using TikTok in the classroom. *Edutopia.* Retrieved from https://www.edutopia.org/article/headache-helpful-teachers-using-tiktok-classroom

Twenge, Jean M. (2017, September). Have smartphones destroyed a generation? *The Atlantic.* Retrieved from https://www.theatlantic.com/magazine/archive/2017/09/has-the-smartphone-destroyed-a-generation/534198/

Vadeboncoeur, Jennifer A. (2005). Naturalised, restricted, packaged, and sold: Reifying the fictions of "adolescent" and "adolescence." In Jennifer

Vadeboncoeur & Lisa Patel Stevens (Eds.), *Re/constructing "the adolescent": Sign, symbol and body* (Vol. 33, pp. 1–24). New York: Peter Lang.

Vasquez, Vivian. (2004). *Negotiating critical literacies with young children.* Mahwah, NJ: Lawrence Erlbaum Associates.

Vassallo, Stephen. (2013). Critical pedagogy and neoliberalism: Concerns with teaching self-regulated learning. *Studies in Philosophy and Education, 32*(6), 563–80. https://doi.org/10.1007/s11217-012-9337-0

Walby, Sylvia, Armstrong, Jo, & Strid, Sofia. (2012). Intersectionality: Multiple inequalities in social theory. *Sociology, 46*(2), 224–40. https://doi.org/10.1177/0038038511416164

Wasko, Janet. (2001). Challenging Disney myths. *Journal of Communication Inquiry, 25*(3), 237–57. https://doi.org/10.1177/0196859901025003004

Wasko, Janet. (2016). The Walt Disney Company. In Benjamin J. Birkinbine, Rodrigo Gómez, & Janet Wasko (Eds.), *Global media giants* (pp. 11–25). New York: Routledge.

Watts, Steven. (1997). *The magic kingdom: Walt Disney and the American way of life.* Columbia, MO: Missouri University Press.

Weedon, Chris. (1987). *Feminist practice and poststructuralist theory.* New York: Basil Blackwell.

Wheeler, Joanna. (2012). Using participatory video to engage in policy process: Representation, power, and knowledge in public screenings. In Elizabeth-Jane Milne, Claudia Mitchell, & Naydene De Lange (Eds.), *Handbook of participatory video* (pp. 365–79). Lanham, MD: AltaMira Press.

Williamson, Judith. (1978). *Decoding advertisements: Ideology and meaning in advertising.* London: M. Boyars.

Willis, Paul. (1990). *Common culture: Symbolic work at play in the everyday cultures of the young.* Milton Keynes: Open University Press.

Wineburg, Sam, McGrew, Sarah, Breakstone, Joel, & Ortega, Teresa. (2016). *Evaluating information: The cornerstone of civic online reasoning.* Palo Alto: Stanford Digital Repository. Retrieved from http://purl.stanford.edu/fv751yt5934

Wohlwend, Karen E. (2009). Damsels in discourse: Girls consuming and producing identity texts through Disney princess play. *Reading Research Quarterly, 44*(1), 57–83. https://doi.org/10.1598/rrq.44.1.3

Wohlwend, Karen E. (2012). The boys who would be princesses: Playing with gender identity intertexts in Disney Princess transmedia. *Gender & Education, 24*(6), 593–610. https://doi.org/10.1080/09540253.2012.674495

Wohlwend, Karen E. (2014). Cultural production of Disney princess play worlds. In Carmen Liliana Medina & Karen E. Wohlwend (Eds.), *Literacy, play and globalization: Converging imaginaries in children's critical and cultural performances* (pp. 69–88). New York: Routledge.

Yeoman, Elizabeth. (1999). "How does it get into my imagination?": Elementary school children's intertextual knowledge and gendered storylines. *Gender and Education, 11*(4), 427–40. https://doi.org/10.1080/09540259920492

Yin, Robert K. (2009). *Case study research: Design and methods* (4th ed.). Thousand Oaks, CA: Sage Publications.

Young, Josephine Peyton. (2000). Boy talk: Critical literacy and masculinities. *Reading Research Quarterly, 35*(3), 312–37. https://doi.org/10.1598/RRQ.35.3.1

Yuval-Davis, Nira. (2006). Intersectionality and feminist politics. *European Journal of Women's Studies, 13*(3), 193–209. https://doi.org/10.1177/1350506806065752

Zeisler, Andi. (2016). *We were feminists once: From Riot Grrrl to CoverGirl, the buying and selling of a political movement.* New York: Public Affairs.

Zipes, Jack, Greenhill, Pauline, & Magnus-Johnston, Kendra (Eds.). (2015). *Fairy-tale films beyond Disney: International perspectives.* London: Routledge.

Index

#Black Lives Matter, 217; example of power-to and power-with, 217
#MeToo, 217; example of power-to and power-with, 217

Aarsand, P., 264n6
activism: grassroots examples, 211, 217, 223–4
actual level of analysis for critical social literacy: described, 206t. *See also* ontology
Adbusters, 268n1
advertising: benefits from circulation of fake news, 214; online advertising, 214; as pop culture, 146; as public pedagogy, 165; student responses, 145, 152–3, 153–4; as teaching resource, 151–71
affect: challenges of teaching critical media literacy, 55–6, 178; construction of selfhood, 181; defined, 178; examples in the classroom, 68–9, 71, 74, 77, 82, 98, 99, 106–9, 117, 132, 152–4, 162–3; and gender stereotyping, 123; as humour, 153, 161; and learning about the operation of power, 92; and media consumption, 178; normalization, 55, 186–7; as pleasure, 55; and political action, 224; and redesign, 69, 74–5, 77, 192–3; result of role play, 94, 101; shapes media responses, 177–8; sources, 192; as a teaching resource, 167; versus emotions, 269n5
affective reflexivity: examples, 198; explained, 198; importance to critical social literacy, 224; prompts for students in the Monopoly project, 68; prompts for teacher reflexivity, 199t; teaching prompts for students, 226t
affiliation: versus difference, 180
agency: conflation with power, 23; conflation with resistance, 22–3; as critical meaning making, 29; defined, 12, 22, 23; differentiated from power, 23; as negotiation of identity, 24; politicized, 32, 162; shaped by media, 23–4
Ahmed, T., 269n5
Albers, P., 170, 215
algorithms: challenge for digital literacy, 214–15
Allen, A., 25, 31–2, 35, 162, 179, 261n3
Althusser, L., 147, 151

Alvermann, D.E., 12, 79, 190, 192
American Apparel ad: as a teaching resource, 153–5
analytical reflexivity: described, 223; examples, 197; explained, 197; implications, 197; prompts for teacher reflexivity, 199t; teaching prompts for students, 226t
Anderson, N., 217
Archer, M.S., 178, 205, 219, 221–3, 272n15
Are You Being Hailed?: assessment of learning, 149; factors contributing to success, 164–5, 167, 168; learning objectives, 148–9, 150, 166; learning outcomes, 160, 162, 167; participants, 144–6, 150–1; project activities, 155, 157–65; project setting, 149–50; student redesigns, 155–62, 157, 157f, 158, 159f, 160–1, 162–3, 164f; teacher redesign, 156; teacher reflexivity, 143, 145, 146, 149, 165, 168–9; teaching materials, 149, 170; teaching prompts, 151, 155, 170; teaching for social justice, 170–1; teaching strategies, 145, 164–5; teaching tools, 148–9, 150, 154, 156–7, 168–9; youth responses to marketing culture, 145–6
Arnold, C., 53
art curriculum: relevance for media literacy, 147
assessment: of Are You Being Hailed?, 149; of Celebrity Marketing, 116, 125; of Hunger Games project, 91, 295t (Appendix D); of Monopoly project, 66; of our research, 47
audience: classmates, 181–3; influence on student performances, 182–3; teaching strategies to deal with, 182–3
authors of *Pop Culture and Power*: as feminists, 9, 11

Bansel, P., 216
Barrett, T., 169
Barrow, R., 218
Barthes, R., 55, 178
Be Internet Awesome, 8; criticisms, 8, 258n10
Beauchamp, F., 208
Beauty and the Beast: student responses, 179
Beers, D., 213–14
Bellas, A., 208–9
Berk, R., 219
Beyoncé: competing readings, 185–6; feminist reading of, 136–7; as parody, 136; resource for student projects in Celebrity Marketing, 127; as Sasha Fierce, 142; student responses, 130, 134, 185–6
Bieber, Justin: resource for student projects in Celebrity Marketing, 127, 129
Biesta, G.J.J., 178
Big Data: challenges, 8
Blatt, B., 266n1
Brandes, G.M., 196
Brown, Chris: classroom discussion, 174–7
Brown, W., 230
Buckingham, D., 18, 41, 42, 63–4, 79, 115, 187, 202
Bullen, E., 52
Burbules, N.C., 219
Burn, A., 18, 63–4
Burwell, C., 34
Butler, A.T., 202
Butler, J., 136, 186

"California Gurls": student responses, 125
capital P politics: as active social citizenship, 193; compared to small p politics, 36; defined 36; example, 52
Carney, B., 213–14
cartoons: as a teaching resource, 30
case studies for *Pop Culture and Power*, 20, 59, 60; benefits of, 20. *See also* Are You Being Hailed?; *Hunger Games*; Celebrity Marketing; Monopoly project
celebrities: influence on youth, 113, 130; limitations, 132–3; as a teaching resource, 132–3
Celebrity Marketing: assessment, 116, 125; challenges, 126–7, 128; choosing media, 113, 126; classroom activities, 116–25; focus group recruitment, 133; gender drawings by students, 119ff–22; learning objectives, 115–16; learning outcomes, 1 28–31, 133–7, 138, 141–42; lesson planning, 116–17; pedagogy, 117; project guidelines, 125–6; research assistant, 114; student engagement, 126, 128, 138–9, 141; student project options, 127; student redesigns, 125–31; teacher expectations, 126; teacher participant, 113; teacher reflexivity, 113; teaching prompts, 117, 123; teaching resources, 116–18; teaching tools, 115–16, 137–9
challenges of teaching critical media literacy: commodification of pop culture, 141; digital technology, 212–18; lack of teaching resources, 16–17, 41–2; limited experiences of youth, 185–6; normalization of market relations, 78–9, 80, 85; normalization of meaning, 25, 28, 135; parental investments in education, 15; peer judgment of student media production, 140; personal identities of learners, 180–3; spread of mis/disinformation, 8, 212–25; teacher as learner, 193; time management, 139; unexpected student responses, 83, 173–7
Chanel advertisement: as teaching resource, 152
Cheung, C., 81
Christensen, L., 30
Chung, S.K., 28
cigarette advertising: as a teaching resource, 28
Cinderella: as a teaching resource, 208
cisgender: normalized in media, 136
Class Struggle: as a teaching resource, 81
classroom activities: Are You Being Hailed?, 155, 157–65; Celebrity Marketing project, 117–28; Hunger Games project, 92–102; in our seminar, 49–50, 51, 52–3, 53–4, 55–6; Monopoly project, 65–6, 67–72; to promote critical social literacy with Disney fairy tales, 208–11
classroom dynamics: as gendered, 137, 138–9
classroom resources for student media production: Are You Being Hailed?, 149, 170; Celebrity Marketing, 116–18; *Hunger Games*, 92, 98; Monopoly project, 66, 71

classroom settings: Celebrity Marketing, 116; *Hunger Games*, 89–90; Monopoly project, 65. *See also* Are You Being Hailed?; project setting
clickbait: example, 212–13
cloaker: described, 214
Cloudflare: lack of accountability, 213–14
code of online conduct, 228–9; example of power-with, 228–9; result of collaborative reflexivity, 228–9
Colbert Report, The: as a classroom resource, 7
collaborative interrogation, 223; encourages political affiliation, 223; examples, 223–4, 228–30
collaborative learning: challenges, 183; examples, 182–3, 184; source of pleasure, 191–3; teaching strategies, 183
collective empowerment: as solidarity, 35
collective intelligence, 37; defined, 84
Conli, R., 121
Connell, R.W., 11, 24
cool hunting, as a classroom activity, 52. *See also* political economy
copyright issues of using pop culture in the classroom, 260n22, 262n8
Corbett, B.A., 257n3
corporate media production: analytical significance, 20; versus everyday cultural production, 19–20; example of, 210–11; as an exercise of power, 51–3, 206t; impact of, 215–16
Couldry, N., 212, 215–16, 257n1
counter-ads: examples, 155–62, 160–1, 162–3, 164f
Coyne, R., 262n12

creative pleasure: explained, 190–1; materials needed, 190; source, 190–1; as a teaching resource, 190–1
Creaven, S., 205
critical discourse analysis: used in Are You Being Hailed?, 156–7; used in Celebrity Marketing, 123; reveals the operation of power, 204; support for critical media literacy, 204; used in our seminar, 48–58
critical framing, 197
critical media literacy: and advertising, 148–9; our approach, 20–1; compared to conventional media literacy, 12, 207; components, 12; as critical judgment, 6; critical social literacy as an alternative, 218–21; critique of critical media literacy as skills, 218–19; as denaturalization, 135; described, 10; goals, 6, 8–9, 23, 27, 38, 39–40, 48, 172; as interrogation, 9; origins, 27; pedagogy for, 6, 172; as skills, 218–19; and social justice, 36, 144; taxing criteria of a metalanguage, 57–9. *See also* challenges of teaching critical media literacy
critical realism: influence on our ontology, 205, 206t
critical social literacy: as an analytical sensibility, 202, 218–21; components, 217; concept map with related terms, 228f; explained as levels of interrogation, 205, 206t, 207, 209; goals, 59; illustrated through classroom activities, 207–11; as informed judgment, 218–21; as an interrogation of power, 203; modes of reflexive interrogation, 220–7, 226–7t; origin of term, 271n5; in relation to reflexive interrogation and informed

judgment, 229f; and related terms, 59, 228f; support for social change, 230; support for social justice, 205
critical thinking: compared to criticality, 6; compared to reflexive interrogation, 219; educators' views, 39–40
criticality: social in character, 219
Criticizing Art: as a teaching resource, 169
Crosby, T., 211
cultural reification, 27; example, 262n6. *See also* normalization
cultural studies: contribution to research on media literacy, 22
culture jamming: activities in the classroom, 33; components, 162; defined, 32; examples, 32–3, 162–3, 164f; as "talking back," 33. *See also* Are You Being Hailed?
Currie, D.H., 180
cyber-pessimism, 262n12
cyberbullying: classroom activity, 52–3; example of, 228

Dahlgren, P., 261n5
Daily Show with Jon Stewart, The: as a classroom resource, 7
data colonialism: explained, 215–16
data for *Pop Culture and Power*, 59–60
Davies, B., 59, 205, 216, 271n5
Dehli, K., 18, 36
De Lissovoy, N., 216
de Roock, R.S., 217
deep real level of analysis for critical social literacy: described, 206t; illustrated, 210–11. *See also* ontology
Def Poetry Jam: as a teaching resource, 221–2
Delwiche, A., 84, 107
democracy. *See* participatory democracy

demographics of research setting, 44–5
design, 5
design research: employed by teachers, 44; explained, 43; goals, 41
DeVault, M.L., 262n10
digital capitalism: challenges for media literacy, 212–17
digital divide: policy orientations, 258n3; statistics, 257n3
digital remix: as a metaphor for new literacy, 258n8
digitized selfhood, 215–17; and new social media, 216. *See also* subjectivity
disciplined pleasure of student media production: explained, 187–8; promotes learning, 187–8; through role play, 187–8
discourse: as normalization, 204; as practice, 47–8; as a regulatory framework, 203–4
disjuncture: as a potential for alternative meaning making, 54, 265n13
Disney: construction of girlhood, 211; as a corporation, 210–11; Disney Princess culture, 211; learning outcomes when using, 122–3; and normalization of corporate power, 210–11; normalization of gender relations, 207–8; and offshore production, 211; stereotyping, 207–8; student responses, 88, 118, 122, 179; as a teaching resource for Celebrity Marketing, 118
distributed cognition, 36–7
diversity: as a teaching resource, 152, 167, 209
documentaries for teaching critical media literacy, 121–2
double standard in media: student analysis in Celebrity Marketing, 129

Dove Onslaught(er): example of culture jamming, 32–3
Duff, P.A., 182
Duncan, B., 268n1
Duncum, P., 165, 170
Dyson, A.H., 182

Eklund, K., 81
Ellsworth, E., 50, 148
embodiment: influences redesign, 156, 163, 166; in learning, 91, 169, 180–1; learning in the Hunger Games project, 106, 107–8; and meaning making, 34; reading as an embodied activity, 152, 154, 209; through role play, 112
empirical level of analysis for critical social literacy: described, 206t. *See also* ontology
empowerment: through critical media literacy, 84; differs from creative pleasure, 191; discourse in advertising, 157, 160–1, 162; versus resistance, 32
Ericsson, S., 121
ethical reflexivity: example as Monopoly project, 225; explained, 198, 224; illustrated, 227–30; prompts for teacher reflexivity, 199t; teaching prompts for students, 227t
ethics of research with teachers, 42. *See also* Appendix C
ethics of research with youth, 46, 264n6, 264n7. *See also* Appendix C
experiential knowledge: challenges of language, 262n10; as a limitation, 80; as practical consciousness, 54; as a resource for redesign, 74, 80–1, 82, 185; as a source for change, 54; as support to exercise power-to and power-with, 202; supports learning, 189; as a teaching challenge, 185. *See also* embodiment

fact checking: limitations, 218
fairy tales: as a teaching resource, 207–11. *See also* Disney
fake news, 8, 258n9; challenges for critical social literacy, 201, 212–15; interrogation of, 212–15; and power of media, 201; spread by youth, 218
fan fiction: as a teaching resource, 209; used in our seminar, 56
fanfiction.net, 56; example of classroom activity, 56
femininity: emphasized femininity defined, 11; normalization through media, 28–9
feminism: of authors, 9, 11; responses among youth, 14, 180, 185–6, 223, 224
Ferreday, D., 177
figured world: activity from our seminar, 51; in ads, 147, 189; example in the Hunger Games project, 101, 187–8; explained, 48–9; of *Monopoly*, 78; in Monopoly project, 188–9, 192; as normalization, 48–50
Fiske, J., 19
Fit Pregnancy: as a teaching resource, 156, 164–5, 185. *See also* critical discourse analysis
Fleetwood, S., 205
focus group discussions with student participants: Celebrity Marketing project, 133; Hunger Games project, 102; Monopoly project, 78
Forsberg, L., 264n6
Foucault, M., 204, 270n3
Freebody, P., 57

Friedman, S., 211
Fuchs, C., 271n9
Fujino, D.C., 10

Gainer, J.S., 34, 132, 258n8
game construction: elements, 63–4
game literacy, 63–4
game play: engagement, 83–4; as pedagogy, 66–7, 77, 107–8, 109; for teaching for social justice, 79; by youth, 85
games: board, as a teaching resource, 63–4, 81–2; promoting literacy, 77; versus video games, 265–6n7
Gamson, J., 132
"Gangnam Style": as a potential teaching resource, 113, 132
Gay, R., 111
Gee, J.P., 9, 48–9, 91, 101, 108, 111, 147, 155–60, 207
gender analysis: a challenge for critical media literacy, 14; challenges of sexualization, 135–7; of Disney media, 208–9, 211; of music videos, 115–16. *See also* heterosexual matrix
gender privilege in the classroom, 138; as a teachable moment, 138
gender stereotyping: an example in advertising, 160; student analysis, in Celebrity Marketing, 128–9; student responses, in Celebrity Marketing, 124. *See also* girlhood
gendered responses: of students to music videos, 137
gendered violence: feminist strategies, 176; intersectionality as a tool, 177; student responses, 174–6, 224; teaching risks, 174–5; teaching strategies, 175–7
Ghettopoly: normalization of racialized relations, 85

Gill, R., 177
Girl Power, 24
girlhood: as a construction, 24, 208–9; as emphasized femininity, 24; as expression of agency, 24; as media construction, 211
Giroux, H.A., 11, 14, 22, 39
Giver, The: as a teaching resource, 88, 266n1
Goering, C.Z., 214
Gonick, M., 24
Gonzalez-Bailon, S., 38
Greenpeace International: and culture jamming, 32–3
Greno, N., 121
Grossberg, L., 39

Hagood, M.C., 12, 79, 190, 193
Haight, M., 257n3
hail: activity in our seminar, 49–50, 51; classroom activity in Are You Being Hailed?, 151–5; explained in Are You Being Hailed?, 151; in film studies, 148; student responses in Are You Being Hailed?, 152–3; and subjectivity, 153; in texts, 147
Hall, S., 29, 50, 207
Hammer, R., 12
Hardingham-Gill, T., 176
Harold, C., 32, 33, 148
Harry Potter: and an example of power-with, 37; and redesign, 37
Harste, J.C., 170, 215
Heath, J., 268n1
Hebdige, D., 22
Hepp, A., 212, 257n1
heterosexual matrix: explained, 267n6; a teaching challenge, 136
heterosexuality: as a social and cultural construction 48; as textually mediated discourse, 48–9
hidden operation of power, 212–14

Hill, M.L., 24
Hines, S., 210
hip-hop: challenging racism, 221–2; example of classroom activity, 221–2; parental responses, 15; as a teaching resource, 15, 221–2
Hobbs, R., 214, 218
Hoechsmann, M., 32, 110, 212, 215, 220, 258n10
Hoffman, J., 175–6
Hogg, D., 223
Holland, D., 48–9
Hollister ad: student redesign of, 163, 164f; as a teaching resource, 153–5
home culture: importance, 196
Hopewell, J., 211
Howard, B., 121
Hunger Games: described, 88–9; re-enactment, 98–100, 107; student responses to violence, 110–11; as a teaching resource, 88, 92, 107, 108, 185; and teaching for social justice, 89
Hunger Games project: alliances, 98, 99–100, 104; assessment, 91; challenges, 98–9; character cards, 91–2; costumes, 95, 96; cross-gender role play, 94, 107; fairness as a student concern, 104–5, 105–6; group discussion prompts by researchers, 104, 105–6; learning on government, 101–2, 108–9; learning objectives, 91, 92, 95, 102, 103, 108–9, 112; learning on power, 101–2, 103–6, 107, 109; learning on rules, 103, 105–6; learning on social justice, 108; lesson planning, 88; playing field, 98; pleasure of role play, 97, 109; research assistant, 88; role play guidelines, 92, 93; School Plan, 88–90; school setting, 89–90; stage presentations, 96–7; student construction of props, 95–6, 96f; student engagement, 93, 94–5, 95–9, 101, 108, 100f; student experiences of the game, 103; student experiences of power, 100–1; student participants, 90; student strategies for the game, 103; student suggestions on rules, 105; teacher participant, 87–8; teacher reflexivity, 106–7; teaching prompts, 94, 99, 101; teaching resources, 92; teaching strategies, 97, 101–2, 107, 108; teaching tools, 90–1, Appendix D; typology of power, 101–2
Hyslop, K., 8

"Ice Cream": teaching prompts, 123; as a teaching resource, 116; student meaning making, 137; student responses, 124
identity: building, 52, 115–16; in the classroom, 183; and the hail, 153; impact of normalization, 179; as intersectional, 55, 258n11; normalization challenged by critical media literacy, 179–81; normalized, 179; as social position, 24; student identity validated in redesign, 166–7; student responses, 123–4; as a teaching challenge, 55, 180–1; teaching prompts, 123; teaching prompts in Are You Being Hailed?, 151; as a teaching resource, 180–1, 189; as a tool for redesign, 163
ideology: everyday meaning, 261n5; as meaning making, 27–8; origins of term, 261n5
ideology critique: criticisms, 165–6; defined, 27; as a first step, 166; limitations, 27; as a teaching strategy, 165–6

If: as a teaching resource, 70–1
imagery: importance in critical literacy, 170
imitation: differs from negotiated redesign, 189
information and communication technologies: labour conditions, 52; production of, 52
informed judgment: facets of, 221; illustrated, 221–2; need for, 218; promoted by reflexive interrogation, 206t, 219–21; through social interaction, 219
Ingraham, C., 136
inner conversation: and informed judgment, 222; interlocutors in, 272n15. *See also* reflexivity
intellectual property rights, 262n8
interpellation, 49; explained, 147. *See also* Are You Being Hailed?
interrogation: and critical social literacy, 207; examples of, 209; of fake news, 212–15; of power of media texts, 208–11; as tool for critical media literacy, 51
intersectionality, 55, 177, 259n11
intertextuality: example in student meaning making, 135–6, 142; examples of, 156, 184; explained, 184; as a teaching challenge, 184, 186; as a teaching resource, 184, 185, 186

Jacobson, N., 92
Janks, H., 6, 12, 15, 22, 30, 36, 39, 40, 61, 198, 225, 259n17
Jenkins, H., 8, 9, 18, 32, 33, 36, 37, 73, 77, 79, 108, 111, 219
Jepsen, Carly Rae: resource for student projects in Celebrity Marketing, 127
Jhally, S., 121

jouissance: explained, 178
judgment by peers: in Celebrity Marketing, 139–40

K-pop: as a teaching resource, 116, 133, 267n4
Katz, J., 122
Kellner, D., 12, 36, 41, 47, 53, 55, 77, 80, 111, 115, 202, 220
Kelly, D.M., 10–11, 53, 196
Kenway, J., 52
Keslassy, E., 211
key informants for *Pop Culture and Power*, 3
Kilik, J., 92
Kindergarten Cop: as an activity to challenge stereotyping, 53–4; as a teaching resource, 53–4
"Kiss You": teaching prompts in Celebrity Marketing, 123; as a teaching resource, 116
Knight Abowitz, K., 189
Knobel, M., 33
knowing versus knowledge, 29, 37
Kornfield, S., 107
Kress, G., 4–5, 203
Kupiainen, R., 37

lack of teacher preparation for media literacy, 16–17
lack of teaching resources for media literacy, 16–17, 41–2
Lady Gaga: resource for student projects in Celebrity Marketing, 127; student responses, 129, 131; as a teaching challenge, 13, 35
Landlord's Game, 81. *See also* Monopoly
Lankshear, C., 33
Lapp, D., 34, 258n8
Laughter, J., 33
Lazar, M.M., 269n1

learning from peers, 70, 75
learning objectives: for Are You Being Hailed?, 148–9, 150, 166; for Celebrity Marketing, 115–16; for Hunger Games project, 91, 92; for Monopoly project, 67
learning outcomes: Are You Being Hailed?, 160, 162, 167; Celebrity Marketing, 128–31, 133–7, 138, 141–2; Hunger Games project, 87, 101–2, 103–6, 107, 108–9; Monopoly project, 69, 73, 79, 85
Lee, J., 211
Levy, P., 84
Lieb, K.J., 177
literacy dimensions: distributed, 66; operational, 66; operationalized in the Monopoly project, 66; transformational, 66
Lopez, E., 218
Love, M., 165
Lucey, T.A., 108
Luckin, R., 34
Luke, A., 9, 24, 50, 57, 201, 257n3
Luke, C., 35, 60, 187
Lukes, S., 25, 31

male gaze: explained, 159–60; illustrated in advertising, 160
Mamikonyan, T., 218
Mansell, R., 258n3
Marciniak, K., 178
Marshall, E., 29, 89
Mason, J., 42
Mason, L., 261n2
materialism: as an approach to critical media literacy, 201–2; defined, 9–10; need for, 204–5; ontology for, 203–7; and social justice, 10–11; as support for teaching for social justice, 26–7; to understand power, 26
McGrew, S., 218

McLaren, P., 27
McRobbie, A., 23
Meagher, M., 176
meaning making: as Available Design, 47–51; as embodied, 10; importance, 9; prompts to interrogate, 58t; by youth, 19
media: definition, 18–19; our focus, 19; normalization of social identities, 25, 28–9, 208–9, 211; and power, 6. *See also* ontology
media appeal to youth: example, 114
media as ideology: critique of, 49–50
media as promotion of false consciousness, 12; limitations, 12
media critique: example, 28; utility for critical media literacy, 28
media engagement: as change, 4–5; as an embodied activity, 210; as social, 56; as two-sided, 4
media information: trustworthiness, 8, 218
media literacy: described, 46–7; for our seminar, 47; as social practice, 18–19. *See also* critical media literacy; critical social literacy
media literacy as cognitive defence, 165–6; criticisms, 166
media-literate person, 46–7
media production by students: benefits, 16; and new technology, 53; as pedagogy, 53–4; as pedagogy for critical media literacy, 53; risks, 16; teacher hesitations, 16. *See also* redesign
media regulation in Canada, 211, 213–14
media texts: as coordinators of social practice, 47; as symbolic communication, 209–10
media usage: by Canadian youth, 3, 257–8n3

Index 311

mediatization: addressed by critical social literacy, 217–21; implications for critical media literacy, 217; origin of term, 212; versus mediation, 257n1
Medina, C.L., 211
Mehan, H., 41, 43
Mejias, U.A., 215
Mickey Mouse Monopoly: student responses, 179; as a teaching resource, 117–18
Middaugh, E., 218
Mirra, N., 10
misinformation: spread by youth, 8, 218
Miss Representation: as a teaching resource, 122
mode of address: examples of classroom activity, 51, 94; explained, 50, 148; in games, 77; in Hunger Games project, 107; as refusal, 50; as a teaching resource, 117
Moje, E.B., 24, 50
Mollet, T., 208
Monopoly: normalizes economic competition, 185; promoting social justice, 78–9; as a teaching resource, 64, 79
Monopoly project: challenge of making rules, 74, 75–6; classroom resources, 66, 71; goals, 66; learning objectives, 67, 68; learning outcomes, 69, 73, 79, 85; *Pencil Hockey League* game, 75–6; *Shopping Cart* game, 73–4; student engagement, 68, 71–2, 73, 75–6, 77; student redesigns, 265n4; teachable moment, 82; teacher reflexivity, 63, 64, 67, 79, 85–6; teaching prompts, 67, 68–70, 71; *Truth or Dare* game, 76–7
Moon, J.S., 12, 192
Morley, D., 257n1
Morriss, P., 31

multiliteracies: Celebrity Marketing as an example, 141; contrast to conventional media literacy education, 5–6; origins, 4–5; pedagogy, 5
multimodal texts, 212; challenges for critical social literacy, 212–15; lack of accountability, 214
multiple case study: data analysis, 61
music videos: as a teaching resource, 115–16, 123–5, 136–7, 176–7

Nair ad: an example of parody, 190; student analysis, 157f; student redesigned, 162, 166–7; as teaching resource, 190
naturalization. *See* cultural reification; normalization
negotiated pleasure of student media production: and experiential knowledge, 188–9; explained 188–9
neoliberal selfhood, 216; challenges for teaching critical social literacy, 216; neoliberalism, 259n13
New London Group, 4–5, 7–8, 36, 57, 59, 197, 200, 258n5
new social media: and data colonialism, 215–16; as an exercise of power-with, 38; impact, 206t; and subjectivity, 216–17
Newsom, J.S., 122
Nixon, R., 176
normalization of meaning: through pop culture by commodification, 75, 81–2; as regulation, 48–51
Norris, P., 262–3n12

O'Connor, K., 6
offshore media production: of Disney media, 211; of media technology, 52
online game play: sources of pleasure, 84

online media engagement: challenges, 8
ontology: for critical social literacy, 205–7, 206t; for *Pop Culture and Power*, 18–19
Orenstein, P., 211
outrage media: appeal, 218; described, 218

parental investment: in media literacy, 15–16, 195–6; in our research, 44; resistance to using pop culture, 15–16
participants: key informants, 13; research assistants, 64, 88; students, 65, 90, 144–6; teachers, 57, 63, 87–8
participatory democracy: as active social citizenship, 11, 39, 261n2; as capital P politics, 193; defined, 10–11; and pedagogy, 36, 211, 230; and pop culture, 24, 214, 262–3n12
participatory pedagogy: example of results, 73, 75–6; promoting productive explorations, 73
participatory redesign: elements, 37
Patterson, N., 176
pedagogy for critical media literacy, 36–7; as collaborative learning, 36; contrast to conventional pedagogy, 36; of our seminar, 46–7
Penuel, W.R., 6
personal reflexivity: described, 223; examples, 197, 223; explained 197; illustrated, 227–30; promoting social change, 230; prompts for teacher reflexivity, 199t; teaching prompts for students, 226t, 230
Picker, M., 179
plaisir: explained, 178
play: as source of learning, 111

pleasure: as collaboration, 191–3; from compliance to rules, 83; through creative expression of redesign, 190–2; through disciplined reading, 147, 167, 178; from the exercise of power-to, 132; guilty pleasure, 143; harnessed to learning, 166; of problem solving, 73; promoting learning, 108; of redesign, 67, 74–5; sources, 188–93; as teaching prompt, 56; types promoted through student redesign, 187–93
Pokémon: as collective intelligence, 36
political agency: a goal of critical media literacy, 38
political economy: example of teaching resource, 210–11; tool for critical media literacy, 51–3
political reflexivity: described, 223; explained, 198; illustrated, 223–4, 227–30; prompts for teacher reflexivity, 199t; and social justice, 198; teaching prompts for students, 227t
politics of critical media literacy, 15–16, 169–70, 198
politics of pleasure: explained, 187; promoting social change, 60; as research question, 60; as a teaching challenge, 187
Pomerantz, S., 271–2n10
Pompe, C., 193
pop culture: challenges of teaching with, 13; competing definitions, 20, 260n21; origin of term, 19; our definition, 19–20; and power, 11; teacher views on using, 63, 66, 87–8, 113, 114, 143–5; using in the classroom, 13–14; and youth, 13
Pop Culture and Power: ethical commitments, 46, Appendix C; goals, 9, 25, 28, 38, 40; key

informants, 3; parental concerns, 44; recruitment brochure, 45; research goals, 12; research questions, 3, 35, 46, 60; research strategy 18, 20–1, 62; themes, 12

pop culture versus commercial culture, 257n2

pop music: as political performance, 136–7; as a resource for teaching critical media literacy, 132–3; student responses, 134. *See also* music videos

postfeminism, 177, 269n1

Potter, A., 268n1

power: analysis of, 52t; concepts, 25, 26f; conflation with agency, 25; conflation with domination, 25; defined, 23–4, 25; experienced through critical media literacy, 181; as social position, 25; teaching in support of social justice, 102

power/knowledge: as mystification, 204

power of advertising: student interpretations in Are You Being Hailed?, 163

power of media: analysis of, 58t; central to critical media literacy, 202–3; as constitutive, 206t; as construction of selfhood, 50–1; as corporate relations, 210–11; hidden through new technologies, 213–15; origins, 205; as situation specific, 48; as textually mediated discourse, 203, 206t

power-over: of advertising, 166–7; as authoritative, 30–1; challenges when exercised by teachers, 194; as domination, 27–31; as parenting, 31; as teaching, 30–1, 35; through textually mediated discourse, 28–9

power-to: as culture jamming, 32–3; defined, 31–2, 162; exercised as redesign, 32, 161; promoted by analytical reflexivity, 223; promoted by personal reflexivity, 223; promotes power-with, 180

power-with: as collaborative redesign examples, 224, 227–30; defined, 35; elements, 77; example, 37; and pleasure, 83; as solidarity, 35

Poyntz, S.R., 32, 110, 212, 215, 220, 258n10

pranking, 148; through redesign, 33

praxis: described, 42

preferred reading: classroom activity, 158; explained, 50; prompts to interrogate, 58t; refusal of, 50

prescribed learning outcomes: British Columbia, 91

Pretty Little Liars: critique, 208–9

Princess Diaries, The: critique, 208–9

Princess Industrial Complex: described, 211

procedural literacy: defined, 77

productive diversity, 36

professional development seminar for *Pop Culture and Power*, 20; assessment, Appendix B; classroom activities, 49–50, 51, 52–3, 53–4, 55–6; components, 45; considerations, 57; goals, 47; pedagogy, 57, 270n1; syllabus, Appendix A

protectionism: critique of, 146–7; as media literacy, 146; problems of, 196

public pedagogy: explained, 14; power of pop culture as, 84; remix as, 34

qualitative research: characteristics, 42

Quan-Haase, A., 257n3

racialized identity: student responses, 7, 152, 162, 163, 166, 180, 189

racialized stereotypes: absence of student responses, 134; in Disney films, 208

314 Index

racism: analysis, 107, 217, 264n3; anti-racist teaching activities, 81–2, 133, 169, 221–2, 228–30; student responses, 118, 134; in youth media production, 7, 34, 35

Rebel Sell: Why the Culture Can't Be Jammed, 268n1

recruitment: of students, 46; of teachers, 39, 45–6

redesign: challenges in the classroom, 6–8; example of market logic, 194; examples, 6; examples of student logic, 188–9, 190; as an exercise of power, 82; of fairy tales, 208–11; influence of market logic, 194; as media production, 5; pedagogical elements, 34; as power-to, 32; resources needed, 32; and self-reflexivity, 66; as social change, 5, 79, 204–5; source of pleasure, 82

redesign of fairy tales: classroom activities, 208–11; as power-to, 210; as power-with, 210

reflection-in-action: explained, 31; as goal of reflexivity, 227; as reflexive interrogation, 227

reflexive interrogation: challenges, 220; compared to critical thinking, 219; as an exercise of power, 225; as forms of dialogue, 221; modes, 220–7, 226t; and politicization, 221; promotion of, 220–1; and social change, 220–1, 225, 227–30; in support of social justice, 225; teaching prompts for students, 220–30, 226t

reflexivity: defined, 219; explained, 196; as inner dialogue, 219; as mediator of agency and power, 219; as mediator of social action, 219

Reitman, I., 53

relations of ruling, 29

remix: defined, 33–4; limitations, 34; versus mashup, 33; as participatory culture, 33; as public pedagogy, 33; teaching media literacy, 33–4. *See also* redesign

research: as regulation of youth, 46

research design for *Pop Culture and Power*, 41, 42–3; benefits, 42–3; challenges, 43, 44; goals, 42

researcher stances towards study of media: 269–70n8

resistance: defined, 32

resistant pleasure: explained, 189–90; as parody, 190; as political agency, 189–90; as reversing the power of advertising, 162–5

Rihanna: antifeminist responses, 224; classroom discussion, 174–7; resource for student projects in Celebrity Marketing, 127; as teaching resource, 175–7

Rodier, K., 176

Rogers, M., 7, 48, 203–4

role play: affective results, 101; character cards for the Hunger Games project, 91–2; cross-gender roles in the Hunger Games project, 94, 107; as disciplined pleasure, 187–8; engagement in *Hunger Games*, 188; of fairy tales, 210; figured world, 101; guidelines for the Hunger Games project, 92, 93; learning in the Hunger Games project, 103, 107–8; learning about power, 91–2, 112, 180; promotion of media literacy in the Hunger Games project, 102; as relationship building, 95; rules of, promoted learning, 187–8; as safe space, 188; a source of pleasure, 97, 109; strategies for immersion in roles, 95; student responses in the

Hunger Games project, 93, 94; as teaching for social justice, 188
Rosati, M., 89
Ross, G., 92
Rossi, C., 228–9
rules of game play: challenges, 84; learning about power, 109; shape player agency, 63–4
Rymes, B., 269–70n8

Sadker, D.M., 138
Sadker, M., 138
Samsung: offshore production, 52
Schäfer, Mirko Tobias., 217
Schickel, R., 208
Schön, Donald, 31
school culture: importance, 183
school settings: for Celebrity Marketing, 114–15; the Hunger Games project, 89–90; importance, 195; the Monopoly project, 65
school violence: student responses, 223–4
Sears, C.A., 176
selfhood: constructed through media, 50–1, 56; digitized, 215–17. *See also* girlhood
Sensoy, Ö., 29
sexualized media: in advertising, 161; challenges for teaching critical media literacy, 133–4; challenges in teaching gender analysis, 186
Share, J., 36, 41, 47, 53, 55, 77, 115, 202, 218, 220
Silverstone, R., 220
Simmons, A.M., 111
Singh-Joseph, R., 229
small p politics: compared to capital P politics, 35–6; defined, 30, 259–60n17; of teaching, 15, 30, 193, 198, 202; transformed into capital P politics, 61, 203

Smith, D.E., 27–9, 37, 47, 50, 54, 59, 80, 204, 216
Snow White and the Seven Dwarfs: student responses, 117–18; as a teaching resource, 208
social class analysis, 160, 267–8n10
social identity: as teaching resource, 117, 150–5
social media: and critical social literacy, 201; and digital selfhood, 215–17; impact of, 259n12; and political agency, 38; promoting social change, 6; student code of conduct, 228–30; usage by youth, 258n4; used in a teaching activity, 124, 127
social practice: embodied by media texts, 209–10
solidarity: example, 229–30
Stack, M., 7, 34, 39, 61
stereotyping: in ads as a teaching resource, 165; challenges for critical media literacy, 133–5; in Disney, 118, 207–10; explained, 29–30; as a limitation in teaching critical media literacy, 132–3; as a marketing strategy, 133; as normalization, 29–30, 135; as a teaching tool, 30. See also *Mickey Mouse Monopoly*
Stone, Z., 133
Storey, J., 19, 260n21
student agency as meaning making: factors that shape, 173
student diversity: as a teaching challenge, 181, 183; as a teaching resource, 152
student gender drawings for Celebrity Marketing, 119f, 120f, 121f, 122f
student meaning making, 56; as agency, 141; complexity, 195; example of intertextuality, 135–6; examples, 74, 75, 80–1; as exercise of power, 141; experience as a resource, 34;

student meaning making (*continued*): factors, 177; about gender, 131, 119f, 119–20, 120f, 121f, 122f, 128–9; in the Hunger Games project, 100–1; importance of independence, 193
student media production: benefits, 16, 37–8, 63, 191; examples, 7, 34–5, 53–7, 58t; risks, 34–5. *See also* student redesign
student redesign: challenges, 7–8, 127, 128; example of student innovation, 69f; examples, 72–7, 123, 127, 155–62, 157, 157f, 158, 159f, 160–1, 162–3, 164f; as fun, 76–7; the issue of imitation, 79–80; need for self-reflection, 7; teacher redesign, 156; teaching prompts, 68, 70; unintended output, 6–7, 71–2, 76
student redesign of games: challenge of making rules, 74, 75; challenges, 74, 79–80, 81; examples, 72f, 73–4, 75–6, 76–7; examples of decision making, 75; gender influences, 74, 76; influences, 74, 79, 82; and the market economy, 75, 80–1
student reflexivity, 223–30; teaching prompts for students, 226t
student responses to media: social class differences, 181; as a teaching challenge, 54–5
students: as peer audience, 181–3
subjectivity: and new social media, 216–17; as subjectification, 261n3; validated through redesign, 192
subvertising, 32–3; examples, 155–62, 160–1, 162–3, 164f
Sunder, M., 262n8
surveillance creep, 271n9
Swift, Taylor: resource for student projects in Celebrity Marketing, 127; student redesign, 130–1, 190; student responses, 130, 134
Szucs, E., 6

Taboola: as data broker, 215; role in fake news, 213
"Take a Bow": student responses, 173–7
Talreja, S., 121
Tangled: as a teaching resource, 121, 123
teacher as co–participant in learning, 168
teacher as learner, 193–5; need for flexibility, 194; reflexivity about, 194
teacher education: call for, in media analysis, 17–18; fairy tales as a unit in, 205–11; *Pop Culture and Power* as contribution to, 18, 20, 41–2, 45, 61–2. *See also* professional development seminar for *Pop Culture and Power*
teacher media education: need for, 41–2, 202
teacher reflexivity: administrative challenges, 195; choosing media, 15, 17–18, 35, 38–9, 63–4, 113–14, 132; collaborative learning, 183; described, 196; dimensions of, 197–200; learning outcomes, 79; lesson planning, 113, 143–6, 181; limitations of, 200; pedagogy, 149, 168–9; as power, 200; prompts for, 199t; student identities, 116, 145, 181–2; student learning, 79, 91, 143–4, 146, 172, 174; student meaning making, 193; student redesign, 63; student responses to feminism, 14; using pop music, 15; working conditions as context of, 195–6
teacher resistance: to teaching for social justice, 39
teaching challenges: on government, 91
teaching critical media literacy: administrative challenges, 195;

challenges, 4, 80, 83, 139, 141–2, 172; classroom challenges, 193–5; constraints, 135–6, 138–9, 262n13; as an exercise of power, 31; importance of understanding power, 202–3; lack of teacher preparation, 16–17; lack of teaching resources, 16–17, 41–2; teacher hesitations, 195; tools, 51–3, 57, 58t, 90–1, 101–2, 116–17, 137–8; unexpected messiness, 173–7
teaching critical media literacy to youth: challenges of fake news, 212–15; participant views, 63, 66, 87, 113, 114, 128, 143
teaching for social justice, 10–11; challenges, 11; constraints, 11, 14, 17; goals, 193; pedagogy, 10–11, 172; political resistance, 263n13; teacher resistance, 39
teaching strategies: for advertising, 145, 151–2, 156–9, 162; avoidance, 35; to deal with affect, 179–81; for music videos, 140. *See also* participatory pedagogy
teaching: as power-over, 30–1, 35
technological challenges of student media production, 140, 141
technoromanticism, 262n12
teen screen: critique, 208–9
textual fetishism: compared to critical social literacy, 205; as misdirection, 206t; normalization of meaning, 205
textually mediated discourse, 28, 49; power of, 28–9; as support for social practices, 50
textually mediated ruling, 217
Thomas, P.L., 214
Tiffin, J., 209
TikTok: as a teaching resource, 271–2n10

Tough Guise: as a teaching resource, 121
Trottier, D., 271n9
Tutt, P., 271–2n10
typology of power: for *Hunger Games*, 101–2

Usher: resource for student projects in Celebrity Marketing, 127; student responses, 131
using pop culture: challenges, 13; participant views, 63, 66, 87–8, 113, 114, 143–5; relevance of media, 13–14

Vadeboncoeur, J., 46
Vancouver Courier: source of fake news, 212–13
Vasquez, V., 170, 215
violation of classroom rules: as pleasure, 192
violent media: enhances learning, 110; research claims on impact, 111; revenge fantasy in commercial media, 177; a source of fun, 110; student responses, 109–10
visual elements of critical media literacy, 167; example from Are You Being Hailed?, 159–60; as pleasure, 167

Wasko, J., 208, 210
Watts, S., 208
West, Kanye: resource for student projects in Celebrity Marketing, 127
What's Up Doc?, 7
Williamson, J., 147
Willis, P., 22
Wohlwend, K.E., 211
World without Oil: as a teaching resource, 81

Yin, R.K., 61
Young, J.P., 31